FUNDAMENTALS OF PRETRIAL TECHNIQUES

THOMAS A. MAUET

Director of Trial Advocacy
and Professor of Law
University of Arizona

Little, Brown and Company
Boston   Toronto

LIBRARY OF CONGRESS CATALOG CARD NO. 87-83341

ISBN 0-316-55094-9

ALP

Published simultaneously in Canada
by Little, Brown & Company (Canada) Limited

PRINTED IN THE UNITED STATES OF AMERICA

This book is dedicated to my father,
Rudolf B. Mauet

SUMMARY OF CONTENTS

CONTENTS

III. LEGAL INVESTIGATION

IV. CASE EVALUATION AND STRATEGY

PART B
CONDUCTING THE LITIGATION   99

V. PLEADINGS

VI. DISCOVERY

VII.   MOTIONS

VIII.   PRETRIAL CONFERENCES AND SETTLEMENTS

PREFACE

New litigation lawyers are quickly faced with an uncomfortable reality: Civil litigation is vastly different from studying civil procedure in law school. For civil litigators the procedural rules are primarily functional tools that regulate the pretrial stage of the litigation process. The new litigator's primary concern is not to "miss the boat."

Helping that litigator not to miss the boat is this book's purpose. Whether a third-year law student in a clinical program or a litigator in the first years of practice, you must approach every lawsuit systematically to make sure that you think through the important considerations and take all timely steps during the investigation, pleading, discovery, and motion practice stages of the pretrial process. Only then have you adequately prepared for settlement or trial.

This text approaches litigation the same way. It presents a methodology for preparation, and reviews the procedural rules and thought processes a litigator should utilize before and during each stage of the process. In addition, it discusses and gives examples of how these litigation skills translate into pleadings, discovery, and motions. In litigation, as in trials, there is no one "right way" to litigate. Consequently, while the text presents standard ways of drafting pleadings and motions and of conducting discovery, there are actually numerous ways of effectively conducting pretrial litigation. The examples set forth in the text are only one approach and are there to illustrate how these steps, in recurring situations, can be accomplished.

This text is of necessity an overview of the basic steps in the litigation process. Because any single-volume work must limit how much space can be devoted to any specific topic, compromises and hard choices were inevitable. In making them, I followed a basic rule: Provide an overview that gives inexperienced litigators the basic information they need to handle routine civil cases. What they *need* was arrived at by reflecting on my beginning years as a litigator and by discussing the book's scope with a number of inexperienced litigators. Sometimes their suggestions were surprising. For example, almost all recommended an overview of joinder, jurisdiction, and venue, since these are such complex, technical areas. They did not mean to suggest that some topics were more important than others, rather these inexperienced litigators felt they were weak in some areas and stronger in others. In many ways their suggestions corresponded with my experiences and account in large measure for the text's coverage.

The text focuses on federal district court practice and the Federal Rules of Civil Procedure. This is done for two reasons. First, the federal rules have been adopted by many state jurisidictions. Most other states have modern code pleading rules that are very similar to the federal rules. Second, solid planning, investigation, and drafting are essential skills regardless of the particular jurisdiction, and the text's emphasis is on those skills. Hence, the book is designed to be a basic resource regardless of where a case is to be litigated.

Rather than using case references, this text cites basic treatises commonly used by litigators. These are the single-volume treatises, Wright; James & Hazard; Friedenthal, Kane & Miller; the two-volume treatises, Moore's Manual and Shepard's Manual of Federal Practice; and the multi-volume treatises, Moore's Federal Practice and Wright & Miller. The citations to these treatises should be much more useful in researching legal issues that may arise than individual case citations. Most topics discussed in this text begin with a footnote that provides citations to the relevant portions of these treatises. The citations generally appear in this order.

As always, a book is the result of much more than just the author's efforts, and this one is no exception. Instrumental in creating this text were my editors at Little, Brown and Company, who for a long time encouraged me to write this companion to my other text, Fundamentals of Trial Techniques. Also of considerable help were Gloria Torres, John Thomas, Abby Jones, and Merle Turchik, who reviewed the text and made numerous constructive suggestions. Finally, I must thank my former students at the University of Arizona College of Law who researched, edited, and provided suggestions. I owe a great deal to them all.

Thomas A. Mauet

Tucson, Arizona
March 1988

CITATIONS

For ease in citing, the text uses the following abbreviated citations:

Wright
Law of Federal Courts, Charles Alan Wright (4th ed. 1983)

James & Hazard
Civil Procedure, Fleming James, Jr. & Geoffrey C. Hazard, Jr. (3d ed. 1985)

Friedenthal
Civil Procedure, Jack H. Friedenthal, Mary Kay Kane & Arthur R. Miller (1985)

Moore's Manual
Moore's Manual — Federal Practice and Procedure, James W. Moore, Allan D. Vestal & Philip B. Kurland (supplemented annually)

Shepard's Manual
Shepard's Manual of Federal Practice (3d ed.) (supplemented annually)

Moore's Federal Practice
Moore's Federal Practice, James W. Moore, et al. (2d ed.) (supplemented annually)

Wright & Miller
Federal Practice and Procedure: Civil, Charles Alan Wright & Arthur R. Miller (supplemented annually)

FUNDAMENTALS
OF PRETRIAL TECHNIQUES

Part A
INVESTIGATING AND PLANNING THE LITIGATION

I
INTRODUCTION TO LITIGATION PLANNING

§1.1. Introduction

You have just been called into the office of a partner in the firm that recently hired you. The partner tells you that a prospective client will be coming to the office shortly who has a "problem" that might lead to litigation. The partner tells you that this problem appears to be just right for you to manage. With a smile, he hands you a note containing the prospective client's name and appointment time. Apprehensively you walk out of his office, thinking: "My God. What do I do now?"

What you do, when you do it, how you do it, and why you do it is what this book on civil pretrial litigation techniques is all about. This first chapter is an overview of the litigation process, and discusses how to organize a coordinated litigation plan. Each step in the plan will be discussed in detail in the other chapters.

§1.2. Organizing litigation planning

Litigation planning deals with two basic questions. First, what overall litigation strategy will best serve the client's realistically attainable goals? Second, how does each piece of the litigation plan contribute toward achieving those goals? Addressing these two questions early, and constantly keeping the answers to them in mind, will do much to develop and implement an intelligent, realistic litigation plan.

An effective litigation plan obviously requires structure. That structure should trigger the important thinking, at the right times, so that you will not "miss the boat" during any step in the litigation process. The basic steps in this plan are listed here followed by a discussion of each step.

1. Establish the terms of the attorney-client relationship.
2. Determine the client's needs and priorities.
3. Determine the elements of potential claims, defenses, remedies, and counterclaims.
4. Identify likely sources of proof.

5.   Determine what informal fact investigation is necessary.
6.   Determine what formal discovery is necessary.
7.   Identify solutions.
8.   Devise a litigation strategy.
9.   Devise a litigation timetable.

1.   Establish the terms of the attorney-client relationship

The first step in any litigation plan is to formally establish the attorney-client relationship. This is best done through a written agreement, unless the client is a regular client with whom you have an established business relationship, because an attorney-client agreement is a contract between the attorney and client, and general contract principles apply.

The agreement should spell out who the client is, who will do the work for the client, what work will be done, how you will be compensated, and when the client will be billed for costs and legal work. All too often either a clear understanding with the client is never reached or all likely issues are not covered, causing serious problems later. Representing a client in litigation is difficult enough without having client relationship problems adding to the difficulties.

Before entering into an agreement, of course, you must first decide if you should take the case. In a simple case you can frequently make an intelligent decision after interviewing the potential client and reviewing available records. For example, in a personal injury case arising out of an automobile accident, you can probably determine whether the client's case has merit by interviewing the client to get the history of what happened, and by reviewing available records, such as police reports and medical records. In more complicated cases, substantial investigation may be necessary.

Establishing the attorney-client agreement is discussed in §4.3.

2.   Determine the client's needs and priorities

People seek out lawyers when they have problems that need to be managed and solved. The lawyer, therefore, should first identify the client's problems and needs, viewing them broadly. The client's needs, seen from his perspective, may well be in conflict with possible solutions; however, finding out what the client wants to have happen is the beginning step in dealing with the problems that brought him to a lawyer in the first place.

Keep in mind that the client's needs must be considered in the long-term as well as the immediate sense. Clients often demand a lawsuit against every imagined wrongdoer, when any lawsuit may be against the client's best interests. You need to assess what can be gained by a lawsuit, and then see how a suit would affect the client in the long-term. For example, consider the frequently encountered situation of a client who wishes to sue another party with whom there is an ongoing business relationship. While the particular matter may have merit, suing the other party may put in jeopardy that valuable relationship and adversely affect current deals with that party. A lawsuit that may vindicate the client on one deal may not make sense when viewed in light of the overall picture.

You will also need to assess the client's priorities. Clients rarely get everything they want, so they must develop a scale of priorities that will help you fashion the litigation strategy. For example, suppose your client wants to sue another party over a contract dispute. Does he want a quick, inexpensive resolution to preserve an ongoing relationship? Does he simply want the other party to live up to the agreement, or is he primarily interested in money damages because he considers the relationship destroyed? These possibilities must be arranged to reflect their relative importance to the client before you can sensibly decide how best to help that client.

Determining the client's needs and priorities is discussed in §2.3.

3. Determine the elements of potential claims, defenses, remedies, and counterclaims

The initial client interview will often identify the legal areas involved. At this early stage, however, it is better to think expansively and consider all legal theories that might apply to the case. For example, while a "contract case" will obviously involve contract claims, it might also involve UCC claims, state and federal statutory claims such as securities and product safety statutes, and business torts. It's best to include all of them in your initial thinking.

After you have identified the possible applicable legal theories, determine what the legal requirements are for each theory. This is best done by looking at the applicable jurisdiction's jury instructions. Most jurisdictions have approved pattern jury instructions for commonly asserted claims and defenses. These will tell you what the required "elements" are for a particular claim or defense. If pattern instructions are unavailable, you should consult practice manuals that cover the particular field or research the cases and statutes to learn the elements for the applicable law.

The same type of analysis must be made for remedies. The availability of remedies is related to the choice of claims, and some remedies are broader than others. For example, in a contract dispute, contract damages will be an available remedy. However, if the dispute has fraud aspects, you may be able to bring a business tort claim and have broader damages rules apply.

Potential counterclaims must also be considered. Before bringing a lawsuit, always check on what the other side has against your client. There is little point in starting a lawsuit if it succeeds in provoking a large, previously dormant counterclaim.

Evaluating potential claims, remedies, defenses, and counterclaims is discussed in §3.3. Developing a litigation chart is discussed in §2.2.

After you have identified the possible applicable legal theories and the elements for each of them, it's best to set up some type of litigation chart, or diagram, to list the theories and elements. For experienced litigators planning routine cases, this may not be necessary. New litigators, however, should develop a chart system to systematically analyze cases from the beginning by correlating the elements of claims and defenses, sources of proof, informal fact investigation, and formal discovery. When fully developed, the litigation chart will form the basis for your trial chart, should the case eventually go to trial.[1] For now, the chart will be the basis for your strategic litigation planning. Litigation charts are commonly organized like the one below.

Example:

Assume you represent the plaintiff in an automobile negligence case.[2]

LITIGATION CHART

Elements of Claims	Sources of Proof	Informal Fact Investigation	Formal Discovery
1. Negligence			
(a) negligence			
(b) causation			
(c) damages			
(1) lost income			
(2) med. expenses			
(3) disability			
(4) pain and suffering			

4. Identify likely sources of proof

Most litigation involves events or transactions that have occurred in the past. The likely sources of proof will be centered on those witnesses who have some knowledge of, and exhibits that contain information about, past events or transactions.

The usual witness sources include your client, other witnesses to the events or transactions, the opposing parties, witnesses who have no direct

---

1. See T. Mauet, Fundamentals of Trial Techniques §1.3 (2d ed. 1988).

2. The elements of negligence claims are duty, breach of duty, proximate cause, injury, and damages. Duty is a legal question, however, so the terminology used here fits more to the trial proof.

knowledge of the events or transactions but may have useful circumstantial information, and experts. Exhibit sources include physical objects, photographs, police reports, business records, transaction documents, and any other paperwork that has a bearing on the events or transactions involved. At this stage it is best to think expansively. Develop a long, thorough list early and refine it over time.

Finally, list the likely sources of proof of the elements of the possible legal theories on your developing litigation chart.

Example:

LITIGATION CHART

Elements of Claims	Sources of Proof	Informal Fact Investigation	Formal Discovery
1. Negligence			
(a) negligence	plaintiff police officers bystanders defendant		
(b) causation	plaintiff defendant treating doctors police officers police reports		
(c) damages			
(1) lost income	plaintiff employer employment records		
(2) med. expenses	med. bills treating doctors pharmacy bills		
(3) disability	plaintiff treating doctors employent records		
(4) pain and suffering	plaintiff treating doctors		

Identifying the likely sources of proof is discussed in §2.2.4.

5. Determine what informal fact investigation is necessary

Once you have identified the likely sources of proof, you then need to decide how to acquire information from those sources. Your choices are two-fold: informal fact investigation and formal discovery.

Inexperienced litigators frequently use formal discovery as the principal fact-gathering method. This is often a serious mistake. It is vitally important to acquire as much information as possible *before* filing suit while formal discovery methods usually are unavailable. As a defendant, you will most likely begin the investigation after the suit has been filed, but you should still consider informal sources of proof. Rule 11 of the Federal Rules of Civil Procedure requires that a lawyer make a "reasonable inquiry" to determine if a pleading is well grounded in fact before signing the pleading.

Informal fact investigations are principally conducted by interviewing witnesses and obtaining documents, records, and other data from willing sources, and getting expert reviews of the case. These investigations have advantages and disadvantages. On the plus side, they are relatively quick and inexpensive and can be done without other parties being present. This is important because evidence can become lost unless identified and obtained quickly. On the negative side, while such investigations can yield important information, it is usually not developed in a way that makes it directly admissible at trial. For example, taking a written statement from a witness during an interview does not normally create a statement that is admissible as an exhibit at trial. At best, the statement is useful for impeachment.

When you have identified the witnesses and exhibits that are best reached through informal investigations, note on your litigation chart how you plan on getting the necessary information from those sources.

Example:

LITIGATION CHART

Elements of Claims	Sources of Proof	Informal Fact Investigation	Formal Discovery
1. Negligence			
(a) negligence	plaintiff police officers bystanders defendant	interview interview interview	
(b) causation	plaintiff defendant treating doctors police officers police reports	interview interview interview request letters	

(c) damages			
(1) lost income	plaintiff employer employment records	interview interview request letter	
(2) med. expenses	med. bills treating doctors pharmacy bills	pl. possession interview pl. possession	
(3) disability	plaintiff treating doctors employment records	interview interview request letter	
(4) pain and suffering	plaintiff treating doctors	interview interview	

Informal fact investigations are discussed in Chapter 2.

6. Determine what formal discovery is necessary

Formal discovery can ordinarily be used only after suit has been filed. For that reason, it is the last stage of the fact-gathering process. It also has benefits and risks. On the plus side, it is usually the only way to get information from the opposing party and other hostile or uncooperative witnesses. In addition, the information is often in a form that makes it admissible at trial. For example, obtaining business records from an opposing party or a nonparty will generate an exhibit that will usually be admissible at trial. On the negative side, formal discovery is time consuming and expensive. In a case with a modest litigation budget, formal discovery may be substantially curtailed because of its cost.

Once you have decided which witnesses and exhibits must be reached through formal discovery, you have to decide which of the discovery methods are best suited to obtaining the necessary information. Each of the formal discovery methods — interrogatories, documents-production requests, depositions, physical and mental examinations, and requests to admit facts — is particularly suited to obtaining certain types of information. To be both effective and cost efficient in obtaining the missing information, the methods must be carefully selected and used in the proper sequence.

When you have identified the witnesses and exhibits that must be reached through formal discovery methods, note on your litigation chart what discovery methods you plan to use to obtain the missing information.

Example:

LITIGATION CHART

Elements of Claims	Sources of Proof	Informal Fact Investigation	Formal Discovery
1. Negligence			
(a) negligence	plaintiff police officers bystanders defendant	interview interview interview	deposition? deposition & interrog- atories
(b) causation	plaintiff defendant treating doctors police officers police reports	interview interview interview request letters	deposition deposition?
(c) damages			
(1) lost income	plaintiff employer employment records	interview interview request letter	request to admit
(2) med. expenses	med. bills treating doctors pharmacy bills	pl. possession interview pl. possession	deposition? request to admit
(3) disability	plaintiff treating doctors employment records	interview interview request letter	deposition?
(4) pain and suffering	plaintiff treating doctors	interview interview	deposition?

Formal discovery is discussed in Chapter 6.

7. Identifying solutions

There are many ways to deal with conflict, and litigation is only one of them. Before a decision to litigate is made, a client's problems should be considered in broad terms to determine what approach will best serve the client's immediate and long-term interests. The best approach must be arrived at through discussion with the client, with whom the decision about what to do ultimately rests. There are several basic possibilities:

    a. Do nothing.
    b. Seek an informal resolution.
    c. Seek formal dispute resolution.
    d. Litigate.

Doing nothing should always be considered. The case may simply be a high-risk case. The amount realistically recoverable may not be enough to justify the financial cost of seeking it. In addition, the noneconomic costs should always be assessed. Your client may not have the resolve to get involved in a lengthy fight. He may not want to take his time, and that of others, away from other pressing concerns. He may have more important ongoing business, professional, or personal relationships with the adversary. Finally, negative publicity surrounding the disputed matter may make litigation prohibitive. If you decide nothing should be done, let the client know and get his agreement in writing so you can formally end the case.

If your client decides to push ahead, you should always consider resolving the dispute informally. Your adversary may also wish to avoid a lengthy, expensive battle. He may admit liability, and dispute only damages. It is always worthwhile to look at informal solutions before battle lines are drawn.

If informal solutions are impossible, think next about alternative dispute resolution, such as mediation, arbitration, and summary trials. These can be relatively quick and inexpensive, and frequently are required in commercial contracts. By getting an impartial, experienced outside party involved, the adversaries can frequently get advisory opinions or binding decisions on both liability and damages.

The last possibility is formal litigation. Keep in mind that litigation is expensive and time-consuming and that a litigant is rarely made whole. These realities must be driven home to the client. The worst thing that can happen is for a lawyer to quickly yield to a client's insistence to sue, only to have that client become disinterested, then uncooperative, as the realities of litigation set in.

Identifying solutions is discussed in §4.5.

8. Devise a litigation strategy

Up to now you have been thinking expansively, to ensure you are not "missing the boat" on anything that might influence the case. If you and the client have decided that litigation is the only solution, it is time to focus your thinking and begin making choices.

Assume that your client has valid claims, that attempts to resolve them informally have failed, and that the client agrees that the only recourse is formal litigation. What do you do now?

Everything you do in litigation must have a purpose. A common mistake inexperienced litigators make is to conduct litigation mechanically so that it becomes an end unto itself, rather than becoming a means to an end. Always ask yourself two questions. What are my client's goals in this lawsuit? How does each thing I do help achieve those goals? Only if you constantly focus on the desired result will the individual steps in the process help achieve it. Perhaps the easiest way to think of litigation strategy is to consider its principal parts:

  i.   Is my primary purpose settlement or trial?
 ii.   What claims should I plead?
iii.   How extensive should discovery be?
 iv.   What motions should I make?
  v.   When should I explore settlement?

First, look at litigation strategy in terms of settlement versus trial. Statistically, over 90 percent of civil cases are settled before trial. With experience, lawyers learn what cases are likely to be settled or tried. The client's needs, resources, and goals will affect whether you anticipate an early settlement, a settlement some time before trial, or an actual trial. If you expect to settle the case, your handling of the case and your relationship with your adversary may be quite different than where a trial is likely.

Second, how "big" a lawsuit do you want? This decision, of course, comes at the pleading stage. There is a world of difference between a simple contract case involving two parties and a complex commercial case involving multiple parties. You have to keep in mind the consequences of your pleadings. Multiple claims frequently require multiple parties, which in turn usually generate extensive pleadings, discovery, and motions; just because the claims are there does not necessarily require that you assert them. Also, litigation must be cost conscious. Inexperienced litigators sometimes allege every conceivable claim, with the result that the client becomes immersed in expensive, time-consuming litigation, which may not be in his best interests. This is the time to review your litigation chart, see which claims and remedies are the most meritorious, and structure a lawsuit that will serve the client's interests, and that is feasible in light of the client's economic resources.

When you have decided on appropriate claims and remedies, you must determine where, and against whom, you can bring the suit. In federal district court, as well as in state court, there are several procedural issues that must be considered:

  a.   What parties must or can I join?
  b.   Will I have subject matter jurisdiction over the claims?
  c.   Will I have personal jurisdiction over the parties?
  d.   Where will proper venue lie?

Asking and answering these questions is critical because they determine what actions can properly be brought in a particular court. The questions are interrelated. For example, choosing the claims and parties is affected by whether you have subject matter jurisdiction over these claims in a particular court. The choice of parties is necessarily related to the question of whether you can get personal jurisdiction over them. These decisions in turn influence the determination of where venue is proper. In short, each of these questions is to varying degrees dependent on the others.

Third, once you have decided on the pleadings, you need to select the discovery that is appropriate for your case and your purposes. What do you need to know that you don't already know or can find out through informal fact investigation to assess the case for settlement purposes? What witnesses do you need to "pin down" with depositions? What should you do during discovery to prepare for a possible trial? What are your cost constraints? What order, and when, should you engage in formal discovery? How extensive should each discovery method be? Again, many inexperienced litigators mechanically begin a standard discovery sequence — interrogatories, documents production, depositions, physical examination, and requests to admit — without a clear idea of what information is needed and how best to get it. Without a consistent overall litigation strategy, the case then bogs down as discovery assumes a life of its own.

Fourth, what motions should I make? Your motions strategy must be part of, and coordinated with, your overall litigation plan. For instance, if you plan on moving for summary judgment on some counts, or on the liability issues, your discovery must be focused on getting the facts that will support your motion. Now is the time to plan on making those dispositive motions and to make sure that your litigation plan, principally the pleadings and discovery, is thought through to support those motions.

Finally, when should I explore settlement, if my opposing party doesn't? Since most cases are settled before trial, you need to think through what your position on settlement should be at those points when the issue is likely to come up. This includes assessing the "value" of the case at various times, as well as the financial and emotional benefits of settlement.

Devising a litigation strategy is discussed in §4.5.

9. Devise a litigation timetable

The last step in the litigation plan is to create a realistic timetable that will control the litigation. As plaintiff, you have substantial flexibility. Unless there is a statute of limitations problem, a short notice of claim period, or a particular reason to file suit quickly, you will have the advantage of time to think through your litigation plan before filing the complaint. Once the complaint is filed, the litigation timetable is largely controlled by procedural rules and judges' practices. Many judges will hold a scheduling conference after the pleadings are filed to establish a timetable for discovery, motions, and the final pretrial conference. For example, a judge may order that all discovery be concluded within six months and that any dispositive motions be filed within thirty days of the discovery cut-off date, and then schedule a pretrial conference in nine months. Even where the judge does not establish a timetable, every jurisdiction has an informal set of expectations in routine cases that you should usually follow.

When you have structured a realistic timetable for your litigation plan, it is best to plot it out on a calendar to ensure that you don't omit any steps or lose track of when particular steps should be taken.

Example:

Litigation Timetable

1/1 (today)	Client interview
by 2/1	Interview bystander witnesses Get pl.'s medical records Get pl.'s employment records Get police reports Interview police officers
by 3/1	File complaint
by 4/1	Interrogatories to def. Documents request to def. Deposition notice to def.
by 5/15	Depose def.
by 7/1	Depose other witnesses? Depose physicians?
by 8/1	Requests to admit to def.
by 10/1	Prepare pretrial memorandum
11/1	Pretrial conference
12/1	Anticipated initial trial date

Devising a litigation timetable is discussed in §4.5.8.

§1.3. Conclusion

This overview chapter has discussed the basic sequential steps in litigation planning. The critical concept is that every step of that plan is interdependent with every other. Each step you take influences what happens later, and the various steps you take will make sense only if they are part of an overall plan. When you are immersed in the technical details of any particular step in the process, it is easy to lose sight of that overall plan.

Consequently, before doing anything, always ask yourself two questions. Why am I doing this? How does it promote my overall litigation plan? If you never lose sight of the big picture and keep your long-term objectives in mind, you will have a much better chance to conclude your litigation with satisfactory results.

II
INFORMAL FACT INVESTIGATION

§2.1. Introduction

Preparation and planning for litigation are the critical initial components of the litigation process. Too many lawyers, however, rush to court and file a complaint to get the process started without thoroughly investigating the facts and the law and without devising a coordinated litigation strategy. Small wonder, then, that the results are frequently disappointing.

Most cases are decided by facts, not law. Litigation outcomes are usually decided according to which party's version of disputed events the factfinder accepts as true. Hence, litigators spend much of their time identifying and acquiring admissible evidence that supports their contentions and evidence that refutes the other side's contentions. The party that is more successful in doing this will have a better chance of convincing the factfinder that its version of the facts is what "really happened."

§2.2. Structuring fact investigations

There are two ways of "getting the facts." You can get the facts informally before filing suit, and you can get them through formal discovery after suit is filed. A common mistake inexperienced litigators make is using the investigation, such as an initial client interview and the reviewing of an accident report, only to decide whether to take the case, and using formal discovery methods as the principal fact-gathering method. This is a serious mistake. First, information is power, and the party that has a better grasp of the favorable and unfavorable facts is in a stronger position to accurately evaluate the case. Second, information obtained early on, particularly from witnesses, is more likely to be accurate and complete. Third, information sought before the action is formalized is more likely to be obtained, since a lawsuit often makes people cautious or uncooperative. Fourth, information obtained before suit has been filed is less expensive to acquire. Formal discovery is the most expensive way to get information. It is usually more effective and less expensive to use informal discovery before filing suit, and to use formal discovery methods to obtain missing information, pin down witnesses, obtain specific information and records from the opposing party, and for other such focused purposes. Fifth, Rule 11 of the Federal Rules of Civil Procedure requires that a lawyer conduct a reasonable inquiry into the facts to ensure a pleading that is well grounded. Finally, you can get information informally without the opposing parties participating, or even being aware that you are conducting an investigation. For all these reasons, then, you should use informal discovery as much as possible.

1. When do I start?

The best time to start is immediately, particularly in cases that are based primarily on eyewitness testimony. For example, a personal injury case should be investigated as soon after the accident as possible. Witnesses forget, or have second thoughts about being interviewed; witnesses move away and disappear; physical evidence can be lost, altered, or destroyed. In this type of case, where liability will be determined largely by eyewitness testimony, it is best to start quickly.

On the other hand, an immediate investigation is not always required. For example, in contract and commercial cases, where the evidence will primarily consist of documents, correspondence, and other business records, and there is no danger that records will be lost or will disappear mysteriously, a prompt fact investigation may not be essential. Contract and commercial cases may have complex legal questions that must be researched and resolved before you can start an intelligently structured fact investigation. In addition, delay sometimes helps. For a defendant who expects to be sued, starting an investigation may only serve to stimulate the other side into investigating the case. Unless the defendant needs to investigate an affirmative defense or counterclaim, a sound approach may be simply to wait for the other side to do something.

2. What facts do I need to get?

Your job as a litigator is to obtain enough admissible evidence to prove your claims and disprove the other side's claims. Therefore, you need to identify what you must prove or disprove. This is determined by the substantive law underlying the claims, relief, defenses, and counterclaims in the case. However, how do you research that law if you do not yet know what the pleadings will allege? What do you research first, the facts or the law?

There is no easy answer here. In litigation, the facts and law are intertwined. The investigation of one affects the investigation of the other. You will usually go back and forth periodically as you develop your theory of the case.

Example:

You have what appears to be a routine personal injury case. From your initial interview of the client it appears to be a simple negligence case against the other driver. You do preliminary research on the negligence claim to see if the damages are sufficient to warrant litigation. You then continue your fact investigation and discover that the defendant is uninsured. Because of this, you start wondering if there may be a claim against the municipality for not maintaining intersection markings and safe road conditions. Of course you need to research the law here. If there is a legal theory supporting such a claim, you then need to go back and see if there are facts that support that theory. Back and forth you go between getting the facts and researching the law until you have identified those legal theories that have factual support.

3. How do I structure my fact investigation?

The easiest way to give structure to your investigation is to use a system of organizing the law and facts based on what you will need to prove if your case goes to trial. In short, this is a good time to start a "litigation chart."[1] A litigation chart is simply a diagram that sets out what you need to prove or disprove in a case and how you will do it. The chart is a graphic way of identifying four major components of the litigation plan:

    (a) Elements of claims
    (b) Sources of proof
    (c) Informal fact investigation
    (d) Formal discovery

Start with the "elements" of each potential claim, relief, and defense in the case. Most jurisdictions have pattern jury instructions for commonly tried claims, such as negligence, products liability, and contract claims. The elements instructions will itemize what must be proved for each claim, relief, or defense. If pattern jury instructions don't exist, more basic research will be necessary. If the claim is based on a statute, read the statute and look at the case annotations that deal with elements and jury instructions. If the claim is based on common law, consult treatises covering the claim and research the recent case law in the applicable jurisdiction. Regardless of where the applicable law is, you must find it and determine what the specific elements are. When you have done this you will have completed the the first step on your litigation chart.

---

1. The litigation chart will become a "trial chart" if the case is ultimately tried. See T. Mauet, Fundamentals of Trial Techniques §1.2 (2d ed. 1988); F. Lane, Goldstein Trial Techniques Chs. 2-4 (3d ed. 1986).

Example:

You represent the plaintiff in a potential contract case. Your client says she obtained goods from a seller and paid for them, but the goods were defective. From your initial client interview, and from reviewing the documents and records she provided, you decided to bring a contract claim against the defendant. Your jurisdiction's pattern jury instructions for contract claims list the elements you must prove to establish liability and damages.

LITIGATION CHART

Elements of Claims	Sources of Proof	Informal Fact Investigation	Formal Discovery
1. Contract			
(a) contract executed			
(b) pl.'s performance			
(c) def.'s breach			
(d) pl.'s damages			

This approach should be used for every other possible claim. For example, since the contract is for the sale of goods, a claim based on UCC warranties may be appropriate. If so, you should put the elements of this claim on your litigation chart.

The litigation chart has two principal benefits. First, it helps you identify what you have to prove or disprove so that you can focus your fact investigation on getting admissible evidence for each required element. Second, a litigation chart helps you pinpoint the strengths and weaknesses of your case as well as your opponent's case. In most trials the side that wins is the one that convinces the factfinder to resolve disputed issues in its favor. The litigation chart will help you identify the disputed matters on which you will need to develop additional admissible evidence to strengthen your version and rebut the other party's version.

4.   What are the likely sources of proof?

Facts come from five basic sources: the client, exhibits, witnesses, experts, and the opposing party. Of these categories, most can often be reached by informal investigations. The client, of course, must be interviewed.

Whenever possible obtain exhibits in your client's possession, other evidence such as physical objects, photographs, documents, and records in the possession of third parties. Witnesses can frequently be interviewed. You can hire consulting experts to help analyze and prepare your case.

On the other hand, formal discovery may sometimes be the only way to get essential information. For example, important witnesses may be uncooperative and need to be deposed. Exhibits in the possession of uncooperative third parties may need to be subpoenaed. Information from the opposing party can usually be obtained only through interrogatories, depositions, and other discovery methods. However, it is always worthwhile to try the informal approach first, since it is quicker, less expensive, and may be more accurate and complete. The only exception concerns other parties: Ethics rules forbid you to make direct contact with an opposing party whom you know is represented by counsel.[2] You must deal with the other party's lawyer. What constitutes a "party," however, is an imprecise thing. Many lawyers feel that any employee of a corporate party, and any expert employed by a party, are included in the rule that prohibits an interview without the lawyer's permission. This position is supported by the Federal Rules of Evidence, Rule 801(d)(2)(D), which makes statements of agents and servants, concerning a matter within the scope of their agency or employment, made during the existence of the relationship, an admission that is admissible against the principal. Model Rule of Professional Conduct 4.2 would also bar a lawyer from communicating with employees having a managerial responsibility within the organization that is an adverse represented party, and with any other person whose statements may constitute an admission on the part of the organization.

While informal fact investigations should always be conducted, their usefulness depends significantly on the particular case at hand. Some cases can be almost completely investigated through informal means, while others must rely principally on formal discovery. For example, in a routine personal injury case based on an automobile accident, you should be able to get all the basic information informally, since the principal sources will be your client, police officers, police reports, medical reports, and disinterested nonparty witnesses. By contrast, in a products liability case brought against the manufacturer of a consumer product, most of the information about the product's design, manufacture, distribution, and safety history will be in the possession of the defendant manufacturer and can be obtained only through formal discovery methods.

Regardless of the type of case, you must first identify the likely sources of proof, then decide how that proof can be obtained. The second step on your developing litigation chart is to list the likely sources of proof and correlate them to the required elements of the claims.

---

2. See Model Code of Professional Responsibility, Rule 7-104(A)(1) (1980); Model Rules of Professional Conduct, Rule 4.2 (1984).

Example:

In a contract case, determine the witnesses and exhibits that will provide the facts about the case. Your client, the plaintiff, is an obvious witness, and the contract is a central exhibit. Other than these obvious sources, where else can you go for proof? For example, what proof is there that the plaintiff performed his obligations under the contract? The plaintiff is again a source of proof. In addition, the plaintiff may have business records showing his performance. The defendant may have written letters acknowledging the plaintiff's performance. The defendant may have business records proving performance. There may also be nonparty witnesses who have knowledge of the plaintiff's performance.

Continue this type of analysis of each element of every claim you are considering, and put those sources on your developing litigation chart.

Example:

LITIGATION CHART

Elements of Claims	Sources of Proof	Informal Fact Investigation	Formal Discovery
1. Contract			
(a) contract executed	plaintiff defendant contract pl.'s secretary		
(b) pl. performed	plaintiff pl.'s records def.'s records		
(c) def. breached	plaintiff pl.'s correspon- dence def.'s correspon- dence pl.'s records def.'s records experts		
(d) pl.'s damages	plaintiff pl.'s records replacement vendor replacement ven- dor's records experts		

The third step is to determine whether these sources of proof can be reached by informal fact investigation and, if so, what method is best suited to getting the necessary information. Witnesses can be interviewed; exhibits in your client's possession should be obtained and reviewed; exhibits possessed by third parties can frequently be obtained from friendly or neutral third parties simply by requesting them; experts can be interviewed, and you can sometimes obtain their reports. Once again, think expansively here, since obtaining information informally is quicker, less expensive, frequently more candid and accurate, and can be obtained without the opposing party participating or perhaps even being aware that you are investigating the case. Put the methods by which you plan to obtain the information on the litigation chart.

Example:

LITIGATION CHART

Elements of Claims	Sources of Proof	Informal Fact Investigation	Formal Discovery
1. Contract			
(a) contract executed	plaintiff defendant contract pl.'s secretary	interview obtained from pl. interview	
(b) pl. performed	plaintiff pl.'s records def.'s records	interview obtained from pl.	
(c) def. breached	plaintiff pl.'s correspondence def.'s correspondence pl.'s records def.'s records experts	interview obtain from pl. obtain from pl. interview	
(d) pl.'s damages	plaintiff pl.'s records replacement vendor replacement vendor's records experts	interview obtain from pl. interview request letter interview	

The last step is to decide what to use formal discovery methods for, and how and when to use them. These considerations are discussed in Chapters 4 and 6.

5.   What is my litigation budget?

You can't buy a Cadillac on a Ford budget, and the same holds true for litigation. The client's financial resources are an important consideration. The "value" of the case, the amount you can reasonably expect in a jury verdict, is another. The amount of work the case requires for adequate preparation is a third consideration. Consequently, you need to estimate how much work the case will require, and see if it is feasible that you can accomplish the work given the resources involved. You need to prepare a litigation budget.

How do you do it? First, you need to estimate how much time you can devote to the case and whether the case can be adequately handled within that time. If a client has a limit on what he can spend, that is the outside limit. Simply divide your hourly rate — if you are billing by the hour — into the fee limit, and you will know the total number of hours you can devote to this case. If your fee is a contingency fee, you can still do the same type of calculation. Start with the dollar amount of a reasonably expected verdict after a successful trial. Reduce that amount by the likelihood that liability will not be proved. For instance, if you have a 50 percent likelihood of proving liability, reduce the expected verdict by that percentage, then divide that dollar amount by your usual hourly rate, and you will again determine the total hours you can devote to the case and still reasonably compensate yourself. Once you determine the total hours, estimate the time you will need to spend on each part of the litigation process: preliminary investigation, pleadings, discovery, motions, and trial.

Think you can't do it? You'd better start. Insurance companies and businesses, increasingly conscious that litigation makes sense only if it is cost-effective, frequently require litigation lawyers to prepare budgets. Keep in mind that your time *estimates* are only that, and it is sometimes appropriate to have a range for your estimates.

Example:

You represent the plaintiff in an automobile accident case. Your fee is one-third of any recovery, after expenses. Assume that if you win at trial, your client can realistically expect a verdict of about $50,000. However, you estimate your chances of proving liability at 60 percent. You estimate litigation costs at $3,000. This reduces the "value" of the case to about $25,000, of which you will earn about $8,000. Your time is presently billed at $60 per hour. This means you can devote up to 133 hours on the case and still be paid a fee equal to your hourly rate.

The case will take approximately two days to try and require about four days of trial preparations, for an estimated total of 48 hours. How do you allocate the remaining 85 hours? Your prefiling investigation — client interviews, witness interviews, exhibits acquisition, legal research, and just plain thinking about the case — may require about 25 hours. Preparing and responding to pleadings may take about 10 hours. Preparing and responding to discovery will require the largest amount of time, approximately 50 hours.[3] Making and responding to motions may take another 10 hours. Preparing pretrial memoranda and attending pretrial conferences may require 20 hours. How does your budget add up?

Investigation	25 hrs.
Pleadings	10 hrs.
Discovery	50 hrs.
Motions	10 hrs.
Pretrials	20 hrs.
	115 hrs.

You didn't come within the allocated 85 hours, but your initial time estimates are reasonably within range. With experience, you will become more accurate in estimating time requirements of particular cases and in estimating the likelihood and amounts of a recovery. This will help you determine if you should take a case to begin with, and, if you do, how much time you can realistically expect to devote to the various stages of its preparation and trial.

However, always keep in mind that your ethical obligations to the client must ultimately control your handling of the client's case. You have an obligation to handle the case competently: your performance is determined by the requirements of the case, not the anticipated fee.

6.   What sources should I investigate?

The basic sources for informal investigations are four-fold: the client, exhibits, witnesses, and experts. Your litigation chart will provide the directions for your informal fact investigation. That investigation should focus on obtaining basic facts — favorable and unfavorable — about the case, and identifying credible, admissible evidence for each claim you are considering.

---

3. Determining how to allocate these 50 hours among the various discovery methods is discussed in detail in §6.3.

How extensive should your fact investigation be? It needs to be thorough enough to fill out your litigation chart, to the extent that you can do so through informal fact investigation, while meeting the cost constraints you have established. Practically, this means several things. First, the client must be interviewed as often as necessary to learn everything she knows about the case. You will also need to interview her periodically as you gather additional information from other sources.

Second, you should try to obtain all key documents, records, and other exhibits. In a personal injury case, this includes the police accident reports, hospital and doctor's records, insurance claims records, and employment history. These can often be obtained informally, and many jurisdictions have statutes that require they be released to the client on request. In a contract case, this includes the contract, correspondence, invoices, shipping records, and related business records. Where physical evidence is important, it should be safeguarded or photographed before such evidence is altered or possibly lost.

Third, witnesses usually need to be identified, located, and interviewed, although what you do will depend on the particular case. In most cases, what witnesses say is critical. For example, in a personal injury case, where the plaintiff and defendant are likely to have contradictory versions of how the accident happened, the testimony of neutral witnesses will frequently control the liability issue. You need to identify, locate, and interview them whenever possible. On the other hand, witness testimony is not invariably critical at trial. For example, in a contract or commercial case, the issues are frequently decided by the documents, records, or substantive law. In such a case there may be no advantage in interviewing witnesses quickly.

Finally, in some cases you will need to consult appropriate experts early in your investigation. For example, in medical malpractice and products liability cases, plaintiff's lawyers usually have the case reviewed by a physician and a technical expert before filing suit. You might as well see what a qualified expert thinks of the strengths and weaknesses of your case now.

§2.3.   Client interviews[4]

Client interviewing has two components: what information to get, and how to get it. What to get will be determined by your litigation chart. How to get it is based on interviewing techniques that must be fully understood in order to get the important information from the client.

---

4. There are several excellent texts that discuss and illustrate in detail the dynamics of client interviewing. See, e.g., D. Binder & S. Price, Legal Interviewing and Counseling (1977); K. Hegland, Trial and Practice Skills (1978).

1. Client attitudes and disclosure

The typical client is unsure of his rights and obligations, and a lawyer's office is an unfamiliar, imposing environment. The lawyer who empathizes with the client's psychological needs knows the factors that promote and inhibit client disclosure and will be more sucessful in getting an accurate picture of the problems that brought the client to a lawyer in the first place.

A client comes to a lawyer to determine if there are actual legal issues relative to his problems and, if so, how to deal with them. The lawyer needs to interview the client so he can identify the legal issues, get all relevant available information, and discuss with the client how the problems can best be handled. How does a lawyer go about getting that information from the client?

There are several factors that can inhibit a client from a full disclosure of information. First, a client being interviewed often feels that he is being judged. This causes the client to withhold or distort facts that may create negative impressions about the client or his case. Second, a client being interviewed often tries to satisfy what he feels are the lawyer's expectations. This causes the client to tell the lawyer what he thinks will be a pleasing story and, again, to withhold negative and contradictory facts. Third, a client may have a variety of internal reasons, such as embarrassment, modesty, and fear that, once again, prevent him from disclosing all information.

On the other side, there are positive factors that promote full disclosure. First, a client is more likely to disclose fully if he feels that the lawyer has a personal interest in him. A friendly, sympathetic lawyer is more likely to get "all the facts" from a client. Second, a client is more likely to disclose fully if he senses that the lawyer is identifying with him. The lawyer who lets the client know that "she's been there too," or is familiar with and understands the client's situation, is more likely to draw out all the facts. Third, some clients enjoy being the center of attention. Supplying critical information makes the client feel important and may stimulate his supplying more information. Fourth, a client enjoys feeling that he is doing the right thing. The lawyer who can instill the feeling that full disclosure is the proper, decent approach is more likely to achieve it.

Lawyers will obtain the fullest possible disclosure by stressing the positive psychological influences and by understanding and minimizing negative influences that inhibit disclosure. Lawyers who create a comfortable physical environment and show an understanding and appreciation of the client will be more successful in obtaining "all the facts," both good and bad. This sensitivity will establish a positive context for client relations during the course of the litigation process.

2. Interview preparation

Interview preparation has several components. What kind of physical setting should you have? How will you record what the client says? What should the client do to prepare for the interview? What topics will you cover during the actual interview?

Many clients will be uncertain and insecure during the first interview. After all, it may be the first time they have ever been to a lawyer's office. A physical setting that is informal, friendly, and private will help make a client feel relaxed and comfortable. A lawyer's private office is a good place to conduct an interview; a small conference room is another.

Strive for informality. Sit in a place other than behind your desk, have coffee and soft drinks available, perhaps play quiet background music. Avoid interruptions. Leave the telephone alone, and close the door to keep others out. Schedule the interview so that you will have enough time to accomplish what you have planned. An initial interview with a client can easily take one or two hours, but perhaps much more. If possible, schedule client interviews as the last appointment for the day, provided you are still mentally sharp at that time. This will allow you to continue the interview without running out of time because of other appointments.

A principal function of a client interview, in addition to establishing rapport and gaining the client's trust, is to obtain information. This information needs to be recorded and there are several ways to do this. First, you can take notes yourself. This has the advantage of allowing for privacy, but has the disadvantage of interfering with your interview. Second, you can have someone else, a secretary, clerk, or paralegal, take notes. Here the advantage is that you are relieved of note-taking, but it puts a third person into the interview environment, which may be an inhibiting influence, particularly during the client's first interview. Third, you can tape-record the interview with the client's permission. Here the advantage is completeness. However, you will still need to make a summary of the interview, and many clients are uncomfortable having their statements recorded.

The paramount consideration is creating an atmosphere in which the client feels comfortable and tells everything he knows about the problems that brought him there. Most lawyers conduct the initial part of the interview without note-taking. After the client becomes comfortable with you and the interview environment and you begin to get the details of his story, you can discuss the need to record what he says and then ask him if he will feel comfortable with the method you suggest. Once you explain why it is so important for you to have an accurate record of what he says and how the attorney-client privilege will prevent anyone else from getting it, the client will usually agree.

What can you have the client do to prepare for the first interview? First, the client should be told to collect all available paperwork, such as letters, documents, bills, and other records. Second, many lawyers ask the client to write down everything he can remember about the legal problems, particularly if they involve a recent event. If the memo is directed to the lawyer, and no one outside the lawyer's staff is permitted to see it, the memo should be protected by the attorney-client privilege, even though the attorney-client relationship may not yet formally exist.[5] The records and memo should be brought to the initial interview.

3. Initial client interview

The initial client interview should have several objectives. First, conduct yourself in a manner that establishes a good working relationship. When the client arrives at your office, don't make him wait. Greet him personally. Have the client make himself comfortable in your office or conference room, and spend a little time making small talk — about traffic or the weather, for instance. Offer him coffee or a soft drink. Remember that the client is sizing you up both as a lawyer and as a person. Second, spend a few minutes learning about the client's background. This shows the client that you see him as a human being and not just as another case. It also helps you evaluate the client as a witness and provides important biographical and financial information. Third, let the client know what is going to happen during the interview, what you need to accomplish, and the reasons for it. Explain that you need to get all the important facts in order to intelligently identify and analyze his legal problems.

Fourth, have the client identify the general nature of his problems. You will usually have a general idea — a "car accident," a "contract problem" — when the client makes the appointment. However, it is always useful to have the client initially tell his story his own way, without interruptions, sizing him up as a trial witness. You may also discover facts you might never otherwise have stumbled upon, and it allows the prospective client to get the matter off his chest in his own words. These considerations are well worth "wasting time" on, even if the client talks about seemingly irrelevant things. The usual way to get the client to tell the story his way is to ask open-ended, nonleading questions. For example, simply asking "I know you were in an accident. Why don't you tell me what happened in your own words?" will usually get the client started. While the client tells his story, listen not only to what he says but also note things he omits, things that would usually be mentioned. When the client is done, you can paraphrase what he has said. This serves as a check on accuracy and shows the client that you have been listening carefully.

Fifth, after the client has told his story, you need to get a detailed chronological history of the events and other background facts. It is frequently advantageous to make an outline or checklist so that you do not overlook important topics. Your litigation chart, setting out the elements of the claims you are considering, should provide a start. It is sometimes useful to look at interrogatories and deposition checklists for this type of case and witness.[6] These may help you develop ideas for the topics and necessary detail as you go through the history of the case. However, don't use a checklist as a questionnaire, since your interview will quickly lose

5. See Wright & Miller §2017; McCormick on Evidence §§88-89 (3d ed. 1984) Fed. R. Civ. P. 26.
6. See, e.g., D. Danner, Pattern Discovery (series 1981-1986).

the personal touch. The standard method is to use the chronological story-telling approach. Most people think chronologically, and that is usually the best way to elicit details. While your checklist should be tailored to fit the particular case involved, you will usually cover the same basic topics regardless.[7]

Sixth, you need to ask follow-up questions on potential problem areas. Here it is best to use specific, focused questions. A client naturally wants to impress his lawyer and convince her that the case is a good one, so he will often give only "his version" of what are disputed facts and omit altogether the unfavorable ones. It is always better to get the bad news early. Remind the client that your job is to get all the facts, both good and bad, so you can accurately assess the case and represent him effectively.[8] Remind him that the opposing lawyers will discover the bad facts soon enough, so it is better to deal with them now. This will usually keep him from adopting an "I thought the lawyer was on my side" attitude.

Where do you probe? Look for information that might adversely affect the client's credibility. Are there problems with the client's background? Is there a spotty work history? Are there prior convictions or other such trouble with the law? Clients frequently omit negative facts in their background. Therefore, you should be asking what the client has left out of the story. For example, in an automobile accident case, has the client omitted the fact that he was given a traffic citation? Was driving with a suspended license? Was drinking? Had just left a bar before the accident happened? Or was using a car without permission? A useful device in getting out these kinds of facts, without directly suggesting to the client that you don't believe his story, is to get the client to be a kind of devil's advocate. Ask him what the other side is probably going to say to his lawyer about the event. This will frequently draw out the "other side's version" of the disputed facts. Keep in mind that under Rule 11 it is at your peril that you accept your client's version of the facts. The client needs to be pushed, probed, even cross-examined to test the facts he gives you. You may need to verify his version of the facts with an independent examination.

The usual topics you will need to discuss with the client during the initial interview include the following.

a. Liability

Facts bearing on the liability of all parties must be developed fully. Details are critical. Here a chronology of events usually works best. For example, in an automobile accident case, you will need to explore how the accident happened step by step. You need to get a detailed description of the scene of the collision. Diagrams and charts are very helpful.

---

7. See D. Baum, Preparation of the Case §§1.10-1.21 (Art of Advocacy Series 1984); J. DeMay, The Plaintiff's Personal Injury Case: Its Preparation, Trial and Settlement (1977); R. McCullough & J. Underwood, II Civil Trial Manual 57-72 (1980); J. Werchick, California Preparation and Trial §§1.2-1.6 (1981).

8. This is required in any event by Rule 11's "reasonable inquiry" duty.

You need to establish the location of each car involved before the collision occurred, at the point of impact, and after the accident had run its course. You need to get details on speed, distance, time, and relationship to road markings.

b. Damages

Damages information must be obtained, for both your client and all other parties. The permissible damages for each possible claim should already be on your litigation chart. For example, in an automobile collision case, damages should include out-of-pocket expenses, lost income, future expenses, and future lost income, as well as intangible damages such as permanence of injury, and pain and suffering. Find out if the client suffered an injury, the extent of it, how he was treated, how he felt then and feels now, and how the injury has affected his life. Find out if he had a preexisting condition that could affect damages. You should also explore insurance coverage for all parties, as well as collateral sources such as health insurance, employer benefits, and government entitlements (e.g., Social Security and Veterans Administration benefits). In contract and commercial cases, and cases in which equitable relief is sought, you need to determine if the injuries to the client can be measured in monetary terms.

You must determine if the defendant has the ability to pay a judgment. Find out if the defendant has insurance, the amount of the policy's coverage, and if the policy covers the event or transaction. Determine the defendant's income sources and assets, particularly those that can easily be attached to collect a judgment.

c. Client background

Your client's background is important for several reasons. The client's personal background — education, employment, family history — is important for assessing the client's credibility as a trial witness. His financial background — income and assets — is important for assessing damages. Finally, the client's financial picture bears on a mundane but obviously important question: Does he have the ability to pay you? You need to get this background information from the client early on, but be sure you let the client know why this personal information is important for your evaluation of the case.

d. Parties

It is frequently difficult to ascertain who all the parties to an event or transaction are and, if businesses are involved, their proper legal identities. Often the client does not know and has given little thought to this aspect of the case. Now is the time to begin obtaining the facts that will help you identify those parties. Once again, Rule 11 requirements must be kept in mind. For example, in an automobile accident case you will need to know not only who the other driver was, but also who owns the other vehicle and whether it is a business or rental vehicle, or was loaned or stolen. You will also need to know where the accident occurred and need to determine who owns, or is in control of, the accident location, since that entity may be responsible for designing, building, and maintaining the roadways.

From your fact investigation you will usually be able to identify the parties you will want to name in your lawsuit. However, identifying parties is not the same thing as learning the proper technical identity of parties. For example, just because the truck that ran into your client had the name "Johnson Gas" on its side does not necessarily mean that the Johnson Gas Company is a properly named party. The potentially liable party may be a sole proprietorship or a corporation with a different name entirely. You need to find this out.

For individuals, learn their correct full names. For corporations, partnerships, unincorporated businesses, and other artificial entities, you must not only learn the proper names, but also whether they are subsidiaries of other entities that should be brought in as parties. Each state's Secretary of State or Corporation Commission usually has a list of domestic and foreign corporations licensed to do business within that state. Such lists usually show the state of incorporation and principal place of business, which is useful for determining if diversity jurisdiction exists, and state who the resident agent is for service of process. If the party is an unincorporated business operating under an assumed name, you may be able to determine the true owners and properly named parties by consulting an assumed-name index, required by many jurisdictions.[9]

e. Defenses, counterclaims, and third-party claims

Plaintiffs and defendants alike must look closely at a frequently overlooked area: What do they have on us? And who else can be brought into the case? Cases are legion where a plaintiff has filed an action only to be hit with a much larger, previously dormant, counterclaim. Think expansively, particularly in the commercial area, since the parties usually will have had previous dealings that could give rise to counterclaims or third-party claims. You should look at both related and unrelated transactions, since liberal joinder rules may permit raising unrelated claims in the same action.

f. Witnesses

The client must be questioned on all possible information sources, whether eyewitnesses, experts, or anyone else who possibly has useful information. Get names, or information that will help to identify and locate people with information. Think expansively here, and don't be con-

9. The capacity of individuals, corporations, and unincorporated associations to sue is governed by Rule 17, which refers to state law. Hence, you must always check state law to determine whether a party has capacity to sue or be sued, and what the technically proper party is.

cerned with the admissibility of testimony at this point. Find out who your client has already talked to about the case, and what he has said.

g.   Records

The client should bring to the interview all paperwork in his possession, such as accident reports, insurance claims, bills, checks, personal records, business records, and correspondence. If the client does not bring them, have him do so as soon as possible. You should keep these records; if the client needs them, make photocopies for him. Learn what other records may exist and who has them, so that these can be obtained now, or later through discovery.

h.   Physical evidence

Does the case involve objects such as vehicles, machinery, or consumer products? While most common in negligence and products liability cases, such evidence can exist in other cases as well. How to locate, obtain, and preserve physical evidence is discussed in §2.4.

i.   Other lawyers

Clients often shop around for lawyers. While a client has a perfect right to talk to more than one lawyer about taking a case, there are always clients who go from door to door until they find a lawyer willing to take it. It is important to find out if the client has seen other lawyers about the case. On the theory that lawyers turn down cases because the cases lack merit, you should be appropriately cautious.

j.   Client goals

What does the client really want? In some cases, such as personal injury, the answer is often simple. The plaintiff basically wants money damages and the defendant wants to avoid paying them. But even then it is important to probe deeper. What does the client view as a favorable outcome? Does he want the case to go to trial, or is he willing to have it settled? Is he looking for vindication, revenge, or other satisfaction not related to money damages? In other cases, such as contract and commercial disputes involving businesses, the answer may be difficult to discern. Money for damages is not always what the client wants or needs. The dispute may be with another business with which the client has an ongoing relationship, and that relationship may be more important than the money damages. Perhaps relief such as specific performance is more important than money damages. Now is the time to find out what the client thinks he wants and begin assessing whether his expectations are realistic or need to be modified.

k. Next steps

Following a client interview, write a short memo evaluating the client and his story. It is easy to forget your specific impressions of a client, yet his credibility as a trial witness will often be critical to his case's success. This is particulary important where more than one lawyer will work on the file.

If you conclude from the initial client interview that you will take the case, you will need to discuss the details of a contractual relationship, including fees, and you should let the client know what steps you will take concerning his problem. These are discussed in §4.3.

4. Follow-up client interviews

Many things should be done during the initial interview of the client. Some cases are relatively simple, and interviewing a well prepared client can take less than an hour. Many cases, however, will require more than one session to collect the basic information. Accordingly, you might use the first session just to build rapport with the client, get the client's story out, and compile a chronology of events. A second session could then be used to review the client's records and ask focused follow-up questions about problem areas. In more complicated cases, it may take several client interviews to acquire the necessary information.

Follow-up interviews will also be periodically necessary during the litigation process. Whenever you receive additional information, through informal fact investigation or during formal discovery, you should review it with the client. The new information may differ from what the client previously told you. Obviously the contradictory information must be evaluated, discussed with the client, and dealt with. In some cases the client may admit that what he previously told you was not entirely true, and change his story. In others, he may deny the new information and stick to his version of the facts. Whatever the client's position, the new information, if it is at odds with the client's story, must be dealt with. Is it true? Is it more accurate? What does the new information do to the client's story? This is an ongoing process, but the key point to remember is that the client must be kept informed as the fact-gathering process progresses.

§2.4. Exhibits acquisition

Your interviews with the client should also identify future exhibits. These include the scene, physical evidence, documents, and records. In addition, interviews with witnesses and your review of exhibits when you get them, particularly documents and business records, may disclose additional exhibits.

You need to acquire these exhibits, get copies of them, or protect them from being lost or altered. The order in which you do things will depend on how important it is to obtain the particular exhibits. For example, physical evidence, such as the condition of a vehicle, machine, or consumer product, should be acquired quickly, before it is repaired, altered, destroyed, or becomes lost. Some records, such as a police accident report, are essential for you to begin your investigation.

The basic types of exhibits are the following.

1. Scene

If a lawsuit involves an event, such as an automobile accident, investigating the scene is vital. Whenever possible, the lawyer should visit the scene, even if someone else will do the technical investigation. That should include taking photographs of all locations from a variety of perspectives and making all necessary measurements so that you can make scale diagrams. Photographs should be both in black and white and in color and be enlarged to 8 inches × 10 inches for courtroom use. Diagrams for courtroom use should be at least 24 inches × 36 inches. While photographic enlargements and courtroom diagrams need not be made until shortly before trial, the necessary preparations should be made now. You should visit the scene at the same time and day of week on which the event occurred, so your photographs will accurately show the relevant lighting, traffic, and other conditions. You might also find additional witnesses to the event — people who are there each day at that time.

If you are reasonably proficient in taking photographs and have the equipment to take photographs that can be processed and enlarged with sufficient quality to make effective courtroom exhibits, you can take them yourself. This will not create a problem for you, a lawyer in the case, becoming a witness, since any person familiar with how the scene looked at the relevant time is a competent qualifying witness. However, where you will be the only person who can qualify the admission of the photographs, obviously someone else must come along because the lawyer cannot usually be a witness in a case she is trying. If you are not a proficient photographer, hire a commercial photographer to accompany you. You must tell the photographer specifically what pictures you will need.

Numerous photographs should be taken from a variety of perspectives. For example, in an intersection collision case, you will normally want pictures of how the intersection looked to each of the drivers as they approached it. Accordingly, pictures should be taken, in the road from the appropriate lane, with the camera held the same distance above the road as the driver's head. Several pictures should be taken, starting from perhaps 300 feet away, then moving to 150 feet, and so on. The photographs will then show what each driver saw as he approached the intersection. In addition, photographs should be taken from where other eyewitnesses, such as other drivers and pedestrians, were when the crash occurred. Finally, if there are nearby buildings, it's always useful to have overhead, bird's-eye-view pictures taken that will show lane markings, pedestrian walkways, traffic signs, and signals in the intersection. You must review witness statements beforehand to know where the witnesses were, and what they saw and did, before you can know what photographs you will need.

Diagrams present a different problem. Since the person who took the measurements and made a scale diagram is often the only witness who can qualify the diagram for admission in evidence, it is better to have someone other than the lawyer do this.

2. Physical evidence

Physical evidence, such as vehicles, machinery, and consumer products, if not already in the possession of police, other investigative agencies, or your client, must be obtained and preserved for possible use at trial. This includes not only locating them, but also keeping them in the same condition and establishing chains of custody. This is particularly important if the evidence will be tested by experts before trial. When you cannot take or move evidence for safekeeping, take a thorough series of photographs and sufficient measurements so that you can make accurate diagrams and models for trial.

Preserving physical evidence often requires that you act quickly. In an automobile accident case, for example, skid marks and the condition of the vehicles involved will be lost as the skid marks wear off and the vehicles are repaired. In these situations you must take immediate steps to prevent the loss, destruction, or alteration of the evidence and ensure a chain of custody when such a chain will be an admissibility requirement.[10] Have someone such as an investigator do this, since he may be a necessary witness at trial.

How do you actually "preserve" physical evidence? Two concerns are involved. First, you must gain actual physical possession of the objects so that they are kept in the same condition until the trial. Second, you must either label the objects or, if they cannot readily be labeled, put them in a container that can be sealed and labeled. Both of these steps ensure admissibility at trial by establishing the two basic requirements — identity and same condition. The usual way to accomplish this is to have someone like an investigator, who can serve as a trial witness, get the objects from wherever they are, label or put them in a container that is sealed and labeled, and have them taken to your office for safekeeping. This label should describe the object, show where it came from, who obtained it, when it was taken, and who received it at your office.

Evidence is frequently in the possession of third parties, such as police departments and repair shops. If the evidence does not belong to your client, the third parties are probably under no legal obligation to preserve the evidence for you. However, most will be cooperative when they learn that what they have is important evidence. They will usually keep the evidence in an unaltered condition until you have had an opportunity to photograph and measure it. You should check if someone

---

10. See McCormick on Evidence §212 (3d ed. 1984).

else, such as an investigator from the police department or insurance company, has already taken these steps. Finally, a third party will sometimes agree to preserve evidence until you can serve the party with a subpoena, or have the court issue a protective order.

Many times, of course, a client comes to a lawyer too late to take these steps, and the evidence will be lost. If the client comes to you shortly after the event, however, you should always act quickly to preserve the evidence. Many cases, particularly in the personal injury and products liability areas, are won or lost on this type of evidence.

3. Records

You should obtain all available documents and records from your client. You may as well obtain everything your client has because once suit is filed the opposing party will be able to discover from your client anything that is relevant and not privileged. If important documents and records are in the hands of third persons, see if those persons will voluntarily turn them over or provide copies. Public records are usually available on request. In many jurisdictions persons have a statutory right to obtain certain records on demand, such as their own medical reports. A written demand on behalf of the client, coupled with his written authorization, will usually suffice. If not, contact the sources to learn the required procedure for obtaining the records. These records are, of course, available by subpoena after suit is filed, but it is better to get them as soon as possible, since the records may be essential to evaluate the case before suit is filed. For example, in a personal injury case, you will need to review police accident reports, doctor's reports, hospital reports, employment records, and perhaps others.[11] In a contract action, you will need to get the contract itself, and records that bear on the performance and nonperformance of the parties, such as orders, shipping documents, invoices, and payment records.

If you can get these kinds of records from third parties, maintain them properly. Keep the records you receive together, in order, and do not mark them. Keep a record of how, from whom, and when you got them. Make additional copies that you can mark up and use during client and witness interviews.

§2.5. Witness interviews

After you have interviewed your client, and obtained the available exhibits, the next stage of your informal fact investigation is interviewing witnesses. Here a great deal of flexibility is possible, and it is particularly important to plan ahead.

---

11. Since some records, such as hospital reports, will be technical, get a good dictionary or encyclopedia to help you understand them.

1. Who and when to interview

The more you know, the more accurately you can assess the strengths and weaknesses of your case. It makes sense, then, to interview every witness, favorable, neutral, and unfavorable, to find out what each knows. The benefits of interviewing everyone, however, are always tempered by economic realities. There are few cases in which you can simply interview everyone regardless of expense. On the other hand, every case has critical witnesses that you must try to interview regardless of the cost. In addition, once taken, the case must be handled competently regardless of cost contraints. Between these two extremes, you need to decide whether you should try to interview a particular known witness and attempt to identify and interview others. For example, suppose you represent a party in an automobile collision case. From your client and the accident reports, you learn what persons were present. If a police report identifies an eyewitness, you need to interview him; but what else should you do? Should you interview the police officer who wrote the report and other officers present who did not write reports? Should you try to locate bystanders who were present but have not been identified?

How far you go is determined by three basic considerations. First, you need to interview all critical witnesses regardless of cost. A competent lawyer simply must always do this. The critical witnesses are the eyewitnesses to an event, the participants to a business transaction, and other persons such as the principal investigating officers. Such witnesses will probably be witnesses at trial. In the above hypothetical, this would mean interviewing the known eyewitness, the police officer who prepared the accident report, and other eyewitnesses whose identity you are able to learn. Second, with witnesses who are not critical, interviewing *is* influenced by your cost constraints. For example, canvassing homes and stores near the accident scene may turn up someone else who saw the accident; however, doing this is expensive and may produce nothing useful. Attempting to identify and interview such possible witnesses may be worthwhile in a $200,000 lawsuit in which liability is unclear, but cannot be done in a $10,000 case where liability is clear. Third, how far you go in locating and interviewing witnesses depends on what you have developed so far. For example, if your client and two solid eyewitnesses clearly establish liability, it may not make sense to find other eyewitnesses who can corroborate the client. On the other hand, if your client's version is contradicted by one eyewitness, it is obviously important to locate and interview other witnesses to see which version they support.

When you have decided on the witnesses you need to interview, you must decide the order in which to interview them. Here again flexibility is required. It is frequently better to interview favorable and neutral witnesses first, before you interview the unfavorable ones, since you will have better success in pinpointing the differences in their stories. Identifying and interviewing the favorable and neutral witnesses first will give you the basis for your side's version of any disputed events and will help you identify the areas of disagreement when you interview the unfavorable witnesses. These areas can then be explored in detail. Frequently, however, you won't know for sure whether a given witness will be favorable.

On the other hand, there are advantages in interviewing unfavorable witnesses early before their attitudes and recall have solidified. For example, in an accident case you know a witness will be unfavorable because that witness is quoted in a police accident report. It may be useful to interview that witness quickly. He may change his mind, or tell you that he "didn't really see it happen," or "isn't sure" about important facts. You may minimize the impact of the witness through an early interview.

2.   Who should do the interviewing?

Either the lawyer or an investigator should conduct the actual interviews. There are advantages and disadvantages with each approach. If the lawyer interviews, the advantages are that no additional investigator costs are incurred, and he can get a first-hand impression of the person as a trial witness. This is particularly important with key witnesses. On the other hand, lawyer interviews can create impeachment problems. If at trial the witness denies making an inconsistent statement to the lawyer, the lawyer will have to be a prove-up witness. This puts the lawyer in conflict with ethical rules that generally prevent a lawyer from being a witness in a trial in which the lawyer represents a party.[12] A common approach is to have the lawyer personally interview witnesses known to be favorable, but have another person present when interviewing neutral or unfavorable witnesses. That person can then prove up impeachment at trial if necessary.

If an investigator interviews witnesses, the advantages are economic and practical. An investigator's time will usually be less expensive than the lawyer's, so there may be cost savings for the client. However, the time saving may be minimized, since the lawyer must spend time educating the investigator about the known facts, the issues, and about what direction the interviews should take. The principal benefits of a properly experienced investigator are that he will probably be better at locating witnesses, and will be an available impeachment prove-up witness at trial.

When hiring an appropriate investigator, you should establish a contractual relationship and give him specific instructions. A contract with the investigator will prevent misunderstandings about what work will be required, what the cost limitations of the case are, and how the investigator will be paid. The contract should expressly state that the investigator will be an employee of the lawyer, and that everything the investigator learns and obtains during the investigation will be reported only to the lawyer and will otherwise be kept confidential. This will improve the chances that the investigative reports will be protected from disclosure by the attorney's work-product privilege.[13] As always, it is best to put the

12. See Model Code of Professional Responsibility, Rule 5-101(B) and 5-102; Model Rules of Professional Conduct, Rule 3.7.

13. See Rule 26(b)(3). A witness statement is usually not discoverable under Rule 26(b)(3).

agreement in writing, either in a simple contract or in a letter to the investigator.

3. Locating witnesses

Lawyers are perfectly capable of locating many witnesses. The client frequently knows the important ones. Records, such as business records and accident reports, will usually identify others. When their names are known, it is surprising how many witnesses can be located over the telephone or by checking basic, available sources. The telephone book, neighbors at a previous address, workers at a former job, friends and relatives are all good sources in locating a known witness. It is often the case that a witness has merely changed a telephone number, moved to a different apartment, or changed jobs, and tracking her down is relatively simple. If these leads do not work, check with the post office, voter registration and motor vehicle departments, utility companies, and other government agencies such as the Veterans Administration, Social Security office, and unemployment and welfare agencies. If the witness is important to you and cannot be located through these types of leads, you may need an experienced investigator.

4. Purposes of the interview

There are several purposes you should try to accomplish during a witness interview. These purposes usually should be pursued in the following order. First, learn everything the witness knows and does not know that is relevant to the case. Have the witness tell what he knows, by using open-ended questions. These can be followed later with specific, focused questions; however, you want details only of the critical events and transactions, not everything the witness knows that may possibly be relevant. When learning what the witness knows, make sure you pinpoint the admissible facts based on first-hand knowledge, separating them from opinion, speculation, and hearsay. With witnesses who have unfavorable information, you should try to limit the damage by limiting the witness' testimony. Find out what the witness does not know, is not sure of, is only guessing about, or has only second-hand information about.

Second, pin the witness down. This means going beyond generalizations and getting to specific, admissible facts. For example, "driving fast" must be changed to an approximation of speed in miles per hour. "He looked drunk" should be pursued to get the details underlying the conclusion, such as "staggering, glassy eyed, and smelling of alcohol." Getting only generalizations and conclusions makes it easy for a witness to change his testimony later.

Third, get admissions. With unfavorable witnesses, having the witness admit that he "isn't sure," "didn't really see it," "was only guessing," or "was told" all serve to prevent the witness from changing or expanding his testimony at trial.

Fourth, get information that might be used for impeachment. If an unfavorable witness says something that later may be useful to impeach him, pin him down. For example, if an unfavorable witness to an accident says he was 200 feet away when it happened, make sure you commit him to that fact. Use "200 feet" in other questions, and recommit him to that fact, since at trial he may claim that the distance was shorter.

Fifth, get leads to other witnesses and information. It is surprising how often a witness will name other witnesses or divulge information not previously mentioned in any report. For example, asking a witness if anyone else was present at an accident scene will sometimes get a response like: "Sure, Ellen, my secretary, was standing right next to me and saw the whole thing."

Finally, try to record the interview or get some type of written statement. How to do this is discussed later in this section.

5. Arranging the interview

Often the most difficult part of witness interviews is getting witnesses to agree to be interviewed in the first place. With favorable witnesses this is not usually a problem, and selecting a convenient time and place for the interview is a routine matter. Unfavorable witnesses, however, are frequently reluctant. Here you can take either of two approaches: attempt to arrange an interview, or attempt a surprise interview. A reluctant witness may agree to be interviewed at a convenient time and place, where privacy is assured, and if the interview won't take too long. Let such a witness know that cooperating now may eliminate the need to be deposed later, and suggest that an interview at home would be both convenient and private. If the witness senses that the real question is where and when, rather than if, he is more likely to agree to an interview.

If a witness will not agree to an arranged interview, the only alternative is the unannounced interview. Frequently, a witness who doesn't want to be bothered will nevertheless agree to talk when an investigator "pops into" the witness' office or "stops by" the house. Again, it may help to reassure the witness that the questions won't take long and may eliminate the need for further involvement. However, a witness has a perfect right to refuse to be interviewed, and you cannot harass or badger the witness hoping to change his mind. The only alternative is to depose the witness later.

6. Structuring the interview

How do you go about structuring a witness interview? First, review the case file, which should contain client interviews, exhibits such as police reports, perhaps other witness interviews, and the developing litigation chart. Second, get copies of any diagrams, photographs, and records you may use during the interview. Third, decide if and how you will record the interview. Finally, prepare an outline for the interview. A frequently followed order for witness interviews is the following:

    a. Witness background
    b. Story in witness's own words
    c. Detailed chronological story
    d. Questions focused on your theory of the case

First, witness background is important for assessing witness credibility and determining if there is any bias, interest, or other facts that affect credibility. Most witnesses don't mind talking about their work, family, and home. Asking these background questions usually puts witnesses at ease. Some witnesses, however, may resent what they consider to be intrusions into their private lives. In such cases you may want to slip the background information into the interview, or simply touch on it at the end. Second, let the witness tell her story in her own words, even at the price of hearing irrelevant facts. It gives you a good picture of the kind of witness she will be at trial, and you may discover important facts that would never have come to light. Third, go over the story in chronological order and in detail. Get specifics on what the witness saw, heard, and did at all important times, and what she saw others do and say. Find out what exhibits the witness knows of, and other witnesses she is aware of. Find out what the witness personally knows and what is only opinion, speculation, or hearsay. Find out to whom the witness has talked. Finally, ask focused questions based on your theory of the case. For example, if the witness gives information that contradicts your version of the events, see how you can minimize its effect. If the witness is "not sure," "guessing," "didn't see it myself," or says other things that lessen the damage, make sure you note it. In addition, see if the witness can corroborate something useful to your side. Witnesses are rarely completely unfavorable; a little searching will often turn up something positive.

7.   Recording the interview

Regardless of the witness, you should make a record of the interview. There are several possibilities:

    (a) Use a court reporter
    (b) Make a tape recording, with the witness' consent
    (c) Obtain a written, signed statement
    (d) Take notes during the interview
    (e) Have another person take notes during the interview
    (f) Make notes after the interview

The approach you use depends on what will best serve your interests and what the witness will permit. If you expect the witness to give favorable information and be cooperative, a short, written and signed statement is often best. After interviewing the witness, simply type a summary of his story and ask him to sign it. Another method is to send the witness a confirming letter summarizing what he said, and ask the witness to sign and return a copy acknowledging its accuracy. This will lock a favorable witness into his basic story, and there is no damage if the opposing side obtains the statement during discovery.[14] With unfavorable witnesses, it is often advantageous to get a detailed statement. This improves your chances of getting contradictions, admissions, and impeachment that may be valuable at trial. Using a court reporter or a tape recorder is probably the most reliable method. Get the witness' permission if you plan to tape record, since surreptitious recordings are illegal in some jurisdictions. Avoid later criticism that the recording does not include everything the witness said by being mindful of when conversation is off-the-record.

What is best, and what a witness is willing to do, are two different things. Many witnesses are reluctant to talk, and they are usually under no legal obligation to talk to anyone, unless compelled by legal process. Of those willing to talk, many are understandably reluctant to give a signed statement or to have their statements recorded or reduced to a writing. Hence, your priority should be to get the witness to tell what he knows so you will learn what his trial testimony is likely to be, and get leads on other witnesses and evidence. Only then should you try to get the most reliable type of statement the witness agrees to give. In short, it is usually better to conduct an interview without any recording than to have no interview at all. You can always dictate immediately afterwards what the witness has said.

8. Interviewing techniques[15]

Every witness is influenced by both positive and negative factors that affect the witness' willingness to be interviewed and disclose what he knows. An interviewer, therefore, should understand these factors and use them to accomplish his primary purpose of finding out what the witness knows. These factors bear on both friendly and hostile witnesses. Hostile witnesses may be unwilling to talk at all; friendly witnesses, although willing to talk, may be influenced by a variety of negative and positive factors.

Negative factors inhibit witness disclosure. Some witnesses feel that they are being judged by the interviewer. Others tell the interviewer what she apparently wants to hear. Still others become inhibited by emotions such as fear or embarrassment. The interviewer must learn to recognize

---

14. While witness statements are usually not discoverable, under Rule 26(b)(3) even trial preparation materials are not absolutely protected from discovery. Upon a showing of substantial need and undue hardship, such materials are discoverable, except that "mental impressions, conclusions, opinions, or legal theories of an attorney or other representative of a party" are always protected from disclosure.

15. See D. Binder & S. Price, Legal Interviewing and Counseling (1977), which covers these basic concepts in great detail.

situations in which these factors exist and use interviewing techniques that reduce their effect.

Positive factors promote disclosure. Witnesses usually respond favorably when the interviewer shows a personal interest in them. Witnesses like to feel that they are doing the decent thing by talking to the interviewer. They tend to identify with the side that values their testimony. Witnesses enjoy feeling important, and may be more likely to help if they feel that the information they can provide is important to resolve a dispute fairly. Positive reinforcement is a strong motivator.

Getting witnesses to disclose fully and accurately is best achieved by minimizing the negative factors and reinforcing the positive ones. Accordingly, pick a convenient time and place for the interview. When scheduling the interview, remind the witness that it's always better to talk when the events are fresh in his mind. Remind him that it is natural to want to help others, and that his disclosing information will help ensure a just and accurate result. Point out what other witnesses have said about the case so as to give him an opportunity to correct inaccuracies. Finally, show interest in the witness. Empathy is a strong motivator, and a witness naturally will want to please someone who appears interested in him.

An interviewer can use either open or closed questions to achieve desired results. Use open-ended, direct-examination questions to get the witness talking, to obtain the basic story, and to pursue leads. For example, questions in a "describe how" and "tell me" format will force the witness to give descriptive answers. But use closed, cross-examination questions to pin the witness down and develop potential impeachment. This question form can focus on specific, isolated facts. For example, to pin a witness down, ask him: "You're sure the car was going 40 mph?" and "She couldn't have been going faster than that, could she?"

The content of questions can also effectively influence responses. Let the witness know your attitude on the matter being discussed, since he has a psychological interest in satisfying his listener's expectations. For example, telling a witness that you feel badly about your client having been cheated by the defendant may get a more sympathetic story from the witness. Second, word choices can influence responses. For example, it is well known that using the word "how fast" rather than "how slowly" will increase estimations of speed. Third, leading questions are more likely to get the kind of answer you want. For example, asking a witness "That car was going faster than the speed limit, wasn't it?" is more likely to elicit a "yes" response. Fourth, knowing what other people have said or what other evidence has already shown can influence witnesses, since witnesses prefer consistency and disdain conflict. For example, telling a witness that another eyewitness has already stated that the car was speeding will often influence the witness.

9. Evaluating witnesses

Following a witness interview, write a short memo evaluating the witness and his information. It is easy to forget your impressions of the witness, yet witness credibility is frequently the critical component in case evaluation. The memo is particularly important if more than one lawyer will work on the file. The memo should evaluate the witness' credibility and effectiveness as a trial witness, note the witness' attitude toward the case, and summarize where the witness' anticipated testimony will help and hurt your case.[16]

§2.6. *Expert reviews*

Wrongful death, medical malpractice, product liability, major negligence, and commercial cases almost always use expert witnesses at trial. The plaintiff's case will probably require expert testimony to establish a prima facie case on liability and causation and to make out a solid case on damages. The defense case will probably have opposing experts. Accordingly, your investigation is frequently incomplete unless you have the file reviewed by appropriate experts.

You may need two experts: one to review the file and consult with you in order to develop facts and theories for trial, the other to be a trial witness. Of course, one expert can and often does perform both roles. Remember, however, that under Rule 26(b)(4) the facts and opinions of a consulting expert are usually protected from discovery, absent exceptional circumstances, but the identity and substance of facts and opinions of experts expected to be witnesses at trial are discoverable. Hence, having a separate consulting expert will usually limit what is discoverable by other parties, and should be valuable in developing theories and evidence for trial. Make sure that your agreement with the consulting expert clearly shows her status, and requires that she communicate only with you, so that her work comes under the Rule 26 protection.

If a case is complex and will involve substantial work, it may be advisable to insist that the case be reviewed by an expert before you agree to take it. The cost of the review should be paid by the prospective client. While the lawyer can usually advance the cost of the review, requiring the client to pay for the review in advance is often an effective way of weeding out clients who already know they have a weak case. Such clients will often refuse to pay for the review, which should make you think carefully about taking the case in the first place, particularly where the client has the ability to pay. This is a sensible approach whenever you have a case that will require expert witnesses. Regardless of how the review comes out, both you and the client will benefit. If the case is complex and will require expert witnesses, Rule 11 may require an expert's review before filing suit.

---

16. Such a memo should also be absolutely privileged as work product and therefore not discoverable. See Rule 26(b)(3).

Do not send out a file for expert review until you have collected the reports and records the expert will inevitably need. Make sure the written materials you send her give a complete and neutral picture of the case, but do not give the expert privileged materials. Keep in mind that an expert who becomes the testifying expert at trial can often be deposed and forced during cross-examination to produce all materials she received for her review. Factual materials that the lawyer gives to the expert may not be protected by the work product privilege,[17] therefore, do not give an expert any materials that contain your mental impressions and thought processes. In addition, rather than have the expert review the file generally, direct the expert to specific areas where you see potential problems. This is best done in conversations with the expert, after you have sent her the necessary materials. For example, in a medical malpractice case you might tell the expert that your potential theory of liability is that the anesthetic was improperly administered, and ask the expert if the standard of reasonable care was breached. A focused review is usually more productive.

While Rule 26 makes important discovery distinctions between consulting and testifying experts, hiring an expert as a consultant does not prevent you from using her as an expert at trial. That decision may have to be made at the discovery stage, however, since a standard interrogatory asks that you identify all experts expected to testify at trial. Again, if you list the consulting expert as a trial witness, she can often be deposed and forced to produce all materials she has reviewed.

Because an expert is so important, and because a consulting expert may later be the testifying expert at trial, you must be careful in selecting one. Perhaps the best way to select an expert is simply to ask litigators you know to recommend one who is knowledgeable in the subject area of your particular kind of case, is willing to work with and educate you, and will be an effective trial witness. If this fails, or you need an expert in an extremely specialized area, some lawyers' groups, such as the American Trial Lawyers Association, maintain expert directories, and law libraries sometimes have directories for various specialties.[18]

§2.7. The "small" case

This book discusses how to organize and investigate a case using the litigation-chart method. This approach integrates the legal and fact investigations so that you can intelligently plan the litigation before filing suit, or responding to one. These are steps that every litigator should take when handling any litigation matter.

When a case is sufficiently large, perhaps with $20,000 to $30,000 in issue, it obviously makes economic sense for the litigants to devote sub-

17. See, e.g., Bogosian v. Gulf Oil Corp., 738 F.2d 587 (3d Cir. 1984).
18. See e.g., H. Philo et al., Lawyers Desk Reference (6th ed. 1979), which lists experts by category. TASA, the Technical Advisory Service for Attorneys, is an organization that refers experts in numerous fields. Many legal newspapers and journals also contain listings and information about experts. Local universities are also a good source.

stantial legal resources to achieve the best possible result. In such cases, the lawyers representing the parties will usually be able to do all the things a conscientious litigator should do, without being constrained by cost. However, consider the client with a "small" case, involving less than $10,000, who comes to you. His case, although appearing to have merit, involves so little money that it is not economically possible to handle it competently and receive adequate compensation for the work involved. What do you do?

This is hardly a theoretical question. The "average" case filed in state and federal courts today involves perhaps $15,000 to $20,000.[19] If that is the typical case, there are obviously numerous cases involving smaller amounts. Automobile accidents involving a few hundred dollars in direct losses, and consumer contract matters involving similarly small sums, are common disputes, and some are litigated.

The inherent conflict can be stated simply. On the one hand, every lawyer has a professional obligation to represent each client competently. On the other hand, a lawyer needs to be compensated to stay in business. How do you resolve this conflict?

The very small cases present less difficulty. Most jurisdictions have small claims courts in which the litigants can represent themselves at trial. Many jurisdictions do not allow lawyers in small claims courts, and judges hear the cases informally without adhering to strict rules of procedure or evidence. They frequently have brochures that explain how to bring a claim in small claims court and how the case will be heard. In addition, some jurisdictions have special procedures for other small cases. These frequently include restriction or elimination of discovery. The intent of both types of procedures is to bring down the cost of trying a case so that it makes economic sense to bring a lawsuit to enforce a claim in the first place. The cases that are too large to be brought as small claims, yet too small to make normal litigation cost effective, cause the greatest problems. These are the cases in the $1,000 to $10,000 range. What can you do when presented with such cases? These small cases are particularly problematical, because a case that is small in dollar amounts may be just as legally and factually complex as a larger case. However, keeping several concepts in mind can at least reduce the concerns.[20]

First, screening small cases is particularly important. This involves carefully assessing liability, damages, and the other party's ability to pay a judgment. There is nothing more unproductive than taking a small case with questionable liability or filing an action against a party who is effectively judgment proof. Small cases must be screened quickly before any substantial investment in time is made.

19. See Trubek, et al., The Costs of Ordinary Litigation, 31 UCLA L. Rev. 72 (1983). The authors conducted a study of approximately 1600 civil cases in five federal districts in 1978; half were state cases, half federal. They found that over two-thirds of the cases involved tort and contract claims, and the average amount at stake was approximately $10,000 (in 1978 dollars). Over 90 percent of the cases settled before trial. The median amount of time a lawyer devoted to a single case was 30.4 hours.

20. See Adelman & Halderman, The Dog Case, 10 Litigation (no. 3, Spring 1984).

Second, the client must understand what you can realistically do given the size of the case, and agree to your approach. For example, if the case is not worth the filing of a suit, perhaps you can attempt to get a settlement. If the case is large enough to bring suit, but formal litigation would be prohibitively expensive, perhaps you can handle this particular case without formal discovery or with limited discovery. Frequently the lawyers can agree to limit discovery by agreeing not to use depositions or informally interviewing the parties. Whatever your approach, make sure the client knows what it will be and the reasons for it, and also agrees to it in writing.

Third, make sure you get your costs covered in advance, and let the client know the overall anticipated costs. A client who has paid the anticipated costs in advance has a direct financial interest in the litigation and will usually be more cooperative and realistic. A client who understands how costs, such as a medical expert's fee, can devour any recovery will have a better grasp of what can realistically be done.

Fourth, get the client to do as much work as possible, such as obtaining documents and records and locating witnesses. This can substantially reduce costs. You can also tell the client that you will not take the case until he has done this kind of preliminary work. Again, this not only reduces expenses but also involves the client in the litigation.

Fifth, you can sometimes economize without seriously compromising the preparation of the case. The largest savings can be made in the area of formal discovery, particularly depositions. Sometimes depositions need not be transcribed. Sometimes you can avoid depositions of witnesses entirely and rely on witness statements. Sometimes the opposing lawyer will agree to reciprocal informal interviews of parties in place of depositions. These savings, of course, must be discussed with the client, and he must agree to the procedures you take.

Sixth, the paramount rule, regardless of the size of the lawsuit, is always the same: The client's case must be competently handled. This means that you must do whatever is necessary to uncover the important facts and witnesses, even if it is not cost effective. If the opposing lawyer will not agree to informal interviews of the parties and it is essential to discover what the party will say at trial, you simply must depose that party. If the case cannot be settled short of trial, you simply must try the case. Lawyers, wittingly or not, sometimes take cases that are uneconomic from the lawyer's point of view. Once taken, however, the lawyer has the same professional obligation to prepare that case competently as she has for any other case.

Finally, keep in mind that when lawyers take cases, they frequently do so for reasons other than the compensation they will directly receive from that particular case. In small cases, accept the fact that you simply will not be paid at your usual rate. However, that fact alone should not prevent you from taking certain cases, since lawyers frequently take cases for reasons other than producing income. The case may be from a regular client, whom you want to ensure remains satisfied with your overall representation. The case may come from a new client who may become a regular client if he is satisfied with the way in which you handle a small matter. The case may be legally or factually challenging. The case may be a high profile case that will enhance your reputation among lawyers and in the community. The case may be a new type of case and involve an area you have become interested in. Finally, you may decide to take a case to meet your pro bono obligations as a lawyer.

The high cost of litigation is a serious concern in our society and has sparked considerable discussion among the public, government, and the organized bar. Litigation procedures have become more streamlined in small cases; alternative dispute resolution is becoming common; judges are taking a more active role in settlement discussions. If a lawyer decides to take a case, however, the cardinal rule is that he always has a professional obligation to represent a client competently. That the client's matter is a small case cannot serve as an excuse for the lawyer to avoid professional obligations. The realities of your professional life as a lawyer are that once you agree to take a case, adequate planning and preparation are required to resolve the matter, regardless of its size. Accordingly, the basic steps discussed in this book must be followed to ensure that your representation is adequate.

III

LEGAL INVESTIGATION

§3.1.   Introduction

As you conduct your informal fact investigation, you must also evaluate the various legal considerations that arise in every lawsuit. These include determining what jurisdiction's substantive law applies; what claims, remedies, or defenses to pursue; what parties must be joined; whether the court has subject matter jurisdiction over the claims; whether the court has personal jurisdiction over the parties; and where venue is proper. This chapter discusses the legal choices a plaintiff must make before filing a lawsuit, and a defendant must make before responding to one, as well as the interdependence of these legal considerations. While this discussion is based on federal district court litigation, the basic analytical sequence is also applicable to state court lawsuits.

A note of caution is in order. Issues dealing with choice of law, legal theories of recovery, joinder, subject matter jurisdiction, personal jurisdiction, and venue can be complex and the literature about them is extensive. A single volume can hardly deal with these issues in depth, much less one chapter in a general text on pretrial techniques. This discussion's purpose is necessarily limited to getting the new litigator to think intelligently about these legal considerations in broad terms to avoid "missing the boat" on vital issues. Where a serious legal issue exists, it must always be researched thoroughly before filing suit. As always, remember that Rule 11 requires that a lawyer conduct a reasonable inquiry into the law and determine that the pleading is well grounded before signing the pleading. The rule, in short, requires that you do your homework.

§3.2.   Choice of law[1]

Before you can determine what claims, relief, or defenses you can raise in your case, you need to know which jurisdiction's substantive law applies.

---

1. James & Hazard §§2.33-2.37; Friedenthal §§4.1-4.7; Moore's Manual §§3.01-3.05; Moore's Federal Practice §§0.301 et seq.; Wright & Miller §§4501 et seq.

In federal court, where plaintiff brings a claim under the court's federal question jurisdiction, the resolution is simple: federal substantive law applies.[2] However, if plaintiff brings a claim under the court's diversity jurisdiction, and the claim is based on a substantive right created by state law, two types of choice-of-law questions arise.

1. When will a state's substantive law apply in federal court?

The question of when state law will be considered "substantive" and be applied in federal court is the so-called *Erie* problem, based on the landmark case of Erie R.R. Co. v. Tompkins, 304 U.S. 64 (1938). In *Erie* the Supreme Court held that whenever a federal court applies state substantive law, it must apply not only its statutory law, but its case law as well. The principal impact of *Erie* is on diversity cases, where a federal court must apply the appropriate state's substantive law.

The question of what is substantive law, as opposed to procedural, is unfortunately not always clear. For example, a state's basic negligence law is clearly substantive, and its discovery rules in civil procedure acts are clearly procedural. However, matters such as statutes of limitations, privileges, and burdens of proof can arguably be both. The Supreme Court has periodically grappled with the substantive-procedural distinction since deciding *Erie*.

In Guaranty Trust Co. v. York, 326 U.S. 99 (1945), the court announced what has come to be called the "outcome determinative" test. When a state law, if applied in federal court, would substantially affect the outcome of the case, the state law is substantive and must be applied. In several later cases the Court has modified the outcome-determinative test. For example, in Byrd v. Blue Ridge Rural Electric Cooperative, 356 U.S. 525 (1958), the Court held that the federal right to a jury trial on a claim prevailed over a contrary state rule; in Hanna v. Plumer, 380 U.S. 460 (1955), the Court applied the federal service-of-process rules over a conflicting state rule; and in Wallace v. Armco Steel Corp., 446 U.S. 740 (1980), the Court applied a state rule defining how an action is to be commenced for statute of limitations purposes over the conflicting Rule 3 in the Federal Rules of Civil Procedure. However, to date the Court has yet to fashion a rule that can be confidently applied to determine if a state law will be characterized as substantive and therefore be applied in federal court. Instead, the Court has essentially decided substantive-procedural questions on a case-by-case basis. Accordingly, any lawyer faced with an *Erie*-type question must thoroughly research the decided cases to determine how the problem is likely to be resolved.

2. What is the state's substantive law?

The second choice-of-law issue deals with multi-state events and transactions. If, for example, an Arizona driver is suing a California driver over

2. In some instances, as with the Federal Tort Claims Act, the federal substantive law refers to the forum state's substantive law.

an automobile accident in Nevada and brings a diversity action in federal court, which state's tort law applies? Does it matter where the action is filed?

The Supreme Court in Klaxon Co. v. Stentor Electric Manufacturing Co., 313 U.S. 487 (1941), held that in a federal diversity action the forum state's conflict-of-law rules govern in determining which state's substantive law will apply. In the above example, if plaintiff brings suit in federal district court in Arizona, then Arizona's conflicts of law rules govern. While the rule attempts to restrict shopping between federal and state forums, a plaintiff who can bring an action in more than one venue may still be able to acquire a more advantageous forum. For example, if the Arizona plaintiff can file suit in Arizona, the Arizona conflicts rules govern, which may result in Arizona substantive law being applied, since Arizona has an interest in applying its own law to its own citizens. If the Arizona plaintiff can file suit in Nevada, the Nevada conflicts rules govern and Nevada may apply its substantive law, since the accident occurred within its borders. If Arizona and Nevada tort law differ and the plaintiff has a choice of forums in which to bring suit, he will obviously pick the more advantageous one.

When the choice of law issue has been resolved, it is sometimes difficult to determine what the applicable state's substantive law actually is. State law, of course, is what a particular state's legislature and supreme court have declared it to be. What happens, however, if there is no controlling statute and the state's high court has not spoken on a particular question of law? How should a federal district court decide what the applicable state law is? The Supreme Court has held that in such cases a state appellate court decision will be highly persuasive, although not binding.[3] If there is no appellate court decision, the district court can certify the question to the state supreme court. If there is no such procedure, the district court can look at any available sources to determine what the state law is likely to be were the state courts presented with the question. Finally, if the district court feels that an antiquated state law would no longer be followed, the court may determine that it is not bound by precedent and can instead fashion a rule that the state courts would likely create if again faced with the issue.[4] In such circumstances, of course, thorough research is required.[5]

§3.3. Legal theories for claims, relief, and defenses

One or two theories for claims or defenses probably provided the initial direction for your fact investigation. Before filing suit or responding to one, however, you should always explore whether the presently available facts will support other legal claims or defenses. There are dangers in

3. Commissioner v. Estate of Bosch, 387 U.S. 456 (1967).
4. Bernhardt v. Polygraphic Co. of Am., 350 U.S. 198 (1956).
5. See Friedenthal §4.6 for an excellent discussion of how a district court determines applicable state law.

prematurely labeling a client's legal problems. Think expansively, so that all reasonably assertable claims are considered before deciding which ones to raise in your initial pleading. However, there are contrary considerations that must be remembered. Rule 11 provides sanctions for improper pleadings when the attorney has not conducted a "reasonable inquiry" of the facts and law, or has filed for any improper purpose.[6] In addition, more claims usually create a more complex and costly lawsuit, something that may not be appropriate in a particular case.

This discussion obviously cannot review the numerous legal theories on which claims and defenses can be brought. However, it is always useful to review checklists of potential theories for claims, remedies, and defenses before filing the initial pleading. Doing so will at least get you to consider other similar theories, both statutory and common law; to review the required elements of each theory; and to analyze the advantages and disadvantages of each in light of the existing facts.[7] Each of these theories, with its required elements, should be put on your litigation chart.

When you have identified all possible theories of claims or defenses, how do you find the "elements" for each of them? Perhaps the best place to start is with the standard jury instructions used in the applicable jurisdiction. These usually exist for common claims and defenses with the required elements of a prima facie case itemized. Additional research will usually be necessary, particulary if the claims or defenses are not based on routine tort or contract theories. For common law claims and defenses, the best starting point is usually a hornbook or treatise on the substantive area involved. For statutory claims, you should obviously start with the statute involved and check the case annotations for elements and jury instructions. After checking these basic sources, check the recent cases interpreting and applying the substantive law. Computer searches on LEXIS or WESTLAW, two legal research systems, are frequently useful. Finally, many states have practice manuals that cover types of litigation that are common to the jurisdiction; frequently these prove to be excellent practical reviews. With this type of research, you should have enough to "mull over" the pros and cons of the various legal theories that can be supported by the available facts.

For example, assume you represent the plaintiff in a personal injury case arising out of an automobile accident. You consider, of course, a negligence claim against the other driver and a claim based on violating the "rules of the road." However, is there a claim based on negligent maintenance of the defendant's vehicle? If the defendant had been drinking, can the drinking support a negligence or statutory claim? Again, the point is to think expansively so that you consider every theory of recovery that can be supported by provable facts.

What claims you decide to bring in a lawsuit is influenced not only by theories of recovery, but also by the remedies permitted under each legal

---

6. See discussion of Rule 11 in §5.2(f) infra.
7. See, e.g., Actions and Remedies (C. Friend ed. 1984).

theory. Your choice of remedies will significantly influence what proof is relevant at trial and the scope of discovery.[8]

Under the Federal Rules of Civil Procedure, a party is not usually limited to the relief requested, and pleadings can ordinarily be amended. Nevertheless, it is always preferable to frame your pleadings so that they accurately reflect all the types of relief to which your client may be entitled. In addition, the remedies you seek will, like all the allegations in the pleadings, determine what will be relevant for discovery purposes. The distinction between legal and equitable actions no longer controls what remedies are permissible, since federal courts, like most jurisdictions, have merged courts of law and equity and have power to order any appropriate relief. Hence, it is important to review all potentially available remedies, legal and equitable, and request all that are proper. The simplest way to look at remedies is to review first the general types of legal and equitable relief, then relate that relief to the specific claims you are considering, and finally review any statutes and court rules that permit additional relief.

First, legal remedies (historically, those remedies permitted for actions in a court of law) include money damages, restitution, and recision. Money damages, the most frequently sought relief, can be compensatory, consequential, or punitive. While compensatory damages are always permitted, consequential or punitive damages are usually permitted only where statutes or case law permit them. Equitable remedies (historically, those remedies granted by a court of chancery when legal remedies were inadequate or inflexible) include injunctions, specific performance, reformation, unjust enrichment, accounting, constructive trust, equitable lien, and reclamation. Any of these remedies should be requested if appropriate to the circumstances, regardless of the kind of claims brought.

Second, the precise measure of the allowable money damages, frequently controlled both by statute and case law, depends on the type of claim being asserted. For example, damages for breach of contract depend on whether the contract involves land, personal property, construction, or employment. Tort damages also vary considerably, depending on whether the claim is based on personal injury, survival, wrongful death, undue influence, fraud, defamation, intentional tort, or statutory actions. Where a claim is statutory, the allowable damages are frequently specified in the statute.

Third, you must check to see if there are any statutory provisions for allowing recoveries for other damages, court costs, and attorney's fees. This includes checking not only the statutes providing for specific causes of action, but also federal and state procedural rules.[9] State civil practice

---

8. The leading treatise on remedies is Dobbs, Hornbook on Remedies (1973).

9. There are over 100 federal statutes that permit awarding attorney's fees and other costs to the successful litigant. Common examples include §1983 civil rights actions, employment discrimination actions under Title VII of the 1964 Civil Rights Act, consumer products warranty actions under the Magnuson-Moss Warranty Act, and actions under the Freedom of Information Act. See E. R. Larson, Federal Court Awards of Attorney's Fees, (1985); Dobbs, Awarding Attorney Fees Against Adversaries: Introducing the Problem, 1986 Duke L.J. 435.

rules often have provisions for costs and fees that, if viewed as substantive, may be applied in federal diversity actions.

For example, assume you represent the plaintiff in a contract dispute over the sale of goods. The plaintiff delivered the goods but has not been paid. Certainly, the plaintiff can receive compensatory damages, but are other remedies possibly available? Can the plaintiff support a claim for consequential damages? Is the defendant guilty of bad faith, or is there some other basis for a punitive damages claim? Are there any statutory means by which you can recover for the plaintiff's attorney's fees and other costs? Once again, the point is to think expansively so that you consider every theory of relief that the law provides in your case.

Remedies issues should always be researched carefully to learn the full measure of damages permitted for the claims involved. A good place to start is with the damages instructions in those jurisdictions that have standard jury instructions.

§3.4. Joinder of parties and claims

Joinder-of-parties issues are best addressed by asking a series of questions that parallel the analytical sequence involved. These are:

1. Who is the real party in interest?
2. Does that party have capacity to sue?
3. Is joinder of parties required?
4. Is joinder of parties permitted?
5. Do any special pleading rules apply?
6. Is joinder of claims permitted?

1. Real party in interest[10]

Rule 17(a) requires that an action be brought "in the name of the real party in interest." That party is the one who, under applicable substantive law, has the right that the lawsuit seeks to enforce. The purpose of the rule is to ensure that the parties with the real interests are the ones actually prosecuting cases. Potential issues arise when personal representatives are named parties.

The applicable substantive law in diversity cases is the state law applicable under the Erie R.R. Co. v. Thompkins, 304 U.S. 64 (1938), analysis. For diversity jurisdiction purposes, the citizenship of the real party in interest is controlling.

Rule 17(a) also specifies exceptions to the general rule by providing that an "executor, administrator, guardian, bailee, trustee of an express trust, a party with whom or in whose name a contract has been made for

---

10. Wright §70; James & Hazard §10.3; Friedenthal §6.3; Moore's Manual §13.01; Shepard's Manual §§3.106-3.110; Moore's Federal Practice §§17.07-17.15; Wright & Miller §§1543-1558.

the benefit of another, or a party authorized by statute" may sue in his own name. While the plaintiff has the burden of showing he is the proper real party in interest, the exceptions to Rule 17(a) have largely eliminated controversy in this area. The only areas where disputes still arise are assignments and subrogation. While a complete assignment makes the assignee the real party in interest, 28 U.S.C. §1359 expressly provides that such an assignment cannot be used to "create" diversity where it would otherwise not exist. If an assignment or subrogation is only partial, both parties to the assignment or subrogation are usually considered real parties in interest.[11]

If the wrong party is sued, Rule 17(a) provides that no dismissal should be entered unless after a reasonable time following an objection a proper substitution of parties is not made or the real party in interest ratifies the action.

2. Capacity to sue[12]

A lawsuit must be brought by and against parties that have a legal capacity to sue. Capacity to sue is governed by Rule 17(b), which in turn refers to state law. In the case of an individual, capacity to sue is determined by the state law of the individual's domicile. For corporations, capacity is determined by the law of the state of incorporation. In other cases, including those involving representatives, the law of the forum state controls capacity to sue. The forum state's laws control partnerships and unincorporated associations, except that, regardless of the forum law, partnerships and unincorporated associations always have capacity to sue over substantive federal rights. Finally, under Rule 17(a) an infant or incompetent can sue or be sued in the name of a representative. If no representative has been appointed, a guardian ad litem can bring suit or be appointed for the sued party.

If a defendant wishes to challenge plaintiff's claim of capacity to sue, the defendant must, under Rule 9, deny the claim "with particularity." Failing to make the denial in a responsive pleading will usually result in any error being deemed waived.

3. Required joinder of parties[13]

Joinder of parties is governed by Rules 19 and 20. The joinder rules address a basic question: As plaintiff, what parties must, should, or may be, brought into the lawsuit so that the claims can be properly decided? What

11. Wright §70; James & Hazard §§10.4-10.5; Moore's Manual §13.01; Shepard's Manual §3.109; Moore's Federal Practice §17.05; Wright & Miller §§1545, 1546.
12. Wright §70; James & Hazard §10.7; Friedenthal §6.3; Moore's Manual §13.02; Shepard's Manual §§3.111-3.117; Moore's Federal Practice §§17.16-17.27; Wright & Miller §§1559-1573.
13. Wright §71; James & Hazard §§10.11-10.15; Friedenthal §6.5; Moore's Manual §§13.04-13.07; Shepard's Manual §§3.120-3.124; Moore's Federal Practice §§19.05-19.21; Wright & Miller §§1601-1624.

parties must, or should be, joined is governed by Rule 19; what parties may be brought in is governed by Rule 20.[14]

Needless to say, these esoteric distinctions have been the source of much debate and litigation over the years. The present joinder rules are an attempt to get away from rigid labels and move toward a pragmatic analysis of the competing interests involved. On the one hand, there are legal and social interests in giving every party an opportunity to litigate and at the same time avoiding multiple suits over the same issues. On the other hand, there are corresponding interests in permitting some claims to be adjudicated, rather than none. The modern approach to joinder, as represented by Rules 19 and 20, is to resolve joinder issues by focusing on those competing interests.

Rule 19, dealing with required joinder, is divided into two basic rules. Rule 19(a) governs what parties are to be joined "if feasible"; Rule 19(b) governs what the court should do if all required parties cannot be joined.

Under Rule 19(a), a party should be joined if that party's presence is (1) required to grant "complete relief," or (2) the party has an interest in the action so that the party's presence is, practically speaking, necessary to protect his interest, or the party's absence may expose other parties to double or inconsistent obligations. Such a party should be joined unless he cannot be served with process, or the party's joinder would defeat federal subject matter jurisdiction. While the rule appears complex, in practice its application is not particularly problematical. As a practical matter, a plaintiff should join any potentially liable party who can be served, if the party's joinder will not defeat subject matter jurisdiction (and, of course, the Rule 11 requirements are met).

Rule 19(b) governs the situation where a party who should be joined cannot be because the party cannot be served with process, or because the party's joinder would defeat federal jurisdiction. The issue before the court then is whether to proceed without the party or dismiss the action. Rule 19(b) states four factors the court must balance in reaching an equitable decision: (1) whether nonjoined and existing parties will be prejudiced, (2) whether an order can minimize any potential prejudice, (3) whether any judgment without the absent party can be adequate, and (4) whether the plaintiff will have an adequate remedy if the action is dismissed.

These practical concerns frequently compete with each other, but certain conclusions are likely. First, if the consequence of a dismissal is that the plaintiff is left without any state forum in which to pursue claims against all parties, it is highly unlikely that the court will dismiss the action. Second, if an absent party can be brought in as a third-party defendant, there is strong ground for rejecting a present defendant's claim of potential prejudice. The possibility of intervention is also a strong ground for rejecting the claim of prejudice to an absent party. Third, the possi-

---

14. The "must-should" categories roughly approximate the traditional "indispensable-necessary" distinction; the "may" category approximates the traditional "proper" label. These traditional terms are now considered outdated.

bility of incomplete relief to the plaintiff will usually be rejected as a reason for dismissal, since that result alone prejudices no one. In short, the judicial tendency has been to retain federal jurisdiction rather than dismiss the case.

4. Permissive joinder of parties[15]

Permissive joinder, governed by Rule 20, resolves the question of who may be joined as a proper party. Rule 20 provides two tests, both of which must be met before joinder will be permitted. First, there must be a question of law or fact common to all parties arising out of the action. Second, each plaintiff must have a right of relief, either jointly, severally, or alternatively against each defendant based on the same occurrences or transactions, or series of transactions or occurrences.

The language of Rule 20 is broad, and permits joinder whenever there is a legal or factual relationship between the parties making it sensible to have all these parties present in one lawsuit. On the other hand, permissive joinder can operate to delay the litigation and make it unfairly expensive and burdensome on certain parties. For that reason, Rule 20(b) gives the court broad regulatory powers, including the power to order separate trials to prevent any unfairness.

Where there is improper joinder, Rule 21 provides simply that the case cannot be dismissed. Rather, the misjoined parties are dropped and nonjoined parties added by court order.

5. Special pleadings rules

Required and permissive joinder rules, set forth in Rules 19 and 20, are not the only rules that regulate whether parties can be joined in a lawsuit. There are several pleading rules that govern a number of special types of actions. These are:

> Counterclaims — Rule 13
> Cross claims — Rule 13
> Impleader — Rule 14
> Interpleader — Rule 22
> Intervention — Rule 24
> Class actions — Rule 23
> Shareholder derivative suits — Rule 23.1

These pleadings, and their special requirements, are discussed in Chapter 5.

15. Wright §71; James & Hazard §§9.7-9.8; Friedenthal §6.4; Moore's Manual §14.01; Shepard's Manual §§3.118-3.119; Moore's Federal Practice §§20.05-20.08; Wright & Miller §§1651-1660.

6. Joinder of claims[16]

Joinder of claims, governed by Rule 18, is always permissive. Each party can bring as many claims as the party has against every other party. These include both present and contingent claims. Deciding what claims to bring against another party is principally a practical matter.[17]

§3.5. Subject matter jurisdiction in district courts

Subject matter jurisdiction refers to the power of a court to hear particular matters. Federal district courts are courts of limited jurisdiction and cannot hear a case unless it falls within their power, as defined in Article III of the United States Constitution, and Congress has extended jurisdiction over the particular type of case.

Because federal district courts are courts of limited jurisdiction, a party seeking to invoke the court's jurisdiction must affirmatively plead and demonstrate proper subject matter jurisdiction.[18] The basis for jurisdiction must appear on the face of a well-pleaded complaint and cannot rest on counterclaims, defenses, or anticipated defenses. On the other hand, any party or the court can raise lack of subject matter jurisdiction. Although most commonly raised by a Rule 12 motion to dismiss, it can be raised at any time, even after judgment or on appeal. If the court has no jurisdiction over the subject matter, the case must be dismissed.

1. "Case or controversy"[19]

The court must have an actual "case or controversy" that is ripe for adjudication. Put another way, the court will not hear moot or collusive cases, render advisory opinions, or hear controversies that are essentially political or administrative issues. This requirement limits cases to those involving real controversies in which parties have a direct stake in the outcome and will actively represent their interests.

The question of whether there is an actual case or controversy, and the related issue of standing, arises frequently in public interest, constitutional, and administrative litigation. For example, a suit to enjoin enforcement of a city regulatory code provision, brought by a local resident, will raise both issues. In private litigation, there will ordinarily be an obvious controversy, with the parties having obvious standing, particularly since declaratory judgment acts have been upheld. In public interest liti-

16. Wright §78; James & Hazard §9.4; Friedenthal §6.6; Moore's Manual §10.06; Shepard's Manual §§3.163-3.166; Moore's Federal Practice §§18.03-18.11; Wright & Miller §§1581-1594.

17. See §4.5.

18. See §5.2.

19. Wright §12; Moore's Manual §1.01(1); Shepard's Manual §1.4; Wright & Miller §3529.

gation, on the other hand, these issues are common as well as complex and must be researched thoroughly.

2. Federal question jurisdiction[20]

28 U.S.C. §1331 provides that "district courts shall have original jurisdiction of all civil actions arising under the constitution, laws, or treaties of the United States." Section 1331 is generally referred to as conferring "general" federal question jurisdiction. This distinguishes §1331 from other "specific" grants of jurisdiction found in §§1333 et seq. and from other non-Title 28 grants.

The general-versus-specific distinction is important because of the requirement that a party invoking the court's jurisdiction must affirmatively show the basis for jurisdiction. Issues over jurisdiction seldom arise when the basis is a specific grant in a statutory provision. Problems frequently exist, however, when the basis for jurisdiction is the general grant under §1331.

a. "Arising under" [21]

Jurisdictional issues occur under §1331 because its arising "under" language is so general. Section 1331 provides that jurisdiction can arise "under the Constitution, laws or treaties of the United States." The constitutional provisions are contained in Article III, §§1 and 2. However, §1331, which contains the same language as Article III, §2, has been interpreted much more narrowly than the parallel constitutional language.

The basic requirements for jurisdiction under §1331 are that the claim be based on federal law, which must be demonstrated in the complaint, and that the federal claim be substantial rather than frivolous.[22] For example, plaintiff brings an action for patent infringement. This raises federal question jurisdiction because it is brought under the Patent Act. Another plaintiff brings an action for an unlawful search of his house. This raises federal question jurisdiction because it is brought under the Fourth Amendment of the U.S. Constitution. Where federal law expressly creates a remedy, jurisdiction will be found. However, where a federal statute, although declaring rights, does not expressly confer a remedy, complex issues exist, and they center on whether an implied remedy exists that is recognizable under §1331. On these issues the courts are frequently divided; therefore, the law must be thoroughly researched.

20. Wright §§17-22; James & Hazard §2.5; Friedenthal §2.3; Moore's Manual §§5.02-5.05; Shepard's Manual §§1.59-1.66; Moore's Federal Practice §0.62(2.-1); Wright & Miller §§3561-3567.2.

21. Moore's Manual §5.02-5.03; James & Hazard §2.6; Friedenthal §2.3; Shepard's Manual §§1.60-1.66, §§1.80-1.108; Moore's Federal Practice §0.62(2.1); Wright & Miller §3562.

22. Since the complaint must affirmatively show that federal jurisdiction exists, it follows that raising a defense based on federal law cannot create jurisdiction.

b.   Specific grants of jurisdiction

There are several other sections of Title 28 that grant federal courts jurisdiction to hear particular matters. These include:

§1333 — admiralty
§1334 — bankruptcy
§1336 — ICC/commerce
§1337 — commerce/antitrust
§1338 — patent, copyright, trademark, unfair competition
§1339 — postal
§1340 — IRS/customs
§§1341-1364 — miscellaneous provisions

Finally, there are numerous statutory provisions outside of Title 28 that also confer jurisdiction on district courts. The more important ones are:

Jones Act, 46 U.S.C. §688
Federal Employer's Liability Act, 45 U.S.C. §56
Securities Act, 15 U.S.C. §77
Civil Rights Act, 42 U.S.C. §1983

Where jurisdiction is based on these specific grants, the same pleading requirements apply: A plaintiff wishing to invoke the court's jurisdiction must always affirmatively plead a proper jurisdictional basis.

Keep in mind that these federal grants of jurisdiction can be exclusive or concurrent with state courts. In several areas, notably admiralty, bankruptcy, and patent and copyright cases, the district courts have exclusive jurisdiction.

c.   Pendent jurisdiction[23]

A claim can properly be brought in federal court if the basis for jurisdiction is a federal question. What happens, however, if plaintiff has other claims, not based on federal question jurisdiction? Can these be brought with the federal claim? If the other claims each have a separate proper basis for federal jurisdiction, such as diversity jurisdiction, no problems arise. However, if there is no such basis for the claims, the question arises of whether the other claims can be "joined" to the federal claim.

The concept of pendent jurisdiction addresses this question and strikes a compromise between the usual requirement that federal jurisdiction must be strictly construed and the obvious advantage of hearing at

---

23. Wright §19; James & Hazard §2.7; Friedenthal §2.13; Moore's Manual §5.15; Shepard's Manual §§1.109-1.112; Moore's Federal Practice §18.07(1.2); Wright & Miller §§3567, 3937.

one time all claims that can be brought by one party against another. A simple answer is to deny federal jurisdiction on the non-federal claims, the result being that a plaintiff who wants to pursue all claims in one action must do so in a state forum. However, this option is not available when the federal claim is one over which federal courts have exclusive jurisdiction. In this situation the options are to try all claims in federal court or to split the claims between federal and state courts.

The Supreme Court in United Mine Workers of America v. Gibbs, 383 U.S. 715 (1966), set forth the standards in deciding whether to permit joining federal and non-federal claims. "Pendent jurisdiction," i.e., that jurisdiction over the non-federal claims, will be permitted if both the federal and non-federal claims "derive from a common nucleus of operative fact." Id. at 725. In short, if the non-federal claims are based on the same set of facts as the federal claims, joinder of the claims is proper, although the court retains discretion to reject the pendent claim.

d.   The United States as a party[24]

When the United States is a plaintiff, no special jurisdictional problems arise. However, the United States cannot be sued unless it has waived its sovereign immunity and consented to the action. A plaintiff suing the United States, therefore, must expressly demonstrate the statutory basis under which the government has consented to be sued. The most frequently used grounds are the Court of Claims Act,[25] Tucker Act,[26] and Federal Tort Claims Act.[27]

Frequently, however, a plaintiff may wish or need to sue a federal official or federal administrative agency, rather than the United States directly. In this situation there must be a specific statute that permits suit against the agency or a named federal official. Such statutes frequently permit suits brought to challenge administrative agency decisions. For example, suit is frequently brought against the Secretary of Housing and Urban Development for denial of claimed Social Security benefits.[28] Where there is no statute permitting suit against a federal official or agency, it is still sometimes possible to sue an official individually for an alleged improper act. Finally, there are a number of federal entities, which may be incorporated or unincorporated, of which the United States is whole or part owner. Examples include the Federal Deposit Insurance Corporation and Federal Housing Authority. Whether such quasi-governmental entities can be sued in federal court is heavily regulated by statute and, sometimes, by case law.

---

24. Wright §22; James & Hazard §2.5; Friedenthal §2.10; Moore's Manual §13,078; Shepard's Manual §§1.128-1.135; Moore's Federal Practice §17.24; Wright & Miller §§3651-3660.

25. 28 U.S.C. §1491.

26. 28 U.S.C. §1346(a).

27. 28 U.S.C. §1346(b).

28. 42 U.S.C. §405.

3. Diversity jurisdiction[29]

Section 1332 provides for the jurisdiction of federal courts in civil actions involving diversity of citizenship, and parallels the constitutional grant of power found in Article III, §2 of the Constitution. This provision of Title 28 sets out four categories of actions for which diversity jurisdiction is proper:

   (i)   Between citizens of different states

  (ii)   Between citizens of a state and citizens or subjects of a foreign state

 (iii)   Between citizens of different states and in which citizens or subjects of a foreign state are additional parties

 (iv)   Between a foreign state as plaintiff and citizens of a state or of different states

Of these four categories, the first is the predominantly used section. The other three are usually referred to as the alienage sections. Diversity jurisdiction does not apply to domestic relations and probate matters, which are considered local matters properly raised only in state courts.

a. "Citizenship" requirement[30]

Section 1332 is based on "citizenship," an imprecise term. The citizenship of natural persons is the state of domicile, and no person can have more than one domicile at a time. For corporations, §1332(a) provides that its citizenship is both the state where incorporated and the state where it has its principal place of business, which is usually defined as where a majority of its business is conducted or, if that is unclear, where the corporate headquarters is located. In direct actions against liability insurers, the insurer is considered a citizen of the state where the insured is domiciled.[31] Unincorporated associations present particular difficulties. If the association is not an entity entitled by state law to sue or be sued in its own name, its citizenship is that of each of its members. If the association is an entity entitled to sue or be sued, the prevailing rule is that here also the association is considered to be a citizen of each state of which a member is a citizen.

Needless to say, what constitutes citizenship for diversity purposes when artificial entities are involved can be a complex issue involving law that is frequently unsettled; thorough research is essential.

29. Wright §§23-31; James & Hazard §2.5, Friedenthal §§2.5-2.7; Moore's Manual §5.06; Shepard's Manual §§1.19-1.58; Moore's Federal Practice §§0.71-0.85; Wright & Miller §§3601-3610.

30. Wright §§24, 26; James & Hazard §2.5; Friedenthal §2.6; Moore's Manual §5.06; Shepard's Manual §§1.24-1.33; Moore's Federal Practice §0.74; Wright & Miller §§3601-3642.

31. Some states have so-called direct action statutes that permit suits that are brought directly against an insurance company. The typical situation is an automobile accident involving the insured.

b. Complete diversity requirement[32]

The requirement that diversity must be "complete" in order for the federal district courts to have jurisdiction means that each plaintiff must have a different state citizenship from each defendant. Stated another way, if any plaintiff and any defendant are citizens of the same state, diversity will not be complete. For example, if citizens of Illinois and California sue citizens of Maine and Vermont, complete diversity exists. If citizens of Illinois and California sue citizens of Maine, Vermont, Connecticut, and California, complete diversity does not exist.

The complete diversity requirement applies to every party that is actually joined, regardless of whether that party is required or permissive. To retain the required complete diversity, a plaintiff can dismiss all but indispensable parties from the action. In addition, a plaintiff may manipulate the parties to create complete diversity. Because of this, a party's characterization as a plaintiff or defendant in the complaint is not controlling. Parties will be realigned as plaintiffs or defendants, and nominal or formal parties will be ignored, to determine if complete diversity actually exists. In the case of legal representatives, such as a trustee or guardian, the citizenship of the representative is controlling. However, where the legal representative is nominal, such as with a guardian ad litem, the citizenship of the represented party is determinative for diversity purposes. Collusive assignments, made solely to create diversity, are also ignored.[33]

The complete diversity rule is somewhat misleading because it applies to the original plaintiffs' claims against original defendants and does not apply to many other situations. The concept of ancillary jurisdiction, which applies to counterclaims, cross-claims, impleader, and interventions as of right, significantly modifies the complete diversity requirement.

Complete diversity is determined according to the citizenship of parties at the time the initial complaint was filed. Later changes in citizenship by a party will not defeat jurisdiction.

c. Jurisdictional amount requirement[34]

Section 1332(a) requires that the "matter in controversy exceeds the sum or value of $10,000, exclusive of interest and costs." The plaintiff's complaint is the sole basis for determining if the requirement has been met. The allegations are controlling unless there is a "legal certainty" that the jurisdictional amount cannot be obtained. This will occur only when plaintiff requests damages, such as punitive damages, to which he is not entitled under the applicable substantive law, and those damages are necessary to reach the jurisdictional amount.

The principal issue in this area involves the problem of valuation, particularly where equitable relief is requested. With injunctions, where

---

32. Wright §§23-31; James & Hazard §2.5; Friedenthal §2.6; Moore's Manual §5.06; Shepard's Manual §1.34; Wright & Miller §3605.

33. See 28 U.S.C. §1359.

34. Wright §§32-37; James & Hazard §2.5; Friedenthal §2.8; Moore's Manual §§5.07-5.14; Shepard's Manual §§1.72-1.79; Moore's Federal Practice §§0.90-0.99; Wright & Miller §§3701-3712.

this problem most frequently occurs, the measure of damages is the value of the right sought to be enforced or the value of the avoided injury. The value may be different, depending on whether it is measured from the plaintiff's or the defendant's perspective. The courts are divided on which view of the measure of damages is appropriate, although more appear to use the plaintiff's loss approach. For example, suppose the plaintiff brings suit to enjoin the enforcement of certain statutes, such as zoning ordinances or health regulations, and to have them declared unconstitutional. The court must look to see what the amount of the loss to the plaintiff would be if the statutes continue to be enforced.

Another issue involves aggregation of claims to meet the jurisdictional amount. Here there are four basic situations. First, where there is one plaintiff and one defendant, the plaintiff can aggregate all claims against the defendant to meet the jurisdictional amount requirement. For example, a plaintiff has two claims, each involving $6,000, against one defendant; the claims involve two separate, unrelated contracts. The plaintiff can properly aggregate the claims. Second, where there is one plaintiff and multiple defendants, plaintiff can aggregate claims only if the claims are joint rather than several and distinct. For example, a plaintiff has two claims, each involving $6,000, against two defendants; the claims involve two separate, unrelated contracts. The plaintiff cannot aggregate these claims. However, if the liability is joint, as would be the case if the defendants are partners jointly liable on a partnership obligation, aggregation is proper. Third, where there are multiple plaintiffs and one defendant, the plaintiffs cannot aggregate separate and distinct claims. The plaintiffs can aggregate only if the claims are undivided and a single title or right is involved. For example, two plaintiffs each have a $6,000 claim against one defendant; the claims involve two separate, unrelated contracts. The plaintiffs cannot aggregate these claims; however, if the two plaintiffs are partners suing to recover a debt owed to the partnership, aggregation is proper. Finally, where there are multiple plaintiffs and multiple defendants, the above analysis applies to the individual claims.

Interest and costs raise fewer questions. Costs include attorneys' fees only if a contract or statute permits them. Interest, which is ordinarily incidental to the action, is included for purposes of determining if the jurisdictional amount is met only if the interest itself is the basis of the action.

4. Ancillary jurisdiction[35]

Because federal courts are courts of limited jurisdiction, the question must arise of whether a federal court can have jurisdiction over claims for which no federal jurisdictional basis exists. The competing interests

35. Wright §9; James & Hazard §2.7; Friedenthal §2.14; Moore's Manual §5.15; Shepard's Manual §§1.109-1.112; Moore's Federal Practice §8.07(5); Wright & Miller §§3523, 3567.

are closely related to pendent jurisdiction issues. On one hand, federal jurisdiction is ordinarily interpreted narrowly. On the other hand, it makes sense, for the sake of judicial economy and consistency, to try all related claims at one time. The issue of ancillary jurisdiction arises whenever a plaintiff has a proper claim and another party wishes to file a counterclaim, cross-claim, or third-party complaint, but the latter claim does not have an independent jurisdictional basis.

The Supreme Court in Owen Equipment Co. v. Kroeger, 437 U.S. 365 (1978), held that ancillary jurisdiction should be conferred where there is a "logical dependence" between the claim having an independent jurisdictional basis and the nonindependent claims. While an imprecise standard, the decision recognizes that the test can only be applied on a case-by-case basis. If the subsequent claim arises out of the same transaction or occurrence as the plaintiff's original claim, it makes sense to try the claims together.

The concept of ancillary jurisdiction is important because it permits certain types of pleadings involving claims that do not have an independent basis for federal jurisdiction. These include compulsory counterclaims, cross-claims, interpleader, intervention of right, and impleader. Such pleadings commonly involve indemnity. For example, consider a plaintiff who properly brings a claim in federal court that has proper subject matter jurisdiction. The defendant wishes to bring in a third-party defendant on an indemnification theory. Indemnification raises no federal questions, however, and since the defendant and third-party defendant are citizens of the same state, diversity is lacking. Yet, in this situation the court will have ancillary jurisdiction over the third-party claim.

5. Removal jurisdiction[36]

The removal jurisdiction of federal district courts is governed by 28 U.S.C. §§1441-1452. Since it is a jurisdictional statute, it is strictly construed and its requirements must be followed closely to ensure that removal is properly made.

Removal is the procedure in which a case, already filed in a state court, is transferred to the federal district court for the same district in which the state action is pending. The first requirement, then, is that the case has already been filed in state court. To determine if removal is proper, you must look to the complaint at the time the removal petition is filed. The removal cannot be based on defenses or counterclaims. Further, the state court where the action is pending must have both subject matter jurisdiction over the action and personal jurisdiction over the defendants. If it does not, removal is improper, even if the federal court could have had original jurisdiction over the action.

36. Wright §§38-41; James & Hazard §2.9; Friedenthal §2.11; Moore's Manual §§8.01-8.13; Shepard's Manual §§1.149-1.173; Moore's Federal Practice §0.155; Wright & Miller §§3721-3740. The mechanics of the removal procedure are discussed in §7.6 infra.

Second, all defendants, except nominal ones, must join in the removal petition. Since removal is for the benefit of defendants, each must agree to the removal; a "defendant" for removal purposes is each party against whom the original plaintiff brought a claim in state court.

Third, the removal petition must, under §1446(b), be filed within 30 days of the time the defendant receives a copy of plaintiff's initial pleading in state court, or within 30 days of receiving summons if the initial pleading under state practice is not required to be served on the defendant, whichever is shorter. The short time period, like all the removal requirements, is strictly enforced. Once the petition is filed, it operates as a stay on any state court proceedings.

Fourth, removal is generally proper if the federal district court could have had original jurisdiction over the action had it been filed in federal court. For this reason you must determine if the federal district could have had proper subject matter jurisdiction over the plaintiff's original complaint.

There are three basic grounds for removal: diversity, federal question, and special removal statutes. Under §1441, removal jurisdiction can be based on diversity; this is usually proper when each plaintiff has a different citizenship from each defendant. The complete diversity rule for removal has one important exception: §1441(b) prevents removal if any proper defendant is a citizen of the state where the action was brought. This exception is based on the notion that a principal reason for permitting removal in diversity of citizenship cases is the possibility of local prejudice against noncitizen parties, which fails if a party is a citizen of the forum state. Accordingly, the diversity jurisdiction for removal is narrower than diversity for original diversity jurisdiction purposes. In addition, complete diversity must exist both when plaintiff's original action was filed in state court and when the removal petition is filed.

Removal can also be based on federal question jurisdiction. If an action could have been brought in district court on federal question grounds, it can ordinarily be removed. Removal generally cannot be allowed unless the claim could be brought as an original action in federal court.

The removal sections also provide for removal in certain special circumstances. These include:

§1441(d) — civil actions against foreign states
§1441 — federal officers
§1442a — members of armed forces
§1442 — civil rights actions
§1444 — foreclosure against the United States

Section 1445 makes certain actions nonremovable. These include actions under state workers' compensation acts; actions against railroads, their receivers, or trustees; and against a common carrier, its receivers, or trustees, arising under specific federal statutes.

Where it later develops that removal was improperly granted, §1447(c) provides for remand to the state court at any time before final judgment.

A plaintiff who wishes to file and keep a lawsuit in state court can use certain strategies to defeat removal. First, where diversity would otherwise permit removal, plaintiff can add a defendant who either is not diverse from the plaintiff or is a citizen of the forum state. So long as such a joinder is not fraudulent in the sense that plaintiff does not really wish to prosecute a claim against that party, it will defeat removal. Second, where diversity does not exist, plaintiff can draft the complaint to avoid pleading a claim that would permit removal based on federal question jurisdiction. Where plaintiff has decided that a state forum is preferable, it is often possible to structure the claims and select the defendants to prevent removal.

§3.6. *Personal jurisdiction*[37]

Personal jurisdiction refers to the power of a court to bring a party before it. A judgment is not enforceable against a party unless that party can lawfully be brought into court and has received notice of the lawsuit. Thus, constitutional concepts of due process underlie this requirement.

Jurisdiction to adjudicate can be in personam, in rem, or quasi in rem. An in personam jurisdiction over a party is necessary for full enforcement of a judgment against a party and for the concepts of res judicata and collateral estoppel to operate. An in rem action is one that involves property over which the parties have some dispute, and jurisdiction over the party exists by virtue of the party's ownership of the property. Finally, a quasi in rem action refers to an action brought to subject only certain property to the claims asserted. This is frequently done by seeking to attach property of a known party to satisfy a future judgment. These distinctions have less significance today at the federal court level, where the critical concerns involve the constitutional limits of personal jurisdiction and the issue of whether service was properly made. Hence, issues surrounding personal jurisdiction involve two separate questions:

1. Can the defendant constitutionally be subject to the court's jurisdiction?
2. Was service of process on the defendant proper?

The first question involves the due process limitations on personal jurisdiction, and the second involves the service-of-process requirements of Rule 4.

37. Wright §§64-65; James & Hazard §§2.14-2.25; Friedenthal §§3.1-3.28; Moore's Manual §§6.01-6.19; Moore's Federal Practice §§0.219-0.229; Wright & Miller §§1061-1075.

1. Due process requirements

Due process issues do not arise for plaintiffs, since by initiating suit a plaintiff is considered to have voluntarily submitted to the court's jurisdiction for all purposes, including being required to respond to counterclaims and other claims brought in that action. Where a defendant is a resident of the forum state, due process problems do not arise, since by virtue of residency it is fair to require the defendant to defend against an action in the forum state. When a nonresident defendant, however, is sued in the forum state and does not consent to the jurisdiction of the court, due process problems may prevent that defendant from being required to defend there. Determining what the due process limitations are is a difficult question that the Supreme Court has considered several times. The question is raised with increasing frequency as more businesses engage in national and international commerce.[38]

The leading constitutional cases include International Shoe Co. v. State of Washington, 326 U.S. 310 (1945), and World-Wide Volkswagen Corp. v. Woodson, 444 U.S. 286 (1980). Recent significant Supreme Court cases are Burger King Corp. v. Rudzewicz, 471 U.S. 462 (1985), and Asahi Metal Industry Co. v. Superior Court, (1987).

In *International Shoe* the Court addressed the question of what activities by a corporation within a particular state will subject it to suit within that state consistent with due process concepts. It held that where a corporation's "minimum contacts" in the forum state were such that being forced to defend a suit in that state would not offend " 'traditional notions of fair play and substantial justice,' " jurisdiction was proper. Id. at 316, quoting Milliken v. Meyer, 311 U.S. 457, 463 (1940). Many subsequent decisions, of course, expounded on what minimum contacts satisfied due process. One of these, *World-Wide Volkswagen*, appeared to narrow the scope of such contacts. There the Court rejected the argument that an out-of-state seller should be subjected to suit in another state simply because it was foreseeable that the vehicle sold might be involved in a collision in another state. Instead, the Court stressed that minimum contacts protect a defendant from being sued in a remote or inconvenient forum, and that foreseeability does not by itself create such contacts as would satisfy due process requirements. Requiring a defendant to defend in the forum state, the Court held, must be fair and not impose unreasonable burdens on the defendant.[39]

The minimum-contacts analysis applies with equal force to in rem and quasi in rem actions.[40] Because of this, distinctions such as in rem or

38. The issue rarely arises in tort litigation, because a tort is usually seen as an event caused by a defendant that subjects him to the court's jurisdiction, and because state automobile statutes usually impose a "consent to be sued" fiction on out-of-state motorists.

39. In *Asahi Metal*, a closely divided court held that merely placing a product into the stream of commerce is not an act that will subject a party to the forum state's jurisdiction, even if the party was aware that the stream of commerce would sweep the product into the forum state. Minimum contacts requires some action purposely directed toward the forum state.

40. The Supreme Court so held in Schaffer v. Heitner, 433 U.S. 186 (1977), deciding that a defendant's ownership of property by itself did not establish such contacts as would

quasi in rem have no direct bearing on the due process question of a defendant's amenability to suit in a particular forum. However, the distinctions are still important for determining the enforceability of judgments.

2. Service-of-process requirements

It is important to keep in mind that amenability to process is different from, and independent of, the adequacy of service of process. If a party is not constitutionally amenable to process, any service on that party will have no effect unless the party waives objections to the service. If a party is amenable to process, service of process on that party must still be properly made.

Service must be properly made because due process considerations require that service be made in a manner that will reasonably put a defendant on notice that he has been sued.[41] Since Rule 4(e) now permits service by any method allowed by the state law in which the district court is sitting, this means, in practical terms, that an out-of-state defendant can be served under the forum state's long-arm statutes.

Service of process under Rule 4 is discussed in §5.3.

§3.7. Venue[42]

A lawsuit must be filed in a proper place. Where a lawsuit can be filed is governed by venue statutes. Those statutes determine the geographic districts where the case can properly be heard.

Since venue provisions are designed in part to protect a defendant from being forced to litigate in an "unfair" forum, it follows that a defendant can waive the benefits of the venue rules. Hence, a defendant must raise improper venue in a timely manner, either by a Rule 12 motion or in the answer, otherwise objections will be deemed waived.

Because a plaintiff may sometimes have more than one available venue, the question of which venue to choose may arise. This question involves both practical and legal considerations. On the practical side, convenience and the cost to the plaintiff, the plaintiff's lawyer and witnesses will frequently dominate the decision. The plaintiff's own district will often be the choice, if it is available. If the plaintiff's principal witnesses are in another district, that should be considered. On the legal side, choice-of-law decisions may be critical, since applicable substantive law may differ for such matters as statutes of limitations, elements of claims, and allowable damages. Further, since the subpoena power of a

---

create proper personal jurisdiction over the defendant, where the claims were not related to the property.

41. See Mullane v. Central Hanover Bank, 339 U.S. 306 (1950).

42. Wright §§42-44; James & Hazard §§2.10-2.11; Friedenthal §§2.15-2.17; Moore's Manual §§7.01-7.15; Shepard's Manual §§2.1-2.78; Moore's Federal Practice §§0.140-0.148; Wright & Miller §§3801-3868.

district is generally limited to its geographical boundaries, if uncooperative witnesses are out-of-state, you may need to choose another available forum to reach these witnesses. Finally, considerations such as the choice of judges, the desirability of prospective jury pools, and length of time until trial should all be considered.

1. Determining venue[43]

The general venue statute for federal district courts is §1391, which has two basic provisions. Under §1391(a), if jurisdiction is based solely on diversity, venue is proper in the district where "all plaintiffs or all defendants reside, or in which the claim arose." For example, a plaintiff, a resident of Arizona, sues two defendants, residents of Nevada and California, for injuries caused by an automobile collision in Utah. Venue is proper only in Arizona and Utah. Under §1391(b), if jurisdiction is based other than solely on diversity, venue is proper only in the place where "all defendants reside, or in which the claim arose," unless a special venue statute applies. For example, a plaintiff, a resident of Georgia, sues two defendants, residents of Florida and Alabama, for patent violations that occurred in Louisiana — venue is proper only in Louisiana.

Unfortunately there are numerous such special venue statutes, both in the Title 18 venue section and elsewhere. The special provisions begin with §1394. Other venue provisions are scattered throughout the United States Code, usually as part of the substantive statute that creates a cause of action.[44] Consequently, you must always check whether a special venue statute exists that overrides the general provisions of §1391.

In addition, §1392 governs venue in "local" actions that are actions involving property. Whether the action is in rem, so that §1392 applies, is controlled by the nature of the remedy sought. Ordinarily, if the remedy is specific to the property, the action will be local, and §1392 makes the venue that of the res involved.

Once the applicable statutes are determined, the question of a party's residence arises, since §1391 is based on residence. For venue purposes "residence" is viewed in much the same way as citizenship. An individual's citizenship is where the individual is domiciled. A corporation under §1391(c) is considered a resident of any district "in which it is incorporated or licensed to do business or is doing business." Unincorporated associations, if they have no capacity to sue under state law, are residents of each district in which any member of the association resides. If the association is an entity entitled to sue under state law, the association is a citizen of the district where it conducts its business. Aliens under §1391(d) can be sued in any district. Finally, where a defendant is the United States, its agencies, officers or employees, §1391(e) controls and provides that venue is generally proper — unless law provides otherwise

---

43. Wright §42; James & Hazard §2.10; Friedenthal §2.15; Moore's Manual §§7.02-7.11; Shepard's Manual §§2.1-2.12; Wright & Miller §3801.

44. For a list of such venue statutes, see Moore's Federal Practice §0.142.

— where the defendant resides, where the action arose, where property involved in the action is located, or where the plaintiff resides if no property is involved.

The venue provisions control where a plaintiff files the initial complaint against the original defendants. They do not apply to counterclaims, cross-claims, or third-party claims, since these are seen as ancillary to the initial suit and hence raise no additional venue issues.

2.   Change of venue[45]

A change of venue can be based on two grounds: improper venue, governed by §1406; and inconvenient venue, governed by §1404. Under §1406, the court has discretion either to dismiss or to transfer to a proper venue any case that has been filed in an improper venue. Since the statute encourages transfers "if it be in the interest of justice," this is the usual approach. Keep in mind that proper venue is a personal right. A plaintiff, by filing an action in an improper venue, waives the right to object to it. A defendant must raise any venue objection either by a Rule 12 motion or in the defendant's answer, otherwise objections will usually be considered waived.

Under §1404(a), the court may transfer a case from a proper venue to another venue, "where it might have been brought," "for the convenience of parties and witnesses, in the interest of justice." This section recognizes that a plaintiff frequently has venue choices, and that the plaintiff's choice, while proper, may not be the most convenient forum for the case seen as a whole. If this situation exists, the court can transfer the case to the more convenient forum, the only restriction being that the new forum must be in a district in which the plaintiff could have filed the action and where the court could have obtained personal jurisdiction over the defendants.

When a case is transferred from one venue to another, the substantive law follows the case. This is important in diversity cases, where the forum state's substantive law, including its conflicts of law rules, is applied. When a case is transferred to another district, in another state, the original substantive law is still applied to the case. This rule avoids forum shopping by the defense in an attempt to get more favorable law applied to the case.

45. Wright §44; James & Hazard §2.11; Friedenthal §2.17; Moore's Manual §7.12; Shepard's Manual §§2.52-2.74; Moore's Federal Practice §§0.145-0.148; Wright & Miller §§3841-3855.

IV

CASE EVALUATION AND STRATEGY

§4.1. Introduction

Case evaluation requires that you gather enough facts and consider sufficiently the legal issues to decide intelligently whether to take the case. Then, if you decide to take it, the evaluation requires that you devise a realistic, cost-effective litigation plan. This chapter discusses making the initial decision to take a case, establishing the attorney-client relationship, developing a litigation strategy, and completing prefiling requirements.

§4.2. Taking the case

You should take those cases that have factual and legal merit and are economically feasible, and you should usually decline the others. But just how and when do you decide if you should take a case?

Your litigation chart, which sets out the potential legal claims and required elements of proof for each claim, provided the direction for your factual and legal investigation; you also prepared a litigation budget. These provide the framework from which to analyze the case. In addition, keep in mind Rule 11, which provides that an attorney's signature on a pleading constitutes a verification that the attorney has conducted a "reasonable inquiry" into the facts and law.[1] Hence, you cannot plead claims, relief, or defenses that you have not adequately investigated to determine whether they are well grounded.

As the lawyer for a prospective plaintiff, you should take a case only if you can realistically expect to prove a prima facie case on at least one theory of recovery. You should already have some admissible proof for each element of each asserted claim or have a reasonable basis for believing you will get such missing proof during formal discovery. In addition,

1. See discussion of Fed. R. Civ. P., Rule 11 in §5.2.4.

the potential recovery must be large enough to justify the work and risks of litigation. Many lawyers, for example, refuse even a simple case on a contingency fee basis unless a realistic recovery is in the several-thousand-dollars range because the fee, usually one-third of any recovery, will simply not provide reasonable compensation for the work and risks involved. In a complex case, such as a medical malpractice claim, the realistic damages might have to be in the $30,000 to $50,000 range to make it economically feasible to take the case.

When to decide, as a plaintiff's lawyer, to accept or decline a case depends on the type of case and the factual and legal issues involved. For example, you might accept a simple automobile collision case after merely inteviewing the client and reviewing the police accident report. Sometimes such a limited investigation will be enough to assess whether the client "has a case," whether, economically speaking, the damages are substantial enough to make it worth pursuing, and whether a judgment can actually be collected. In more complex matters, however, such as medical malpractice, products liability, or commercial cases, you may need to do substantial legal research, extensive factual investigation, and have an expert review the case before you can make this decision. The basic question is always the same: Do I know enough from my fact investigation and legal research to conclude that the client has a provable case with substantial damages that can be collected? If the case appears weak, involves a great deal of work, and would be taken on a contingency fee basis, the best time to turn it down is now. Every lawyer has taken cases and later regretted it. The best way to avoid this is by rejecting the marginal cases early.

There are exceptions. First, where a plaintiff is in imminent danger of having an applicable statute of limitations run, your first obligation is to file a claim to prevent the statute from running, even though you have not had an opportunity to investigate the facts and research the law. Protecting the plaintiff's claim from a limitations bar must take precedence over other considerations.[2] Second, keep in mind that lawyers frequently take cases for reasons other than the income that the case will produce.[3]

If you decide to take a case, you need to enter into a contract with the client. If you turn down the case, you need to send out a letter declining representation. These steps are discussed in the following sections.

As a defendant's lawyer, the decision whether to take a case is in one way easier and in another way more difficult. It is easier from the economic point of view, since defendant's cases are not taken on a contingency basis. So long as the defendant agrees on how to pay the lawyer for the legal services, there are no economic risks in taking a weak case. However, the decision is more difficult in the sense that the lawyer and the defendant must agree on how best to defend the case. If the client realizes the case is not defensible on the merits, the client may try to pressure the lawyer to drag out the case or file unfounded counterclaims. But

---

2. Protecting the plaintiff's claim under these circumstances should not constitute a Rule 11 violation. See Boone v. Superior Ct., 145 Ariz. 235, 700 P.2d 1335 (1985).

3. See §2.7. The "small" case.

a defense lawyer has the same obligations, under codes of professional ethics as well as under Rule 11, as the plaintiff's lawyer. Such conflicts are best handled at the outset by letting the client know what you can and cannot do in defending the case, and by reaching agreement on how you plan to defend.

§4.3. Establishing the terms of the attorney-client agreement

The attorney-client relationship should be formally established with a written agreement. There are three reasons for this. First, any contractual relationship is best established by a written instrument. Second, the agreement will prove the existence of an attorney-client relationship for privilege purposes. Third, it will establish the work to be done, what will not be done, and the basis for compensation, all of which are necessary for a good working relationship with the client.

Unless your client is sophisticated and has experience working with lawyers, the client will have little understanding of the legal work involved in litigation and the various fee arrangements that can be made. It is in everyone's best interests that the client be educated on these matters. You should discuss how you set your fees, and the expected costs, with the client.

In some jurisdictions the agreement, particularly a contingency agreement, must be in writing. It is most common to use either a written contract or a letter to the client, a copy of which the client signs and returns. Regardless of which method is used, it should be sufficiently detailed to cover all aspects of the relationship. Unfortunately, disputes between lawyers and clients are common, but they can largely be avoided by making sure that the agreement is drafted in clear and simple English, covers all likely issues, and specifies what is not covered. Ambiguities and omissions in attorney-client agreements will usually be strictly construed against the lawyer.[4] The agreement should cover the following basic subjects.

1. Work covered

The agreement should specify what work will be performed and what will not be. For example, the agreement might be to prosecute a negligence claim arising out of a car accident on a certain date and time. If you will not handle any appeal, or if there will be an additional charge for any appeal, the agreement should specify this. If you will not handle a workers' compensation claim, insurance claim, or other related matters, the agreement should say so. In general, you must guard against a client thinking that you would do more than you agreed to do. Spelling out what is not covered should prevent this from happening.

4. See S. Speiser, Attorney's Fees (1978).

2. Lawyer's fee

A lawyer's fee is the compensation the lawyer will receive for professional services rendered on behalf of the client. The amount of the lawyer's fee, the way it will be determined, and when it will be paid must be spelled out. The total fee must be reasonable in light of the work to be done, the difficulty of the work, the amount of time it will involve, and the customary range of fees for similar work in your locality.[5]

The agreement should specify how the fee will be determined. Three approaches are commonly employed: an hourly rate (common in corporate, commercial, and insurance defense cases), a fixed flat fee (common in criminal defense cases and in family law), and the contingency fee (common in plaintiff's personal injury cases). Obviously the agreement can specify any number of combinations or modifications of these basic approaches, unless the fee is regulated or set by statute. For example, agreements frequently specify a minimum retainer fee, paid up front, that is credited against an hourly billing rate. When the fee is based on an hourly rate, the client must understand that what is being paid for is the lawyer's expertise and time. Hence, any time expended on a client's case will be billed to the client, regardless of whether the time is spent on court appearances, conferences, research, on drafting documents, or on making telephone calls.

The agreement should define how the fee amount is determined and when it should be paid. For instance, in personal injury cases where the plaintiff's attorney's fees are usually a percentage of any recovery, it is important to specify whether the percentage is computed before or after costs are deducted and that the fee is due when any judgment is actually collected.

If a fee will be shared with another lawyer outside the principal lawyer's firm, you must disclose this fact to the client and obtain his consent. The division of fees must be proportionate to the work and responsibility of each lawyer.[6]

A lawyer has an ethical duty to make the fee reasonable. This may mean that the lawyer must review the fee, even in a contingent fee situation, to make sure it is in fact reasonable before submitting it to the client.[7]

Many statutes and rules regulate and limit attorney's fees. For example, statutory causes of action frequently either limit attorney's fees or make them subject to court approval.[8] Make sure that your agreement complies with any applicable statutes and rules.

An attorney's lien can usually be imposed on a judgment to ensure payment of the fee. This is frequently done in contingent fee situations.

---

5. See Model Code of Professional Responsibility, Rule 2-106; Model Rules of Professional Conduct, Rule 1.5.

6. See Code of Professional Responsibility, Rule 2-107; Model Rules of Professional Conduct, Rule 1.5(e).

7. See, e.g., In the Matter of Schwartz, 686 P.2d 1236 (Ariz. 1984).

8. See, e.g., Federal Tort Claims Act, 28 U.S.C. §2678; M. F. Derfner & A. D. Wolfe Court Awarded Attorney Fees (1983).

In some jurisdictions an attorney's lien is only enforceable if the client expressly agrees to it. Hence, it is good practice to discuss the lien with the client and have the agreement show that the client agrees to it.

3. Retainers

In some situations a lawyer should insist on a retainer to ensure payment of the fee and other costs. A retainer is simply a cash payment of a sum of money to the lawyer before work begins on the client's case. This makes sure that the lawyer will get paid for the work and that costs the lawyer advances will be reimbursed. A common arrangement is to insist on a retainer, and then periodically deduct fees and costs as they are incurred. Regardless of the precise arrangement, the agreement must specify the amount of the retainer, when it must be remitted, and what fees and costs will be deducted from it.

Whenever a lawyer receives advanced funds from a client, the funds must be put in a separate client trust account. Under no circumstances can any client's funds be commingled with the lawyer's funds.[9] Funds of all of a lawyer's clients can be held in one trust account; however, a separate ledger must be kept for each client showing receipts and disbursements. A number of states have adopted, through statutes or court rules, the Interest on Lawyer's Trust Accounts (IOLTA) system, which requires holding client funds in interest-bearing accounts.

4. Costs

The agreement should distinguish between fees due the lawyer for professional representation and the costs and expenses incurred during the course of that representation. The agreement should note anticipated costs, such as filing fees and other court costs; expert witness fees and expenses; court reporter fees; travel expenses; photocopying, mailing, and long distance calls. It is sometimes a good idea to estimate the usual costs for the type of case involved. The agreement should also specify when the costs will be paid; customarily the client is billed at regular intervals, such as monthly or quarterly. The agreement should make clear that costs are the client's obligation, even if no recovery is obtained.

Plaintiff's personal injury cases present a special situation. The reason for accepting a contingency fee arrangement — that the client is otherwise unable to pay for legal representation — also bears on the propriety of advancing costs. A lawyer may advance costs, such as court costs, deposition expenses, investigator fees, and expert witness fees; however, the client ultimately is still responsible for paying those costs. The most common approach is to reimburse costs to the lawyer when a judgment is actually paid. If there is no recovery, the client is still respon-

9. See Model Code of Professional Responsibility, Rule 9-102; Model Rules of Professional Conduct, Rule 1.15.

sible for paying the costs, although a client without money will probably not be able to reimburse the lawyer. For this reason, some lawyers accept contingency fee arrangements for cases that will have substantial costs only if the client advances a sum of money sufficient to cover the expected costs.

5. Billings

The agreement should specify when fees and costs will be billed. While monthly billing is normally best for both lawyer and client, less frequent billings are sometimes appropriate, particularly for regular business clients, or if little work is done in any given month.

6. Authorization to file suit

The agreement should contain a statement that authorizes the lawyer to file suit on behalf of the client or, if a defendant, authorizes the lawyer to defend the suit. The terms of the agreement should then be put in writing, either in a letter to the client or a written agreement.

Example (hourly fee agreement letter):

Dear Mr. Jones:

As we discussed in my office yesterday, I have agreed to represent you in the divorce proceedings recently started by your wife Joan. I will handle all negotiations necessary to attempt a property settlement before trial. If a trial becomes necessary, I will represent you to the conclusion of the trial.

Fees for representing you will be based on the time expended on your case, the nature of issues presented, and the services rendered. My present hourly rate is $100 per hour. You have agreed to provide a retainer of $1,500 within one week. My usual total fee in divorce cases, assuming that no unusual problems arise, is approximately $1,500 if we agree on a property settlement, and approximately $3,000 to $4,000 if the case must be tried.

In addition to my fee, there will also be certain costs expended on your case, such as court filing fees, court reporter fees, long distance telephone and photocopying charges. You will be responsible for paying all such costs, regardless of the outcome in the case.

I will send you an itemized statement each month showing the time I have spent on your case and the other costs that have been incurred. I will subtract each monthly statement from the $1,500 retainer until it has been used up. I will then bill you directly, and you have agreed to pay those monthly statements in full when you receive them.

Please confirm that this letter correctly reflects the terms of our agreement by signing and dating the enclosed copy of this letter on the spaces provided.

Upon receipt of the signed letter and the $1,500 retainer I will begin work on your case.

Sincerely,

/s/ *John Smith*

Agreed: _____

        John Jones

Dated: _____

Example (contingency fee agreement):

AGREEMENT

Date: _____

I agree to employ John Smith and his law firm, Smith & Smith, P.C., as my attorneys to prosecute all claims for damages against Frank Johnson and all other persons or entities that may be liable on account of an automobile collision that occurred on June 1, 1986, at approximately 3:00 P.M., near the intersection of Maple and Elm Streets in this city. I authorize you to file suit on my behalf.

I agree to pay my lawyers a fee that will be one-third (33⅓ percent) of any sum recovered in this case, regardless of whether received through a settlement, lawsuit, or any other way. The fee will be calculated on the sum recovered, after costs and expenses have been deducted. The fee will be paid when any moneys are actually received in this case. I agree that John Smith and his law firm have an express attorney's lien on any recovery to ensure that their fee is paid.

I agree to pay all necessary costs and expenses, such as court filing fees, court reporter fees, expert witness fees and expenses, travel expenses, long distance telephone costs, and photocopying charges, but these costs and expenses will not be due until a recovery is actually received in this case. I understand that I am also responsible for paying these costs and expenses, even if no recovery is received.

I agree that this agreement does *not* cover matters other than those described above. It does not cover an appeal from any judgment entered, any efforts necessary to collect money due because of a judgment entered, or any efforts necessary to obtain other benefits such as insurance, employment, Social Security and Veteran's Administration benefits.

Agreed: _____

        John Jones

I agree to represent John Jones in the matter described above. I will receive no fee unless a recovery is obtained. If a recovery is actually received, I will receive a fee as described above.

I agree to notify John Jones of all developments in this matter promptly, and will make no settlement of this matter without his consent.

Agreed: _____

     John Smith and
      Smith & Smith, P.C.

7. Next steps

Once you have decided to take the case and have reached an agreement with the client, there are several steps you should take to get the new relationship started on the right track and make sure that it stays on that track. First, if your agreement includes an express attorney's lien, send a notice of your attorney's lien to the opposing party's lawyer and any insurance carriers. Most jurisdictions have standard attorney's lien forms used in litigation. Sending out the notices will ensure that your fee is paid when any judgment is paid.

Second, you should have the client sign authorization forms that will allow you to obtain certain records before filing suit. Depending on your jurisdiction's laws and practice, you may need signed authorizations to get police reports and motor vehicle records; hospital, doctor, employment, and insurance records; Social Security, Veterans Administration, and other governmental records. Find out what type of authorization is necessary, and become familiar with the statutes requiring that such documents be made available to the client or his lawyer on request. You can also call the particular agency to learn its requirements and procedures. Some agencies have standard authorization forms.

Third, your client needs advice on what he should and should not do. He should be told not to talk to anyone about the matter. Explain that persons may try to interview him or get him to make or sign statements. He should tell such persons that he is represented by a lawyer, and he should notify you of all such attempts. Explain that he is generally not required to talk to anyone unless required through the formal discovery process; he should direct all requests for information to you. He should not sign anything without first discussing it with you. He should be told to save and collect all relevant records, documents, bills, checks, and paperwork of any kind in his possession and deliver them to you; he should send records and documents that subsequently come into his possession to you as well.

Fourth, your client needs a blueprint for the proceedings, since he may have little idea how civil litigation is actually conducted. He should be told what needs to be done before suit is filed, what happens during the pleadings, discovery, and motion practice stages of the litigation process, and what his role in this process will be. He should have some idea of how much time each of these stages takes and how far in the future any trial is likely to be; at the same time he should be aware that most cases are settled before trial. He also needs to be reminded of the risks and costs of any lawsuit, including the risk of an adverse verdict after trial. A well-informed client will understand the process he is a part of and will be likely to assist you throughout. Some lawyers use a follow-up letter or brochure that repeats this advice and contains a chronology of likely events. This is a sound practice that can easily be tailored to your litigation practice.

Finally, maintain communication with your client. Litigation goes in spurts; a period of activity is often followed by weeks of inactivity. If your client has not heard from you recently, he may erroneously conclude that you don't care about him or have lost interest in his case. Accordingly, make sure you maintain contact. Send him copies of all pleadings, discovery, motions, and other court papers, as well as copies of correspondence. Write him periodically to let him know what is going on in the case. If nothing is happening, let him know and explain why. A well-informed client will usually be a cooperative, satisfied client.

§4.4. Declining representation

A lawyer may not always be able to take a case. The matter may not be within the lawyer's expertise. It may not have merit or be large enough to justify a suit, or the defendant may not be able to pay a judgment. The lawyer may be too busy or have a conflict of interest. Or the lawyer may be unable to agree with the client on a fee. Whatever the reason, when a lawyer declines a potential case, it should be put in writing, usually in a letter to the prospective client.

Where a lawyer represents one party but cannot represent a related party because of a potential conflict of interest, the related party should be sent a letter in which the lawyer declines the offer of employment. Also, if an attorney withdraws from representing a client, an appropriate letter should be sent. It is important to make a decision and send the notification promptly, since a person's rights may be affected by any delay.

The letter declining the case ensures that the party clearly understands that you will not be representing him, and can help resolve any question about whether the attorney had a duty to protect the party's interests even though he was never a client.[10] If you decide not to represent a party, you nevertheless have an obligation to warn him if a statute of limitations or other notice statute may run shortly, so that he can get another lawyer in time.[11]

10. See J. M. Smith, Preventing Legal Malpractice 4-5 (1981).
11. See, e.g., Togstad v. Vesely, 291 N.W.2d 686 (Minn. 1980).

Example (letter):

Dear Mr. Jones:

As we discussed in my office yesterday, I will not be able to represent you for any claims you may have based on an automobile collision that occurred near the intersection of Maple and Elm Streets in this city on June 1, 1986, at approximately 3:00 P.M.

Since I cannot take your case, you may wish to see another lawyer about handling this matter for you. As we discussed yesterday, if you wish to have another lawyer represent you, you should do so promptly. If you do not, there may be legal problems, such as a statute of limitations bar, that might prevent you from pursuing your claims. Since your accident happened on June 1, 1987, and the statute of limitations for tort claims in this state is two years, if you wish to file a lawsuit you must do so *before* June 1, 1989. To avoid such problems, I recommend that you find another lawyer promptly, so any rights you have can be protected.

Enclosed are the originals of the police reports and insurance claim forms you brought to my office.

Sincerely yours,

/s/ *John Smith*

The letter should be sent by registered mail, return receipt by addressee only requested. When you get the signed return receipt, staple it to the copy of your letter. This will be persuasive evidence to rebut any later claim that you never actually declined the case.

§4.5. *Planning the litigation*

Assume you have accumulated the facts available through informal discovery; researched the possible legal claims, remedies, defenses, and counterclaims; put them on your litigation chart; researched other procedural questions; reached an agreement with the client to represent him; and have no timing problems. Now is the time, before filing your initial pleading, to structure a litigation plan.

A litigation plan consists of defining the client's objectives and developing a strategy to achieve those objectives. Once you develop a strategy in broad terms, you can then divide the strategy into its component, chronological parts.

Even if you think a litigation plan can't be developed, your client will think it can. Sophisticated commercial clients, such as insurance companies, require a litigation plan before authorizing a lawsuit or, if a defendant, after receiving the complaint. The litigation plan requirements usually include an explanation of what claims, relief, or defenses you will raise; a description of the basic facts, including the anticipated factual issues; an explanation of the planned discovery; a description of anticipated legal issues; an assessment of settlement possibilities; an assessment of the likely trial outcome; and cost projections for each stage of the plan. If sophisticated users of legal services have found that a detailed litigation plan promotes cost-effective representation, doesn't it make sense to make such a plan in every kind of case?

After you have completed your informal investigation, the basic steps in developing a litigation plan are the following:

1. Reevaluate the client's objectives, priorities, and cost constraints
2. Define the client's litigation objectives
3. Develop a "theory of the case"
4. Plan the pleadings
5. Plan the discovery
6. Plan the dispositive motions
7. Plan the settlement approach
8. Develop a litigation timetable

1. Reevaluate the client's objectives, priorities, and cost constraints

When the client first came to you for legal advice, he had one or more "problems" he told you about. One of your first steps was to identify his legal problems and objectives, and develop a scale of priorities for those objectives. Now is the time to reassess those problems and objectives. You will have the benefit of your partially completed litigation chart showing the fruits of your research and informal fact investigation. You will also know the client's cost constraints. Finally, time has passed. All of these may influence what the client's current objectives and priorities are. You need to sit down with the client, review what you have done to date, determine if the client's thinking is the same or has changed, and analyze those objectives and priorities to see if they still make sense in light of what you now know about the case.

2. Define the client's litigation objectives

If the client's thinking is unchanged and the dispute cannot be resolved short of litigation, you next need to decide on broad litigation objectives that serve the client's overall objectives and priorities. Always remember that the client controls the objectives of the litigation, and the lawyer decides on the means to achieve those objectives. For example, suppose that your plaintiff-client wants an early settlement of the case and to keep expenses at a minimum. Your strategy may be to keep the pleadings simple, to push for focused discovery, and then to start settlement discussions. On the other hand, suppose that your plaintiff-client anticipates that a trail will be necessary. Your strategy may be to use broad pleadings with alternative theories of recovery, to engage in extensive discovery, and to prepare thoroughly for trial. Your litigation objectives will then form the basis for the remainder of your litigation plan.

3.   Develop a "theory of the case"

Your side's "story" is a critical part of the litigation plan. You need to review what you presently know about the uncontested and contested facts, and ask some basic questions. Is your side's story complete or are there significant missing pieces? Are your witnesses reliable? Do their stories make sense? Is your side's story one that has jury appeal? Where does your side's version and the other side's version of the facts clash? How do you plan to win the credibility battle over the disputed facts?

Trial lawyers frequently call their side's position the "theory of the case."[12] Those with experience know that most trials are won on the facts, not the law. The winning side usually organizes credible witnesses and exhibits into a believable story, and wins the war over the disputed facts by presenting more persuasive evidence on its side of the dispute. This will only happen if you take the time to develop a coherent, persuasive theory of the case before drafting the pleadings.

4.   Plan the pleadings

Pleadings are the vehicle by which you bring your theory of the case to court. Seen this way, you will not make the mistake of (and violate Rule 11 by) raising a number of allegations in your pleadings and then wondering how you can find facts that fit into the theories of recovery.

What claims, relief, or defenses should you assert? Inexperienced litigators often "throw the book at them" and plead every conceivable claim, remedy, or defense that meets Rule 11 requirements. This illusion of safety can come at a high price. By adding claims, a case becomes more complex, with its additional costs and time requirements. Adding claims frequently results in adding parties, again making the litigation more involved. Adding claims also broadens the scope of discovery with the danger that discovery, always expensive and time consuming, may escalate out of control. While you must protect the client's legal interests by advancing essential claims, you should also consider the costs and disadvantages of pursuing every supportable claim against every proper party.

The better approach is to begin with your theory of the case. What claims, remedies, or defenses are reasonably supported by the facts that you have obtained through informal discovery or that you reasonably can expect to support with the fruits of formal discovery? Beyond that, do you have a realistic ability to prevail on each legal theory?

Once you have decided on what legal theories can be supported, it's time to decide which ones to raise in a pleading. You again need to reflect on your overall litigation objectives. For example, if an objective is to hold down litigation costs, it may make little sense to raise numerous legal theories. Simplicity in the pleadings will better serve your objective.

12. See T. Mauet, Fundamentals of Trial Techniques §1.4 (2d ed. 1988). See also D. Binder & P. Bergman, Fact Investigation: From Hypothesis to Proof ch. 9 (1984); J. McElhaney, "The Theory of the Case," in Trial Notebook (2d ed. 1987).

What do your proposed pleadings do to your discovery plan? The more complex the pleadings, the more expansive and expensive the permissible discovery. The scope of the pleadings controls the scope of discovery, and often its costs, because anything relevant, that is not privileged, is discoverable; so the more things that are raised by the pleadings, the greater the areas that are now relevant for discovery purposes. There is little point in pleading a variety of legal theories, just to be "safe," only to have the litigation get out of control. For example, consider a plaintiff who wishes to bring a negligence claim against a trucking company because of a vehicle collision. The plaintiff is considering whether to plead a claim for punitive damages. Doing so, however, will greatly expand the relevant scope of discovery, since the defendant's financial and safety history will now be discoverable. If the likelihood of getting punitive damages is small, does it really make sense to push such a claim? You may well be undertaking substantial additional work without a corresponding benefit to your client. On the other hand, plaintiffs frequently want broad discovery, at least compared to defendants. By adding peripheral parties, consistent with Rule 11 requirements, you make discovery easier, since discovery can be more broadly applied to parties than nonparties.

When you have decided which of the possible legal theories to raise in the initial pleading, you will still need to consider the related legal issues. The plaintiff must appreciate how the choice of claims will affect such issues as the choice of parties that must be brought into the suit, whether subject matter jurisdiction exists for each claim, whether personal jurisdiction exists for each defendant, where venue is proper and, if more than one venue, where the best place to file suit is. These questions are all interrelated, and substantial legal research will be necessary when the issues are complex. The time to research is now, not when you are suddenly faced with a motion to dismiss for lack of subject matter jurisdiction or for failure to join an indispensible party.

5. Plan the discovery

The discovery stage is usually the largest part of the litigation process, the one that consumes the most time and money. Hence, it is particularly important to plan discovery to serve your client's overall objectives and cost considerations. Without planning, discovery usually becomes unfocused and expensive — two disasters you should always avoid.

Planning discovery is essentially a seven-step process:

(i)   What facts do I need to establish a winning case on my claims (or to defeat the opponent's claims)?

(ii) What facts have I already obtained through informal fact investigation?

(iii) What "missing" facts do I still need to obtain through formal discovery?

The answers to the above questions should already be established on your litigation chart. You must consider four other questions:

(iv) What discovery methods are the most effective for obtaining the missing facts?

(v) What facts and witnesses, that you already know through informal investigation, do you need to "pin down" by using formal discovery methods?

(vi) What restrictions does your litigation budget place on your discovery plan?

(vii) Finally, in what order should you execute your discovery plan?

These questions obviously require some time to think through. When you have decided on what discovery methods to use for particular information, exhibits, and witnesses, put them on your litigation chart and your litigation timetable.[13]

6. Plan the dispositive motions

What dispositive motions, such as summary judgment, should you plan? Will your planned discovery provide the basis for succeeding on those motions? On the other hand, if the other side will be making the motions, what discovery have you planned that will defeat them? The motions stage of the litigation process will only be successful if you have coordinated your discovery with your motions plan. This means that you must look down the road before filing the pleadings to see what motions will be realistic, and use discovery to obtain the facts necessary to prevail when the motions are later made.

7. Plan the settlement approach

Your sense of when to discuss the possibility of settlement with the opposing party must be part of your overall litigation plan. When the client's objective is to settle quickly and keep costs down, you might consider discussing settlement early, such as after the pleadings have been closed or after a critical witness has been deposed. Otherwise, you will probably want to consider settlement after discovery is closed, after dispositive motions have been ruled on, or when you are preparing for the final pretrial conference. At these later stages you will have a better grasp of the case's strengths and weaknesses, but you will have incurred substantial litigation expenses.

8. Develop a litigation timetable

After developing and coordinating each of the preceding steps in your litigation plan, you should draw up a realistic timetable. For this you need

13. This process is discussed in detail in §6.3.

to consider the case's complexity, the likely responses of the opposing party, and the usual time between the filing of a complaint and trial date in the jurisdiction where the case is brought. You can then put the steps into a chronological sequence, and include them on your master calendar to remind yourself of the due date for each step in this particular case.

The planning of litigation must be an integrated, creative, flexible, continuing process. The plan needs to be integrated because each step should be tailored to achieving your client's litigation objectives while keeping in mind that each step influences the other steps. It should be creative because every case is different and must be planned out to account for the conditions of the particular case, rather than plugging the conditions into a standard formula. Finally, it must be flexible and continuing because developments invariably occur during the litigation process that require changes in your plan.

§4.6. *Example of litigation planning:* Novelty Products, Inc. v. Gift Ideas, Inc.

The following example illustrates the thought process that is involved in each step of a coordinated litigation plan.

Facts

Novelty Products, Inc. ("Novelty") is a corporation that manufactures novelty items that are sold to gift shops throughout the United States. Its corporate headquarters and manufacturing plant are in Buffalo, New York. Gift Ideas, Inc. ("Gift") is a corporation that owns a chain of gift shops located throughout California. Its corporate headquarters is in Los Angeles.

Over the past five years Gift has periodically ordered products from Novelty under an established procedure. Gift's purchasing department places orders over the telephone, and Novelty sends a written confirmation of the order before delivering it. Gift then pays for each shipment within thirty days of receipt.

One of the items Gift has ordered from Novelty during that time is a patented tabletop electric cigarette lighter called the "Magic Lite." Gift has ordered the lighter, in increasingly large shipments, approximately every six months. The lighter now accounts for about half of all sales from Novelty to Gift. The latest lighter order, for $30,000, was made the usual way, and was shipped last month.

A few days ago Gift notified Novelty that the latest shipment of lighters would be returned unpaid. Gift has just decided to make and market a tabletop electric cigarette lighter itself, and from now on its shops will only carry its own lighter. The Gift lighter, called the "Magic Flame," is almost identical in appearance and design to the Novelty lighter. A few months ago Novelty's design chief left the company and began working for Gift.

The shipment of lighters has been returned to Novelty, but Novelty has been unable to find another buyer for the lighters. Since Novelty will soon be marketing a new version of the lighter, finding a buyer seems unlikely.

The president of Novelty now comes to you for help.

Assume you have researched potential claims against Gift, determined the elements of those claims, identified the sources of proof, and completed an informal fact investigation. You have interviewed your client and appropriate employees, and have reviewed your client's records and correspondence along with what you could obtain from other nonparty sources. At this time your litigation chart appears as follows:

LITIGATION CHART

Elements of Claims	Sources of Proof	Informal Fact Investigation	Formal Discovery
1. Contract			
(a) contract executed	pl.'s records pl.'s witnesses def.'s records def.'s witnesses	obtained from client interviews	request to produce depositions, interrogatories, request to admit
(b) pl.'s performance	pl.'s records pl.'s witnesses def.'s records def.'s witnesses	obtained from client interviews	request to produce depositions, interrogatories, request to admit
(c) def.'s breach (nonpayment & return of goods)	pl.'s records pl.'s witnesses def.'s records def.'s witnesses shippers	obtained from client interviews	request to produce depositions, request to admit subpoenas
(d) pl.'s damages	pl.'s records pl.'s witnesses 3d parties who rejected lighters	obtained from client interviews interviews	subpoenas

The litigation chart would be continued for every other potential claim you have been considering. In Novelty's case, these would include:

(2) Bad faith
(3) Theft of trade secret
(4) Trademark
(5) Patent
(6) Unfair competition

Now is the time to develop the litigation plan. The steps are:

1. Reevaluate the client's objectives, priorities, and cost constraints
2. Define the client's litigation objectives
3. Develop a "theory of the case"
4. Plan the pleadings
5. Plan the discovery
6. Plan the dispositive motions
7. Plan the settlement approach
8. Develop a litigation timetable

1. Reevaluate the client's objectives, priorities, and cost constraints

From your interviews with Novelty's president, the company's objectives have become clear: Novelty wants to be paid the $30,000 due under the contract, yet it also wants to maintain its other ongoing business with Gift. It wants to accomplish these dual objectives quickly at a minimum cost. After your demand that Gift pay the contract amount has been rejected, Novelty's president agrees that litigation will be necessary. The president still feels that litigation, if kept simple, will not adversely affect Novelty's ongoing business relationship with Gift. These client objectives remain unchanged.

2. Define the client's litigation objectives

Since Novelty's president has authorized litigation, you need to decide on the basic litigation objectives and then get the client's approval. In this case Novelty has three possible approaches: it can keep the case simple and bring only a contract claim against Gift; it can bring the former design chief in as a defendant by alleging theft of a trade secret; or it can expand the case against Gift by alleging bad faith, copyright, trademark, and unfair competition claims. Which one of these litigation objectives will best serve Novelty's overall objectives?

You first recommend not pursuing a case against the former design chief, since he was not under contract with Novelty, and you have no proof that he helped Gift design its new lighter. Pressing a theft-of-trade-secrets claim against him has Rule 11 problems and runs counter to the client's preference for handling the case simply, quickly, and cheaply.

You next recommend not pursuing the complex case involving the patent, trademark, and unfair competition claims. You have doubts that Novelty will prevail on these claims on both legal and factual grounds. In addition, such claims would undoubtedly destroy the continuing business dealings between Novelty and Gift, which remain important to Novelty. The claims would also create lengthy, expensive, and publicity-generating litigation, all things Novelty needs to avoid. Novelty could always decide to bring a separate suit on these claims if circumstances require it, since joinder of claims is always permissive and there are no statute of limitations that are about to run.

This leaves the basic contract claim against Gift, based on either common law or the UCC sales provision. The advantages of taking this approach are that you have an excellent chance of winning on the merits, and the case can be handled relatively quickly and inexpensively. The disadvantages are that damages may be low since a party has a duty to mitigate damages. However, to date Novelty has been unable to resell the returned lighters, so damages near the contract price may be appropriate. You also consider adding a bad faith claim, which, if permitted under the applicable jurisdiction's substantive tort law, might permit compensatory or punitive damages. Your thinking is that Gift is more likely to settle the case for the contract price when faced with a bad faith claim. However, your research of current bad faith law, under both New York and California law, reveals that such a claim probably cannot be brought in a contract case under your facts. Bringing such a claim would probably violate Rule 11.

You then develop a litigation budget for the proposed contract claim against Gift. You project the following amounts of time will be necessary:

Fact and legal investigation	15 hrs.
Pleadings	5 hrs.
Discovery	50 hrs.
Motions	15 hrs.
Pretrial conference	15 hrs.
Trial and trial preparation	50 hrs.

The client has already paid for the fact and legal investigation. The total projected time remaining, without a trial, is about 85 hours; with a trial, the total time will be about 135 hours. Your hourly rate is presently $100. Accordingly, the cost to the client of resolving the dispute through a trial will be around $14,000. Since you feel the contract claim is strong and that under the circumstances getting $30,000 in damages is realistic, bringing the case — and trying it if necessary — still makes economic sense to the client. This holds even though Novelty will have to bear its own legal expenses, based on your research finding that no applicable law permits the recovery of attorney's fees in this situation.

You meet with Novelty's president and present the above analysis and cost projection to him. He agrees with it, and authorizes you to file suit against Gift on the contract claim. He again reminds you of his wish to settle quickly if possible and to keep the tone of the litigation as a simple dispute between two businesses over which one will bear the loss for an improperly canceled order.

3. Develop a "theory of the case"

Before dealing with the pleadings, you need to consider what Novelty's theory of the case should be. You decide to portray Novelty as a small company that had ongoing business dealings with Gift, a larger corporate chain. The specific transaction was a routine one where Gift made an oral order and Novelty sent a confirming letter, shipped the lighters, and sent a bill. Gift refused to pay for the lighters, but had no valid reason to do so. Gift simply changed its mind after agreeing to buy because it was going to market its own lighter. When the lighters were returned, Novelty could not resell them because it was preparing to market an improved version of the original lighter. In short, according to your theory, Gift welshed on the deal, and therefore owes Novelty the full $30,000. You feel that this theory will both be simple and have jury appeal.

4. Plan the pleadings

So far, you have decided to bring a contract action against Gift; however, many important questions must still be answered. First, what substantive law will apply? Novelty, the plaintiff, is in Buffalo, New York; Gift is based in Los Angeles, California. The offer was made from Los Angeles and accepted in Buffalo. Since the contract was completed in New York and the place of contracting under the standard interests analysis usually controls the choice of the applicable substantive law, New York law will probably be applied, regardless of whether the action is filed in New York or California. Filing the action in New York will also help, since it is the plaintiff's home state.

Since you have decided to sue only Gift, proper parties are not a concern. However, if you file in federal district court, will the court have subject matter jurisdiction over the claims? In this case, jurisdiction can properly be based on the court's diversity jurisdiction under 28 U.S.C. §1332; since the plaintiff is a citizen of New York and the defendant is a citizen of California, complete diversity exists, and the claim is in excess of the required jurisdictional amount.

Can you get personal jurisdiction over Gift? If suit is filed in California, service of process on Gift will be easy, since Gift's corporate headquarters is in Los Angeles. If suit is filed in New York, can Gift be forced to defend a lawsuit there and can Gift be properly served with process? Your research indicates that Gift's dealings with Novelty are adequate "minimum contracts" such that Gift can be required to defend in New York. Moreover, since provisions of Rule 4 of the Federal Rule of Civil Procedure allow for service under the forum state's long-arm statute, you should be able to properly serve Gift if suit is filed in New York.

Finally, where is venue proper? Under 28 U.S.C. §1391, both New York (the Western District) and California (the Central District) are proper places to bring suit. Since the Western District of New York has such obvious advantages to Novelty, suit should be brought there.

5. Plan the discovery

The client has two basic objectives: keep it simple and inexpensive, and try to settle it quickly. The first objective was served by keeping the pleadings simple. The second objective must be remembered when planning the discovery, as well as in the later steps of your litigation plan, since your litigation budget allocates just 50 hours to discovery.

Consult your litigation chart. At this stage the facts you have gathered come principally from Novelty's employees and business records. In a contract case, this is to be expected. The untapped sources, then, Gift's employees and records, must be reached through formal discovery.

Since a basic objective is an early settlement, you don't want to get mired in lengthy discovery. In addition, you have decided to move for partial summary judgment on liability as soon as possible. These objectives — getting the missing information, getting evidence for your summary judgment motion, and pushing for early settlement — can be served by a carefully designed discovery plan.

For example, you decide to use discovery only to get Gift's records and witness testimony that deal with the specific transaction involved. You decide that the evidence of an established course of dealings between Novelty and Gift, which would be necessary at trial to prove the contract terms, can be established by Novelty's records and witnesses. Second, you decide to focus on the contract and its breach, not contract damages, which you can again prove through Novelty's records and witnesses. This will give you the information necessary for your motion for partial summary judgment on liability.

What remains to be decided is which discovery methods to use to execute the plan and what order to use them in. You decide to send a set of interrogatories to Gift dealing with the basic chronological events involved in the transaction. You also decide to send Gift a request to produce all records dealing with the specific transaction. These should, among other things, identify the Gift employees who handled the transaction and were involved in the decision to return the lighters. Finally, you decide to depose those same essential Gift employees in succession, during one or two days, to minimize their contact with each other. When this is done, you will send a request to admit facts that cover the liability facts of the case.

The last decision is when to take these steps. Ordinarily you will want to move quickly to stay ahead of the other side. Here you decide to send out the interrogatories and requests to produce records at the earliest permitted time, and to send out the deposition notices for the necessary depositions a few weeks later. The request to admit facts can then follow on the heels of the depositions.

6. Plan the dispositive motions

Your overall litigation objective is to seek an early settlement, preferably after pleadings are filed or discovery has begun. If this does not work, you plan to move for partial summary judgment on liability as soon as discovery is completed. You will then have the information necessary to support your motion and to create additional pressure for a settlement.

7. Plan the settlement approach

Early settlement has always been a priority in your case. Accordingly, you plan to make settlement overtures, if Gift does not initiate them, after the pleadings are filed, after discovery is well under way and also when completed, after the motion for partial summary judgment is heard, and at the final pretrial conference.

Your approach has been to use focused discovery, particularly the request to admit facts, and the partial summary judgment motion to eliminate liability from the settlement discussions and put pressure on Gift. Since Novelty has been unable to resell the lighters, there is no mitigation of damages problem and damages are likely to be the full contract price. You decide that, with Novelty's consent, you will agree to settle for an amount close to the contract price, minus your total litigation expenses. This puts the settlement "value" of the case in the range of $22,000 to $30,000, depending on how early the case is settled.

8. Develop a litigation timetable

Now that you have developed a litigation plan that will realistically serve the client's objectives and priorities, you need to put the basic components on a timetable. Your basic timetable for Novelty is:

LITIGATION TIMETABLE

1/1 (today)	Complete litigation plan
by 2/1	File complaint
by 3/1	Interrogatories, production requests to def.
by 5/1	Deposition notices to def. witnesses
by 6/1	Depose def. witnesses (same day if possible)
by 7/1	Requests to admit facts to def.
by 9/1	Motion for partial summary judgment on liability
by 10/1	Prepare pretrial memorandum
by 11/1	Pretrial conference
12/1	Initial trial date

These dates can then be put on your general calendar to remind you when the basic steps in this case should be completed.

§4.7. Prefiling requirements

Are you finally ready to begin drafting the pleadings? Not quite. There are still a few matters you need to consider before plunging ahead.

1. Statutory notice requirements

Some actions, primarily tort claims against governmental bodies such as municipalities, often have statutory notice requirements that must be complied with or else suit will be barred. These statutes usually have time limitations substantially shorter than the applicable statute of limitations, often as short as six months or less, and usually have detailed fact requirements. These statutes are usually strictly construed, so each statutory requirement must be closely followed.

2. Contract requirements

Many contracts, particularly insurance and employment contracts and contracts with governmental bodies, have notice and claims provisions that are drafted as conditions precedent. These provisions usually require notice of intent to sue, or presentation of claims before filing suit, and require that notice be given within a short period of time, usually much shorter than the applicable statute of limitations period. Make sure your client has complied with the conditions precedent required by the contract before filing suit.

3. Mediation, arbitration, and review requirements

By statute and contract, many disputes must be submitted to binding or nonbinding mediation or arbitration before suit can be brought. For example, construction contracts frequently have arbitration clauses, and several states require by statute that medical malpractice claims must first be presented to a medical review panel.

4. Administrative procedure requirements

Claims against governmental bodies usually cannot be brought in court until administrative procedures have been followed and exhausted. For example, claims for benefits from the Social Security and Veterans Administrations must ordinarily be pursued through the administrative process before resort to the judicial system is permitted.[14] Accordingly, determine what applicable administrative procedure statutes apply to

14. See 42 U.S.C. §421(c); Administrative Procedure Act, 5 U.S.C. §§551 et seq.

your claim, and make sure that they have been followed before filing suit.

5. Appointment of legal guardian

Some individuals are incompetent to sue in their own name and must have a legal representative or specially appointed guardian litigate for them. Capacity to sue is governed by Rule 17, which generally defers to local law in determining both capacity to sue and the appropriate representative party.[15] Minors and incompetents, for example, can only sue through their legal guardians or conservators. Appropriate state court appointments of guardians, or other legal representatives, must be obtained before suit can properly be brought. When the statute of limitations will run shortly, this is a serious concern since obtaining such appointments may take time.

6. Lis pendens

Some jurisdictions require the filing of a lis pendens notice and service on all interested parties whenever a suit involves an interest in real property or tangible personal property. The notice is filed in the public records, usually property and title records. This gives notice of the pending litigation to parties having an interest in the property. Once notified, any interest in the property they acquire is subject to any judgment that may be entered in that particular litigation. Where your suit involves real or personal property, you should always check to see if any lis pendens rules apply; if so, follow them so that a judgment will be valid and enforceable against such parties. State lis pendens notice requirements are applicable to federal cases involving real estate.[16]

7. Attachment

There are no federal attachment statutes or rules providing for attachment. In some states, however, it is possible to attach property where otherwise jurisdiction over the property might be lost. State statutes often provide for attachment of a debtor's property interest under certain defined circumstances and usually specify the procedures, including service of process and bonds, that must be followed. Some jurisdictions also provide for prefiling attachments or garnishment procedures that may be used to freeze assets that may satisfy any future judgment. There are remedies for wrongful attachment, however, so caution is obviously in order.

15. See §3.4.
16. See Rule 64; 28 U.S.C. §1964.

8. Temporary restraining orders

If you are seeking injunctive relief, you may be able to obtain a temporary restraining order (TRO) to prevent immediate irreparable injury to
your client's interests. A TRO may be obtained under specified conditions for a strictly limited period of time, until a hearing for a temporary
injunction can be scheduled.[17] While it is difficult to obtain a TRO, there
will be times when seeking a TRO is essential to preserve a client's
rights.[18]

9. Discovery before suit

Upon filing a verified petition that complies with Rule 27's requirements,
you may depose a person before suit is filed to perpetuate that person's
testimony. This should be considered whenever it is important to have
testimony from a person who is old, sick, or may leave the jurisdiction.

10. Demand letters

While not legally required, demand letters are frequently used, particularly in tort, contract, and commercial cases. For instance, in anticipatory
breach situations it is advantageous to send a demand letter asserting that
the other side appears to be in breach and requesting assurances of performance. Such letters, if not responded to, may constitute admissions by
silence.

Demand letters also serve practical purposes. In small disputes,
where a compromise is possible, a demand letter that notifies the other
side of your intent to sue unless an acceptable settlement is reached can
often trigger settlement discussions. A demand letter will often generate
a denial letter stating the basis for rejecting your claim, and is sometimes
a good indication of what defenses will be raised if suit is brought later.

In some cases, where your ability to get the facts is limited because
the important records are all in your opponent's possession, it may be
appropriate to send a draft of your complaint to your opponent and
await a response. The opponent may respond by giving you information
that will affect your decision to file the lawsuit or will affect the claims
that you ultimately bring.

---

17. See Rule 65.
18. Obtaining a TRO or preliminary injunction is discussed in §7.5.

Part B
CONDUCTING THE LITIGATION

V

PLEADINGS

§5.1. *Introduction*

Modern pleading rules essentially limit the purpose of pleadings to notice of claims and defenses. Former purposes that included discovering facts, sharpening issues, and disposing of frivolous claims are now controlled by discovery and motion practice. Under modern rules, claims and factual issues will rarely be resolved at the pleadings stage. Hence, don't expect the pleadings to accomplish more than what they are designed to do.

Federal pleadings rules are principally contained in the Federal Rules of Civil Procedure, although other sources exist and must always be kept in mind. Under Rule 83 district courts can create local rules governing litigation in that district. Most have done so. Local rules generally do not affect the substance of pleadings, but ordinarily control mechanics such as the number of copies filed, size of paper, format, and bindings. Particular federal statutory actions, such as bankruptcy and copyright, may also have special procedure rules. Finally, specialized federal courts, such as magistrates, bankruptcy, and claims courts, may have special statutory and local procedural rules. Hence, you should always check procedural statutes and local rules in addition to the Federal Rules of Civil Procedure to determine what rules apply to your particular case.

Good pleadings practice is a combination of two things: a solid litigation plan and technically precise drafting. The litigation plan, which you have already developed, will control the claims and remedies (if a plaintiff), or the defenses and counterclaims, cross-claims, or third-party claims (if a defendant). The drafting of pleadings then becomes the primary concern, since pleadings that are technically precise will avoid attacks by motions and eliminate the need to file amended pleadings to cure defects that should have been avoided in the first place.

§5.2. *General pleading requirements*

The Federal Rules of Civil Procedure have made simplicity and limited purpose the touchstones of the pleadings stage of the litigation process. Under Rule 2, all actions are "civil actions," and under Rule 7(a) the only basic pleadings allowed are complaints, answers, and replies.

1. General "notice" requirements for claims[1]

Rule 8(a) permits four forms of claims:

> complaint
> counterclaim
> cross-claim
> third-party complaint

All forms are actually complaints, since each asks for relief of some kind, but the various labels designate which party is bringing the claim. Since they are all complaints, however, their requirements are the same. Rule 8 requires only a "short and plain statement of the claim showing the pleader is entitled to relief." This commonly, although perhaps inaccurately, is labeled "notice pleading."

Under "notice pleading," the only requirement is that the pleading contain enough information to fairly notify the opposing party of the basis of the claim. It does not require an elaborate narration of facts, nor does it require that a legal theory of recovery or relief be set forth. Previous distinctions about whether a pleading was of fact, law, or conclusion of law now have no significance. Hence, for most allegations the only requirement is a "short and plain statement" that gives fair notice of your claims to the opposing side. Forms 2 through 23 in the Appendix of Forms to the Federal Rules of Civil Procedure contain a variety of legally sufficient pleadings. The safest pleadings approach is to use the forms and modify them to meet the specific requirements of your case. The standard drafting technique is to state just enough facts to identify the events or transactions that your claim is based on and the legal theory of recovery. These techniques are detailed in §5.3.

The only exception to the simple notice pleading requirement is Rule 9, which requires that certain matters, including capacity and au-

---

1. Wright §68; James & Hazard §3.8; Friedenthal §5.7; Moore's Manual §901; Shepard's Manual §3.5; Wright & Miller §§1182-1192; Moore's Federal Practice §§8.02-8.06. The leading case on the simplified pleading requirements of Rule 8 is Conley v. Gibson, 355 U.S. 41 (1957).

thority to sue, fraud, mistake, and special damages, be alleged specifically and particularly. This type of pleading is also discussed in §5.3.

2. Alternative and inconsistent pleadings[2]

Rule 8(e)(2) allows a party to plead multiple claims or defenses in alternative or hypothetical form, either in one or in separate counts or defenses. In practice, each claim is usually put in a separate count and each defense is designated separately. Keep in mind, however, that since pleadings can be read to the jury during trial, alternative or inconsistent pleadings may cast the party in a poor light. Hence, drafting must also be done with an eye toward the impression the pleading will have on the jurors.

3. Format requirements[3]

Format requirements are set forth in Rules 10 and 11. There are several that must be followed for every pleading. Local rules may also specify additional requirements.

a. Caption

The caption of a case refers to the names of the parties, the court in which the case is being filed, and the case number. Every pleading must have a caption containing this information.

b. File number

The file number is the case number that is stamped on the complaint when it is first filed with the clerk of the court. It must appear on all successive pleadings. Although not required, the designation "Civil Action" is usually placed below the file number.

c. Title of action

The complaint must list all the parties to the action. Subsequent pleadings need only list the first plaintiff and first defendant, with an appropriate reference to additional parties, such as "et al."

Make sure that your caption correctly states the proper name and legal description of each party. Under Rule 17, every action must be brought in the name of the real party in interest; and, according to this Rule, the capacity to sue or be sued is controlled by the law of domicile, incorporation, or forum.[4] You must always check Rule 17(b) and (c) to

---

2. Friedenthal §§5.12-5.13; Moore's Manual §§9.05-9.06; Shepard's Manual §3.72.
3. Friedenthal §5.14.
4. See §3.4.

see if a party has capacity to sue or be sued and that the correct person or entity is designated as a party. Common designations include the following:

- John Smith
- Sharon Jones, as guardian of the Estate of Robert Jones, a minor
- Robert Smith, as conservator of the Estate of Ellen Smith, an incompetent
- Frank Watson, as executor of the Estate of James Morley, deceased
- Barbara Myers, as trustee in bankruptcy of the Estate of Robert Jackson, bankrupt
- R. J. Smith Company, a corporation
- Johnson Hospital, a not-for-profit corporation
- Robert Smith, d/b/a Smith Cleaners
- Barnett and Lynch, a partnership
- Western Ranches Association, an unincorporated association

Where a party is being sued both individually and in a representative capacity, it should be spelled out.

Example:

John Smith, individually and as administrator of the Estate of Franklin Smith, deceased

The caption, then, simply lists each party and what side of the action each is on.

Example:

UNITED STATES DISTRICT COURT FOR THE NORTHERN DISTRICT OF NEW YORK

John Smith, and J. W. Smith Company, a corporation, Plaintiffs	
v.	No. _____
Randolph Construction, a corporation, and William Johnson, d/b/a Solar Consultants, Defendants	Civil Action

Sometimes it is impossible to identify a proper party by name before filing. In these circumstances you can designate a party as "John Doe, the true name being presently unknown," and pursue the identity of the party through formal discovery. This sometimes happens when a plaintiff has been able to identify some but not all liable parties.

d. Designation

Each pleading should be labeled to show what type it is, such as a complaint, counterclaim, cross-claim, third-party complaint, answer, or reply. Where multiple parties are involved, it is useful to show against whom the pleading is directed.

Examples:

COMPLAINT

ANSWER TO CROSS-CLAIM OF DEFENDANT FRANKLIN CORPORATION

THIRD-PARTY COMPLAINT AGAINST JONES CONSTRUCTION COMPANY

e. Signing pleadings

Every pleading, or other court paper, must be signed by one of the party's lawyers. The signing must be by an individual, not a law firm, although in practice the lawyer's firm is frequently shown as "of counsel." The pleading must also contain the lawyer's address and, in practice, a telephone number.

Under the federal rules pleadings are not "verified" — that is, signed by the parties and notarized — although this remains proper procedure in many state jurisdictions, and verification may be permitted or required by specific local rules.

4. Rule 11[5]

Under Rule 11, a lawyer's signature on a pleading, motion or other court paper automatically constitutes a certification that the lawyer has read the pleading and that to the best of the lawyer's knowledge, information, and belief the pleading is well grounded in fact and law — or is a good faith argument for a change in law — and is not being filed for any improper purpose.[6]

Rule 11, amended in 1983, significantly increases the lawyer's obligations. A good faith belief that the pleading is well founded is not sufficient: A lawyer must now have made a "reasonable inquiry" into the law

5. Friedenthal §5.11; Moore's Manual §3.70; Moore's Federal Practice §11.02; Wright & Miller §§1331 et seq.

6. Rule 11 parallels the applicable ethics considerations. See Model Code of Professional Responsibility, Rule 7-102 (1980); Model Rules of Professional Conduct, Rule 3.1 (1984). For a useful discussion of Rule 11, see Golden Eagle Distributing Corp. v. Burroughs Corp., 801 F.2d 1531 (9th Cir. 1986).

and facts, and have concluded that there is a sound basis in law and fact for the pleading. What constitutes a "reasonable inquiry" must be considered on a case-by-case basis, and the case law concerning this standard is hardly uniform at this time.[7] Among the factors to be considered are the amount of time available to investigate the law and facts, the reliability of the client as a source of facts, and the extent to which an investigation could corroborate or alter those facts. If a lawyer simply relies on his client's representation of facts, where a reasonable inquiry would show that the facts are otherwise, the lawyer's Rule 11 obligations have not been met.[8] The reasonable inquiry requirement applies not only to theories of recovery and damages against the defendant, but also to every party brought into the case. You must have a reasonable belief, based on a reasonable investigation, that there is a case for every claim against every defendant. Rule 11 applies with equal force to any pleading, or other court paper, filed by any party.

Under Rule 11 the court can impose sanctions for violations of this requirement, which are no longer contingent on subjective bad faith or deliberate harassment.[9] The Rule expressly states that the court "shall . . . impose . . . an appropriate sanction" when a violation of the reasonable inquiry requirement occurs. Sanctions can include all reasonable expenses, including attorney's fees, that were incurred as a result of the improperly brought pleading. The court can impose sanctions in response to the motion of a party or on its own motion, and is not required in all cases to hold a hearing before imposing sanctions. Further, sanctions can be substantial in appropriate circumstances.[10]

The message of Rule 11 should be abundantly clear: Gone are the days when a lawyer could, with relatively little preparation, file an action containing a variety of claims against a multitude of defendants and later simply dismiss those claims and defendants that never should have been raised or brought into the case in the first place. Today the reasonable inquiry requirement has teeth, and judges are increasingly willing to impose significant sanctions for violations.

5. Service and filing

Pleadings and other court papers must be served on all parties in one of the permitted ways. Service of any complaint or summons must be made on the party in accordance with the provisions of Rule 4.[11] When a party is represented by a lawyer, service of pleadings other than a complaint should be made on the lawyer. This is customarily done either by personal delivery or mail, although under Rule 5(b) delivery includes leaving

7. See Nelken, Sanctions Under Amended Federal Rule 11, 74 Geo. L. Rev. 1313 (1986), analyzing the reported Rule 11 cases to date.

8. Coburn Optical v. Cilco, 610 F. Supp. 656 (D.C.N.C. 1985).

9. See, e.g., Eastway Constr. Co. v. City of New York, 762 F.2d 243 (2d Cir. 1985); Rogers v. Lincoln Towing, 771 F.2d 194 (7th Cir. 1985).

10. See, e.g., Calloway v. Marvel Entertainment Group, 111 F.R.D. 637 (S.D.N.Y. 1986), where the court imposed a $200,000 sanction.

11. See §5.3.

it at the lawyer's office with the person in charge, as well as other infrequently used methods. If a party is not represented by a lawyer, the party himself must be served, and the permitted methods essentially parallel those for lawyers.

Unless otherwise ordered, all pleadings and other court papers that are actually served on parties must be filed with the court clerk either before service or within a reasonable time after service. The usual practice is to have the original and appropriate number of copies of the pleading or other court paper taken to the clerk of the court for filing, and have another copy stamped "filed" and dated for your own files. This is usually done the same day papers are being served on the lawyers for the other parties. Local rules often specify how proof of service should be made. The usual practice is to have a certificate or affidavit of service attached to the end of the pleading that shows when and how service was made, and includes the signature of the attorney or the notarized signature of a member of the attorney's staff.

Examples:

CERTIFICATE OF SERVICE

I, ____(attorney)____ , state that I served the above by mailing a copy to the attorneys for ____(plaintiff/defendant)____ at ____(state address)____ on ____(date)____ .

Dated: _____

_____
Name of attorney
Address
Tel. No.

AFFIDAVIT OF SERVICE

I, ____(name)____ , having been first duly sworn, state that I served the above by mailing a copy to the attorneys for the other parties at their addresses of record in this case.

_____
Name

Signed and subscribed to before me on ____(date)____ .

_____
Notary Public

My commission expires on ____(date)____ .

§5.3. *Complaints*

The complaint is the plaintiff's initial pleading, which, when filed, starts the litigation. There are three essential components of every complaint required by Rule 8(a):

1. Statement showing subject matter jurisdiction
2. Statement of claims
3. Statement of relief requested

In addition, the complaint must show a jury demand, if a jury will be demanded, and it must be filed and served on each opposing party.

1. Subject matter jurisdiction[12]

Since federal courts are courts of limited jurisdiction, jurisdiction must be alleged in the complaint; and since jurisdiction cannot be assumed, it must be demonstrated. Care as well as particularity is required. The jurisdictional allegation is usually the first part of a complaint and is customarily labeled as such. There are two principal ways that subject matter jurisdiction can be acquired in federal court.

a. *Federal question jurisdiction*[13]

Federal jurisdiction can be based on a federal statute, constitutional provision, or treaty. To establish jurisdiction in this way, the complaint should cite the particular statute, constitutional provision, or treaty, and perhaps quote the operative wording or paraphrase it. Failure to do so is not fatal, since jurisdictional allegations can be amended[14]; however, citing a federal statute, constitutional provision, or treaty will not conclusively confer jurisdiction, since facts alleged in the complaint can contradict and disprove the jurisdictional allegation. As always, the safest pleading approach is to track the language of the Appendix of Forms to the Federal Rules of Civil Procedure.

Example:

[Caption]

COMPLAINT

Plaintiff Ralph Johnson complains against Defendant Wilbur Jackson as follows:

---

12. Wright §69; James & Hazard §3.24; Friedenthal §5.14; Moore's Manual §10.03; Shepard's Manual §3.6; Moore's Federal Practice §§8.07-8.11; Wright & Miller §§1206, 1208-1209.
   13. See §3.5 supra. The general federal question statute is 18 U.S.C. §1331.
   14. See 28 U.S.C. §1653.

Jurisdictional Allegation

1. Jurisdiction in this case is based on the existence of a federal question. This action arises under [the Constitution of the United States, Amendment _____, §____] [or the Act of _____ ____, ____ Stat. ____, ____ U.S.C. §____] [or the Treaty of the United States _____], as is shown more fully in this complaint.

b. Diversity jurisdiction[15]

Federal jurisdiction can also be based on diversity of citizenship. The jurisdictional allegation must affirmatively show complete diversity of each plaintiff and each defendant. The essential requirement is citizenship, not residence. An individual has only one state of citizenship. A corporation, for jurisdictional purposes, is deemed a citizen of both the state where incorporated and the state where it has its principal place of business. An alien, for jurisdictional purposes, is treated as if the country of foreign citizenship were a 51st state.

Example (individuals):

Jurisdictional Allegation

Jurisdiction in this case is based on diversity of citizenship of the parties and the amount in controversy. Plaintiff is a citizen of the State of California. Defendant is a citizen of the State of Oregon.

Example (corporations):

Jurisdictional Allegation

Jurisdiction in this case is based on diversity of citizenship of the parties and the amount in controversy. Plaintiff is a corporation incorporated under the laws of the State of Delaware having its principal place of business in the State of New York. Defendant is a corporation incorporated under the laws of the State of Georgia having its principal place of business in the State of Florida.

Where the party is a legally recognized unincorporated association, such as a labor union or service organization, it is a citizen of every state of which any of its members is a citizen. Partnerships are considered citizens of each state where a general partner is a citizen. For legal representatives — such as a guardian of a minor, executor or administrator of an estate, and trustee of a trust — the representative's citizenship is usually

15. See §3.5 supra. The diversity jurisdiction statute is 18 U.S.C. §1332.

controlling for diversity purposes, although there may be exceptions in special circumstances.[16]

Where a statute makes notice of a claim a prerequisite to suit, some courts have held that the fact that notice was given is a jurisdictional requirement that must be alleged in the complaint.[17] Diversity jurisdiction under 28 U.S.C. §1332 also requires that the "matter in controversy exceeds the sum or value of $10,000, exclusive of interest and costs."[18] Where the jurisdictional amount must be alleged in the pleadings, it is customary to simply paraphrase the statute at the end of the jurisdictional allegation.

Example:

Jurisdictional Allegation

... The amount in controversy exceeds the sum of ten thousand dollars ($10,000), exclusive of interest and costs.

2.   Statement of claims[19]

Rule 8(a) merely requires that a pleading contain a "short and plain statement of the claim showing that the pleader is entitled to relief." Rule 8(e) states that each allegation in the pleading shall be "simple, concise and direct"; only a few claims, principally fraud and mistake, must be pleaded with particularity. In short, technical requirements have been discarded, the sole requirement now being that enough be pleaded that the other party has fair notice of the claims presented sufficient to defend itself.

Since the requirements for the statement of claims are minimal, great latitude in drafting exists. Hence, the more significant drafting questions are: What is the most effective way to make a statement of the claim in a complaint? Are there any general drafting "rules" that apply?

a.   Use plain English

In recent years the trend in legal drafting has been away from legalese in favor of plain English. The same approach should be applied when drafting pleadings. Commonly used words, short sentences of simple construction, active verbs, and a preference for nouns and verbs over adjectives and adverbs create clear and forceful language. This benefits everyone in litigation — parties, lawyers, judge, and jury.

16. See Wright §29; Wright & Miller §3606.
17. See Shepard's Manual §3.6.
18. See §3.5. The $10,000 matter in controversy requirement applies to diversity cases under 28 U.S.C. §1332; since 1980, it no longer applies to federal question cases under 18 U.S.C. §1331.
19. Wright §68; James & Hazard §§3.14-3.20; Friedenthal §5.15; Moore's Manual §10.14; Shepard's Manual §3.17; Moore's Federal Practice §§8.12-8.17; Wright & Miller §§1215-1254.

b. Keep it simple

Pleadings are not the place to disclose the detailed facts on which you base your claims, nor the place to elaborate on your theories of recovery. The Rules require only a "short and plain statement." You need only allege enough to put the opposing party on fair notice of what your claims against him are. While this must be read in the light of the complexity of the case, with complex cases requiring more detailed allegations, the preference should still be for simplicity.

On the other hand, there are times when making specific factual allegations can be effective, because they are harder for the defendant to deny. In addition, a specific allegation — each should be set out in a separate paragraph — can support a subsequent specific discovery request. If the defendant denies an allegation, then objection can hardly be taken to discovery methods that are directed at uncovering the denied facts.

The official Appendix of Forms gives excellent examples of complaints in common situations that, by virtue of Rule 84, are legally adequate, yet use simple English. The safest approach in drafting pleadings is to modify these forms to your claims whenever practical.

Example (negligence):

1. On August 1, 1985, at approximately 3:00 P.M., plaintiff Jones and defendant Smith were driving automobiles on Elm Street, near Maple Avenue, in Chicago, Illinois.
2. Smith negligently crossed the center lane of Elm Street with his automobile, striking Jones' automobile.
3. As a result Jones received facial injuries, a broken arm, and other injuries, experienced pain and suffering, incurred medical expenses, lost substantial income, and will incur more medical expenses and lost income in the future.

Example (contract):

1. On August 1, 1985, plaintiff Jones and defendant Smith entered into a contract. A copy of the contract is attached to this complaint as Exhibit A.
2. Jones paid Smith $1,000 and has performed all of her obligations under the contract.
3. Smith failed to paint Jones' house as he was required to do under the contract.

The preference for using simple English should also apply to naming parties. Use names rather than the pleading's designations, such as plaintiff, defendant, cross-claimant, or third-party defendant or other legal designations, such as trustee, drawer, or obligor, unless a local pleading rule requires the designation of the party. Using names keeps things clear, particularly where multiple parties are involved.

A common practice is to set out the full name of each party the first time it is used, then show in parentheses how you will refer to that party from then on.

Examples:

Defendant William B. Jones (hereafter "Jones") . . .

The International Business Machines Corporation ("IBM") . . .

c. Plead "special matters" with particularity

Rule 9 is an exception to the liberal "notice pleading" approach of the federal rules. Under Rule 9, certain allegations must be pleaded "specifically" and "with particularity." These include fraud, mistake, and special damages.[20] While capacity and authority to sue and conditions precedent can be pleaded generally, denials must be made specifically and with particularity.

What constitutes appropriate specificity and particularity in pleading these special matters is unclear.[21] While the particularity requirement should be viewed in light of Rule 8's liberal pleading standards, it is safer as well as proper to set forth the specific elements of the special matter being pleaded. This will ensure that the requisite particularity has been established.

Example (fraud):

1. On August 1, 1985, plaintiff Jones and defendant Smith entered into a contract. A copy of the contract is attached to this complaint as Exhibit A.

2. Under the contract, Jones agreed to pay Smith $20,000, and Smith agreed to sell Jones a parcel of land in Atlanta, Georgia. The precise location and description of the parcel are set out in the contract, attached as Exhibit A.

3. Before executing this contract, Smith represented that he had legal title to the parcel, that the parcel had no encumbrances of any kind, such as mortgages, tax liens, or judgment liens, and that Smith would be able to have the property rezoned to a B-2 zoning.

4. Those representations were false and fraudulent, Smith knew they were false and fraudulent when made, and Smith made them to induce Jones to enter into the contract.

5. Jones relied on Smith's representations and was damaged.

d. Use separate paragraphs

The rules require a separate paragraph for a "single set of circumstances" whenever practicable — admittedly an imprecise standard. When

---

20. Subject matter jurisdiction must also be pleaded specifically. See §3.5.
21. See Moore's Manual §9.07.

in doubt, it is probably better to use paragraphs liberally, since this usually makes the pleadings simpler to follow. More important, it makes the complaint easier to answer and will minimize the likelihood that an answer will admit part and deny part of a single paragraph. As a result the positions of the parties will be clearer, benefiting everyone.

Example:

1. On June 1, 1985, plaintiff Jones and defendant Smith entered into a contract, a copy of which is attached as Exhibit A.
2. On June 15, 1985, Jones paid Smith $10,000 as required by the contract.
3. Jones has performed each of her obligations under the contract.
4. Smith failed to deliver 1,000 folding chairs to Jones by June 30, 1985, and has failed to perform his obligations under the contract.

e. Use separate counts

Although not required by the rules, it is customary to state each claim involving a separate theory of recovery in a separate count, even if all are based on the same general occurrence or transaction. This has the advantage of setting out clearly each legal theory that forms a basis for recovery.

Since setting out different theories of recovery in different counts usually requires restating some allegations, it is efficient and proper under Rule 10(c) to incorporate into the later count by reference those allegations made in earlier counts.

Example:

Count II

1-15. Plaintiff adopts Par. 1-15 of Count I as Par. 1-15 of this Count.
16. . . .
17. . . .

It is also useful to label the legal theory for each count and, where different counts are against different parties, show which parties are involved in each count.

Example:

Count I — Contract

(against defendants Jones and Roberts)

1. . . .
2. . . .
3. . . .

<u>Count II — Implied Warranties</u>

(against defendant Roberts only)

f. Use exhibits

Rule 10(c) permits attaching exhibits to pleadings. This is most commonly done in contract cases, where the contract that forms the basis for the claim is attached to the complaint. When attached to the pleading, the exhibit becomes an integral part of it. This is usually a more efficient way of stating a claim than setting out the exhibit's contents in the body of the complaint.

Example:

1. Plaintiff Jones and defendant Smith entered into a contract on June 1, 1985. A copy of this contract is attached as Exhibit A.

Even if the exhibit is attached to the pleading, you can still quote operative language in the complaint.

3. Prayer for relief[22]

Rule 8(a) requires a pleading to make a "demand for judgment for the relief to which [the pleader] deems himself entitled. Relief in the alternative or of several different types may be demanded." The Rule makes no distinction between legal and equitable relief.

Care in pleading relief is important for two reasons. First, since under federal law the nature of the remedy sought is often controlling on the question of the right to a jury trial,[23] the demand for relief should be drafted to ensure the right to a jury trial, or to avoid it, as the case may be. Second, where a default judgment is requested, the method under which default can be obtained is affected by the type of relief sought, and the relief granted is limited to that requested in the pleadings.[24] Since default is always a possibility, you should always draft the prayer carefully.

The prayer for relief should specify the types of relief sought, including legal and equitable remedies, interest, costs, attorney's fees, and any special damages, with sufficient detail. Where several specific types of relief are sought, the better practice is to itemize and number them.

---

22. Wright §68; James & Hazard §§3.21-3.22; Friedenthal §5.15; Moore's Manual §10.15; Shepard's Manual §3.8; Moore's Federal Practice §8.18; Wright & Miller §§1255-1260.

23. See §3.3.

24. See Rules 54 and 55.

Examples:

WHEREFORE, plaintiff demands judgment against defendant for the sum of $15,000, with interest and costs.

WHEREFORE, plaintiff demands a preliminary and permanent injunction, an accounting for all damages, and interest and costs.

WHEREFORE, plaintiff demands:
1. That defendant pay damages in the sum of $12,000;
2. That defendant be specifically ordered to perform his obligations under the contract;
3. That defendant pay interest, costs, and reasonable attorney's fees incurred by plaintiff.

4. Jury demand[25]

Under Rule 38, a party may demand a jury trial, on any claim triable as of right by a jury, in writing at any time after the complaint is filed and "not later than 10 days after the service of the last pleading directed to such issue." The party may specify in the demand which claims he wishes tried to a jury. The rule permits the jury demand to be placed on the pleading itself, and this is the customary method of making the demand. Local rules, however, may have additional requirements for jury demands. A common practice is to place the label "JURY TRIAL DEMANDED" below the case number, and the phrase "PLAINTIFF DEMANDS TRIAL BY JURY" at the end of the complaint. Local rules sometimes have additional requirements, such as the use of jury demand forms and the payment of fees.

If one party makes a jury demand, the other parties are entitled to rely on it. However, if a party makes a jury demand on only some counts, the other parties must make a timely jury demand on other counts. Failure to make a timely demand for a jury trial constitutes a waiver of the right under Rule 38(d), and courts have taken a strict view on waiver and only rarely exercise their discretion and permit a belated demand.[26]

5. Filing and service of summons[27]

Under Rule 3, a federal action is commenced when the complaint is filed with the clerk of the court, and commencement is significant for statute of limitations purposes. In federal question cases, the filing of the complaint tolls the statute of limitations. In diversity cases, however, state law controls, and if state law requires something more than the mere filing of the com-

25. Wright §92; Friedenthal §11.9; Moore's Manual §9.10; Shepard's Manual §§7.20-7.21; Moore's Federal Practice §§38.07-38.46; Wright & Miller §§2318-2322.
26. See Wright §92.
27. Wright §§64-65; Moore's Manual §§6.01-6.19; Shepard's Manual §§3.80-3.94; Moore's Federal Practice §§4.02-4.46; Wright & Miller §§1061-1153.

plaint — usually service of summons on the defendant — state law must be complied with fully before the statute of limitations is tolled.[28]

After the action is commenced, the complaint must be served on each defendant. Under Rule 4, detailed service of summons rules control how the complaint and summons are to be served on defendants. There are several steps involved, and you should check local rules for any additional filing and service-of-summons requirements. For example, most districts require designation or cover sheets and appearance forms to be filed with the complaint and summons.

a.   Issuing the summons

When the complaint is filed, the clerk is directed under Rule 4(a) to issue the summons. In practice, the summons form, which is available from the clerk's office, is usually filled out in advance and taken to the clerk's office when the complaint is filed. To assist in service it is useful to list on the back of the form where and when service on each defendant can most likely be made. For example, if the service is to be made at the defendant's work address, it is useful to put down the working hours and where on the premises the defendant actually works. The clerk then "issues" the summons by signing and stamping it with the court seal, the date, and the case file number. Make sure you have enough copies of the complaint and summons for the clerk's administrative needs, for service on each defendant, and for your own files.

b.   Summons content

Rule 4(b) controls the summons content. The following example contains the standard elements of a summons.

Example:

SUMMONS

To: _____ *(defendant and address)* _____

You are hereby summoned and required to serve upon _____ _____, plaintiff's attorney, whose address is _____ _____, an answer to the complaint that is hereby served upon you, within 20 days after service upon you, exclusive of the day of service.

If you fail to do so, judgment by default will be taken against you for the relief demanded in the complaint.

_____
Clerk of Court

---

28. See Wright §64.

However, if the summons will be served under Rule 4(e) permitting service under state service rules, the summons should conform to the particular state's summons requirements.

c. Persons who may serve the summons

As a general rule, the complaint and summons can be served by any person who is not a party and is at least 18 years old. Service by the U.S. Marshal is now required only in limited circumstances specified in Rule 4(c)(2)(B) — on behalf of paupers or the United States and its agencies, and by court order.

d. Methods of service

How service of summons may be made depends on the entity being served, and is governed by Rule 4(d)-(f).

i. Individuals

An individual can be served a summons in several ways. First, service can be made by personally giving the individual a copy of the complaint and summons. Second, it can be made by leaving a copy of the complaint and summons "at his dwelling house or usual place of abode" with a person of suitable age and discretion residing there. Third, service can be made on an agent authorized by appointment or law to receive process. Fourth, where the individual is out of state, service may be made when any federal statute authorizes out-of-state service, or when a statute of the state in which the district court sits permits out-of-state service. These are the state long-arm statutes, which provide for extraterritorial service on any defendant who has had constitutionally sufficient contacts with that state.[29]

ii. Infants and incompetents

Service on infants and incompetents is made in the same manner as service would be made under the law of the state in which service is to be made. While state laws vary, they usually require service on a parent or a legal guardian of the infant or incompetent.

iii. Corporations, partnerships, and associations

Service on domestic and foreign corporations, partnerships, and unincorporated associations that can be sued in their own name can be made several ways. First, service can be made by personal delivery to an officer, manager, or general agent. Second, service can be made to an agent authorized to receive service of process; the list of domestic and foreign corporations, usually compiled by each state's Secretary of State or Corporation Commission, should show the authorized agent for process. Third, when

---

29. See §3.6.

the corporation is out of state, service can be made under any federal statute providing for service or under any method permitted by a statute of the state in which the district court sits — principally the state's long-arm statute.

iv.   Officers and agencies of the United States, and state and municipal government organizations

Rule 4(d)(4)-(6) details the requirements for service on federal, state, and local governments, as well as on federal agencies and employees. The requirements are technical, and the Rule should always be reviewed before attempting service.

e.   Territorial limits of service

The geographical scope of service is governed by Rule 4(f). There are four basic precepts.

i.   Statewide service

Summons may be served anywhere within the state in which the district court sits.

ii.   The 100 mile "bulge" rule

The 100 mile "bulge" provision provides for some service within 100 miles of the place where the original action commenced, even if state lines are crossed. However, this rule applies only to parties brought in as third-party defendants under Rule 14, or as additional necessary parties to a counterclaim or cross-claim under Rules 13 and 19.

The purpose of the rule is to permit service of process on additional parties that are brought into the action after the original suit is filed and are necessary for a fair and complete disposition of the action. This is an important rule for multi-party litigation in large metropolitan areas such as New York, Chicago, and Washington, which cover several jurisdictions, since otherwise it would often be difficult to serve every party in the suit.

iii.   State long-arm statutes

Rule 4(e) provides for service on parties outside the state in which the district court sits whenever that state permits out-of-state service. The Rule refers, of course, to state long-arm statutes and attachment procedures that create quasi in rem jurisdiction.[30] It puts federal and state process on essentially the same footing as far as territorial limits are concerned.

iv.   Federal statute or court order

Whenever a federal statute or court order authorizes service on a party outside the state in which the district court sits, service may be made in accordance with the statute or order.

30. See §3.6.

f. Timeliness of service

Under Rule 4(j) service of the complaint and summons must be carried out within 120 days after filing of the complaint. Unless good cause can be shown for not having carried out service in time, the action will be dismissed without prejudice as to the unserved defendant.

The complaint, of course, may be refiled against that same party. Refiling after the statute of limitations has run should not create a problem, so long as the original action was properly filed within the limitations period. The reasoning for this is similar to the "relation back" analysis for amended and supplemental pleadings.[31] However, when a state cause of action is asserted and state law requires more than the mere filing of the complaint to satisfy the state statute of limitations, such as actual service of summons, these additional requirements must be met within the limitations period.[32]

g. Proof of service

Rule 4(g) requires that the person serving process establish proof of service promptly and in any event within the time during which the party served has to respond to the process. If process is served by anyone other than the U.S. marshal, proof must be in affidavit form. In practice, the proof-of-service affidavit is usually found on the summons form.

Example:

AFFIDAVIT OF SERVICE

I, _____, having been first duly sworn, state that I served a copy of the summons and complaint on
_____ by _____ at
　　　(defendant)　　　　　　 　(method of service)
_____ on _____.
　　　(address)　　　　　　　　　(date)

_____
(signature)

Signed and sworn to before me
on: _____

_____
Notary Public

My commission expires on _____

h. Informal service

Sometimes you will know the lawyer who will represent the defendant in the lawsuit. You may have already had contact with the defen-

---

31. See §5.13.
32. See Wright §64; Wright & Miller §1057. The leading case is Ragan v. Merchants Transfer & Warehouse Co., 337 U.S. 530 (1949).

dant's lawyer before filing suit, or you may know the lawyer who regularly handles the defendant's legal matters. In such instances, a good practice is to call the lawyer and let her know you are about to file suit. Ask her if she will accept service of process and acknowledge receipt on behalf of the defendant. If so, simply deliver or mail the complaint to her.

If you think the defendant will try to avoid service of process, or will contest the validity of service, serve the defendant formally under Rule 4. Otherwise, informal service can be a convenient approach; it is frequently used in commercial litigation with corporate parties.

§5.4.   Rule 12 responses[33]

When a complaint and summons have been served on a defendant, he can respond in two basic ways. First, he can answer the complaint. Ordinarily, the defendant must answer within 20 days of service. If out-of-state service is made under a state statute, however, the statute determines when the answer is due.

Second, before filing an answer the defendant can make any of three motions attacking claimed defects in the complaint.[34] These are a motion to strike, a motion for a more definite statement, and a motion to dismiss; all of which are governed by Rule 12. Where a defendant decides to attack the complaint with a Rule 12 motion, he must do so within the time permitted for his answer, ordinarily within 20 days of service of the complaint.[35]

1.   Motion to strike[36]

Under Rule 12(f), if the complaint contains "any redundant, immaterial, impertinent or scandalous matter," it can be stricken upon motion. While such a motion is not frequently made, it should be considered where there is a possibility that the complaint will be read to the jury during trial.

33. Wright §66; James & Hazard §4.2; Friedenthal §§5.22-5.24; Moore's Manual §§11.01-11.07; Shepard's Manual §§3.38-3.44, 4.2-4.34; Moore's Federal Practice §§12.05-12.23; Wright & Miller §§1341-1397.

34. See §5.3 for the requirements of a complaint.

35. If a Rule 12 motion is denied, a defendant generally has 10 days to answer the complaint.

36. Wright §66; James & Hazard §4.2; Friedenthal §5.24; Moore's Manual §11.05; Shepard's Manual §§4.20-4.22; Moore's Federal Practice §12.21; Wright & Miller §§1380-1383.

Example:

[Caption]

MOTION TO STRIKE

Defendant Johnson Corporation moves under Rule 12(f) for an order striking certain immaterial and scandalous matters from the complaint. In support of its motion defendant states:

1. Par. 2 of the complaint alleges that the "Johnson Corporation had gross receipts of $102,436,000 for fiscal year 1984." This allegation is immaterial to a contract action and should be stricken.

2. Par. 7 of the complaint alleges that the "Johnson Corporation is an international cartel that dominates the furniture polish industry." This allegation is impertinent and scandalous and should be stricken.

WHEREFORE, defendant Johnson Corporation requests that the court enter an order striking these parts of plaintiff's complaint and requiring plaintiff to file an amended complaint that deletes the stricken matter within 10 days.

2. Motion for a more definite statement[37]

Under Rule 12(e), if the complaint is "so vague or ambiguous" that the defendant cannot respond to it, the defendant may move for a more definite statement. The motion must point out the defects and specify the details that are needed. However, since the complaint need only be a "short and plain statement," and pleadings generally should be "simple, concise and direct," and because discovery is the preferred method for flushing out details, such motions are disfavored and infrequently granted. A more commonly used approach is to move to dismiss under Rule 12(b)(6) for failure to state a claim on which relief can be granted.

Example:

[Caption]

MOTION FOR A MORE DEFINITE STATEMENT

Defendant Johnson Corporation moves under Rule 12(e) for an order requiring plaintiff to provide a more definite statement. In support of its motion defendant states:

1. Par. 3 of the complaint alleges that "plaintiff and defendant and others entered into an agreement in 1984 under which defendant was obligated to deliver such amounts of furniture polish as plaintiff may from time to time request."

---

37. Wright §66; James & Hazard §4.2; Friedenthal §5.23; Moore's Manual §11.07; Shepard's Manual §§4.18-4.20; Moore's Federal Practice §§12.17-12.19; Wright & Miller §§1374-1379.

2. Nowhere else in the complaint is greater detail provided, and no copy of any contract is attached to the complaint. Without additional details, defendant cannot respond to this allegation.

WHEREFORE, defendant Johnson Corporation requests that the court enter an order requiring defendant to serve and file a more definite statement within 10 days showing what date this alleged contract was entered into, where it was entered into, every party to it, the requirements under the contract, and, if in writing, a copy of the alleged contract.

3. Motion to dismiss under Rule 12(b)[38]

Under Rule 12(b), the defendant may raise certain defenses either in the answer or by a motion to dismiss. This is the predominant motion for attacking the complaint, and it has several important characteristics.

a. The one motion requirement

If you decide to respond to the complaint with a motion to dismiss on Rule 12(b) grounds, the Rule requires that you present all defenses that can be raised in one motion to dismiss. In other words, you must consolidate all available Rule 12(b) defenses into one motion. This requirement prevents attacking the complaint on a piecemeal basis.

b. Rule 12(b) defenses

The following defenses may be raised in a motion to dismiss:

(1)   Lack of subject matter jurisdiction
(2)   Lack of jurisdiction over the person
(3)   Improper venue
(4)   Insufficiency of process
(5)   Insufficiency of service of process
(6)   Failure to state a claim upon which relief can be granted
(7)   Failure to join a party under Rule 19

In addition, there is some case law holding that affirmative defenses in Rule 8(c) may be asserted in a Rule 12(b) motion to suppress.[39] Federal practice has eliminated the need for special appearances to contest personal jurisdiction, since under Rule 12(g) the joinder of defenses does not create a waiver of any of them. Hence, a defendant can raise any of the Rule 12(b) defenses by motion and is not held to have waived the right to assert lack of personal jurisdiction.[40]

---

38. Wright §66; James & Hazard §4.2; Friedenthal §5.22; Moore's Manual §11.06; Shepard's Manual §§3.38-3.44, 4.23-4.30; Moore's Federal Practice §§12.07-12.14, 12.22-12.23; Wright & Miller §§1347-1366.
39. See Moore's Manual §1606(3); Shepard's Manual §3.41.
40. See Shepard's Manual §3.41.

c. Waiver

Under Rule 12(g) and (h), defenses not consolidated into one motion to dismiss may be waived, but the waiver rules depend on the defense involved. Lack of jurisdiction over the person, improper venue, insufficiency of process, and insufficiency of service of process are all waived if not included in a motion to strike or, if no motion is made, in the answer. Hence, if any of these grounds are raised in a motion to dismiss, the others must be raised then as well, or they will be waived. Failure to state a claim and failure to join an indispensable party, however, may be raised in the answer, in a motion for judgment on the pleadings, or at trial. Finally, lack of subject matter jurisdiction is never waived and can be raised at any time.

The waiver rules create two categories of defenses to a claim. The procedural irregularity defenses are waived unless timely presented, while substantive defenses to a valid judgment cannot be so waived.

d. Practice approach

The underlying theory of Rule 12 must be kept in mind when deciding whether to present Rule 12(b) defenses in a motion to dismiss or in the answer. The Rule permits certain defenses that may terminate the litigation to be presented and heard early in the litigation process. This is obviously an efficient way to deal with a defective or meritless complaint. If you decide to assert a defense in a motion to dismiss, you should raise the other Rule 12(b) defenses available and assert them in one consolidated motion, because most of those defenses are waived if not raised then.

Second, consider the types of defenses that can be raised. Three of the grounds, lack of jurisdiction over the person, insufficiency of process, and insufficiency of service of process, are essentially procedural defects that usually can be cured. Since the plaintiff can ordinarily file an amended complaint or serve process on the defendant again, there may be little point in raising these defenses if the plaintiff can easily cure them. For example, where there is no proper personal jurisdiction over the defendant because of a defect in the process, but it is obvious that the defendant can be properly served later, there may be little point in raising these defenses even though they are technically available. On the other hand, where personal jurisdiction over the defendant does not properly exist, and probably cannot be obtained, the motion should be made.

If the defense is improper venue, the defense is waived if not included in a motion to dismiss that raises other 12(b) defenses.[41] Hence, if venue is in fact improper under venue rules, and the present venue is a logistically inconvenient location for the defendant, the motion should be made. If granted, the probable result will not be dismissal, but transfer to a proper venue.[42]

41. See §3.7 supra; 28 U.S.C. §§1391 et seq.
42. See 28 U.S.C. §§1404, 1406.

Finally, where the defenses are lack of subject matter jurisdiction, failure to state a claim upon which relief can be granted, and failure to join an indispensable party, the defendant has more flexibility since these may be made either in the answer, by a motion for judgment on the pleadings, or at trial, even if a motion to dismiss based on other Rule 12(b) grounds has been made. Hence, the defendant has the option of including these grounds in a motion to dismiss or raising them later. Raising them by motion to dismiss, of course, will get the issue resolved sooner than by including them in the answer. Regardless of which approach is taken, however, the plaintiff is on notice of a possible defect in his pleading and can usually file an amended complaint correcting the defect.

The history of Rule 12(b) shows that motions to dismiss rarely result in the final disposition of a lawsuit.[43] Indeed, federal pleadings are designed to frame issues, not resolve disputes. Hence, the trend in litigation practice has been to make fewer motions under Rule 12, and to raise those defenses instead in the answer; that is, to raise those defenses in a motion to dismiss only when there is a clear strategic reason to do so, not simply because the Rules permit it.

A motion to dismiss based on Rule 12(b) should clearly set out the defenses being asserted in separate paragraphs.

Example:

[Caption]

MOTION TO DISMISS

Defendant Jones moves under Rule 12(b) for an order dismissing the complaint. In support of his motion defendant states:

1. The court lacks jurisdiction over the subject matter of this action because it appears from the complaint that the alleged claim does not arise under the Constitution of the United States, any Act of Congress, or treaties of the United States.

2. The court lacks jurisdiction over the subject matter of this action because the controversy is not between citizens of different states, and because the amount in controversy between the plaintiff and this defendant is less than $10,000, exclusive of interest and costs.

3. The court lacks jurisdiction over the defendant because the defendant is a corporation incorporated under the laws of the State of Delaware, has its principal place of business in Delaware, and is not subject to service in the State of Maryland where service was attempted.

4. This action has been brought in an improper district, since the complaint alleges that jurisdiction is based on diversity of citizenship, plaintiff is a citizen of the State of California, defendant is a citizen of the State of Nevada, and the claims arose in the State of Nevada. Venue in the district of Arizona is therefore improper.

---

43. See Wright §66.

5. Service of process on the defendant was insufficient because service was made on the defendant's business partner at his place of business, as shown by the proof of service for the summons.

6. The complaint fails to state a claim against this defendant on which relief can be granted.

7. The complaint fails to join all indispensable parties as required by Rule 19 because the Phillips Corporation is an indispensable party, has not been joined as a party, and if brought within this court's jurisdiction would destroy this court's jurisdiction since complete diversity would be lacking.

The basic allegations of Rule 12(b) grounds should be developed both factually and legally. Where facts are necessary, statements in affidavit form and exhibits should be attached to the motion, although the court under the Rule can then treat the motion as one for summary judgment. If case law is pertinent, it should be contained in a memorandum of law accompanying the motion.

The most commonly raised ground for dismissal, of course, is Rule 12(b)(6), failure to state a claim upon which relief can be granted. The motion should be granted if, based on facts alleged and applicable law, there is no possible set of facts that could support the claim under any available legal theory.[44] The motion is conceptually limited to matters alleged in the complaint. If facts outside the pleadings are presented at a hearing on the motion, the court should treat the motion as one for summary judgment and proceed in accordance with Rule 56. If the motion is granted, plaintiff will routinely be given leave to file an amended complaint. However, if the plaintiff is acting in bad faith, has repeatedly failed to amend properly, or obviously cannot amend properly, leave to amend should be denied.[45]

§5.5. Answers[46]

When the plaintiff's complaint has been served, every defendant must respond, either by filing a Rule 12 motion, discussed in the preceding section, or by answering the complaint.

1. Timing

As a general rule, under Rule 12(a) the defendant must serve an answer within 20 days of service of the complaint and summons. Different deadlines may apply if service is made out of state, if the U.S. government is a defendant, or if a specific federal or state statute applies. Where the de-

44. See Conley v. Gibson, 355 U.S. 41 (1957).
45. Forman v. Davis, 371 U.S. 178 (1962).
46. Wright §66; James & Hazard §§4.4-4.8; Friedenthal §§5.17-5.20; Moore's Manual §11.08; Shepard's Manual §§3.28-3.44; Moore's Federal Practice §§8.21-8.29, 12.05-12.07; Wright & Miller §§1261-1279, 1347-1348.

fendant first responds with a Rule 12 motion, the answer is due within 10 days after the defendant receives notice of the court's action on the motion or within 10 days after service of a more definite statement.

2. General requirements

There are several rules that regulate the form and content of the answer. Rule 8(b) requires that an answer shall "state in short and plain terms" the defenses asserted. It must either admit or deny the allegations, or state that the defendant is without knowledge or information sufficient to form a belief as to their truth. Under Rule 8(c), affirmative defenses must be set out in the answer, and under Rule 12(b), the specified defenses may be set out as well. The defenses may be set out alternatively, inconsistently, and hypothetically. A hypothetical defense can be raised to an allegation in a complaint if it is found to be true, thus permitting a response that both denies the allegation and raises a hypothetical defense to it.

Since a complaint must be answered, failing to answer will constitute an admission of all facts alleged in the complaint; this does not apply, however, to the prayer for relief. Answering with a simple "admit," "deny," or "no knowledge or belief" is usually sufficient. Under Rule 9(a), however, where the answer raises an issue as to the "legal existence of any party or the capacity of any party to sue or be sued or the authority of a party to sue or be sued in a representative capacity," the denials must be made with particularity.

To parallel the complaint, the answer must be organized in paragraphs and by counts, setting out separate defenses in separate counts. Where there is only one defendant the answer is simply titled "ANSWER." If there are multiple defendants, however, the title should specify the party answering, for example, "ANSWER OF DEFENDANT ACME TOOL CORPORATION." If a defendant demands a jury trial, the "JURY TRIAL DEMANDED" notice should appear in the caption of the answer, and the words "DEFENDANT DEMANDS TRIAL BY JURY" at the end of the answer. Finally, the answer, like every pleading, must be signed by the lawyer; this signature constitutes a certification that the pleading is made in good faith under Rule 11.

The answer, therefore, may have three parts: responses to the complaint's allegations, affirmative defenses, and Rule 12(b) defenses. A well-drafted answer will set out each part clearly.

3. Responses

Rule 8(b) permits three types of responses to the complaint's allegations. The answer may either admit or deny the allegations, or state that the party is without knowledge or information sufficient to form a belief as to their truth. The format, whether informally brief or more formal, is largely a matter of local custom, although the trend is toward brief responses.

Examples:

[Caption]

ANSWER

Defendant Jones answers the complaint as follows:

Count I

1. Admits.
2. Defendant admits the allegations in Par. 2.
3. Denies.
4. Defendant denies the allegations in Par. 4.
5. No knowledge or belief.
6. Defendant states that she is without knowledge or information sufficient to form a belief as to the truth of the allegations in Par. 6, and therefore denies them.

If the response is "no knowledge or belief," this must be based on good faith. Such a response should not be available on matters that are common knowledge or that can easily be learned by the defendant.[47] For example, if the complaint alleges that the defendant corporation had "gross receipts during 1985 in the amount of $6,450,000," the defendant's lawyer cannot answer "no knowledge or belief" since the lawyer can easily find out if the allegation is true or not.

The answer may admit only part of an allegation and deny the remainder, or may admit having no knowledge or information as to the remainder, as the case may be. Each paragraph of the complaint must be responded to individually, unless the defendant can in good faith collectively deny every allegation of the complaint.

Example:

1. Defendant admits he is a citizen of the State of California, but denies the remaining allegations in Par. 1.
2. Defendant admits he entered into a written contract with plaintiff on June 1, 1985, but denies that the contract was modified under an agreement on August 1, 1985, or on any other date.
3. Defendant denies he owned and operated a business known as Jones Excavating in 1985 or any other year. Defendant does not have sufficient knowledge or information to form a belief as to the truth of the other allegations in Par. 3, and therefore denies them.

Within these guidelines the rules permit considerable drafting flexibility. The modern trend is toward brevity and conciseness. The standard

47. See Moore's Manual §11.08(2).

approach is to simply have counts and numbered paragraphs corresponding to the counts and paragraphs of the complaint. However, it is just as effective to set out admissions, denials, and no-knowledge-or-information responses collectively when the situation is appropriate. If the complaint incorporates several paragraphs in the first count, the answer can do the same.

Example:

Count I

1. Defendant admits the allegations of Pars. 1, 2, 3, 4, 5, and 6 of the complaint.
2. Defendant denies the allegations of Pars. 8, 9, and 10 of the complaint.
3. Defendant states she does not have sufficient knowledge or information to form a belief as to the truth of the allegations in Par. 7, and therefore denies them.

Count II

1. Defendant incorporates her answers to Pars. 1-3 of Count I.
2. Defendant denies all other allegations of the complaint not specifically admitted.

Denying all allegations not specifically admitted is a safe practice, since this prevents a typographical error in the answer from prejudicing your client. Claims under Rule 9(a) of no capacity or authority and claims under Rule 9(c) that conditions precedent have not been performed are raised by denials, but must be particularly specified.

Example:

1. Defendant denies that plaintiff is a legal entity that has capacity to sue in its own name, and specifically denies that plaintiff has any legal existence that permits it to pursue this action in the name of "John Smith Corporation."
2. Defendant denies that plaintiff has performed all conditions precedent as required under the contract, and specifically denies that plaintiff delivered a copy of the contract to defendant within 30 days of execution, although plaintiff was required to do so before the contract would be in force.

Not every allegation in the complaint must be responded to, since not every count, or every paragraph in a count, will contain an allegation directed at your defendant. Where you represent one defendant in a case that has multiple defendants, and some counts or paragraphs do not apply to your defendant, the usual practice is to point this out in your answer. This avoids the possibility of "silence" in your answer being interpreted as an admission.

Example:

Count II

The allegations in this count are not directed to this defendant.

Example:

12. The allegations in Par. 12 of plaintiff's complaint are not directed toward this defendant, so this defendant makes no answer to the allegations.

4. Rule 12(b) defenses

As discussed previously,[48] the defendant can raise Rule 12(b) defenses in a pre-answer motion to dismiss or can include them in the answer. If the defenses are raised in the answer, each should be labeled separately to refer to the specific defense being asserted, preferably by tracking the language of Rule 12(b) and elaborating where necessary.

Example:

FIRST DEFENSE

The complaint fails to state a claim against the defendant on which relief can be granted.

SECOND DEFENSE

This court lacks jurisdiction over the subject matter of this action, since the complaint alleges that jurisdiction is based on diversity of citizenship and there is no allegation that the amount in controversy exceeds $10,000, exclusive of interest and costs.

5. Affirmative defenses

Rule 8(c) sets forth what it characterizes as affirmative defenses:

> accord and satisfaction, arbitration and award, assumption of risk, contributory negligence, discharge in bankruptcy, duress, estoppel, failure of consideration, fraud, illegality, injury by fellow servant, laches, license, payment,

---

48. See §5.4.

release, res judicata, statute of frauds, statute of limitations, waiver, and any other matter constituting an avoidance or affirmative defense.

Keep in mind that other defenses have also been characterized as affirmative defenses.[49] When answering the complaint, the usual practice is to label each affirmative defense separately, and clearly describe the affirmative defense being asserted, preferably by using the language of Rule 8(c) and elaborating where necessary.

Example:

FIRST AFFIRMATIVE DEFENSE

Plaintiff's cause of action set out in the complaint did not occur within two years before commencement of this action, and is barred by the applicable statute of limitations.

SECOND AFFIRMATIVE DEFENSE

Plaintiff's cause of action is barred by defendant's discharge in bankruptcy.

Affirmative defenses are usually considered substantive. In diversity cases, therefore, the trial court will apply the substantive law of the state in which it is sitting.[50] That forum state's law must be researched for the substantive law that will apply under its conflict of law rules and for the recognized defenses. However, under state law an affirmative defense may not necessarily be one that the defendant has the burden of pleading. The danger in asserting such a defense as an affirmative defense in the answer is that the defendant may be held to have undertaken the burden of proof. On the other hand, failing to raise in the answer all affirmative defenses mentioned in Rule 8(c) runs the risk that the defenses will be waived.[51] The safer course is to raise the defense and make it clear that you do not intend to assume a burden of proof not existing under state law.

Example:

THIRD AFFIRMATIVE DEFENSE

Plaintiff was contributorily negligent in sustaining the injuries complained of in her complaint. By raising the defense of contributory negligence, however, defendant expressly does not assume any burden of proof that applicable substantive law may place on plaintiff.

49. See Shepard's Manual §3.35.
50. This is the rule of Erie R.R. Co. v. Tompkins, 304 U.S. 64 (1938). See §3.2 supra.
51. See Shepard's Manual §3.37; Moore's Manual §11.08(4).

6. Practice approach

Drafting answers to complaints involves two basic considerations. First, make sure you respond to every allegation in every paragraph of every count of the complaint, since any allegation not responded to is deemed admitted. A safe practice is to deny all allegations not specifically admitted or otherwise answered. Where the allegations are admitted in part and denied in part, make sure the answer clearly states the facts being admitted and clearly denies all remaining allegations. Clear, simple language is critical here.

There may be times, however, when you may wish to admit an allegation even though you are not required to admit it. Remember that pleadings are always interrelated with discovery. If a fact alleged is denied, a plaintiff will invariably focus some of his discovery efforts on the denied fact. On the other hand, admitting a fact may have the effect of preventing further discovery of information that would prove the fact. When that information contains harmful or embarrassing facts, it may make sense to simply admit the allegation in your answer, although you could have — consistent with Rule 11 — denied it.

Second, set out all Rule 12(b) defenses and affirmative defenses that you can raise in good faith; it is best to list and label them separately. There is no penalty for raising inconsistent, hypothetical, or alternative defenses. If you are in doubt whether a defense is considered an affirmative defense, the safer course is to raise it in the answer. The real danger is that you will fail to raise a defense with the result that it will be waived. If you need additional time to study potential defenses, it is better to move for additional time to respond than to serve a hastily considered answer.

If the plaintiff has not made a jury demand with the complaint and you want a jury trial, you must make an appropriate jury demand on the answer. If the plaintiff has made a jury demand on the complaint, you need not make one, although the safer approach is to make the demand on the answer as well. The jury demand is usually made by putting the words "JURY TRIAL DEMANDED" below the case number and the words "DEFENDANT DEMANDS TRIAL BY JURY" at the end of the answer. Local rules usually have additional requirements, such as jury demand forms and fees.

§5.6. *Counterclaims*[52]

In addition to Rule 12 motions and the answer, both of which are responses to the complaint, a defendant can also counterclaim. This is a pleading brought against a plaintiff within the time the defendant has to answer. The counterclaim is functionally identical to a complaint, and is

---

52. Wright §79; James & Hazard §4.8; Friedenthal §6.7; Moore's Manual §11.09; Shepard's Manual §§3.45-3.50; Moore's Federal Practice §§13.02-13.41; Wright & Miller §§1401-1430.

made part of the answer. As such, the analytical approach and the pleading strategy for the counterclaim are the same as for a complaint. The plaintiff must respond to the counterclaim, either with Rule 12 motions or a reply, within the usual time limits. Counterclaims are either compulsory or permissive, and substantially different rules apply to each.

1. Compulsory counterclaims

Compulsory counterclaims, governed by Rule 13(a), are claims that a defendant is required to bring against the plaintiff. The purpose of the compulsory counterclaim rule is clear: If the court already has jurisdiction over the plaintiff, the defendant, and the subject matter of the lawsuit, it makes sense to hear and adjudicate at one time all claims related to the occurrence or transaction involved.

A claim is compulsory if four requirements are met:

(i)   the claim must already exist when the defendant is required to answer the complaint;

(ii)   the claim must arise out of the same transaction or occurrence on which the complaint is based;

(iii)   the court must be able to obtain jurisdiction over any necessary additional parties; and

(iv)   the counterclaim must not be the subject of a pending action.[53]

No jurisdictional dollar amount is necessary. The court has ancillary jurisdiction over the counterclaim even if the plaintiff voluntarily dismisses the complaint. However, if the complaint is dismissed for jurisdictional defects, the counterclaim will be dismissed unless it has an independent jurisdictional basis.

The principal difficulty with compulsory counterclaims is in determining if the defendant's claim involves the same transaction or occurrence that gave rise to the plaintiff's claim. While this is often easy to determine in tort claims, such as an automobile accident, it is often a difficult question in the corporate and commercial area where numerous lengthy transactions are often involved. Courts have devised several approaches for determining whether the "same transaction or occurrence" is involved. These include deciding whether the legal or factual issues are the same, whether the trial would involve the same proof, and whether the complaint and counterclaim are logically related. The purpose of Rule 13(a) is to promote fairness and efficiency by having related claims heard in one trial with consistent results. Accordingly, the phrase in general has been broadly interpreted. The "logical relation" test, the most flexible approach, has the support of most of the treatises on the topic.[54]

Where there is proper jurisdiction over the plaintiff's complaint, the court will also have ancillary jurisdiction over the counterclaims. In addi-

---

53. See Moore's Manual §11.09(2).
54. See Shepard's Manual §3.46; Moore's Manual §11.09(3); Wright §79.

tion, since the plaintiff by filing suit chose the venue, the plaintiff cannot complain about the same venue for the defendant's counterclaim. Hence, there are no basic jurisdiction or venue problems associated with bringing compulsory counterclaims.[55]

2. Permissive counterclaims

Permissive counterclaims, governed by Rule 13(b), are claims that a defendant may bring, but is not required to bring, against a plaintiff in the pending lawsuit. A counterclaim is permissive if it does not arise out of the transaction or occurrence on which the plaintiff's complaint is based.

A permissive counterclaim, because it is a claim asserting different grounds than the complaint, must have a separate jurisdictional basis. The reasoning behind the requirement is that a defendant cannot use a counterclaim to bring another claim into federal court that could not have been filed there as an original claim. A permissive counterclaim, in other words, cannot enlarge federal jurisdiction. If the permissive counterclaim has an independent jurisdictional basis, but no proper venue exists in the district where the plaintiff's complaint was filed, it also cannot be brought.[56] Both independent jurisdiction and proper venue must exist before the defendant can bring a permissive counterclaim.

The concept behind the permissive counterclaim rule is fairness. Since a plaintiff has total freedom to bring unrelated claims against the defendant, the defendant should have the same freedom, restricted only by the independent jurisdiction and venue requirements. If the counterclaims make the case too complex, the court can order separate trials on the counterclaims.

3. The United States as plaintiff

When the United States is a plaintiff, Rule 13(d) applies special rules. As a sovereign power, the United States has immunity from suit unless it has waived that immunity and has consented to be sued. No procedural rule can enlarge the types of suits that can be brought against the United States. Accordingly, no counterclaim can be asserted against the United States unless the government has expressly consented to be sued on that type of claim. The only exception is recoupment, which can be asserted as a counterclaim to reduce or defeat a claim.[57] This rule does not work the other way around; when the United States is a defendant, there is no equivalent restriction on its right to bring any proper counterclaim against the plaintiff.

---

55. See Moore's Manual §11.09(5); Wright §79.
56. See Shepard's Manual §3.47; Moore's Manual §§11.09(9) and (10).
57. See Moore's Manual §11.09(20); Shepard's Manual §3.49.

4. Statutes of limitations

Statutes of limitations are usually considered substantive law. Federal statutes of limitations apply to federal claims, and state statutes apply to state claims brought under diversity jurisdiction. A counterclaim, like a complaint, must be filed within the applicable statutory period, or it will usually be barred.[58]

5. Waiver and amended pleadings

Failure to plead a compulsory counterclaim bars the defendant from asserting the claim later in another action. Rule 13(a) operates like a statutory bar in both federal and state courts.[59]

If a counterclaim was omitted through "oversight, inadvertence or excusable neglect, or when justice requires," the court may permit an amended answer to include the omitted counterclaim. However, the court cannot allow such a counterclaim if the statute of limitations has run because the concept of relation back applies only to amended pleadings, and a new counterclaim in an amended answer is viewed as a new pleading.[60]

Under Rule 13(e), a counterclaim that matures or accrues after the defendant serves his answer may, at the court's discretion, be raised through a supplemental answer. If the court denies it, no prejudice should occur because such a counterclaim by definition cannot be compulsory and the defendant can always assert it later as an independent claim. Of course, where the defendant requests leave to file a supplemental pleading early in the litigation process and the counterclaim is based on the same transaction or occurrence as the plaintiff's complaint, leave will usually be granted.

6. Practice approach

A counterclaim is simply a complaint brought by a defendant against a plaintiff in a pending suit. In format, content, and signing the counterclaim should be drafted like a complaint.[61] The only difference is that the counterclaim is made part of the defendant's answer and is served on the plaintiff's attorney like any post-complaint pleading, motion, or discovery document. It is usually titled "ANSWER AND COUNTERCLAIM," with separate headings and sections for each. If there are several plaintiffs against whom counterclaims are brought, the titles should be specific.

58. See Moore's Manual §11.09(18); Wright §79. An exception is recoupment, which only diminishes or defeats the plaintiff's claim and is usually viewed as arising out of the same transaction.
59. See Wright §79; this bar is frequently characterized as res judicata, waiver, or estoppel.
60. See Moore's Manual §11.09(17).
61. See §5.3.

If the counterclaim is not included in the answer, it may be waived. To set it off from the answer, it should be clearly labeled a counterclaim; if you are unsure whether the claim is in fact a counterclaim, the safe course is to label it as such, since there are no penalties for an incorrect designation. If you are unsure whether your counterclaim is compulsory or permissive, the safe course again is to assert the counterclaim to avoid a possible waiver. Finally, since a counterclaim is analogous to a complaint, you should make a jury demand on those counterclaims that you want tried to a jury, since failure to do so may constitute a waiver. The plaintiff's demand for a jury trial will not extend to the defendant's counterclaims.

Example:

COUNTERCLAIM

Defendant Acme Manufacturing complains of plaintiff Wilbur Johnson as follows:
    1. [If the counterclaim is permissive, you must allege the jurisdictional basis for bringing the claim in federal court.]
    2. [Draft the pleading in the same manner as any complaint.]

7. Plaintiff's responses

The plaintiff must consider how best to respond to the counterclaim and answer. If the answer merely admits or denies the complaint's allegations, the plaintiff ordinarily need do nothing. However, if the answer contains redundant, immaterial, impertinent, or scandalous matters, you as plaintiff can move to strike. If the answer contains Rule 12(b) defenses or affirmative defenses, you may move to strike "any insufficient defense." In short, you can make any of the Rule 12 motions that are available when responding to a complaint. The plaintiff's responses to an answer that includes a counterclaim are discussed in the next section.

§5.7. Replies[62]

The plaintiff under Rule 7(a) must reply to a "counterclaim denominated as such." There must be a counterclaim in fact, and it must be labeled a counterclaim on the defendant's answer. Only if both requirements are met must plaintiff reply. These requirements relieve the plaintiff of the burden of correctly guessing if the defendant's pleading is a counterclaim or an affirmative defense, since the distinction as a matter of substantive law is not always clear. However, a careful plaintiff will reply to any re-

---

62. Wright §66; James & Hazard §4.9; Friedenthal §5.21; Moore's Manual §12.03; Shepard's Manual §3.55; Moore's Federal Practice §7.03; Wright & Miller §§1184-1188.

sponsive pleading that may be a counterclaim, even to those not so labeled, since pleadings may be read to the jury during trial.

Since a counterclaim is the functional equivalent of a complaint, the plaintiff in responding is in the same position a defendant is in when responding to the original complaint. Hence, the plaintiff can respond to the counterclaim with any Rule 12 motions or may respond with a reply. The reply itself can answer the counterclaim, assert Rule 12 defenses, and raise Rule 8(c) affirmative defenses.[63]

Because a reply is simply an answer to a counterclaim, the reply should be drafted in the same manner as an answer[64] and should be titled "<u>REPLY</u>." When a plaintiff must respond to more than one counterclaim, the reply should show in the title which counterclaim is being responded to.

Example:

[Caption]

<u>REPLY</u>

Plaintiff Wilbur Johnson replies to Defendant Acme Manufacturing's counterclaim as follows:

1. Plaintiff admits the allegations in Par. 1 of the counterclaim.
2. . . .
3. . . .
WHEREFORE. . . .

§5.8. *Cross-claims*[65]

A cross-claim is essentially a complaint brought by one codefendant against another codefendant. Rule 13(g) permits a cross-claim if the claim arises out of the same transaction or occurrence that is the subject matter of the original complaint, or relates to any property that is the subject matter of the original action. If a counterclaim has been brought against two or more plaintiffs, those plaintiffs may cross-claim against each other. Also, if a defendant has brought third-party complaints against additional parties, those third-party defendants may cross-claim against each other.

There are several cross-claim rules that must be understood.

---

63. There is some case law permitting a compulsory counterclaim in the reply as well. See Moore's Manual §12.04.

64. See §5.5.

65. Wright §80; James & Hazard §9.12; Friedenthal §6.8; Moore's Manual §14.04; Shepard's Manual §3.51; Moore's Federal Practice §§13.34-13.35; Wright & Miller §§1431-1433.

1. Discretionary pleading

Cross-claims are always discretionary. A cross-claimant may, but is not required to, bring his claim in the pending action. The cross-claimant can always bring the claim as a separate action. Hence, there are no waiver dangers involved in this decision.

2. Subject matter

A cross-claim must be based on the subject matter of the original complaint, a counterclaim, or property involved in the original complaint. This restriction is designed to protect the original plaintiff from being unfairly forced into litigation that involves a matter totally different from the matters raised in the original complaint, and one in which he may not have any interest. Requiring the cross-claim to arise out of the same transaction or occurrence as the complaint, or counterclaim, or the property involved in the complaint involves the same test and analysis used for compulsory counterclaims.[66]

The rule allows both matured and contingent cross-claims. Accordingly, claims that the coparty "is or may be liable" for all or part of plaintiff's claim against him are properly raised in the cross-claim. In fact, most cross-claims raise just such issues, usually based on active-passive negligence, indemnity, or contribution.

3. When made

Rule 13(g) requires that the cross-claim be made in a party's responsive pleading, usually the answer. Accordingly, just as a counterclaim must be made when answering a complaint, a cross-claim also must be made at that time. This promotes efficient and orderly pleadings.

4. Jurisdiction, venue, and joinder

Since cross-claims must involve the same subject matter as the original complaint or of a counterclaim, jurisdiction over the cross-claim is considered ancillary and venue is considered already established by the original pleading. Hence, there are no jurisdiction or venue problems relative to cross-claims. If the original complaint is dismissed, however, the cross-claim will also be dismissed, unless it has an independent jurisdictional basis.

Difficulties may arise in a related area, however. Rule 13(h) applies the joinder requirements of Rules 19 and 20 to cross-claims as well as to counterclaims. While Rule 13(g) requires that a cross-claim be brought against a coparty, usually a codefendant, additional parties that are indis-

---

66. See §5.6.1.

pensable to the cross-claim must be joined. Where an indispensable party cannot be brought in because jurisdiction over the person cannot be obtained, the cross-claim must be dismissed, although the dismissal will necessarily be without prejudice. The cross-claim can always be brought as an independent action later. Further, if the addition of cross-claims makes the trial too complex, the court can order separate trials under Rule 13(i).

5. Cross-claims against the United States

Cross-claims against the United States cannot enlarge the scope of claims on which the United States as a sovereign power has consented to be sued. The cross-claim, like counterclaims, must be based on a claim that could have been independently brought against the United States. This result appears required by the concept of sovereign immunity, although Rule 13 explicitly requires this only for counterclaims, not cross-claims.

6. Practice approach

The cross-claim, like a counterclaim, must be part of the defendant's answer. It must be served with the answer on existing parties in the same way any pleadings, motions, or discovery documents are served. If the cross-claim brings in new parties that are indispensable under joinder rules, the cross-claim must be served on each new party under Rule 4's summons and service requirements in the same way a complaint is initially served on a defendant.

The cross-claim, like a complaint,[67] counterclaim, or third-party complaint, is a pleading that asks for relief. Hence, it should be drafted like a complaint. The prayer for relief will ordinarily reflect the contingent liability position of the cross-claiming party.

Example:

CROSS-CLAIM AGAINST DEFENDANT JONES

Defendant John Smith cross-claims against Defendant James Jones as follows:

     1. . . .

     2. . . .

WHEREFORE, in the event that Defendant Smith is liable to Plaintiff, Defendant Smith demands judgment against codefendant Jones in the same amount, plus interest and costs.

---

67. See §5.3.

7. Responses to cross-claims

When a cross-claim has been served on a coparty, that party can respond with any of the responses permitted to a complaint. The party can make any of the Rule 12 motions or can answer the complaint and raise Rule 12(b) defenses and affirmative defenses. The party responding to the cross-claim must do so by motion or answer within the required time for answering, normally 20 days.

§5.9. Impleader (third-party practice)[68]

Impleader, also called third-party practice, is governed by Rule 14. It is a method for bringing into the action new parties who may be liable to a defendant for some or all of the judgment that the plaintiff may obtain against the defendant. The original defendant becomes a "third-party plaintiff" filing a complaint against a new party, the "third-party defendant."

Impleader must be distinguished from the filing of counterclaims and cross-claims, both of which involve new claims between original parties to the action. Impleader, by contrast, is a procedure by which new parties, the third-party defendants, are added to the action. The process helps carry out one of the principal purposes of federal pleadings: Whenever possible, consistent with jurisdictional limitations, a court should hear all related claims in one action because this is an efficient way to resolve multi-party disputes and obtain consistent results.

There are several rules for impleader actions that must be understood. The terms usually employed to identify the parties in impleader situations are the original plaintiff; the original defendant, who is now also a third-party plaintiff; and the third-party defendant.

1. Discretionary pleading

Under Rule 14(a), an original defendant can serve a third-party complaint on a third-party defendant without leave of court so long as it is done within 10 days of serving the original answer to plaintiff's complaint. After that time the defendant must obtain the court's permission to do so. The original plaintiff, if served with a counterclaim, may under Rule 14(b) also bring in a third-party defendant.

The court retains discretion to allow or deny impleader, and any party may move to strike a third-party claim.[69] In deciding whether to allow impleader, the court must balance the preference for complete resolution of all related issues with any possible prejudice to the plaintiff.

---

68. Wright §76; James & Hazard §10.18; Friedenthal §6.9; Moore's Manual §§14.02-14.03; Shepard's Manual §§3.125-3.134; Moore's Federal Practice §§14.02-14.37; Wright & Miller §§1441-1465.

69. See Wright §76.

Ordinarily the court should permit impleader; if the case then becomes too complex, it can simply order separate trials on the third-party claims. If the court denies impleader, the third-party claim can usually be brought as an independent action.

2. Subject matter

An original defendant, as a third-party plaintiff, may include in his third-party complaint any claim that asserts that the third-party defendant "is or may be liable to him for all or part of the plaintiff's claim against him." However, the original defendant's right to bring third-party claims is broader than would first appear from Rule 14. There are four types of claims that can be brought under the impleader rule.

First, and most commonly, an original defendant can bring an impleader action based on indemnity, contribution, active-passive negligence, subrogation, or any other theory that passes part or all of the defendant's liability to one or more new parties. Second, the defendant can bring a contingent claim against the third-party defendant. The "is or may be liable" language in the Rule permits accelerated contingent liability claims. Third, the original defendant may be able to bring an independent claim against a third-party defendant, since under Rule 18(a) any party can join claims against another. So long as the defendant has one claim against a third-party defendant that is proper under Rule 14(a), any other independent claims proper under the joinder rules can be added. Finally, the defendant can bring a claim against the third-party defendant that the original plaintiff could not bring directly against the third-party defendant.

3. Jurisdiction and venue

Impleader necessarily involves two related questions: whether the new action is proper under impleader rules, and whether there is proper jurisdiction and venue over the new action. Although an impleader action may be proper under Rule 14, this does not necessarily mean that jurisdiction and venue properly exist.

Where impleader is based on an indemnity type of claim, for instance, ancillary jurisdiction exists and there will be no jurisdiction or venue problems. This situation is much like that which exists with the filing of compulsory counterclaims. Where impleader is based on a claim that is independent of the original plaintiff's claim against the original defendant, however, there must be an independent basis for jurisdiction.[70] This situation is much like that involving permissive counterclaims.

---

70. The leading case is Owens Equip. Co. v. Kroger, 437 U.S. 365 (1978). See Wright §76.

4. Statutes of limitations

As with any complaint, a third-party complaint is subject to all applicable statutes of limitations. In addition, if the original plaintiff files an amended complaint directly against a third-party defendant, it is considered a new cause of action to which the relevant statute applies. The concept of relation back, applicable to amended pleadings, does not apply here.[71]

5. Practice approach

A third-party complaint under Rule 14 is the fourth type of complaint permitted by the federal rules, in addition to complaints, counterclaims, and cross-claims. As such, it should have the three basic parts of any complaint: a jurisdictional allegation, a statement of claims, and a prayer for relief. In short, the approach to drafting a third-party complaint is essentially identical to that of the original complaint, although it should recite the circumstances of the already pending original complaint. The document itself is entitled "THIRD-PARTY COMPLAINT." The caption should clearly show the status of the various parties.

   Where leave of court is required, the defendant must move for permission to bring the third-party complaint against the new party. The usual procedure is to attach the proposed pleading and summons to the motion.

   Since a third-party complaint brings new parties into the suit, each new third-party defendant must be served with the third-party complaint and summons, as required by Rule 4.

Example:

[Caption]

DEFENDANT JOHNSON'S MOTION TO BRING IN THIRD-PARTY DEFENDANT

   Defendant Thomas Johnson requests permission to proceed as a third-party plaintiff against Frank Jones. A copy of the proposed third-party complaint is attached to this motion as Exhibit A. In support of his motion Defendant Johnson states:

   1. . . .

   2. . . .

   WHEREFORE, Defendant Johnson requests that an order be entered permitting him to proceed as third-party plaintiff against Frank Jones, file the third-party complaint (Exhibit A), and to have that

---

71. See §5.13.

complaint and summons served upon Frank Jones as third-party defendant.

_____

Attorney for
Defendant Johnson

Example:

UNITED STATES DISTRICT COURT
FOR THE DISTRICT OF VERMONT

Rebecca Smith, Plaintiff	
v.	

Thomas Johnson,
    Defendant and Third-Party
    Plaintiff
	No. _____
	
	Civil Action

v.	
Frank Jones, Third-Party Defendant	

THIRD-PARTY COMPLAINT

Defendant and Third-Party Plaintiff Johnson complains of Third-Party Defendant Frank Jones as follows:

1. Plaintiff Smith has previously filed a complaint against defendant Johnson. A copy of that complaint is attached as Exhibit A.
2. . . .
3. . . .

WHEREFORE, Defendant and Third-Party Plaintiff Johnson demands judgment against Third-Party Defendant Jones for all sums that Plaintiff may receive in judgment against Defendant Johnson.

6. Third-party defendant responses

A third-party defendant who has been served with a third-party complaint can choose any of the responses of any party served with a complaint. He may make Rule 12 motions, or he may answer the third-party complaint. He can also assert any defenses the original defendant may have against the original plaintiff. This protects the third-party defendant who might otherwise be prejudiced by the original defendant's failure to assert all available defenses against the original plaintiff.

Further, a third-party defendant can counterclaim against the original plaintiff directly, so long as that counterclaim involves the same transaction or occurrence that is the basis for plaintiff's claim against the original defendant. The court will have ancillary jurisdiction over such a counterclaim. He can also assert cross-claims against other third-party defendants under Rule 13.

Finally, a third-party defendant can also bring a third-party complaint against a new party who in turn may be liable to him for all or part of the original third-party complaint filed by the original defendant.

The approach for drafting each of these responses is essentially identical to the approach for responses discussed earlier in this chapter. Make sure that the particular response chosen bears a title that makes clear what type of response it is and identifies the pleading to which it is responding. Where ancillary jurisdiction does not attach to a third-party claim, an independent jurisdictional basis must exist, and there must be personal jurisdiction over the new parties.

While the pleading possibilities under Rule 14 appear complex, its underlying philosophy is simple: The federal rules broadly permit adding parties and claims so that all parties and all aspects of a dispute can be regulated and disposed of in one consolidated proceeding that produces consistent results. If the pleadings make the case too complex, the court can always order separate trials. This in fact is frequently done. The court will try the claims between the original plaintiff and original defendant first. The third-party claims can then be tried later if necessary. Ordering separate trials for the original claims and the subsequent third-party claims will also protect the original plaintiff from any unfairness that might be caused by the addition of the third-party claims.

7. Original plaintiff responses

Under Rule 14(a), after a third-party complaint has been filed, the original plaintiff can file an amended complaint directly against a third-party defendant. This in effect allows the plaintiff to do what could have, and perhaps should have, been done in the first place. However, there must be an independent jurisdictional basis for the amended complaint. If a third-party defendant has counterclaimed directly against the original plaintiff, that plaintiff must reply to the counterclaim within the usual time limits.

§5.10. *Interpleader*[72]

Interpleader is the procedure under which a party, called a "stakeholder," who is or may be subjected to double liability because two or more claimants are making competing claims on a fund or property can resolve these claims. The standard situation involves multiple claims on

---

72. Wright §74; James & Hazard §10.19; Friedenthal §§16.10-16.13; Moore's Manual §14.06; Shepard's Manual §§1.98, 3.135; Moore's Federal Practice §§22.02-22.17; Wright & Miller §§1701-1721.

the proceeds of an insurance policy. If the insurance company does not know who should get the proceeds, it may pay the wrong person and later be forced to pay a second time. Interpleader asks the court to decide who is entitled to the fund or property and in what amounts. In an interpleader action the stakeholder is the plaintiff, and the competing claimants become the defendants.

There are two types of federal interpleader: Rule 22 interpleader, and so-called statutory interpleader under 28 U.S.C. §1335. Each must be considered separately, since substantial differences exist.

1. Rule 22 interpleader

Rule 22 interpleader is in some respects broad, in others restrictive. It is broad because it allows interpleading claims that "do not have a common origin, or are not identical but are adverse to and independent of one another." It also allows the defense that the plaintiff-stakeholder is "not liable in whole or in part to any or all of the claimants." Accordingly, the plaintiff need not deposit the fund in issue with the clerk of the court or post an equivalent bond. The rule allows a defendant in a pending suit to plead interpleader in a counterclaim or cross-claim.

On the other hand, Rule 22 interpleader is restrictive since the usual jurisdiction and venue rules apply. This means that where federal jurisdiction is based on diversity of citizenship under 28 U.S.C. §1332, there must be complete diversity between a plaintiff-stakeholder and each defendant-claimant, a situation that in interpleader cases will rarely exist. The amount in controversy must also exceed $10,000, a determination based on the amount of the fund or value of the property involved. Proper venue is determined under the general venue statute, 18 U.S.C. §1391.

2. 28 U.S.C. §1335 interpleader

Statutory interpleader under §1335, while conceptually identical to Rule 22 interpleader, has significant procedural advantages. First, §1335 relaxes the diversity requirement by requiring that only two of the defendant-claimants have diverse citizenship. Plaintiff's citizenship is not considered. This relaxed diversity requirement allows most interpleader actions to be filed in federal court. Venue under §1397 is proper in any district where one or more of the defendant-claimants resides. Second, the amount in controversy need only exceed $500. Third, under §2361 the court may issue an injunction against any defendant-claimant pursuing another action involving the same fund or property in state or federal courts. Finally, statutory interpleader under §2361 permits nationwide service of process.

Section 1335 requires that the claims be "adverse to and independent of one another," but the claims need not have a common origin or be identical in type. However, the plaintiff must deposit the fund or property with the clerk of the court or post a bond in the amount of the fund or property.

Further, while §1335 itself is silent on whether to allow a statutory interpleader to be asserted in a counterclaim or cross-claim, most courts permit it.[73]

3. Practice approach

An interpleader complaint based on either Rule 22 or §1335 should have all the components of an ordinary complaint: a jurisdictional statement, a statement of claims, and a prayer for relief. Under §1335, the jurisdictional statement should state whether the fund has been deposited with the court or a bond has been posted in the appropriate amount payable to the clerk. The prayer for relief should ask for all relief that is appropriate, including a determination of the amount of liability, if any; a determination of which claimants are entitled to the fund or property and in what amounts; an injuction against any claimants pursuing other actions in state or federal courts based on this claim; and fees and costs, including attorneys fees where permitted.[74]

Example:

Whole Life Insurance Co., a
  corporation,
        Plaintiff

    v.

Thomas Smith
    and
James Smith,
      Defendants

No. _____

Civil Action

COMPLAINT FOR INTERPLEADER

Plaintiff Whole Life Insurance Co. complains of defendants Thomas Smith and James Smith as follows:

Jurisdictional Allegation

1. Jurisdiction in this action is based on 28 U.S.C. §1335. Defendant Thomas Smith is a citizen of the State of Maine. Defendant James Smith is a citizen of the State of Vermont. The amount in controversy exceeds the sum of $500, exclusive of interest and costs.

---

73. See Wright §74.
74. Attorneys fees are permitted where the plaintiff is a passive litigant not disputing that it owes a set amount to someone. See Moore's Manual §14.06(2).

<u>or</u>

1. Jurisdiction is based on Rule 22 of the Federal Rules of Civil Procedure and 18 U.S.C. §1332. Plaintiff is a citizen of the State of New York. Defendant Thomas Smith is a citizen of the State of Maine. Defendant James Smith is a citizen of the State of Vermont. The amount in controversy exceeds the sum of $10,000, exclusive of interest and costs.

2. On June 1, 1984, plaintiff issued a life insurance policy on the life of Franklin Smith. A copy of that policy is attached as Exhibit A.

3. . . .

4. . . .

5. By reason of the defendants' conflicting claims, plaintiff cannot determine with certainty which defendant [, if either,] is entitled to any proceeds of the policy [or, if either is entitled, in what amount].

6. Plaintiff has deposited the face amount of the policy, $50,000, with the clerk of the court. [Required only under §1335 interpleader.]

WHEREFORE, plaintiff requests that the court enter a judgment finding that:

(1) Neither defendant is entitled to recover any money from the policy [permitted only under Rule 22 interpleader];

(2) Each defendant is permanently enjoined from pursuing any other actions or claims on this policy [permitted only under §1335 interpleader];

(3) If this court finds the policy in force at the time of Franklin Smith's death, that the defendants be required to interplead and settle their claims on the policy between themselves, and that plaintiff be discharged from any liability except to any person in such amount as the court adjudges plaintiff is liable;

(4) Plaintiff is entitled to costs [and reasonable attorney's fees if a passive litigant.]

§5.11. *Intervention*[75]

Intervention, governed by Rule 24, is the procedure by which a nonparty having an interest in a pending action can protect its rights by becoming an additional party and presenting a claim or defense. The Rule closely parallels the joinder rules by allowing two types of intervention, intervention of right and permissive intervention.

1. Intervention of right

Rule 24(a) permits two bases for intervention of right. The seldom-used basis is if "a statute of the United States confers an unconditional right to

---

75. Wright §75; James & Hazard §10.17; Friedenthal §6.10; Moore's Manual §14.05; Shepard's Manual §§3.148-3.155; Moore's Federal Practice §§24.02-24.20; Wright & Miller §§1901-1913.

intervene."[76] The frequently used basis is Rule 24(a)(2), which sets forth three requirements for intervention of right.

First, the intervenor must claim "an interest relating to the property or transaction which is the subject of the action" pending. What is a sufficient "interest" remains unsettled, since Rule 24 in its present form was enacted in 1966 and the case law is hardly uniform. Various courts have held that the intervenor's interest must be "direct," "substantial," or "significantly protectable."[77] An analysis of the intervenor's claimed interest, of the relief sought, and of the nature of the claims and defenses asserted in the pending action is required.

Second, the intervenor must be "so situated that the disposition of the action may as a practical matter impair or impede his ability to protect that interest." The critical term "as a practical matter" was included to make clear that this determination should not be limited to legal bars such as res judicata, but should include any substantial functional difficulties that might adversely affect the intervenor's interests.

Third, the intervenor must not be "adequately represented by existing parties." This requires a comparison of the interests of the existing parties with the claimed interests of the intervenor to determine how closely they are related. If the intervenor's interests are essentially identical to those of an existing party, so that the existing party will necessarily assert the same positions as the intervenor would, intervention should be denied.

2. Permissive intervention

Rule 24(b) permits two bases for permissive intervention. The seldom-used basis is if "a statute of the United States confers a conditional right to intervene." The usual situation for such a basis is where the federal or a state government can intervene in a case involving the constitutionality or interpretation of a statute.[78]

The frequently used basis for permissive intervention is Rule 24(b)(2), which permits intervention "when the applicant's claim or defense and the main action have a question of law or fact in common." This involves an analysis similar to that made for the permissive joinder of parties under Rule 20(a). This request to intervene is addressed to the court's discretion, and the court may deny it where the intervenor's request would "delay or prejudice" the rights of the pending parties or inject unimportant issues into the case. If a court denies intervention, there are no adverse legal consequences since res judicata will not apply to the unsuccessful intervenor. The common situation where intervention is permitted is where the intervenor has a claim against the defendant that is factually and legally similar to the plaintiff's pending claim against the defendant.

76. A list of such statutes is found at Moore's Federal Practice §24.06.
77. See Wright & Miller §1908.
78. See Moore's Federal Practice §24.10.

3. Timing

A prospective intervenor must move to intervene in a timely fashion, regardless of whether the intervention sought is of right or is permissive. Both Rule 24(a) and (b) require a "timely application," but where intervention of right is requested, it will ordinarily be permitted, regardless of when the application is made, since the intervenor's right might otherwise be adversely affected. Despite this, it is possible to seek intervention of right so late in the pending action that it is considered untimely and is therefore denied.

When permissive intervention is sought, the court must consider "whether the intervention will unduly delay or prejudice the adjudication of the rights of the original parties." This requires analyzing the relief the intervenor wants, whether the intervenor will be an active or passive party, and particularly the stage that the pending action is in. Intervention obviously will be more favorably viewed when sought early in the pleading stage than if substantial discovery has already been taken.

4. Jurisdiction

The intervenor's addition to the pending action must meet jurisdiction and venue requirements. Where intervention of right is requested, the intervenor's claim is necessarily closely related to the original action and ancillary jurisdiction will attach. On the other hand, if intervention is not based on Rule 24(b)(1), independent jurisdictional grounds must exist.[79]

Venue should not be an issue, since it is viewed as a personal right and the intervenor is generally held to accept the venue that has already been established.

5. Practice approach

Rule 24(c) requires that the intervenor make a timely motion to intervene in the district in which the original action is pending. It must attach an appropriate pleading in the event the motion is allowed. The motion, which must be served on all existing parties, should state the reason why intervention is appropriate under the circumstances.

Example:

Frank Johnson,	
Plaintiff	
v.	No. _____
Wilma Smith,	
Defendant,	Civil Action
Jacob Franklin,	
Intervenor	

79. See Wright §75.

MOTION TO INTERVENE AS A DEFENDANT

Jacob Franklin moves for leave to intervene as a defendant in this action. A copy of his proposed answer is attached as Exhibit A. In support of his motion Franklin states:
1. Intervention is appropriate because. . . .
2. . . .
WHEREFORE, Jacob Franklin requests that he be permitted to intervene as a defendant, file his answer to the complaint, and participate in this action as a party defendant.

ANSWER OF DEFENDANT-INTERVENOR FRANKLIN

Defendant Franklin answers the complaint as follows:
1. . . .
2. . . .

If the motion to intervene is granted, the intervenor becomes a party and has the rights of any party. The intervenor usually cannot contest past orders, but can counterclaim and cross-claim, present any appropriate motions, and fully participate in discovery. Keep in mind, however, that the court has power to limit intervention to certain matters if permissive intervention has been granted.

The denial of a motion to intervene raises the difficult issue of whether the ruling is final and appealable.[80] While there is a split in authority on this question, it appears that a motion for intervention of right is appealable if denied, but the denial of a motion to intervene permissively is appealable only where an abuse of discretion is shown. If the motion to intervene is granted, it is not an appealable order.

§5.12. *Class actions*[81]

The topic of class actions by itself can fill volumes, and literature on the subject in treatises, cases, and journals is extensive. It is obviously a complicated area, one in which the inexperienced litigator should tread cautiously if at all. Hence, this section is limited to a brief overview of the class-action requirements and the initial considerations and steps in such suits. The principal concern of the inexperienced litigator should be determining whether a case can be pursued as a class action. If so, assistance from someone with more experience in this area should probably be sought.

---

80. See Moore's Manual §14.05(6); Moore's Federal Practice §24.15.
81. Wright §72; James & Hazard §§10.20-10.23; Friedenthal §§16.1-16.19; Shepard's Manual §§3.138-3.147; Moore's Manual §14.07; Moore's Federal Practice §§23.01-23.97; Wright & Miller §§1751-1803.

1. General class requirements

Rule 23(a) sets out four class requirements that must be met before the action can proceed as a class action. These apply regardless of whether the class involves the plaintiff or the defendant.

First, the class must be so "numerous that joinder of all members is impracticable." The Rule itself does not define what a class is or how its members should be determined. Impracticability depends on the type of claims asserted and the persons asserting those claims. Because of this, the numbers necessary for a class action are quite flexible, and the ultimate decision whether a class action is the preferred method of dealing with a claim is left to the discretion of the trial court. While it is usually clear that hundreds of potential plaintiffs or defendants make the action suitable for class-action treatment, and that fewer than 30 ordinarily is not enough, the case law on class numbers in the middle range — perhaps 30 to 50 members — shows no particular pattern. Some of such classes have been held to be of an appropriate number, others not.[82] The outcome is as dependent on other considerations as it is on the number of class members.

Second, there must be "questions of law or fact common to the class." This requires the same type of analysis required for joinder and intervention requests.[83]

Third, the "claims or defenses of the representative parties" must be "typical of the claims or defenses of the class." Also, the representatives must be actual members of the class. In addition, the claims or defenses of the class must be reviewed, and there must be enough representative parties to ensure that each claim or defense is represented fairly. This obviously requires that the lawyers closely analyze the facts before selecting actual parties and initiating suit.

Finally, the representative parties must "fairly and adequately protect the interests of the class." This requirement is directed to both the representative parties and their lawyers. The interests of the representatives must be scrutinized to determine if conflicting interests exist. If they do, a possible solution is to certify separate classes. In addition, the lawyers must have sufficient ability and experience to represent the class competently. It may be useful to ask other members of the class to authorize the named parties and their lawyers to represent their interests.

2. General facts requirements

Rule 23(b) sets out three fact situations in which a class action is appropriate.

First, it is appropriate where separate actions would "create a risk of inconsistent or varying adjudications" that would "establish incompatible standards of conduct" for the party opposing the class, or where separate

82. See Moore's Manual §14.07(1); Wright & Miller §1762.
83. See §3.4.

adjudications would "as a practical matter be dispositive of the interests of the others" in the class who are not parties to that adjudication. The former is commonly relied upon in actions against municipal entities to declare actions invalid, such as expenditures and bond issues. The latter is frequently relied upon in shareholder actions against corporations, such as to compel declaration of a dividend.

Second, a class action is appropriate where the party opposing the class has "acted or refused to act on grounds generally applicable to the class." Many of the cases brought on this basis are civil rights actions in which a party is asking for injunctive or other equitable relief under Title VII of the 1964 Act, and some employment discrimination cases.

Third, a class action is appropriate where "questions of law or fact common to the members of the class predominate over any questions affecting only individual members" and a class action is the best method for handling the entire controversy. This has become the most common basis for class actions, and one that is frequently relied upon in antitrust and securities fraud cases. However, a class action under this Rule — Rule 24(b)(3) — is rarely permitted in mass tort cases, such as airline crashes, because the plaintiffs' claims are usually seen as too diverse to justify class action treatment.

3. Jurisdiction

In a class action based on diversity of citizenship, the usual requirement of complete diversity between any plaintiff and any defendant is relaxed. Only the citizenship of the named representatives of the class are considered.[84] Hence, through the simple device of selecting as named class representatives persons who are diverse in citizenship to the nonclass party, diversity for class action purposes can ordinarily be established.

The jurisdictional amount requirement is more problematical and often arises in a Rule 24(b)(3) class action. For a long time the courts have barred aggregating claims to meet the required jurisdictional amount.[85] In a diversity action each plaintiff must have a claim that exceeds $10,000; in a class action, therefore, the claims of the plaintiff class members cannot be aggregated, nor can the claims of the named representatives be aggregated.[86] This means that each named representative of the class must have a claim that exceeds the jurisdictional amount. In many potential class actions, of course, there are numerous members of the class with individual small claims. In these situations the jurisdictional amount requirement in diversity cases cannot be met, and the claim cannot be presented in federal court. However, this problems does not exist when the claim is based on federal question jurisdiction since there is no jurisdictional amount requirement. Therefore, the common approach is to raise a federal question as the basis for jurisdiction whenever possible.

---

84. See Moore's Manual §14.07(6). The leading case is Stewart v. Dunham, 115 U.S. 61 (1885).

85. See Moore's Manual §14.07(6).

86. See Wright §72; Zahn v. International Paper Co., 414 U.S. 291 (1973).

4. Procedure

Rule 23(c) governs the initial procedures in a class action. The first two steps are critical. First, the court must determine "as soon as practicable" if the action can be brought as a class action. This necessarily requires an evaluation of the Rule 24(a) and (b) requirements, a determination of what issues can be tried as a class action, and a determination of what the class or classes will be.

Second, in an action under Rule 23(b)(3), the predominantly used section, the court must direct the "best notice practicable under the circumstances," which includes "individual notice to all members who can be identified through reasonable effort." Aside from related concerns, such as the actual technical requirements for notice, the "opt-out" provision, and res judicata issues, the immediate concern is a practical one. Notice can be an expensive undertaking, sometimes prohibitively so. For class members whose identity can be ascertained with reasonable effort, notice by first class mail is usually required; for unknown class members, some form of notice by publication is required. Since each side must bear its costs of litigation, the expense of actually notifying the individual class members can effectively prevent a claim from being pursued as a class action.[87]

§5.13. Amendments of pleadings and supplemental pleadings[88]

The principal concepts behind the federal rules' pleading requirements are that pleadings should accurately notify the parties of the claims involved and that enough flexibility should be permitted so that substantial justice is achieved in every case. Rule 15, the amendments rule, reflects these concerns. Amended pleadings should be freely allowed when fairness requires it; that is, whenever an amendment would create a more accurate or complete pleading and the opposing parties will not be substantially prejudiced. The Rule applies to all pleadings — complaints, answers, and replies.

1. Amendments as of right

Any party has a right to amend a pleading once, at any·time before a responsive pleading is made. If no responsive pleading is permitted, an amendment by right can be made within 20 days after service, unless the case is already on the trial calendar. A motion that attacks a pleading is

---

87. The Supreme Court has held that in class action suits brought under Rule 23(c)(2) the party seeking the class action must bear the costs of actual notice to the reasonably identifiable class members. Eisen v. Carlisle & Jacquelin, et al., 417 U.S. 156 (1974).

88. Wright §§66, 68-69; James & Hazard §§4.11-4.17; Friedenthal §§5.26-5.28; Moore's Manual §§9.09-9.11; Shepard's Manual §§3.58-3.65; Moore's Federal Practice §§15.02-15.16; Wright & Miller §§1471-1510.

not considered a responsive pleading. If an amendment is by right, it is simply served on the other parties and no court action is needed.

When the amended pleading seeks to add new parties, Rule 15(a), permitting timely amendments of right, seems to conflict with Rule 21, which permits additions of parties only by leave of court. Courts have gone both ways on this issue, some holding that leave is always required, others not.[89]

There is also some conflict between Rule 15(c) and state statutes of limitations, which apply in diversity cases. In circumstances where the federal rule would permit an amended complaint but the complaint would be barred by the applicable state statute, courts have held that Rule 15 controls and permits the amendment.[90]

2.   Amendments by leave of court

Rule 15(a) permits amendments by leave of court. The Rule expressly provides that "leave shall be freely given when justice so requires." The amended pleading can change the jurisdictional allegations, factual claims, legal theories of recovery, events and transactions involved, and even parties to the action.[91] Yet the courts have been indulgent in permitting amendments, and grounds such as oversight, error, or delay by themselves are generally held insufficient to deny leave to amend.[92]

Courts may exercise their discretion and deny leave to amend when, in addition to delay or neglect, there is some actual prejudice to the opposing party. In other situations, the court may grant leave to amend while restricting it to particular matters so that prejudice to an opposing party is minimized. Obviously the amending party should seek leave to amend as early in the litigation process as possible to minimize prejudice. A motion during the pleading stage will in all likelihood be granted. One made after discovery is underway, however, may well encounter difficulties.

When a motion for leave to amend is made after a motion to dismiss for failure to state a claim on which relief can be granted, some courts will not grant leave if it appears certain that plaintiff cannot, under the existing facts, state a proper claim.[93] Courts often look to see if the proposed amended complaint properly states a claim before granting leave to amend. If it does not, leave can properly be denied.

3.   Statutes of limitations and "relation back"

An important concern in amending pleadings is whether the statute of limitations applies to amended pleadings. This question exists only if the

89. See Moore's Manual §909(2).

90. See Wright §59.

91. 28 U.S.C. §1653 provides that "defective allegations of jurisdiction may be amended, upon terms, in the trial or appellate courts."

92. See Moore's Manual §9.09(3).

93. See Shepard's Manual §3.60.

amended pleading is filed after the applicable statute of limitations has run on a particular claim. Whether the statute will bar the amended pleading depends on whether the concept of "relation back," set out in Rule 15(c), will apply. The two principal types of amendments — changing facts and legal theories, and changing parties — must be considered separately.

a. Changing facts and theories

Rule 15(c) states that if the amended pleading's claims or defenses "arose out of" the same "conduct, transaction or occurrence set forth or attempted to be set forth" in the original pleading, the amendment will relate back to the date the original pleading was filed so that the statute of limitations will not operate as a bar. When the amended pleading alleges an entirely new claim, the concept of relation back will not apply. Whether the claims or defenses in the amended pleading "arose out of the same conduct, transaction or occurrence set forth or attempted to be set forth" in the original pleading is an imprecise standard, but courts have been reasonably lenient in permitting amendments, particularly when only a change in legal theory is involved.[94]

b. Changing parties

The more difficult situation concerns changing parties with an amended pleading. Rule 15(c) permits relation back to avoid a limitations bar where the new party added by amendment either actually knew of the suit and would not be prejudiced, or knew or should have known that, but for a mistake in identifying the proper party, he would have been sued.

The first situation involves actual knowledge of the action by the new party. The second involves a misnomer of a proper party, where the proper party knew or should be held to know that it was the target party all along. This is a common problem when commercial parties or the United States government is involved, where determining the technically proper defendants is difficult and sometimes impossible prior to discovery. Cases that have dealt with the question of when a party "should have known" he was the intended party are hardly uniform and should be thoroughly researched.[95]

4. Supplemental pleadings

Under Rule 15(d), a party may move to file a supplemental pleading alleging transactions, occurrences, and events that have occurred since the time the original pleading was served. Permitting the motion is discre-

---

94. See Wright §66.
95. See Shepard's Manual §3.61.

tionary with the court, which can impose any reasonable terms to protect the other parties.

Since a supplemental pleading by definition raises new matters that have arisen since the original pleading, statute of limitations and relation back issues will rarely be involved.

5. Practice approach

A motion for leave to amend, like any other motion, must meet the Rule 7(b) requirements. The motion must state with particularity the grounds for the motion and the relief sought. Timely notice must be sent to other parties. The better practice is to attach the amended pleading as an exhibit to the motion. In addition, it is both more convenient and a safer practice to have a complete amended pleading, rather than incorporate by reference parts of the original pleading. It is simply easier to deal with a complete pleading, and responses will likely be more accurate.

Example:

[Caption]

MOTION FOR LEAVE TO FILE AMENDED COMPLAINT

Plaintiff moves for an order permitting plaintiff to file an amended complaint. A copy of the amended complaint is attached to this motion as Exhibit A. In support of this motion plaintiff states:

1. Plaintiff's original complaint was against one defendant, William Smith, and alleged one theory of liability based on negligence.

2. New information, based on both informal fact investigation and discovery, has revealed that another party, Acme Motors, may be liable to plaintiff and that a valid claim against Acme may exist, based on products liability and implied warranty.

WHEREFORE, plaintiff requests that an order be entered permitting plaintiff to file the amended complaint attached as Exhibit A, which adds Acme Motors as a defendant and alleges two additional counts, based on products liability and implied warranty, against Acme Motors.

Attorney for Plaintiff

If the motion is allowed, or the amended pleading is of right, a party that is required to respond to the amended pleading must do so either within the time remaining to respond to the original pleading or within 10 days of service of the amended pleading, whichever is greater.

Many motions to permit an amended pleading are made after an opposing party has been granted a motion to dismiss under Rule 12. Here the dismissed party should move for leave to file an amended pleading within 10 days of dismissal.[96] The better and more common practice, however, is to move for leave to file an amended pleading and have the motion granted at the hearing on the motion to dismiss, if that motion is granted. In this way the order granting the motion to dismiss will also contain an order permitting the amended pleading.

96. See Moore's Manual §9.09(5).

VI

DISCOVERY

§6.1.   Introduction

Discovery is the principal fact-gathering method in the formal litigation process. In today's litigation environment, the discovery stage is where most of the battles are fought and where the war is largely won or lost. Consequently, understanding discovery so that you can effectively use the permissible discovery methods as tactical and strategic tools is critical for every litigator.

Federal discovery has three principal characteristics. First, it is largely a self-executing process. For the most part, lawyers conduct discovery without judicial approval, participation, or regulation. Second, the discovery rules are flexible and permit any order, and repeated use, of the various discovery methods subject only to court protection against abuse. Third, orders regulating discovery are usually not final appealable orders. Since discovery issues will often be moot by the time a final judgment is entered in the case, appeals are relatively infrequent. This means that issues concerning discovery are principally resolved at the trial court level.

§6.2.   Scope of discovery[1]

Rule 26(b), the basic discovery rule and the rule that controls the scope of discovery, provides that a party may discover "any matter, not privileged, which is relevant to the subject matter involved in the pending action." This section of Chapter 6 discusses what "relevance" means in the discovery context and reviews the specialized areas now expressly regulated by Rule 26: insurance, statements, experts, privileges, and work product.

1. Wright §81; James & Hazard §5.8; Friedenthal §7.2; Moore's Manual §15.02; Shepard's Manual §§5.1 et seq.; Moore's Federal Practice §26.55; Wright & Miller §2007.

1. Relevance

Relevance for discovery purposes is exceptionally broad. Information sought need not be admissible at trial, nor need the information itself be relevant. If the information sought to be discovered "appears reasonably calculated to lead to the discovery of admissible evidence" on the subject matter of the lawsuit, it is discoverable. In short, a "fishing expedition" is proper if it might unveil probative evidence.[2]

Rule 26(b)(1) expressly permits discovery of the "identity and location of persons having knowledge of any discoverable matter," including the names and addresses of those persons. Courts have generally not required production of the names of trial witnesses through discovery, although this is usually required as part of a pretrial memorandum.[3]

Rule 26(b)(1) also expressly permits discovery of "books, documents or other tangible things." However, a recurring unsettled issue is whether the Rule applies only to material usable in a party's case in chief or whether it includes impeachment material as well. The issue is whether the material is usable as substantive evidence or whether its sole potential use is to impeach an adversary's witnesses at trial. If the former, it is clearly discoverable; concerning the latter, the courts are divided.[4]

2. Insurance agreements[5]

To end a long standing dispute over the discoverability of insurance, Rule 26(b)(2) expressly makes discoverable liability insurance held by any party that may satisfy a judgment. Both the existence and contents of the insurance agreement are discoverable. This information is critical for assessing the "value" of a case and the defendant's ability to pay a judgment.

3. Statements[6]

For discovery purposes, there are three types of statements: witness statements, party statements made to the party's attorney, and party statements made to anyone else. Different rules apply to each.

A written statement made by a nonparty witness that is in the possession of an adversary is discoverable since it is a relevant, tangible thing. A problem arises when a witness has been interviewed by an opposing lawyer but no statement was made. Under these circumstances the opposing

2. Wright §81; Moore's Manual §15.02; Shepard's Manual §5.24; Moore's Federal Practice §26.56(1); Wright & Miller §2008.
3. Wright §81; Moore's Manual §15.02; Shepard's Manual §5.27; Moore's Federal Practice §26.57; Wright & Miller §2013.
4. Wright §81; Moore's Manual §15.02(1); Wright & Miller §2015.
5. Wright §81; James & Hazard §5.7; Friedenthal §7.2; Moore's Manual §15.02(1)(c); Shepard's Manual §5.37; Moore's Federal Practice §26.62; Wright & Miller §2010.
6. Wright §82; James & Hazard §5.8; Friedenthal §7.5; Moore's Manual §15.02(4); Moore's Federal Practice §26.65; Wright & Miller §§2027, 2028.

lawyer has no tangible thing that is discoverable, and any notes of the interview that contain the lawyer's impressions of the witness are probably privileged. Of course, the identity and location of such a witness are discoverable.

Statements made by a party to his own lawyer are not discoverable, principally because the attorney-client privilege will usually apply to such communications. However, Rule 26(b)(3) expressly allows a party to obtain his own statement in the possession of anyone else upon demand, without a court order or any showing of need. A party is considered to have a right to his own written or recorded oral statement.

4. Experts[7]

There are three basic kinds of experts: testifying experts, consulting experts, and informally consulted experts. Different rules govern the discoverability of their identity, opinions, and reports.

Rule 26(b)(4)(A) makes discoverable the identity of each party's experts who are expected to be called as witnesses at trial. Through interrogatory answers, a party must also disclose what subject matter the expert will testify about, the substance of the expert's facts and opinions, and a summary of the grounds for each opinion. However, further discovery, such as a deposition of an expert or subpoena of the expert's files, may only be obtained by motion and court order. This Rule protects experts from being drawn into the discovery process directly without prior approval of the court.

Rule 26(b)(4)(B) governs consulting experts, those who have been retained or employed to help the lawyer during the litigation process, but are not expected to be witnesses at trial. Such experts ordinarily cannot be subjected to the discovery process, unless a requesting party can show "exceptional circumstances under which it is impracticable . . . to obtain facts or opinions on the same subject by other means." The Rule in effect establishes a qualified privilege for the work of a consulting expert, one akin to that for a lawyer's trial preparation materials. The only exception is Rule 35(b), which makes the reports of a physician's mental or physical examination of a party discoverable in certain circumstances.[8]

Informally consulted experts, those experts who have not been retained by the lawyer but have provided information, are not governed by discovery rules. Therefore, neither the existence, identity, nor opinions of such an expert is discoverable. This prevents experts with minimal contacts with a lawyer from being drawn into the discovery process.

7. Wright §81; James & Hazard §5.11; Friedenthal §7.6; Moore's Manual §15.02(5); Shepard's Manual §5.36; Moore's Federal Practice §26.66; Wright & Miller §§2029-2034.
8. See §6.7.

5. Privileges[9]

Federal privileges are controlled by Rule 501 of the Federal Rules of Evidence, which continues the development of privileges by case law, statutes, and constitutional provisions.

The first question to ask regarding this aspect of discovery is, What privilege law applies? Rule 501 provides that federal privileges, as developed by the courts, will apply. The exception is that in civil cases for which state law has "supplie[d] the rule of decision" as to an element of a claim or defense, state privileges will apply. This essentially means that in federal criminal cases and in federal civil cases based on federal question jurisdiction, federal privilege law will apply. However, in federal civil cases based on diversity jurisdiction, state privileges rules will apply. Which state's privilege rules will apply is determined by the forum state's choice-of-law rules. Where a privilege is based on the U.S. Constitution, principally the Fifth Amendment's self-incrimination clause, it applies regardless of the type of federal case involved.

The second question that must be asked is, What is the applicable federal or state privilege law? When the Federal Rules of Evidence were enacted, Congress chose not to codify federal common law privileges, preferring to let federal privileges continue to develop in the courts. Therefore, care must always be taken to research the law of the appropriate jurisdiction, because privilege law can vary.

State privileges, by contrast, are developed by both the courts and the legislatures, although in recent years the trend has been to codify privileges. Keep in mind that state jurisdictions vary widely in their privilege law. While all states recognize frequently used privileges such as marital, attorney-client, and doctor-patient, they vary substantially in their recognition of others such as the privilege for accountants, reporter's informants, and governmental secrets. The scope of any privilege, and whether it applies in civil or criminal cases, also varies significantly. This is an area of evidence law that, when joined with choice of law issues, always requires substantial research.

6. Trial preparation materials[10]

Ever since the Supreme Court decided Hickman v. Taylor, 329 U.S. 495 (1947), federal courts have recognized a two-tier privilege rule applicable to an attorney's work product; that rule, with some changes and added details, is now incorporated in Rule 26(b)(3).

The attorney's work product, now called "trial preparation materials," is protected by a qualified privilege. Trial preparation materials in-

9. Wright §81; James & Hazard §5.9; Friedenthal §§7.4-7.5; Moore's Manual §15.02(2); Shepard's Manual §§5.30-5.34; Moore's Federal Practice §§26.60-26.61; Wright & Miller §§2016-2020.

10. Wright §82; James & Hazard §5.10; Friedenthal §7.5; Moore's Manual §15.02(4); Shepard's Manual §§5.35, 5.175; Moore's Federal Practice §26.57(2); Wright & Miller §§2021-2028.

clude any "documents and tangible things" that were "prepared in anticipation of litigation" by another party or that party's "representative." A representative includes not only the lawyer, but other agents such as an insurance adjuster or claims investigator.

If the privilege attaches, it is only a qualified privilege. The Rule permits a party seeking discovery to obtain protected documents and tangible things upon a showing of "substantial need" because the party cannot obtain the "substantial equivalent" by other means without "undue hardship." Under this provision of the Rule, it is clear that undue hardship cannot be shown simply by demonstrating added expense or inconvenience. With witness statements, the area where this issue most frequently arises, there must be some demonstrable reason why the requesting party cannot get the substantial equivalent of the statement himself before production can be ordered.[11]

The second tier of the privilege, the one covering the lawyer's "mental impressions, conclusions, opinions on legal theories," is absolutely protected by the privilege. Hence, disclosure can never be compelled.

§6.3. Discovery strategy

The discovery rules in the Federal Rules of Civil Procedure are both broad and extensive, and in most cases they permit more discovery than either party will wish to make. Consequently, your overriding concern at the discovery stage is, What will be an effective discovery strategy for this particular case? As outlined previously, discovery planning is essentially a seven-step process.[12]

1. **What facts do I need in order to establish a winning case on my claims (or to defeat the opponent's claims)?**

2. **What facts have I already obtained through informal fact investigation?**

These questions should already be answered in your developing litigation chart.

3. **What "missing" facts do I still need to obtain through formal discovery?**

Discovery is the vehicle you use to force other parties, and nonparties, to disclose information they have pertinent to the litigation. Your first ques-

11. Wright §82; Shepard's Manual §§5.35, 5.175; Moore's Manual §15.02(4); Moore's Federal Practice §26.64(3); Wright & Miller §2025.
12. §4.5.5.

tion, therefore, should be, What information do I need to know, that I do not already know from my informal investigation and have not admitted in the pleadings, so that I can thoroughly prepare the case for a possible trial? While the answer will vary with each case, it will usually include some of the following:

(a) Identity of proper parties
(b) Defendant's ability to pay a judgment
(c) Identity of agents and employees
(d) Opponent's factual basis for legal claims
(e) Opponent's position on factual issues
(f) Identity and location of witnesses
(g) Prospective testimony of adverse parties, agents, and employees
(h) Prospective testimony of important witnesses
(i) Identity, opinions, and reasoning of experts
(j) Prospective testimony of experts
(k) Tangible evidence
(l) Documents
(m) Records
(n) Statements of parties and witnesses
(o) Testimony of favorable witnesses that may become unavailable for trial

Not all of this information is necessarily discoverable. However, you should always compile a similar roster for each case — using your litigation chart — since it will control the information you will try to discover.

4. What discovery methods are most effective for obtaining the "missing" facts?

There are five methods of discovery permitted under the federal rules: interrogatories, requests to produce, depositions, physical and mental examinations, and requests to admit. Although there is some overlap, each method is particularly well suited for certain kinds of information.

Interrogatories are most effective for obtaining basic factual data from other parties, such as the identity of proper parties, agents, employees, witnesses, and experts, and the identity and location of documents, records, and tangible evidence. They are also useful in obtaining other parties' positions on disputed facts, and experts' opinions and bases for opinions. On the other hand, interrogatories are not usually effective instruments for getting detailed facts, impressions, or versions of events.

A request to produce documents and tangible things is the discovery method by which one obtains from another party copies of records, documents, and other tangible things for inspection, copying, and testing. Such a request also permits an entry on another party's land or property to inspect, photograph, and analyze things on it. This is the only discovery device that forces another party actually to produce records and things, and to permit entry onto property to copy, photograph, or study evidence in your opponent's possession.

Depositions are most effective in tying down parties and witnesses to details, and in discovering everything they know pertinent to the case. It is the only discovery vehicle that permits you to assess how good a witness a person is likely to be at trial. It is an excellent vehicle to secure admissions or other evidence favorable to your side and it is the only one that can be used on nonparty witnesses. Further, a deposition is the only method to preserve testimony if a witness will become unavailable for trial.

A physical and mental examination of a party can be obtained by court order when the physical or mental condition of that party is in issue, a situation most common in personal injury cases. While other discovery methods can be used to get records of past examinations, this is the only means of forcing a party to be examined and tested prospectively. For that reason it is the best method for evaluating a party on such damages elements as permanence, extent of injury, and medical prognosis.

Finally, requests to admit is the discovery method that forces a party to admit or deny facts or a document's genuineness — a powerful discovery device if used carefully. An admitted fact is deemed conclusively admitted for the purpose of the pending trial. This discovery method is effective if limited to simple factual data, such as someone's employment on a specific date, or the genuineness of signatures on a contract. It is not a good method for dealing with opinions or evaluative information.

There are two more areas where, upon motion and court order, you may obtain additional discovery: expert depositions and trial preparation materials.

Under Rule 26(b)(4) you can obtain through interrogatories only the subject matter, facts and opinions, and a summary of the grounds for each opinion of your opponent's expert's anticipated trial testimony. Upon motion, the court may order further discovery, which will principally involve depositions and production of supporting records. Where the basic issues at trial will center on disputed expert opinions, as in products liability cases, and it is important to get the details underlying expert testing and opinions, this motion should be considered since it is frequently granted. Keep in mind, however, that the court must impose costs for reasonable fees and expenses of such experts.

You can obtain discovery of your opponent's consulting expert only on a showing of "exceptional circumstances under which it is impractical ... to obtain facts or opinions on the same subject by other means." While this is obviously a difficult standard, the Rule contemplates those rare cases, such as where a consulting expert has engaged in destructive testing of a product, where relevant expert information is solely in the possession of one party's expert.

Trial preparation materials, which are protected from disclosure by a qualified privilege, can be obtained from an opponent "only upon a showing of substantial need." The party seeking production must also be "unable without undue hardship to obtain the substantial equivalent of the materials by other means." This exception to the attorney's work product rule arises most often in regard to witness statements, which are not automatically discoverable. Where one side has taken a statement from a witness who now refuses to talk to other lawyers, who cannot be subpoenaed, or who has a lapse of memory, and the substantial equivalent of the statement cannot be obtained, the court may order the production of the statement.

5. What facts and witnesses, that I already know of through informal investigation, do I need to "pin down" by using formal discovery?

There is little point in using formal discovery methods with your favorable witnesses, unless those witnesses are old, sick, or are likely to move away. If this is the case, you will want to take the witness' deposition to preserve the testimony for trial, since the transcript will usually qualify as former testimony.[13]

With unfavorable, hostile, or adverse witnesses and parties, however, there are good reasons for deposing them, even if you already know from your informal fact investigation what they will say at trial. First, there are always benefits in learning in detail what those witnesses will say. Second, witnesses may testify inconsistently in respect to their previous statements, or inconsistently in respect to each other. Third, you may be able to limit the witnesses' trial testimony by getting the witnesses to admit to topics they have no first hand knowledge of, are not sure of, or are only approximating or guessing at. All of these are good reasons for deposing important, unfavorable, or adverse witnesses you expect will testify for the opposing party at trial.

6. What restrictions does my litigation budget place on my discovery plan?

Information gathering, especially formal discovery, is expensive, and any discovery strategy must necessarily consider the expenses involved. While your litigation budget, which you have already prepared, will have analyzed the amount of time you will allocate to discovery, at this point you should give the discovery portion a second look. This should be done for three reasons. First, the pleadings, now completed, may force changes in your discovery strategy. Second, since discovery will usually consume the majority of your pretrial time allotment, it is particularly important to review it. Third, discovery can easily escalate out of control, so staying with your game plan is essential.

Most formal discovery methods are expensive, and responding to discovery, particularly interrogatories and documents requests, can become expensive because of the time involved in researching and preparing responses and reviewing the necessary documents. Depositions are an

---

13. FRE 804(b)(1).

expensive discovery method, and it is here that cost effectiveness is particularly important. Deposition costs include the lawyer's time, witness fees, the court reporter's fees, and transcript costs. Assuming a one-hour deposition, the witness, reporter, and transcript costs will probably be in the $150 range. A lawyer may need two hours to prepare for the deposition and one hour after the deposition to make a summary of her impressions, creating a cost in the $400 range. Even a short deposition, then, can cost several hundred dollars.

Deposition costs, therefore, require that you use this discovery method cautiously. You will probably need to depose your adverse party and critical occurrence witnesses in every case. However, you can often postpone depositions of experts and rely on interrogatory answers and various records for settlement purposes, deposing your adversary's experts only when a trial becomes a realistic possibility. Similarly, consider moving for a physical examination of the opposing party only when a trial becomes likely. Also, use investigators to interview nonparty witnesses who are not central to the case. There are often other ways of getting the essence of a witness' testimony short of a deposition, and you must always balance the additional benefit of depositions with their cost in all cases where litigation costs are a concern.

Example:

Consider a typical automobile accident case, in which you represent the plaintiff. You previously estimated the "value" of plaintiff's case at $25,000, of which you will earn about $8,000 with a successful conclusion. You have made various estimates of time requirements, and have allocated 50 hours to preparing and responding to discovery. How do you estimate how much time you should plan spending on the various discovery methods?

Start by breaking down formal discovery into its component parts to consider what discovery is essential. First, you will need to submit interrogatories to the defendant and answer the defendant's interrogatories. In automobile cases involving simple negligence claims, many jurisdictions use standard sets of interrogatories. Sending interrogatories to the defendant, answering the defendant's, and reviewing the defendant's answers for sufficiency will probably take only a few hours, particularly if you have done your informal fact investigation before filing suit. You estimate interrogatories will take five hours.

Second, you will need to depose the critical witnesses: These will include the parties and occurrence witnesses. You will need to depose the defendant and one bystander, and to prepare your plaintiff for deposition, since the defendant will certainly depose him. In a simple automobile case, the plaintiff's deposition will probably take two hours, the defendant's and bystander's will perhaps take one hour each. Preparation for each deposition will probably take as long as the deposition itself. In addition, you will need to prepare a summary of each deposition immediately afterward and review the transcript of the plaintiff's testimony for accuracy before he signs it. Accordingly, you estimate that these depositions will take approximately 15 hours.

Third, you will need to send notices to produce documents to the defendant, subpoenas to nonparties, and answer the defendant's production requests. You will also need to organize and review all the documents and records you receive. These will include medical records, physician records, employment records, vehicle repair records, police reports, and insurance reports. You estimate that this work will take 15 hours.

Fourth, the defendant may want to have the plaintiff medically examined, particularly if plaintiff is claiming any permanent physical injuries. You will need to review the information that is developed through that examination, which is usually disclosed through interrogatory answers. You estimate this will require two hours.

Fifth, plaintiff and defendant may reciprocally agree to depose each other's medical experts. Defendant will want to depose plaintiff's treating physician and plaintiff will want to depose the defendant's examining physician. Preparing, taking, and summarizing these medical-expert depositions will take substantial time. You estimate this will take 15 hours.

Finally, you may want to send a notice to admit facts to the defendant, and you may have to respond to the defendant's. You estimate this will take eight hours.

Notice that this time estimate already adds up to 60 hours, and not all the variables that exist have been taken into consideration. On the positive side, both parties may not agree to depose each other's experts or the case may settle early. On the negative side, you may need to depose additional witnesses or depose someone a second time, and you may need to file motions to enforce or protect your discovery rights. The point, however, is to analyze the cost considerations as you develop your discovery strategy, because the two must be consistent with each other.

7.   In what order should I execute my discovery plan?

Formal discovery should be used as a progressive device in which each discovery method is utilized as a sequential building block. Under the Rules there is no required sequence. Essentially, each party can engage in discovery when, how, and as often as it wants. The only limitations on discovery are usually not confining. First, a plaintiff must wait a short period of time after service of summons before initiating discovery without a court order, and a defendant is sometimes allowed a longer period to respond to that discovery. These initial time requirements are necessary as a practical matter to allow a recently served defendant to retain counsel and respond to the complaint before being forced to deal with discovery demands. Once a defendant has responded to the complaint, these initial limitations no longer apply. Second, under Rule 26(f) the court has power to devise a discovery plan. The court usually holds a conference with the lawyers to develop a realistic plan. While courts are increasingly using this power, for the most part parties conduct their discovery unhampered and ordinarily the court only sets "cut-off" dates for discovery. For example, the court may order that interrogatories be served within 60 days of the discovery plan conference, and that all depositions of nonexperts be completed within nine months. This process is very effective in avoiding a trial postponement on the usual basis that "we haven't completed discovery yet." Third, the court has power under Rule 37 to issue protective orders and order sanctions for abuse of discovery.

Because the discovery process is so flexible, the relevant questions are, When should I start discovery? In what order should it be carried out?

The initial question can be answered simply. You should start discovery as soon as the Rules permit and as soon as practical. If you have done your prefiling investigation and preparation work, you should be able to begin discovery during the pleading stage. For instance, defendants frequently serve interrogatories with their answers, and sometimes serve notice to take the plaintiff's deposition at the same time. Doing this shows your opponent that you intend to litigate vigorously and gives you a head start on any discovery cut-off dates.

The following is a common discovery sequence:

(a) interrogatories
(b) requests to produce and subpoenas
(c) depositions of parties, witnesses, and experts
(d) physical and mental examinations
(e) requests to admit

This sequence utilizes the building block approach to discovery. Interrogatory answers should identify the opponent's witnesses, documents, and positions on the facts. Once the answers are received, you can serve requests to produce on parties and subpoenas on nonparty witnesses in order to obtain the documents, records, and other evidence identified in the interrogatory answers. After you have received this information you are ready to take depositions of parties, witnesses, and, if permitted, experts. In personal injury cases the physical and mental examinations of parties are ordinarily conducted later in the litigation process, since these examinations usually focus on such issues as permanence of injury, prognosis, and loss of earning capacity. Once these steps have been completed, notices to admit can further pinpoint areas of dispute and eliminate the need to prove uncontested facts at trial.

This sequence, of course, can be and often is modified. Amended, supplemental, or additional pleadings may be filed that will necessarily alter the course of discovery. In addition, there may be tactical benefits in changing the usual sequence or in serving more than one discovery device at the same time. Keep in mind that the discovery process educates your opponents as well as yourself. Lawyers sometimes take the deposition of an adverse party before interrogatories or notices to produce have been sent out on the theory that the adverse party will have neither the time nor the inclination to prepare thoroughly by collecting and reviewing all the pertinent records beforehand. Also, lawyers frequently schedule depositions of the adverse party and that party's employees and agents back to back so that successive deponents cannot review the testimony of earlier deponents before being deposed themselves. Further, lawyers frequently couple interrogatories requesting the existence of documents with a request to produce the documents identified, and use early requests to admit facts in order to narrow the scope of discovery.

There is no magic formula for deciding on the best sequence for discovery. This should be tailored to the specific needs and circumstances of each case. An important point to remember, however, is that discovery should not be used simply because it is available. Each step must have a specific purpose and be part of an overall discovery strategy.

In addition to this basic seven step process, there are two additional considerations you should always keep in mind.

8. How can I conduct discovery informally?

The federal rules prescribe how discovery should be conducted, and a procedurally safe approach to discovery is to always do it "by the book." However, life doesn't always go by the book, nor does discovery in the litigation world. Litigation lawyers usually try to arrange things between themselves informally. This applies to all phases of the litigation process and is permitted and encouraged under Rule 29.

What aspects of discovery can be handled informally? The simple task of scheduling depositions can be. Instead of simply serving notice to your party opponent for his disposition, why not contact the other party's lawyer and try to arrange a mutually agreeable date and time? This will probably avoid any motions to reschedule the deposition, and will usually result in the same courtesy being extended to you in the future. Serve a notice of deposition after you have worked out the arrangement.

With nonparty deponents, whom you must subpoena and usually depose in the location convenient to that party, informal accommodations can be made. Serve the subpoena first, then see if the deponent is willing to come to your office. Offering to pay the witness' reasonable, legitimately incurred expenses in coming to your office, rather than following the formal Rule 45 procedures, frequently benefits everyone.[14]

It is also common to work out the mechanics of documents production informally. Why not call the other party's lawyer and work out how, when, where, and in what order each party will produce the requested documents, along with how they will be photocopied and who will pay for the charges. Another area where "working it out" informally is a common practice is in agreeing to depose each other's experts along with arranging the necessary details.

While there are many other areas where the informal resolutions of problems are common, the point is the same: Whenever possible, it makes sense to try to work out the mechanics and details of discovery

14. See §6.6.1(c).

with the other side and with third parties. Courtesy and reasonableness somehow make the world work better, and discovery in the litigation process is no different.

9. How can I limit discovery against my party?

As the lawyer for a party, you naturally have an interest in limiting the discovery of your case, unless your case is so strong that you don't want to limit it, or where early complete disclosure will force a favorable settlement. There are three basic areas where you can affect whether information can be discovered.

First, if your client is a business entity, take immediate steps to control the paperwork generated in the business that has any bearing on the litigation: If it is not written down, it cannot be turned over under a request to produce. Have the business' employees communicate directly to you about the pending litigation, rather than to supervisors, since this may afford the advantage of bringing the communications under the attorney-client privilege protection.[15]

Second, again, if your client is a business entity, make sure that employees notify you if anyone tries to interview any of them about the case. Since any statements made by the employees may be admissions that are admissible against the business employer under FRE 801, you are probably entitled to treat such an employee as a party. This means that no one can interview the employee without your permission, and you can represent the employee at his deposition. It also means that communications between the employee and you should be protected by the attorney-client privilege.[16]

Third, obtain statements from witnesses that bring the statements under the qualified trial-preparation-materials privilege or, better yet, under the absolute attorney's mental impressions privilege. Verbatim statements from adverse witnesses are useful, since they can be used to impeach. They may be dangerous, however, when taken from favorable witnesses, and so it is safer to have your investigator — or for you yourself to — interview the witness, then prepare a summary of the witness' information with observations on how strong or weak the witness is, what kind of witness she will make at trial, and how her testimony fits into the theory of the case, along with other pertinent mental impressions. You will then have a useful record of the witness, which will probably be protected from disclosure. Even if the other side does obtain it through a showing of substantial need, it will not include any verbatim statements usable to impeach. The observations about the witness, however, should be absolutely protected as the lawyer's work product.

15. See Upjohn Co. v. United States, 449 U.S. 383 (1981). *Upjohn* rejected the "control group" test for determining which corporate employees' communications with corporate counsel will be protected by the attorney-client privilege. Any employee who has information necessary for the corporate counsel to evaluate will have those communications to corporate counsel protected by the privilege.

16. See id.

Finally, consider the ways in which you can protect your expert witnesses from discovery procedures that go beyond those required by Rule 26.[17] Since experts are a fact of life in most litigation, controlling your experts' exposure to discretionary discovery must be part of your overall discovery strategy.

Rule 26 entitles other parties to obtain, through interrogatory answers, certain information about your testifying expert's background, testimony, and reasons for his opinions. If the other parties feel that the information received about your expert is inadequate to learn about his testimony and prepare properly for his cross-examination, they will move for discretionary additional discovery, which can only be obtained by court order. It is this balancing of purposes — limiting the information about your experts, yet not exposing him to additional discovery — that is at the center of expert discovery strategy.

Information about your experts may be requested in an initial interrogatory, before you have decided who your testifying experts will be. The standard interrogatory answer in this situation is "unknown at present," which acknowledges the continuing duty to supplement answers within a reasonable time after deciding who the trial experts will be. Keep in mind that delaying the identity of your experts is a dangerous game, since the court can always impose sanctions for abuse. You may be prevented from calling experts at trial, and other parties might also choose to delay identifying experts. This is a poor place to play games, and a poor place — as always — to have your ethics questioned.

The rules for answering an interrogatory are relatively imprecise, requiring disclosure of the "identity" of experts, the "substance" of their testimony, and a "summary" of the grounds for opinions. How detailed should your responses be? While you may frequently want to minimize discovery, remember that the party serving the interrogatories can always move to compel more detailed answers. It is often a sound strategy to provide broad answers to other parties. This can provide substantial benefits in the future. First, it can forestall motions to compel full and complete answers. Second, it gives you a stronger position from which to resist motions for discretionary discovery. You can object on the basis that your existing answers are fully adequate to inform other parties and to allow them to adequately prepare for cross-examination of your experts at trial, which is the standard inquiry in deciding whether additional discovery should be ordered. Hence, the usual discretionary discovery requests — supplemental interrogatory answers, production of the experts' reports and working papers, and expert depositions — should not be granted. Third, providing complete answers puts you in a stronger position if you are seeking more expert discovery from other parties. Courts quite naturally are inclined to look at scope-of-discovery issues as a two-way street.

Finally, maintain a professional relationship with your testifying expert to minimize the danger of disclosing matters that might be protected by the attorney-client and work product privileges. Allowing your experts

---

17. See §2.6, discussing expert review of cases before filing suit.

to communicate directly with your client is dangerous. Disclosing information to your expert that is work product runs the danger that it may end up being discovered. But since the expert must have sufficient information on which to evaluate the case and develop opinions, the question becomes how to best convey the necessary information to your expert. The safe approach is to divulge only those materials that are discoverable by other parties anyway, and use caution when transmitting additional information to the expert. This will minimize the danger of having your case hurt or of your being embarrassed at trial.

§6.4. Interrogatories

Submitting interrogatories to the opposing parties is usually the first step in the discovery process because interrogatories are the best method for getting basic facts about the other side's case. Once interrogatory answers have been received, further discovery can develop this basic information in greater detail.

1. Law[18]

Although interrogatories are governed by Rule 33, that Rule is often supplemented by local rules because discovery abuse tends to be more extensive with interrogatories than with other discovery methods. These local rules frequently impose additional constraints, most commonly placing limits on the number of interrogatories that can be served and requiring court approval for additional sets of interrogatories. Some districts have approved pattern interrogatories for common cases such as automobile personal injury suits. Hence, you should always check the rules for the particular jurisdiction.

Interrogatories may be used to identify witnesses and experts; to obtain the subject matter, opinions, and basis for the opinions of experts; and to identify documents and other tangible things. Also, they can be used to inquire about any claim or defense, and about any relevant matter that is not privileged, since the scope of discovery is defined by Rule 26(b). However, Rule 33(b) also permits interrogatories that ask for "an opinion or contention that relates to fact or the application of law to fact." The line between what is "opinion" and what is a question of "pure law" is admittedly imprecise and has generated substantial litigation.[19] Because such issues usually become either clearer or moot as discovery progresses, the court may order that such interrogatories remain unanswered until a later time.

18. Wright §86; James & Hazard §5.4; Friedenthal §7.9; Moore's Manual §15.09; Shepard's Manual §§5.10, 5.126-5.144; Moore's Federal Practice §33; Wright & Miller §§2161-2182.
19. Moore's Manual §15.09; Shepard's Manual §5.137; Moore's Federal Practice §33.17; Wright & Miller §2167.

Interrogatories can be served by any party on any other party. They can be served upon the plaintiff after suit is commenced, and upon any other party with or after service of summons and complaint upon that party. In practice, interrogatories are frequently served with the initial pleading or response, or shortly afterwards.

Rule 33 puts no limit on the number of interrogatories one party can serve on another, nor does it limit the number of sets of interrogatories. Frequently, however, local rules limit the number of interrogatories — often to 20 or 30 — and require that court permission be obtained for additional sets of interrogatories; the local rules vary widely and must always be checked. The reason for the local rules is to prevent overly extensive interrogatories, a common means of abusing discovery.

The issue of whether an interrogatory is a single, complete interrogatory or is a compound interrogatory that attempts to get around the local rules limiting the number of interrogatories, frequently arises. This problem is usually controlled by the local rules, which typically provide that subparagraphs of an interrogatory must be directly related to the interrogatory.[20] Hence, an interrogatory with subparts is proper only if it divides a single topic into its component parts. In fact, using such interrogatories is often an effective drafting approach.

Answers are due within 30 days of service of the interrogatories, except that a defendant has 45 days from the time of service of the summons and complaint upon him. The answer must respond to each interrogatory separately with either an answer or an objection. An answer must be a "full" answer that fairly meets the substance of the interrogatory. The answering party has an obligation to find the information if it is within the party's possession, even if not within the personal knowledge of the actual person answering.[21]

Under Rule 33(c) the answering party may specify business records from which an answer may be derived or ascertained, instead of giving a direct answer, if the "burden of deriving or ascertaining the answer is substantially the same for the party serving the interrogatory as for the party served." Where this is the case, the answer need only specify the records in sufficient detail to allow the requesting party to locate and identify the records, and to give the requesting party a reasonable opportunity to inspect and copy them.

An answer must be signed under oath by the person making it. If any interrogatories are objected to, the lawyer making the objection must sign as well.

Finally, an answering party has a continuing obligation to supplement certain answers. Rule 26(e) requires supplementation of responses, even though complete when made, if the interrogatory asked for the identity of persons having knowledge of discoverable matters, or asked for the identity of experts expected to testify at trial and the subject and substance of that testimony. The obligation to supplement is particularly

---

20. See Wright & Miller §2168.
21. Moore's Manual §15.09; Shepard's Manual, §§5.141, 5.155; Moore's Federal Practice §33.26; Wright & Miller §2177.

important in regard to experts since at the time that the answers to the first set of interrogatories are served the answering party will frequently not yet know who the testifying experts will be. Failing to supplement answers within a reasonable time can subject the answering party to Rule 37 sanctions.

2. Practice approach

A lawyer preparing to send interrogatories to another party must ask three basic questions: When should I send out interrogatories? What kind of information should I seek? How should I organize and draft interrogatories to get the desired information?

a. Timing

Since interrogatories may be served upon any other party once the complaint has been served on the party, great latitude exists. The common practice is to send an initial set of interrogatories to each party when the initial pleading is served. For example, although plaintiffs can serve interrogatories on the defendant shortly after the summons and complaint have been served, in practice a plaintiff will usually wait until it is known who the lawyer representing that defendant will be, and then send the interrogatories to the lawyer. In addition, a plaintiff anticipating that the defendant will counterclaim is likely to wait for the defendant's responsive pleading before sending interrogatories. Defendants frequently send interrogatories to the plaintiff at the same time as their initial response to the complaint.

Sending interrogatories out quickly accomplishes two important things. First, it gets the discovery process started, which is particularly important since using the other discovery methods usually depends on the interrogatory answers. With court imposed discovery cut-off dates increasingly a part of the litigation process, efficiency is important. Second, it lets other parties know that you intend to litigate actively and aggressively, an important message to send to your adversaries early on.

b. Topics

Before drafting the interrogatories, ask yourself, What information do I want now so that I can use subsequent discovery methods to develop the information more fully? If you have thought through your discovery strategy,[22] you should know what information you need that is well suited to obtaining through interrogatories. This initial information usually includes the following.

22. §6.3.

i.   Identity of parties, agents, and employees

Frequently in commercial litigation, you will not know the proper formal names of parties, parent corporations, subsidiaries; where they are incorporated or licensed to do business; or the type of legal entities they are or their relationships to other parties. You need to know this information for a variety of purposes, relating to jurisdictional and joinder issues, for instance. You will also need to learn the identity of all agents and employees, and their relationships to the party. Interrogatories are the best method for getting this information.

ii.   Identity of witnesses

Most every lawsuit will have witnesses to the events and transactions on which the claims are based. Interrogatories are a good method for obtaining the witnesses' identities, locations, and relationships to the parties.

iii.   Identity of documents and tangible things

Similarly, most every lawsuit will have certain documents, records, and other tangible things on which the claims are based, or that are relevant to the claims. Interrogatories are the best method for identifying and locating these and for determining who has custody or control of them.

iv.   Identity of experts, facts, and opinions

Under Rule 26(b)(4), interrogatories are the required method for discovering the identity of experts expected to be witnesses at trial, along with the subject matter of their testimony, their opinions, and a summary of the grounds for their opinions.

At this early stage, of course, the answering party may not yet have selected the experts who ultimately will be witnesses at trial. However, Rule 26(e) requires reasonably prompt supplementation of responses when an interrogatory requests this information. Hence, there is a purpose for requesting it in the initial interrogatories. Some lawyers, however, ask for this information in a second set of interrogatories, after a substantial amount of discovery has been taken, the theory being that a useful response is more likely to be received at that time.

v.   Details and sequences of events and transactions

Interrogatories are a useful method for obtaining concrete facts underlying vague or generalized claims. For this reason they are particularly useful in the commercial litigation area where lawsuits are frequently based on a series of events and transactions spread out over time, but are not detailed in any way in the pleadings.

vi.   Damages information and ability to pay

The plaintiff's complaint will often contain only a general request for damages "in excess of $10,000," or whatever the minimum jurisdictional amount is. Damages interrogatories to the plaintiff are useful for drawing out the specific legal theories of recovery the plaintiff is asserting, the dollar amount claimed for each element of damages, and the basis for each claim.

Since it is vitally important for a plaintiff to determine the defendant's ability to pay a judgment, a standard interrogatory should ask about insurance policies that may cover the event or transactions on which the lawsuit is based, and for the details of the coverage. Rule 26(b)(2) expressly makes this information discoverable. If the pleadings, such as a punitive damages claim, make the defendant's financial condition relevant, this information should also be requested.

vii.   Identity of persons who prepared answers and of sources used

Where interrogatories are served on a corporate party, they should ask for the identity of each person who participated in preparing the answers, and ask for the identity of the documents used to prepare each answer. This information will be important in deciding whom to depose and what documents to request.

viii.   Positions on issues and opinions of fact

Interrogatories that ask for "opinions," "contentions relating to facts," or the "application of law to facts," are usually proper. On the other hand, interrogatories that ask for matters of "pure law" are objectionable. The dividing line is unclear, and a great many discovery motions deal with this problem.[23] Where a pleading is vague, however, a proper interrogatory can prove to be a useful request. For example, it is proper in a negligence action to ask what specific conduct plaintiff claims constituted the negligence, just as in a contract action it is proper to ask what conduct plaintiff claims constituted a breach.

The court has the power under Rule 33(b) to postpone answering such interrogatories. Accordingly, many lawyers avoid such requests in the initial interrogatories, since it may trigger objections and delay receiving answers to the more basic interrogatories.

c.   *Drafting the interrogatories*

The drafting lawyer's principal task is to prepare a set of interrogatories that will successfully elicit the desired information. The questions must be drafted so as to force the answering party to respond to them squarely and to eliminate the possibility of evasive, though superficially responsive, answers. Also, the questions must be organized sequentially to make sure that all desired topics are covered. Basic interrogatories for

---

23. Moore's Manual §15.09; Shepard's Manual §5.137; Moore's Federal Practice §§33.12, 33.17; Wright & Miller §2167.

recurrent types of actions are frequently stored in word processors, making them easy to modify for a specific case.

i. Headings

An interrogatory, like any court document, must contain a caption showing the court, parties, and civil case number. Further, the interrogatories should include a heading that identifies which party is raising the interrogatories to which other party. It is also a good practice to label them "First Set," "Second Set," and so on, and to number them sequentially with a later set picking up where the previous set left off. This avoids confusion when references are later made to interrogatories and answers.

Example:

[Caption]

PLAINTIFF JOHNSON'S INTERROGATORIES TO DEFENDANT ACME CORPORATION

(First Set)

Plaintiff Johnson requests that defendant Acme Corporation, through an officer or authorized agent of the corporation, answer the following interrogatories under oath and serve them upon plaintiff within 30 days, pursuant to Rule 33 of the Federal Rules of Civil Procedure:
    1. . . .
    2. . . .
    3. . . .

Example:

[Caption]

PLAINTIFF JOHNSON'S INTERROGATORIES TO DEFENDANT ACME CORPORATION

(Second Set)

Plaintiff Johnson requests that. . . .
    23. . . .
    24. . . .
    25. . . .

ii.   Definitions and instructions

A common practice in more complex interrogatories is to have the actual interrogatories preceded by a definitions and instructions section. Terms used repeatedly in the interrogatories can be defined, making the interrogatories easier to follow, while effectively deterring evasive answers. Terms commonly defined in interrogatories include "record," "document," "communication," "witness," "participate," "transaction," "occurrence," "collision," "state," "describe," and "identify." Use broad descriptions of these basic terms so that the answering party cannot give a superficially accurate but effectively unresponsive answer.

Example:

DEFINITIONS

The following terms used in these interrogatories have the following meanings:

1. To "identify" means to (a) state a person's full name, home address, business occupation, business address, and present and past relationship to any party; (b) state the title of any document, who prepared it, when it was prepared, where it is located, and who its custodian is.

2. A "document" means all written or printed matter of any kind, including but not limited to legal documents, letters, memoranda, business records, interoffice communications, and data stored electronically, which are in the possession or control of the answering party.

3. A "communication" means all oral conversations, discussions, letters, telegrams, memoranda, and any other transmission of information in any form, both oral and written.

It is sometimes useful to have an instruction section detail how interrogatories should be answered. Again, it makes the particular interrogatories easier to understand.

Example:

INSTRUCTIONS

In answering each interrogatory:

(a) state whether the answer is within the personal knowledge of the person answering the interrogatory and, if not, the identity of each person known to have personal knowledge of the answer;

(b) identify each document that was used in any way to formulate the answer.

Finally, in cases where a series of events or transactions is involved, it may be useful to state the time frame the interrogatories are intended to cover.

Example:

Unless expressly stated otherwise, each interrogatory relates to the time period beginning June 1, 1984, through and including the date on which answers to these interrogatories are signed.

Keep in mind, however, that such preambles are useful only in more complex interrogatories. For instance, they are frequently employed in commercial cases. In other cases, such as simple contract or personal injury actions, they are usually unnecessary because they make the interrogatories more complex than they need to be. The intensity of discovery, including interrogatories, must be commensurate with the case's complexity.

In addition, keep in mind that clear, simple interrogatories are more likely to yield clear, simple answers that will provide information that is actually useful. The more complex the interrogatories, the more complex and less useful the answers are likely to be. Accordingly, it is usually better to err on the side of simplicity.

iii.   Interrogatory style

Particular interrogatories must be clear and must adequately cover the necessary subjects. The interrogatories are usually drafted as imperatives, not as actual questions, since the imperative form affirmatively requires the answering party to supply information.

The first purpose of interrogatories is to identify parties, witnesses, documents, and experts.

Example (parties and agents):

1. State the full name of the defendant, where and when incorporated, where and when licensed to do business, where it has its principal place of business, and all names under which it does business.

2. Identify each officer and director of the defendant during the time period of June 1, 1984, through the date answers to these interrogatories are signed.

3. Identify each company, subdivision and subsidiary in which the defendant has any ownership, control, or interest of any amount for the period referred to in Interrogatory #2 above.

Example (witnesses):

1. Identify each person who was present during the execution of the contract that forms the basis of Count I of plaintiff's complaint.

2. Identify each person who participated in or was present during any of the negotiations of the contract executed by plaintiff and defendant on June 1, 1985.

3. State the full name and address of each person who witnessed, or claims to have witnessed, the collision between vehicles driven by the plaintiff and defendant occurring on June 1, 1985.

4. State the full name and address of each person who was present, or claims to have been present, at the scene of the collision during and after the collision, other than the persons identified in Interrogatory #3 above.

5. State the full name and address of each person who has any knowledge of the facts of the collision, other than those persons already identified in Interrogatories #3 and 4 above.

Note that rather than ask for witnesses in a general way, the interrogatories first focus on witnesses to a particular transaction or event, then expand the scope in subsequent questions to ensure that all possible known witnesses are identified. This organizes the information into useful categories.

Example (documents):

1. Identify each document that relates to the contract executed by plaintiff and defendant on June 1, 1985.

2. Identify each document in your possession and control that relates to the accident that is the basis for plaintiff's complaint.

A common practice is to combine an interrogatory that asks for the identity of documents with a request to produce all documents identified in the interrogatory answer. This has the advantage of getting copies of the identified documents more quickly.[24]

Interrogatories are also the required method for obtaining information about experts expected to testify at trial. The use of a basic imperative with subsections is recommended.

Example (experts):

1. As to each expert expected to testify at trial, state:
   (a) his full name, address, and professional qualifications;
   (b) the subject matter on which he is expected to testify;
   (c) the substance of the facts and opinions to which the expert is expected to testify; and
   (d) a summary of the grounds of each opinion.

The above interrogatories are all directed toward obtaining the identity of parties and agents, witnesses, documents, and experts, and are a part of almost every interrogatory set. These questions obtain the hard data that will provide the springboard for further investigation and discovery.

Interrogatories should also ask for the specific facts on which the pleadings are based. This is particularly important since, due to the minimal requirements of federal "notice pleading," the pleadings frequently

---

24. See §6.5 on drafting documents requests.

contain general conclusory language that gives little information about the facts on which claims, defenses, or damages are based. Interrogatories should develop the basic facts so that the parties can focus on specific facts underlying the legal claims.

Example (facts underlying complaint in personal injury action):

1. Describe the personal injuries you sustained as a result of this occurrence.
2. Were you hospitalized as a result of this occurrence? If so, state the name and address of each such hospital or clinic, the dates of your hospitalization at each facility, and the amount of each facility's bill.

If a single interrogatory asks for several categories of information, it is more effective to set out those categories in lettered subsections. This makes it clear what information you want, and makes it more likely that you will elicit complete answers.

Example:

3. Were you treated by any physicians as a result of this occurrence? If so, state:
   (a) the name and address of each such physician;
   (b) each physician's areas of specialty;
   (c) the dates of each examination, consultation, or appointment; and
   (d) the amount of each physician's bill.
4. Were you unable to work as a result of this occurrence? If so, state:
   (a) the dates during which you were unable to work;
   (b) your employers during those dates;
   (c) the type of work you were unable to do; and
   (d) the amount of lost wages or income.
5. State any other losses or expenses you claim resulted from this occurrence, other than those already stated above.
6. During the past 10 years, have you suffered any other personal injuries? If so, state:
   (a) when, where, and how you were injured;
   (b) the nature and extent of the injuries;
   (c) the name and address of each medical facility where you were treated; and
   (d) physicians by whom you were treated for those injuries.
7. During the past 10 years, have you been hospitalized, treated, examined, or tested at any hospital, clinic, or physician's office for any medical condition other than personal injuries? If so, state:
   (a) the name and address of each such medical facility and physician;
   (b) the dates such services were provided; and

(c) the medical conditions involved.

These kinds of questions serve to systematically discover the facts on which the plaintiff's case is based, and the answers will point to the areas that need to be explored in greater detail.

Finally, interrogatories should be used to identify the facts on which specific claims are based. Complaints commonly allege in conclusory fashion that the defendant "breached the contract" or "negligently operated a motor vehicle." An interrogatory is an effective means of developing the facts that the other party claims support the legal contentions.

Examples:

1. State all facts upon which you claim that defendant acted negligently.

2. State the conduct by the plaintiff and any of its officers, employees, or agents that you claim constituted a breach of the contract.

3. Do you contend that Samuel Jones lacked authority to enter into a contract on behalf of the defendant corporation? If so, state the facts on which you base this contention.

iv.   Signing, serving, and filing

The interrogatories must be signed by the attorney, served on each party, and filed with the court. Service is made by any permitted method under Rule 5, most commonly by mailing a copy to the lawyers for the other parties. The original interrogatories, with an attached proof of service statement, is then filed with the clerk of the court.

d.   *Responses to interrogatories*

A party must usually answer interrogatories within 30 days of service of the interrogatories. Since they frequently require a substantial amount of work, information necessary to prepare the answers must be obtained reasonably quickly. If the client is out of town and unavailable, or the interrogatories are lengthy, move for additional time to answer. It is usually a good idea to call the opposing lawyer, explain your problem, and ask the lawyer to agree not to oppose your motion for additional time.

i.   Researching and preparing answers

A common procedure in answering interrogatories is to send the interrogatories to the client and ask her to respond to the request for information from her own records and from personal recall and to then return the information to you, her lawyer. You then draft the actual answers. After the client reviews the answers for accuracy and completeness, the client should sign the document and return it to you. This procedure works well with individual clients. When the interrogatories are complicated, the client and lawyer must work together on preparing the answers.

Corporate parties and other artificial entities, however, present special considerations. First, the lawyer representing the corporation must decide who in the corporation should answer the interrogatories. Ordinarily a corporate officer who has personal knowledge of the transactions involved, or who has knowledge of the corporate record-keeping system, is an appropriate choice. The selection of the person is not as significant as might first appear, however, because although whoever provides the answer will be bound by it, the answer will also be imputed to and be binding on the corporate party.

Second, the corporate party has an obligation to investigate files that are in its possession or control, to collect the requested information, and to put that information in the answer. Records are considered in a party's possession or control if they are records that are kept at the company's offices, or if they are physically in the possession of another, like an accountant or a storage company, but the party has the power to get the records returned. The corporation's duty to investigate is limited only by the extent of its own records, but there is no duty to conduct an independent outside investigation.[25] A corporate party cannot avoid answering a proper interrogatory through the device of selecting someone to answer the interrogatories who has no personal knowledge of any relevant facts.

Third, under Rule 33(c) a party can answer an interrogatory by specifying the business records from which the requested information can be derived if the burden of obtaining the desired information from those records is substantially the same for either party. This is a most useful device, because it avoids "doing the homework" for the requesting party and permits answers to be made more quickly.

ii. Objections

A party on whom interrogatories have been served has two possible responses: an answer or an objection. If the response is an objection, simply state the objection as your answer to a particular interrogatory. There are several bases for objecting. First, a party may object on the basis that the information sought is irrelevant. However, since the Rule 26 definition of relevance for discovery purposes is quite broad, such an objection is difficult to make successfully. In addition, the court can grant sanctions for frivolous objections. Second, a party may object on the ground of privilege, relying on either the privilege for qualified trial preparation materials and absolute mental impressions under Rule 26(b) or on the privileges under Rule 501 of the Federal Rules of Evidence. Third, an objection can be made to interrogatories that ask for information that cannot be obtained by interrogatories, such as an interrogatory that demands the production of records. Fourth, an objection can be made on the basis that the interrogatory is annoying, embarrassing, oppressive, or unduly burdensome and expensive. This is probably the most frequently raised objection, one that has generated a substantial body of case law. Where such an objection is raised, the answering party should move for a

---

25. Moore's Federal Practice §33.07; Wright & Miller §2171.

protective order under Rule 26(c).[26] The claim that an interrogatory is unduly burdensome and expensive requires that the court balance the burden of collecting the information requested with the benefit to the requesting party. Where the work involved in obtaining the information is enormous and the benefit to the requesting party is small in light of the issues in the case, an objection to the interrogatory should be sustained.[27]

Where an objection exists, it should be made on the interrogatory answer.

Example:

Interrogatory No. 8:　State which officers were involved in the sale of forklift trucks to the XYZ Corporation on August 1, 1984.

Answer: Defendant objects to Interrogatory No. 8 on the ground that it asks for information that is irrelevant because it pertains to a transaction with a nonparty, the XYZ Corporation, that has no relevance to the controversy between the plaintiff and defendant.

Interrogatory No. 9: Identify all conversations between defendant's employees and defendant's corporate counsel between August 1, 1983, and the present date.

Answer: Defendant objects to Interrogatory No. 9 on the ground that it asks for material that is privileged under the attorney-client privilege.

iii.　Answers

The other possible response is to answer the interrogatory. There are three basic types of responses.

First, the party can answer the interrogatory by supplying the requested information if it is either known or ascertainable from the party's personal knowledge or records. The answer should be as brief as possible, since you ordinarily don't want to volunteer information that has not been requested. On the other hand, you must answer with the essential facts at your disposal, since failing to disclose can subject you to serious sanctions. In addition, if you have a strong case and are looking toward a favorable settlement, you may want to volunteer information. The lawyer's task in answering interrogatories is to strike an appropriate balance between the advantages of brevity and a full, detailed answer.

Example:

Interrogatory No. 2: Identify each person who was present during the execution of the contract that forms the basis of Count I of plaintiff's complaint.

Answer: John Marlowe and Phillip Johnson.

26. See §6.9.1.
27. See Wright & Miller §2174.

Interrogatory No. 3: Identify each physician who treated you as a result of this occurrence.

Answer: Dr. William Jackson, Mercy Hospital, Seattle, Washington; Dr. Erica Olson, 3420 Cascades Highway, Seattle, Washington; possibly other physicians at Mercy Hospital, whose names are unknown; investigation continues.

Interrogatory No. 4: State the name and address of each person who was present or claims to have been present during the collision.

Answer: Mary Jones, 2440 Congress St., Tucson, Arizona; Frank Wilson, 1831 N. Campbell Ave., Tucson, Arizona; Abby Jones, 2440 Congress St., Tucson, Arizona; Jennifer Jones, 2440 Congress St., Tucson, Arizona; in addition, there were several other pedestrians in the vicinity, but the names and addresses of such persons are presently unknown; investigation continues.

Where the interrogatory asks for information on which the answering party has some personal knowledge but not to the detail requested, and no records exist that can supply those details, the answer should accurately reflect this situation.

Example:

Interrogatory No. 6: Identify each communication between John Marlowe and Phillip Johnson that relates to the contract that forms the basis of Count I of plaintiff's complaint.

Answer: There were several telephone conversations between Marlowe and Johnson during a period of approximately four weeks preceding the execution of the contract. The exact dates and substance of each of these conversations are unknown.

This type of answer is satisfactory when the answer cannot state facts that are not within the knowledge or recall of the answering party and no records exist to supply the details. The better practice is to follow up on this type of response through depositions, which allow the extent and details of the party's recall to be explored and developed.

Where an interrogatory asks for a party's contentions, a more complete answer is called for since the answering party does not wish to limit its proof or theories of liability.

Example:

Interrogatory No. 4: State all the facts on which you claim that defendant acted negligently.

Answer: Defendant (1) drove in excess of the posted speed limit; (2) drove in excess of a reasonable speed under the existing conditions and circumstances; (3) failed to keep a proper lookout to ensure the safety of others; (4) failed to keep his vehicle in the proper lane; (5) failed to yield the right of way; and (6) failed to obey traffic signals, markers, and "rules of the road." Investigation continues.

In this type of answer the "investigation continues" response is important because additional investigation and discovery may develop additional facts to support the negligence claim.

A second type of response is simply to state "no knowledge" where this is accurate. Keep in mind that an answering party must search his own records to determine if the information exists, and, if it does, use the information to answer the interrogatory.

Example:

Interrogatory No. 4: State if any witnesses to the collision prepared written reports of any kind regarding the collision.

Answer: No knowledge.

Rule 26(e) imposes a continuing duty to supplement answers regarding the identity of witnesses, testifying experts, and answers that were incorrect or were correct when made but must be supplemented because failing to do so would constitute knowing concealment. A common response in such instances is to answer based on present knowledge and acknowledge the continuing duty under the Rule.

Example:

Interrogatory No. 2: Identify each person who saw or heard something during the collision.

Answer: Other than plaintiff and defendant, none presently known; investigation continues.

Interrogatory No. 3: Identify each expert expected to be called as a witness at trial.

Answer: None at present; plaintiff is aware of her continuing duty to supplement responses under Rule 26(e)(1)(B).

The third type of answer is to identify business records that provide the answers. Rule 33(c) requires only that the answer specify the records and give the requesting party a reasonable opportunity to examine and copy them. Actual production with the interrogatory answer is not required; however, such records are always discoverable through a notice to produce under Rule 34. For this reason, many lawyers simply attach copies of the pertinent documents as exhibits to the interrogatory answers.

Examples:

Interrogatory No. 5: Identify each communication between Phillip Johnson and Jane East between June 1, 1984, and August 4, 1984, relating to the contract that forms the basis of Count I of plaintiff's complaint.

Answer: Any such communications are kept in the defendant's telephone log-book, the pertinent dates of which may be examined and copied at a reasonable time at the defendant's place of business.

Interrogatory No. 6: Identify each sales transaction entered into between plaintiff and defendant for the period of January 1, 1984, through August 4, 1984.

Answer: These transactions are recorded on the defendant's Sales Records, which are computerized after sales transactions are completed. A printout of these transactions is attached as Exhibit A.

iv.   Signing, serving, and filing

The format for interrogatory answers, like any other court document, should have the case caption and title of the document. The answers must be signed and sworn to by the person making them. If any interrogatories are objected to, the attorney must sign them as well.

The completed interrogatory answers must then be served on each party and filed with the court. Service is made by any proper method under Rule 5, most commonly by mailing a copy to the lawyers for the other parties. The original answer, with an attached proof of service, is then filed with the clerk of the court.

Example:

[Caption]

DEFENDANT ACME CORPORATION'S ANSWERS TO PLAINTIFF'S INTERROGATORIES

Defendant Acme Corporation answers the first set of interrogatories put forth by plaintiff as follows:

Interrogatory No. 1: . . . .

Answer: . . . .

Acme Corporation

By   _____

William Phillips
Vice President for Administration of Acme Corporation

State of Arizona | SS.
County of Pima |

William Phillips, after being first duly sworn, states that he is an officer of Acme Corporation and is authorized to make the above interrogatory answers on behalf of Acme Corporation, that the above answers have been prepared with the assistance of counsel, that the answers are based either on his personal knowledge, the personal knowledge of Acme Corporation employees, or on information obtained from Acme Corporation records, and that the answers are true to the best of his knowledge, information and belief.

_____

William Phillips

Signed and sworn to before me on this _____ day of _____,
_____

_____

Notary Public

My commission expires on _____

§6.5. *Requests to produce documents and subpoenas*

After answers to interrogatories have been received you will usually have enough detailed information to ask for copies of identified documents through a request to produce. Hence, requests to produce are usually the second step in the discovery process, although simple requests to produce documents are frequently served with interrogatories and ask for the production of all documents identified in the interrogatory answers.

1. Law[28]

Requests to produce documents and things and for entry upon land to inspect are governed by Rule 34. A request to produce can be served only upon another party. The scope of the request, like other discovery, is controlled by Rule 26(b), which permits discovery of any relevant matter that is not privileged.

Rule 34 permits requests to produce for three things:

(a) Documents for inspection and copying
(b) Tangible things for inspection, copying, and testing
(c) Entry on land or property for inspection and testing

28. Wright §87; James & Hazard §5.5; Friedenthal §7.11; Moore's Manual §15.10; Shepard's Manual §§5.161-5.194; Moore's Federal Practice §§34.01-34.22; Wright & Miller §§2201-2218.

Of these, production of documents is the principal use of Rule 34 requests. The Rule requires a party to produce all documents that are in that party's "possession, custody or control." This obligates a party to produce all relevant documents, even those not in the party's actual possession, if the party has a lawful right to get them from another person or entity.[29] In short, a party cannot avoid production through the simple device of transferring the documents to another person or entity such as the party's lawyer, accountant, insurer, or corporate subsidiary. When this avoidance device is used the party is deemed to have retained "control" of the documents and is required to get them returned in order to comply with the production request.

A request to produce must describe each item or category to be produced with "reasonable particularity." This is usually read to require that, in the context of the case and the overall nature of the documents involved, a responding party must reasonably be able to determine what particular documents are called for.[30] This is obviously a flexible standard that varies from case to case.

Rule 34 requires that the documents produced for inspection must be produced in either the same order as they are normally kept, or in the order, with labels, that corresponds with the categories of the request. The producing party cannot purposefully disorganize documents and records to make them more difficult to comprehend. Further, the request to produce must specify a "reasonable time, place, and manner" for the inspection. The responding party must serve a written response for each category requested, usually within 30 days of service of the request, stating whether he objects, with reasons for the objection, or will comply.

2. Practice approach

a. Timing

Before serving a request to produce documents or a request for entry upon land to inspect, you need to know what documents you want produced and what things you want to inspect. Rule 34 requires "reasonable particularity." If you have drafted your interrogatories carefully, and have asked for descriptions of relevant documents and for the identity of those whose custody those documents are in, answers to the interrogatories should provide sufficient detail to meet the particularity requirement for production requests. Hence, requests to produce should normally be served as soon as possible after the answers to interrogatories have been received. Sometimes, as previously mentioned, production requests are served at the same time as interrogatories.

29. Moore's Manual §15.10; Shepard's Manual §5.172; Moore's Federal Practice §34.17; Wright & Miller §2210.
30. Moore's Manual §15.10; Shepard's Manual §5.168; Moore's Federal Practice §34.07; Wright & Miller §2211.

This timetable presumes that the party has adequately, and in a timely fashion, answered your interrogatories. If the answering party has objected, failed to answer, or served evasive or incomplete answers, you must resolve the problems through appropriate discovery motions.[31] Doing this, however, will necessarily delay serving the requests to produce. In this situation you should consider serving a request to produce anyway, since you can ordinarily determine in a general way what documents the other party is likely to have and describe them sufficiently by topic or subject matter to meet the particularity requirement. It is easy for discovery to become sidetracked or to stall completely. In these situations you must weigh the benefits and liabilities of waiting or going ahead in light of your overall discovery strategy.

b.   Organization

Before actually drafting the request to produce, you need to organize your thoughts on what you want from the other party. If you have intelligently thought through your discovery strategy, put forth your interrogatories to and received answers from that party, then the bulk of your work is already done. You will know in sufficient detail what documents you want, what documents the answering party admits having, how those documents are described or labeled, and who their custodian is.

If you have not yet received interrogatory answers but have decided to send out requests to produce anyway, you will have to evaluate what documents the other party is likely to have, how they are likely to be labeled and organized, and who their custodian is. If this is difficult or impossible to do, you should consider serving notice for the deposition of that party for an early date in order to question the deponent about his records. In the case of a corporate party, you should also consider deposing the party's custodian of records. This will help you determine what kind of records the corporation generates and maintains, and will in turn help you make a more focused document request.

c.   Drafting requests to produce

i.   Heading

A request to produce should be drafted like any other court document. It must have a caption showing the court, case title, and docket number and be properly labeled. Where a case has several parties, it is useful to designate which party is sending the request to which other party; otherwise, the simple title "REQUESTS TO PRODUCE DOCUMENTS" will suffice.

31. See §6.9.

Example:

[Caption]

PLAINTIFF JOHNSON'S REQUESTS TO PRODUCE DOCUMENTS TO DEFENDANT ACME CORPORATION

Plaintiff Johnson requests defendant Acme Corporation to produce the documents and things listed below, pursuant to Rule 34 of the Federal Rules of Civil Procedure:

1. . . .
2. . . .
3. . . .

ii. Definitions

Requests to produce present the same problems concerning definitions as interrogatories. Accordingly, terms and phrases frequently used, such as "document," "record," "relating to," "transaction," and "occurrence," should be defined. It is best to use definitions identical to those used in the interrogatories.[32]

Example:

DEFINITIONS

The following terms used in this request to admit have the following meanings:

1. A "document" means. . . .
2. A "transaction" means. . . .

iii. Drafting requests

There are three basic requests permitted under Rule 34: to inspect and copy documents, to inspect and examine tangible things, and to enter upon land to inspect and examine things. The requests should follow a basic format.

The requests to produce must specify a reasonable date, time, and place for the production. Rule 34 requires only that this be "reasonable," which must necessarily take into account the volume and complexity of the records sought. Since the Rule requires a response within 30 days of service, the date set for the production should be a longer time period.

Example:

A. Plaintiff requests that defendant produce the following documents for inspection and copying at the offices of Mary Anton, plaintiff's

---

32. See §6.4.

attorney, 200 Main Street, Suite 400, Tucson, Arizona, on August 21, 1986, at 2:00 P.M.:

    1. . . .

    2. . . .

B. Plaintiff requests that defendant produce the following things for inspection, copying, and testing at the offices of Independent Testing, 2000 Main Street, Tucson, Arizona, on August 22, 1986, at 9:00 A.M.:

    1. . . .

    2. . . .

C. Plaintiff requests that defendant permit plaintiff to enter defendant's lumber yard located at 4000 Monroe Street, Tucson, Arizona, for the purpose of inspecting, photographing and measuring the premises on August 23, 1986, at 2:00 P.M.

Most requests to produce involve documents. There are several ways to draft requests that will meet Rule 34's particularity requirement.

First, you can use the interrogatory answers. If those answers have listed and described a variety of documents, referring to the descriptions should be adequate. The responding party will be in a poor position to claim that a description it furnished is now suddenly insufficient.

Example:

1. Each document identified in defendant's answer to Interrogatory No. 6 in plaintiff's first set of interrogatories.

Second, ask for all documents that relate to a specific transaction or event. By making the request specific, it should not be challenged on the grounds of being too vague.

Example:

2. All documents relating to the sale of the property located at 4931 Sunrise St., Tucson, Arizona, entered into between plaintiff and defendant on July 31, 1984.

Third, you can ask for specific types of documents that relate to a more general time frame or course of conduct.

Example:

3. All bills of lading, invoices, and shipping confirmation notices relating to all goods shipped from plaintiff to defendant during the period from January 1, 1985, through April 30, 1985.

In each of the above examples, the party responding to the request to admit should not have difficulty in either understanding the request or identifying the documents requested. In contrast, a request calling for the production of "all documents relating to the allegations in plaintiff's complaint" or similarly vague language, is defective and unenforceable since it does not meet Rule 34's specificity requirement.

It is possible that the responding party will not object to a general request, but, regardless, it is usually not an effective approach for discovery. Requests to produce should balance the safety of inclusiveness with the utility of a more focused request. A request that is too broad may result in a huge volume of paperwork being deposited in your office; you may have neither the time nor assistance to review all of it in order to extract the few documents that are relevant to your case.

Fourth, it is always useful to ask for the identity of any documents that existed at one time but have since been destroyed. This prevents the literally true but misleading response that there are "no records" of the description requested.

iv. Signing, serving, and filing

The request to produce should be signed by the lawyer, served on each party, and filed with the court. Service is made by any permitted method under Rule 5, most commonly by mailing a copy to the lawyers for the other parties. The original requests to produce, with an attached proof-of-service statement, is then filed with the clerk of the court.

d. *Responses to requests to produce*

A party served with a request to produce usually must respond within 30 days of service of the request. Even though the lawyers for the requesting and responding parties frequently reach an informal agreement on how and when to produce documents and conduct inspections,[33] the responding party should serve and file a response, since this is required by Rule 34.

i. Researching and preparing responses

If the preliminary investigation has been done, and answers to interrogatories have been prepared and served, you already will have done most of the initial work involved in responding to requests to produce. In addition, you should always send the requests to your client and ask the client a couple of questions about the requests. First, does the client know what the requests actually call for? If not, you may want to object on grounds of vagueness. Second, how much effort will be required to collect the documents requested? If it is substantial and the case is not complex, you may be able to object on the grounds that the requests are unduly burdensome and move for a protective order, or at least for additional time to respond.

After your party has collected the documents, review the material to determine if all of it is relevant. If there are any privileged communications, now is the time to object, since privileges are waived unless timely asserted. Finally, make sure that those documents are in

---

33. See §6.3.8.

fact all the available documents your party has in his possession, custody, or control. You can be sure that your party, and other witnesses, will be questioned about the completeness of the tendered documents during their depositions. Now is the time to review the documents for completeness with your party.

ii. Objections

As with interrogatories, a party on whom requests to produce have been served has two possible responses: an answer or an objection. If the response is an objection, there are several possible bases. First, an objection may be made on the ground that the documents sought are irrelevant. However, since Rule 26 has such a broad definition of relevance for discovery purposes, this is a difficult ground on which to prevail. Moreover, this ground will probably have been ruled on if the same objection was made to the interrogatory that asked for the identity of the documents. Second, an objection can be based on a privilege, either the privilege for trial preparation materials and mental impressions under Rule 26(b), or the privileges recognized under Rule 501 of the Federal Rules of Evidence. Third, an objection can be based on the request being annoying, embarrassing, oppressive, or unduly burdensome and expensive. Here the answering party should seek a protective order under Rule 26(c); still, an objection to a request to produce should be made on the response.[34]

Example:

[Caption]

RESPONSE TO PLAINTIFF'S REQUESTS TO PRODUCE

Defendant Acme Corporation responds to plaintiff's Requests to Produce Documents as follows:

1. Defendant objects to plaintiff's Request No. 1 on the ground that it requests documents the disclosure of which would violate the attorney-client privilege, since the request on its face asks for the production of "all correspondence from corporate officers to corporate counsel regarding the contract dated July 1, 1984."

Frequently a request may be objectionable in part. Where this is so, the response should make clear what part is being objected to and what the responding party agrees to produce. Such an objection is a common response to a broad request asking for a variety of documents, some of which may be privileged.

---

34. See discussion in §6.4.2(d).

Example:

2. Defendant objects to plaintiff's Request No. 2 to the extent it asks for privileged communications protected by the attorney-client privilege. Plaintiff's Request No. 2 asks for the production of "all memoranda by defendant's subsidiary, Acme Productions, relating to a bid on U.S. Government Contract No. 84-3287, commonly known as the 'Tristar Contract.' " These memoranda include documents prepared by Acme Productions officers and employees, documents prepared at the request of and sent to Acme Corporation's General Counsel, which relate to the pending litigation and are protected from disclosure by the attorney-client privilege.

iii. Answers

If a request to produce is not objected to, it must be answered. An answer involves two considerations: the formal response, and the practical concerns involved in arranging for the actual production of the documents. There should be a formal answer even if, as is often the case, the production is worked out informally between the attorneys, since Rule 34 requires a response.

Example:

[Caption]

RESPONSE TO PLAINTIFF'S REQUESTS FOR PRODUCTION AND INSPECTION

Defendant Acme Corporation responds to plaintiff's Requests for Production of Documents and Inspection as follows:

1-8. Defendant has agreed to produce the documents requested in plaintiff's Request Nos. 1 through 8 at the offices of plaintiff's attorney on or before August 15, 1986.

9. Defendant has agreed to permit the inspection of the items described in plaintiff's Request No. 9 at its manufacturing plant located at 9000 Main St., Tucson, Arizona, at a mutually agreed upon date and time, but not later than August 31, 1986.

_____
Attorney for Defendant
Acme Corporation

If records requested do not exist, the response should clearly establish this fact.

Example:

3. There are no documents in the possession, custody, or control of defendant Acme Corporation requested by plaintiff's Request No. 3.

Most production requests are worked out informally between the lawyers, who usually call each other and agree on the mechanics of delivering and copying the pertinent records. This will usually include when and where the documents will be produced, how the documents will be organized, and who will perform and pay for the actual copying. The usual procedure is for the documents to be produced at, or delivered to, the requesting attorney's offices on an agreed upon date. The responding party has the option of producing the records either in the order in which they are ordinarily kept, or labeled to correspond to the categories of the request. Since most production requests overlap on particulars to ensure completeness, a common approach in responding is to produce the documents in their usual order since this is easier for the responding party.

Regarding an informal agreement on the mechanics of reproducing the records, the rule requires only production — not copying — by the responding party. However, it is usually desirable for the responding party to make copies so as to retain possession of the original documents. For this reason it is common for the responding party to make copies of the records that comply with the requests; the cost of reproduction is then paid by the requesting party. As the lawyer for the answering party, make sure you keep a copy of everything submitted to the opposing side so that no issues arise later over what was actually delivered.

When the documents involved are so voluminous that copying all of them would be prohibitively expensive, a common solution is to have the lawyer for the requesting party review the documents at the offices of either the answering party or the answering party's lawyer. The requesting lawyer can then select the relevant documents for photocopying.

iv.   Signing, serving, and filing

The response to requests to produce must be signed, then served on every other party and filed with the court. Service is made by any permitted method under Rule 5, most commonly by mailing a copy to the lawyers for the other parties. The original response, with an attached proof of service, is then filed with the clerk of the court.

3.   Subpoenas to nonparties

Requests to produce documents apply only to parties to the action. Hence, when you need to obtain documents, records, and tangible things from nonparties, you will need to use a subpoena duces tecum, which is governed by Rule 45.

Rule 45 applies only to subpoenas for witnesses to attend a judicial proceeding such as a deposition, hearing, or trial. In conjunction with the proceeding, such a subpoena can also direct the person to produce books, papers, documents, and tangible things at the proceeding. The person is *not* required to deliver those records to anyone before the proceeding, although a cooperative witness will frequently do so. A subpoena for records that directs the witness to produce them at a time and place when no judicial proceeding will occur is defective and may be quashed.

When a party wishes to obtain records or tangible things from a nonparty before trial, the only proper discovery procedure is to subpoena that witness for a deposition and include in the subpoena a command to produce and permit inspection and copying of designated records and things. This procedure is governed by Rule 45(d) and is discussed in greater detail in §6.6 infra.

§6.6. Depositions

Depositions are usually taken after both interrogatory answers and responses to documents requests have been received, since those answers and documents will usually be used to plan an intelligent deposition. Although depositions are both expensive and time consuming, they are quite useful in assessing witness credibility, learning what witnesses know, and pinning witnesses down. They are the only discovery method that can be used on nonparties, and the only method in which the opposing counsel does not directly control the responses. For these reasons, depositions play a critical role in the discovery plan of virtually every case.

Rules 27 through 32 govern depositions. Rule 30, which regulates oral depositions, is the principal one, however, since oral depositions are the predominant way in which depositions are taken.[35]

1. Law[36]

a. Timing

Oral depositions may be taken of any party or nonparty, and can be taken after commencement of the action without court order. Court approval is required under Rule 30(a) only if the plaintiff wishes to take the defendant's deposition within 30 days of service of the summons and complaint, unless the defendant has already served notice for the plaintiff's deposition. This Rule allows the defendant time to retain a lawyer and respond to the complaint before having to submit to a deposition.

---

35. Depositions on written questions, governed by Rule 32, and letters rogatory, governed by Rule 28(b), are rarely utilized.

36. Wright §84; James & Hazard §5.3; Friedenthal §7.7; Moore's Manual §15.06; Shepard's Manual §§5.55-5.117; Moore's Federal Practice §§30.01-30.64; Wright & Miller §§2071-2157.

b. Notice

Whenever a deposition will be taken, the party taking the deposition must give "reasonable" notice to every party to the action. Rule 30(b) does not specify what is reasonable, although some local rules specify minimum requirements, frequently five days. Also, many courts have addressed the question, most finding that reasonable notice is a flexible standard that depends on the nature of the case and the deponent involved.[37]

The notice must state the name and address of each person to be deposed. If the name is not known, the notice must describe the person to be deposed in sufficient detail to identify that person individually or as part of a class or group. This is frequently the case with corporations and other artificial entities, where the actual name of the proper person to be deposed is unknown. In such a case the corporation, or other entity, must designate an officer, director, managing agent, or other person to testify on its behalf. The notice must also state the time and place for the deposition.

In addition to the notice to other parties, of course, the person to be deposed must also be notified. Where the deponent is also a party, the notice of deposition is sufficient. Where the deponent is a nonparty, he must be subpoenaed in accordance with Rule 45 — this is called a subpoena ad testificandum. Witness fees and mileage costs must accompany the subpoena, as set by 28 U.S.C. §1821. A problem that frequently arises concerns the amount of fees and costs that the witness is entitled to receive. A common practice is to tender the witness a check for the probable mileage and one day's witness fees, and to take care of any differences after the deposition.

Finally, the deponent can be commanded to produce records, documents, and tangible things for inspection and copying at the deposition. With parties, this is simply achieved by serving on the deponent a request to produce under Rule 34 for the same date and place on which the deposition will be held. Nonparties can also be commanded to produce records by serving a subpoena under Rule 45(d) — a subpoena duces tecum. Where such a subpoena is served, a copy of it must be sent to each party by attaching the copy to the notice of deposition.

c. Location

Rule 30 does not specify where a deposition may be conducted. Accordingly, the deposition of a party can be held anywhere. If for some reason the location is unreasonable, the deposed party must seek a protective order under Rule 26(c).[38]

The deposition of a nonparty must comply with Rule 45(d), which has serveral technical requirements concerning location. First, the subpoena of the witness must be issued by the clerk of the district in

---

37. Wright §84; Moore's Manual §15.06; Shepard's Manual §5.82; Moore's Federal Practice §§30.56-30.57; Wright & Miller §2106.
38. See §6.9.1.

which the deposition is to be taken. The clerk, however, will only issue the subpoena if you have served a notice of deposition on all parties and have proof of service. Accordingly, you should get a duplicate original or a certified copy of the notice and proof of service and present it to the clerk when you request that a Rule 45 subpoena be issued. Second, the Rule includes location limitations that are designed to protect a nonparty witness from undue inconvenience. Ordinarily, the witness can be required to attend a deposition only in the county in which the witness resides, is employed, or personally conducts business, unless the court orders otherwise. If the witness is a nonresident of the district where the deposition is to be held, the witness can only be required to attend in the county where he was served with the subpoena, or within 40 miles of the place of service, unless the court orders otherwise. These limitations prevent requiring the witness to travel great distances to a deposition. The statutory preference is that the lawyers should do the traveling for the convenience of the witness. It is common practice, however, for lawyers to offer a witness travel and lodging expenses, and perhaps reimbursements for lost income, if the witness will agree to be deposed at the lawyer's convenience. It is usually cheaper, in the long run, for the witness to travel to the lawyers, than the other way around.

d. Recording

A deposition must be taken in the presence of someone authorized to administer oaths, and who can stenographically record the testimony. Invariably, a certified court reporter is also a notary public and therefore able to perform both functions. Rule 30(b)(4) now allows the parties to agree to recording the deposition by means other than stenographically, using another reliable method such as audio- or videotaping. Rule 30(b)(7) also authorizes depositions taken by telephone. While the predominant means of recording remains the court reporter, since this method produces a written transcript, the other methods are being utilized more as ways to reduce costs or to make a more vivid recreation of the deponent's testimony. These other methods have become a common way of recording experts' depositions when the experts are not expected to testify at trial and their depositions will be introduced in evidence during the trial. Video depositions are also a good idea if the opposing counsel is unduly interfering when you are taking the deposition, such as by repeatedly making objections that serve no proper purpose and are made only to coach the witness on a desirable response.

e. Signing, correcting, and filing

There is no requirement that a deposition be transcribed. If any party requests it, however, the court reporter must prepare a transcript. The witness has the right to make corrections, which the reporter must enter on the deposition along with a statement of the witness' reasons, and to sign the deposition. These rights can be and sometimes are waived, however.

The reporter must certify that the witness was sworn and that the transcript is accurate. The reporter should then seal the original, which should include any exhibits that were marked and used during the deposition, and file it with the clerk of the court.

f. Objections

Rule 30(c) provides that the reporter shall note on the deposition all objections to the qualifications of the reporter or other officer, to the procedure, evidence, and conduct of parties, as well as any other objections. The Rule states that "[e]vidence objected to shall be taken subject to the objections," the intent being that the witness should answer the questions asked with all objections being noted. This permits a judge to rule on the objections later, in the event that any party wishes to use the transcript at trial.

Under Rule 32(d), objections to a witness' competency, or the materiality or relevance of the testimony, need not be made during the taking of the deposition, unless the ground for the objection could have been eliminated if made known at that time. However, objections to the form of questions, and other errors that might have been cured if the objection had been made, are waived unless timely made.

Neither Rule 30 nor 32 addresses the special problems concerning privilege objections. The usual procedure of requiring answers "subject to the objection" will not work. If the answer is privileged, providing the answer will constitute a waiver of the privilege. Therefore, a timely objection must be made, and if the deponent is a party, the deponent's lawyer should instruct the deponent not to answer.[39] The party taking the deposition then has the option of moving for an order to compel discovery under Rule 37.

If the examination is being conducted in bad faith to annoy, embarrass, or harass the deponent, then a party or the deponent can demand that the deposition be suspended so that the party or deponent can move for a protective order under Rule 32(d) to terminate or limit the examination.

---

39. The problem is more complicated with nonparty witnesses who are not represented by counsel. Can a lawyer for a party make an objection for the witness? Under DR 7-104(A)(2), the usual answer is no. Since a party's lawyer does not represent the witness, the lawyer ordinarily cannot give legal advice to the witness other than recommending that the witness get advice, particularly since the witness may have interests that are, or may be, adverse to the party's. However, there is nothing improper in objecting to a question on behalf of your client; state the basis of your objection, and suggest that the witness talk to a lawyer before answering the question. There is nothing wrong in suggesting to anyone that he ought to talk to his own lawyer and get proper legal advice.

The problem also arises with employees of business entities. The lawyer for the business will usually treat the employee as her client and represent the employee at the employee's deposition. The theory is that since the employee's statements may be admissible at trial as admissions against the business, the lawyer for the business has a right to represent him (unless, of course, the employee is also a party or has his own lawyer). See §6.3.9.

2. Practice approach

Deposition rules are sufficiently broad that they rarely restrict the deposition process in any meaningful way. Since the rules permit such latitude, the principal concerns are the practical ones of using depositions effectively as part of your overall discovery strategy. There are several questions that you should always ask.

a. Should I take a deposition?

Depositions are probably both the most effective discovery vehicle when used properly and the most ineffective one when misused. You should consider the pros and cons of depositions in general and weigh these considerations when deciding if a particular witness should be deposed in a pending case.

On the plus side, depositions are by far the most effective discovery device for obtaining detailed information, primarily since the deposition is taken in question and answer form, which permits follow-up questioning on promising topics. Second, a deposition commits the deponent to the details of his story. This will tell you what the witness is going to say at trial, and gives you an opportunity to investigate those facts to see if contrary evidence can be obtained to refute the testimony. Third, the deposition gives you an opportunity to develop specific facts that may be used as impeachment at trial. Fourth, a deposition is in many respects a trial simulation, so you can evaluate the deponent as a trial witness. Finally, opposing counsel has only limited objection rights, making depositions the only discovery method in which counsel does not prepare the responses.

On the minus side, depositions are expensive. Even a short deposition will cost a couple hundred dollars in lawyer's fees, reporter's fees, transcript costs, and possibly the witness' lodging and mileage fees. Where the amount at issue in a dispute is modest, costs are usually the primary reason for limiting the use of depositions. Second, depositions can perpetuate unfavorable testimony. Taking a deposition simply to find out what a witness will say can come at a price, if that witness is unfavorable and later becomes unavailable for trial. Third, a deposition educates your opponents as much as it educates you. Where you believe your opponent will learn more from the deposition than you, or you can get the same information informally such as by having an investigator interview the witness, taking the deposition can be counterproductive. Fourth, taking depositions may motivate an inactive opponent to prepare and pursue discovery. Unless your opponent has been using delaying tactics, motivating an opponent rarely does you any good.

b. Whose deposition should I take?

The cost-benefit factors discussed above must be used in deciding which witnesses to depose. There are three basic categories of witnesses you need to consider.

First, the opposing parties should always be deposed. You obviously will want to tie them down to the detailed facts and their versions of disputed events and transactions, and evaluate them as potential witnesses. The only exception might be nominal parties, such as a guardian or administrator of an estate. When the party is an artificial entity like a corporation, the officers and employees directly involved in the transactions and events at issue should be deposed.

Second, consider deposing the principal nonparty witnesses you have identified. In personal injury cases, this would include eyewitnesses to the event involved, as well as witnesses to the major damages elements. In contract and commercial cases, it would include the witnesses to the conversations, agreements, and conduct that are relevant to the transactions involved, and witnesses to any breaches and resulting damages.

The nonparty witnesses category obviously has the potential to be the largest one, and it is here that you need to consider how far to go in keeping with cost-effectiveness. While you obviously need to learn what the testimony of important witnesses will be, there comes a point at which the information obtained from witnesses who are merely corroborative and peripheral is not worth pursuing through depositions.

A good rule of thumb for depositions is that you should depose your opponent's witnesses, not your own, since there is usually no benefit in deposing witnesses you know will be favorable. However, where such a witness is elderly or in poor health, or may leave the jurisdiction and be unavailable for trial, you should always consider taking the witness' deposition to preserve the testimony. Hence, at the beginning of the depositions stage, lawyers will usually depose a favorable witness that is known to have strong testimony in order to guard against disaster. If the witness becomes unavailable, a deposition will usually qualify as former testimony under Rule 804(b)(1) of the Federal Rules of Evidence. If this is your purpose, make sure that the deposition is conducted so that the transcript is clear and complete. Consider taking a videotaped deposition, since this is probably the most effective method of presenting former testimony to a jury.

Third, consider what experts you need to depose. While you may not depose an expert as of right, the court can order expert depositions on such conditions as are reasonable. The information about experts obtained through interrogatory answers and reports generated through Rule 35 mental and physical examinations is frequently not the detailed information you need for trial, and tells you little about the kind of witness the expert will make at trial. Where the relative persuasiveness of opposing experts will be a major trial consideration, deposing the expert is a practical necessity. Most courts recognize these realities and are usually indulgent in permitting both expert depositions and the production of related documents that are necessary to prepare for the depositions.[40]

Fortunately, deposing the experts is usually worked out informally. Where both sides have experts that are expected to testify at trial, there are obvious reciprocal interests in deposing each other's experts. Experts

40. See discussion of experts in §6.3.9.

are usually not opposed to being deposed, so long as it can be done at a reasonable time and place and they will be compensated for their time. In such circumstances, the parties and experts usually make informal arrangements for the necessary depositions, although it is a good idea to draft a written stipulation of the arrangement under Rule 29 and file it with the court because a written agreement will avoid later misunderstandings.

Where the expert is outside the court's jurisdiction and it is anticipated that the expert will not come forward voluntarily to testify, the expert is considered "unavailable" for the purposes of FRE 804(a)(5). Since an expert cannot be compelled to testify at trial, the expert's deposition will often be admitted at trial as former testimony under FRE 804(b)(1). For this reason, the deposition of such an expert should be taken to ensure that the questions and answers will be available for admission at trial. It is particularly important that an "unavailable" expert's testimony be clear and complete. A videotaped deposition should be considered here for this purpose. A video deposition has the advantage of presenting a vivid recreation of the deponent's testimony to the jury. Its disadvantage is that taking the deposition and then editing out objectionable questions and answers is expensive. Nevertheless, a video deposition of an expert, if done carefully, is a vastly superior method of presenting the absent expert's testimony.

c. When should I take depositions?

Since under Rule 30(a) oral depositions can be taken at almost any time, the timing of depositions is determined primarily by tactical considerations.

First, depositions can be taken before an action has been commenced if Rule 27(a) requirements are met. Those requirements are technical and detailed; they include drawing up a verified petition that sets out the facts of the anticipated suit, the details expected from the witness, and the reasons a deposition is necessary. The petition must be served, with a notice of deposition, to each anticipated adverse party that can be found. The amount of work required under Rule 27(a) is at least as much as is required to prepare, file, and serve a complaint and summons. For that reason, Rule 27(a) is ordinarily used only in those circumstances where service on the adverse party cannot be made with due diligence.

Second, another possiblity is to depose your opponent shortly after the suit has been commenced. This may be necessary in certain situations, such as when you need facts to support a jurisdictional motion, or when you need to learn the identity of proper parties and officers and agents of such parties, or when you want to depose a custodian of records to learn about your opponent's records so that you can prepare a more focused documents request.

An early deposition may also catch your opponent unprepared and result in a more useful deposition. The witness may disclaim knowledge of certain facts, or assert facts that can be disproved. These can be used as admissions and for impeachment at trial.

On the other hand, there are obvious risks. Without interrogatory answers and documents received through documents requests, your preparation cannot be nearly as thorough as it should be. While the discovery rules do not bar repetitive discovery, your opponent may seek a protective order if you serve notice to him for a second deposition after other discovery has been received, and he may succeed in preventing a second deposition. In short, taking an early deposition with the idea of taking a second detailed one later involves risks.

Third, the usual approach is to take depositions after initial interrogatory answers and documents have been received. Only then will you have the necessary facts and materials to prepare thoroughly and take the kind of detailed, complete deposition you will want to take. This is particularly important when deposing adverse parties, where the party can only be pinned down when you have the preliminary discovery on hand.

Deciding when to take a deposition can only be done on a case-by-case basis. Your decision must balance the benefits of an early deposition against a later one based on the extent of your knowledge from existing discovery. The important concept to keep in mind is that the question of when to take a particular deposition should never be a routine matter, but should always be decided by weighing the benefits, disadvantages, and risks of a particular course of action.

d. What order of depositions should I use?

There are several approaches to establishing the order of depositions, and the approach that will be effective in a given case depends on the issues, parties, and witnesses involved.

First, continuing with the concept that discovery should be a building process, a common approach is to depose neutral and unfavorable witnesses first, then adverse employees, officers, and parties to the action, and finally, the adverse parties' experts. Arranging the depositions in this order allows you to use information obtained from witnesses to prepare for depositions of parties to the action and, in turn, the experts.

This approach, however, has built-in disadvantages, since every deposition educates both you and the other parties. Every witness deposition you take before taking the adverse party's deposition functions to prepare that party to be deposed.

The second approach, therefore, is to reverse the order and depose adverse parties first, then the nonparty witnesses. This has the advantage of pinning down the adverse parties to detailed testimony before hearing other witnesses, who may have conflicting testimony.

The third possiblity is to schedule a series of depositions back to back so that later deponents do not have time to review the transcripts of the earlier depositions. This works well with unfavorable witnesses and adverse parties, who might otherwise try to find out what an earlier witness said and then tell a consistent story. If you see a danger of this happening in a particular case, simply schedule the first deposition for the morning, the second for early afternoon, and so on, allowing enough time so that you can realistically keep to the schedule. For example, when deposing corporate employees, it is often effective to schedule them back to back, starting at the bottom and working up to management. You are more likely to get inconsistencies this way.

As with the decision on when to depose, a decision on the order of depositions can only be made on a case-by-case basis. Deciding on the order should not be a routine matter, but should always involve weighing the advantages, disadvantages, and risks of a particular approach.

e. What must I do to schedule a deposition?

Scheduling a deposition involves two decisions: when and where. When has been discussed above. Where depends on your personal preference and what the Rules allow. Rule 30 does not deal with location, so it leaves the choice up to the party taking the deposition of another party. However, Rule 45(d) has specific location rules for deposing nonparty witnesses. In general, such a witness can only be deposed in the county where he resides, is employed, or personally transacts business. When planning depositions, in short, you can make a party come to you, but you must go to a nonparty witness.

The usual location for deposing a party is in your own offices. You will be comfortable there, have your files with you, and have your deponent away from familiar surroundings. If you have previously obtained responses to your documents requests, there should be no need to be at the deponent's place of business.

To depose a nonparty witnesses, you will usually have to go to the witness' county, unless you can get the witness to come to you. While the Rule is designed to convenience nonparty witnesses, it can have the effect of inconveniencing everyone else. Therefore, it is usually a good idea to try to have the witness come to you. If, in addition to the mileage and witness fees, you offer to compensate the witness for actual travel expenses and lost wages, the witness may be more likely to come to your offices to be deposed. This is often preferable, since it saves you time and, in the long run, saves your client money.

To depose experts, it is frequently better to visit the experts at their offices. It will be convenient for the expert, and you will have access to the expert's reports, records, and reference material. This will avoid what otherwise is a common problem: the expert who, for one reason or another, fails to bring all necessary paperwork, thereby making a thorough deposition impossible. Make sure, however, that you bring everything you need to the expert's office.

After you have selected a time and place for the depositions, you must do the following:

(i)   Send notices to parties
(ii) Serve subpoenas on witnesses
(iii) Send notices to produce or serve subpoenas duces tecum
(iv) Reserve a suitable room for the deposition
(v)   Arrange for a court reporter
(vi) Reconfirm deposition date and attendance

The notices to parties and subpoenas to witnesses, along with any notices to produce or subpoenas duces tecum, should be served with a reasonable lead time. Given the busy schedules of most people, 20 or 30 days notice is certainly appropriate. When deposing a party, it is always a good practice to call that party's lawyer and select a mutually convenient time before preparing the notices. This avoids delays, avoids motions to reset deposition dates, and generally helps create good working relationships between lawyers, which benefits everyone. With nonparty witnesses, it is frequently a good idea to serve a subpoena first, and subsequently try to arrange for the witness to travel to your office.

The notices must be sent to every party to the action. If the deposition is for a party, nothing else need be done, unless you also need to send a notice to produce records. If the deposition is for a nonparty, you must serve a subpoena on that witness, or a subpoena duces tecum for records, if necessary. Keep in mind that the subpoena under Rule 45(d) must be issued by the clerk of the district in which the deposition will be taken. The clerk will only issue a subpoena to a nonparty if you demonstrate that you have given notice of the deposition to all parties. Bring a duplicate or, if the clerk's office requires it, a certified copy of the notice and proof of service to the issuing clerk.

Example:

[Caption]

NOTICE OF DEPOSITION

To: *(defendant's attorney)*

Please take notice that I will take the deposition of Rudolf Watson, defendant, before a notary public, or any other authorized officer, on August 30, 1986, at 2:00 P.M., at Room 201, 400 Elm St., Chicago, Illinois, pursuant to Rule 30 of the Federal Rules of Civil Procedure. You are required to have the deponent present at that date, time, and place for oral examination.

Attorney for Plaintiff

If you wish to have the party deponent produce records, simply add, "The deponent shall produce the following documents and records," and attach a list describing the relevant documents. If the deposition is of a nonparty, the notice should have a copy of the subpoena attached if possible. It is also a good practice to send a copy of the notice to the court reporter who is scheduled to take the deposition. The subpoena for a nonparty will be on a standard form that is presigned and sealed and issued by the appropriate clerk's office. Make sure you attach a check for the necessary witness and mileage fees.[41]

After the notice and subpoena have been served, arrange for a suitable place in which to take the deposition. Make sure a court reporter is scheduled and told where and when the deposition will be held. Those who should be present include the deponent, the court reporter, the lawyers for the parties, and perhaps the parties themselves. A conference room or private office in your law office suite is usually the best place to take the deposition. You will be comfortable there and have all your files available. However, if you want to be particularly accommodating to a witness for tactical reasons, use a location convenient for the witness. If the deponent is required to produce documents and you are afraid she will not fully comply, depose her where the records are kept.

Finally, it is always a good idea to reconfirm the deposition with the parties, lawyers, witnesses, and court reporter involved. Rule 30(g) provides for costs against the deposing party where a notice to depose a witness is given, the witness is not served, and other parties and lawyers are not notified of this fact. Where a witness cannot be served and the deposition must be canceled, notify all other persons involved promptly.

f. How should I prepare for taking a deposition?

Taking a good deposition obviously requires preparation. You must collect all the documentation that has any bearing on the witness' anticipated testimony, review it, and have copies available for use during the deposition. A copy can be marked by the witness during the deposition, in which case it should be given to the court reporter to attach as an exhibit to the deposition transcript.

When you have reviewed the available material, you should begin to outline how you will take the particular deposition. This depends on several considerations: Is the deponent an adverse party, unfavorable witness, or friendly witness? What information do you need to obtain? What foundations for exhibits do you want to establish? What admissions or impeachment should you try to obtain? Are you taking the deposition only to discover information, or should you take it with an eye toward preserving the witness' testimony for possible later use? What are the risks involved in deposing this person? These considerations must be evaluated so that you have good answers to the fundamental question you must ask yourself: Why am I taking this deposition?

These considerations affect how you will take a particular deposition. Regardless of your approach, your questioning should be thorough, because a basic purpose for depositions is to find out what the deponent knows. It is usually a good practice to make an outline of your anticipated topics with suitable references to the exhibits you will want to use. While such an outline must obviously be tailored to the facts of each case, certain general topics should usually be explored. There are numerous books available that contain checklists for various types of cases and wit-

41. 28 U.S.C. §§1821 et seq.

nesses. These are useful for considering the types of topics that can be explored and the sensible order for them, but such checklists should never be a substitute for tailoring your questions to the particular deponent.

Example (preliminary matters):

(1) Background
   Name and address
   Personal and family history
   Education
   Job history
(2) Documents and records
   Notice to produce and subpoenas
   Record keeping
   Records search
   Identifying produced records
   Names and addresses of other persons and entities that may
      have records related to case
(3) Identity of party
   Officers, directors, employees, agents
   Parent corporation and subsidiaries, licensees
   Incorporation and places of business
   Residence
   Place where licensed to do business
   Names used in business
(4) Witnesses
   Names and addresses of persons witnessing events and
      transactions
   Names and addresses of persons deponent has communicated
      with
   Names and addresses of persons who may know something
      about case

These background topics should be pursued regardless of the deponent. When the deponent is a party, most of this information should already have been received in the interrogatory answers, but you should have the deponent reconfirm the information and explain them in greater detail where necessary.

Once you have organized your preliminary matters, you should outline the substantive areas, which depend on the type of case, legal and factual issues, and the witness' relationship to them. The key to the deposition here is detail. You need to make sure that the outline covers all the topics and is logically organized — usually chronologically — which helps you to be thorough and avoid mistakes. Sometimes it may be useful to vary your topics from a strictly chronological order so that the deponent cannot anticipate questions.

The deposition should extract from the witness everything the deponent knows that is pertinent to the case. Remind yourself that you usually get only one opportunity to depose a person, so you must be prepared to get the most out of that opportunity.

Example (plaintiff in personal injury case):

(1) Background questions
     (Preliminary matters as outlined above)
     Health history before accident
(2) Vehicles involved
     Make, year, registration
     Insurance
     Condition, inspection, repair records
(3) Scene of collision
     Neighborhood
     Roads
     Traffic markings and controls
(4) Weather and road conditions
(5) Events before accident
     Activities earlier in day
     Food, alcohol, drugs
     Physical condition at time
     Earlier activities
(6) Events immediately before collision
     Location and direction of vehicles
     Passengers
     Traffic conditions
     Visibility and weather conditions
     Other distractions
     Where first saw defendant's car
     Marking diagrams and photographs
(7) Collision
     Speed of cars before impact
     Traffic signals
     Braking and other conduct of plaintiff
     Braking and other conduct of defendant
     Point of impact
     Where cars ended up
     Marking diagrams and photographs
(8) Events after collision
     Bystander activities
     Police activities
     What plaintiff and defendant did
     What plaintiff and defendant said
     Plaintiff's and defendant's condition after collision
     Ambulance
(9) Medical treatment
     At hospital — diagnosis and treatment
     Doctors visits after discharge — treatments
     Medication, therapy

(10) Present physical condition
       Any physical limitations
       Medication
(11) Damages
       Vehicle
       Hospital expenses
       Doctor's bills
       Lost wages
       Insurance payments
       Other claimed losses

Example (corporate plaintiff in contract breach case):

(1) Background questions
       (Preliminary matters as outlined above)
(2) First contact with defendant
       Reasons — how came about
       Persons involved
(3) Course of dealing up to contract
       Types of business conducted
       Business practices
       Specific contracts entered into
       Performance history
(4) Negotiations leading up to contract
       Dates, times, places, participants
       All communications
(5) Contract execution
       Date, time, place, participants
(6) Conduct following execution
       Performance by each party
(7) Breach claimed
       When, what
       Witnesses
(8) Conduct following breach
       Attempts to mitigate
(9) Damages claimed
       Breach damages
       Consequential damages

Example (physician in personal injury case):

(1) Professional background
       Education
       Internship and residency
       Licenses and specialty boards
       Description of practice
       Experience in type of injury involved here
(2) Physician's medical records and reports
       Identify them

       Treatises he relies on
       Consultations
(3) First contact with plaintiff at hospital
       Where and when
       History
       Symptoms
       Examination and findings
       Tests
       Diagnosis
       Treatment
(4) Subsequent contacts with plaintiff
       Where and when
       Symptoms
       Examinations and findings
       Tests
       Prognosis
(5) Opinions and conclusions
       Extent of injuries
       Permanence of injuries
       Effect on plaintiff
       Causation
       Why physician disagrees with other experts
(6) Fees
       How much
       Future fees

g. How do I start the deposition?

If all goes well, the parties' lawyers, the court reporter, and the deponent will all appear at the designated place, date, and time. You should also consider having your client attend, since this will educate the client. This is a particularly good idea when the deponent will testify to conversations and transactions with your client, in which case the deponent is more likely to be truthful and candid when your client is listening to the testimony. After routine introductions have been made, the participants have settled down in the deposition room, and the court reporter has set up the stenographic equipment, you are ready to begin the oral deposition. Start by giving the court reporter a copy of a pleading with a complete caption; also, the reporter should be given the correct spelling for the names of all persons present. Then proceed.

First, ask the court reporter to swear in the witness, and have the transcript affirmatively show that the witness was sworn.

Second, make an introductory statement for the record that identifies whose deposition it is, the date and place, and everyone present. Also, the statement should reflect that notice was given, that the deposition is being taken under the Federal Rules of Civil Procedure, and that the witness has been sworn. In some jurisdictions this is sometimes done by the court reporter, making it unnecessary for the lawyer to do it.

Example:

> *Q.* The record should show that this is the deposition of the plain-
> tiff, Margaret Singer, being taken in the case of Margaret Singer
> v. Robert Johnson, Case No. 85C 483 in the United States Dis-
> trict Court for the Northern District of Ohio. It is being held at
> the law offices of Marlyn Anders, 200 Main Street, Suite 400,
> Cleveland, Ohio. Today's date is August 15, 1986. Present in ad-
> dition to Ms. Singer are myself, Marlyn Anders, attorney for de-
> fendant Johnson, Sharon Witts, attorney for plaintiff Singer,
> and Darlene Winters, a certified court reporter and notary pub-
> lic. Mrs. Singer, you were just sworn to tell the truth by the court
> reporter, correct?
>
> *A.* That's right.

When the deponent is a party, he will usually have been prepared
for the deposition, will know what to expect, and will be familiar with the
procedure. When the deponent is a nonparty, however, this may not be
the case, and it is sometimes worthwhile, if you want this particular witness to be relaxed and comfortable, to explain the deposition procedure
and its importance. This prevents a witness from later claiming, if im-
peached from the transcript, that he was confused or was being pressed
by the lawyer.

Example:

> *Q.* Mr. Johnson, have you ever attended a deposition before?
> *A.* No.
> *Q.* Do you know how a deposition works?
> *A.* Not really.
> *Q.* Mr. Johnson, I'm going to ask you questions about this accident,
> and you'll have to answer them under oath. The other lawyers
> can also ask questions if they want to. Afterward the court re-
> porter will type up everything said here today. If you want to,
> you can review the transcript to check if it is accurate and make
> any corrections before signing it. Do you understand?
> *A.* Yes.
> *Q.* It's important that you understand the questions and give accu-
> rate answers. If there's anything you don't understand, or any-
> thing you don't know or aren't sure of, you let us know, all
> right?
> *A.* Yes.

Where the deponent is a party that has also been served with a request to produce, or the deponent is a witness that has been served with a
subpoena duces tecum, have the deponent produce the records or documents on the record, even if he voluntarily sent them to you in advance.
Identify them for the record, make copies of them and give the court
reporter a copy to attach to the transcript, and mark them as exhibits.

Example:

Q. Ms. Jones, you received a subpoena for certain records of your company along with the subpoena to appear, correct?
A. Yes.
Q. Did you comply and bring the records?
A. Yes.
Q. May I see them? (Lawyer obtains them from witness.) For the record, the witness has handed me photocopies totaling five pages. I'll mark them Deposition Exhibit A. Page one is an invoice, page two a bill of lading, page three is a shipping notice, and pages four and five are account ledgers. Each page bears the name of ABC Shipping Company. Ms. Jones, does that accurately describe these five pages?
A. Yes.
Q. These are all business records of ABC Shipping?
A. Yes.
Q. Did you search the company records for all records relating to the transaction described on the subpoena served on you?
A. Yes.
Q. These five pages are the only ones that exist?
A. Yes.
Q. Other than these records, does your company make other records for a transaction of this kind?
A. No.

If you anticipate the need to introduce the records in evidence at trial, it is always a good procedure to qualify the witness as a "custodian or other qualified witness" and establish a business records foundation under Rule 803(6) of the Federal Rules of Evidence. If the witness is a party of agent of the party, the testimony will qualify as an admission; if a nonparty, the testimony should qualify as former testimony if the witness is unavailable at trial.

Finally, good practice requires that you put any stipulations on the record and state expressly what they are. Parties frequently deal with the status of objections, sometimes stipulating that all objections are preserved or that all objections are preserved except those directed to the form of the question. This can be useful because it eliminates the need to make most objections during the deposition, allowing for a much clearer and shorter transcript. Objections can then be raised later if the transcript will be used during trial.

h. What questioning styles should I use?

The questioning style you employ during the deposition must be consistent with your purpose. Are you taking the deposition primarily to gather information from a witness? Are you taking a party's deposition to pin the party down on details, to obtain admissions, and to develop impeachment? Are you deposing a favorable witness to preserve the witness' testimony in the event he becomes unavailable for trial? The different purposes will affect how you conduct the deposition.[42]

Regardless of your purposes, you should always keep two concerns uppermost in your mind: Have I clearly and unambiguously stated questions and received answers? How will this sound if it is read to a jury during trial?

i. Getting information

When your principal goal during the deposition is to gather information, it is frequently a good approach to let the witness ramble on rather than control the witness with narrow, focused questions. You are more likely to have the witness volunteer useful information if you ask broad questions in a friendly, informal way. You can always steer the witness to the topics that need to be covered and use follow-up questions to tie down the details. Whether the questions and answers violate evidentiary rules, such as leading or hearsay, is unimportant, if your only goal is to get information.

ii. Eliciting detail and pinning down specific facts

When deposing an adverse party, you usually have dual purposes: finding out what the party knows in detail, and pinning the party down to specific, hopefully harmful, facts. Ask open, nonleading questions to try to get the deponent to talk and to fully detail what he knows. If the opposing lawyer has done his homework, of course, the party will be loathe to volunteer information not specifically asked for. However, it is always good to use this approach since even a well-prepared party may sometimes divulge something you would never have uncovered.

The second purpose, pinning the party down, is usually accomplished by using leading, focused, cross-examination type questions. One of the most common mistakes is to let the witness give ambiguous or qualified answers that do not make for effective impeachment at trial. If the party hedges, ask follow-up questions that pin him down. If the party refuses, try to get him to admit that he is only "guessing," "approximating," or that he simply "doesn't know." Parties have a predictable talent for improving their recall of facts and details at trial. Therefore, getting an "I don't know" or an "I can only approximate" response can be useful for impeachment purposes if the party at trial claims to know specifically.

iii. Preserving testimony

When deposing someone to preserve testimony, your principal concern is to create clear, progressive testimony that will not run afoul of evidentiary rules. Keep in mind that, absent any contrary stipulations,

---

42. The actual questioning techniques for examining a deponent are much the same, and as varied, as conducting direct and cross-examinations of witnesses at trial. For a discussion of these techniques, see, e.g., P. Bergman, Trial Advocacy in a Nutshell (1979); K. Hegland, Trial and Practice Skills (1978); J. Jeans, Handbook on Trial Advocacy (2d ed. 1975); and T. Mauet, Fundamentals of Trial Techniques (2d ed. 1988).

Rule 32(d) preserves all objections to questions and answers except those directed to form or others that could have been cured had they been made promptly. Therefore, unless the witness is an adverse party or witness, use nonleading questions. Avoid objectionable forms of questions, such as those that can be considered leading, compound, argumentative, speculative, ambiguous, or narrative. Don't ask questions that call for hearsay or improper opinions.

Deposition purposes, of course, do not always separate out with such clear definition. For example, even when you are deposing a witness and are trying to pin the witness down with leading questions, you may want to use that witness to establish the foundations for records, documents, and other exhibits for possible use at trial.[43]

Some lawyers, at the end of a deposition, ask the deponent if he would like to correct anything he has said, or whether he has any additional information pertinent to the case that he has not been asked about. If the witness answers no, you can use this answer to impeach him at trial if he testifies inconsistently or testifies to new facts not previously disclosed, suggesting to the jury that the new or different testimony is a recent creation.

i.   How should I handle objections?

When you are taking depositions, there are three basic types of objections.

First, an objection can be made to the form of the questions or answers; however, Rule 32(d) requires that unless an objection is made promptly, it is waived. Even after a timely objection is made, the witness must still answer the question "subject to the objection." If you are taking the deposition only to gather information, you can safely ignore the objection. If you may use the transcript later at trial, however, determine if the objection has possible validity. If it does, rephrase the question properly to overcome the objection. Remember that you can never be totally sure that you will not need to use the transcript during trial.

Second, an objection can be made on evidentiary grounds other than privilege. However, since it is not necessary to object if the grounds are relevance, hearsay, or if the objection is not based on form, the other parties can reserve objections until such time as the deposition is used at trial. That is, if such an objection is not made at the deposition, it can be made at trial — and this is the customary procedure. If made at the deposition, the deponent must still answer. Again, however, if you plan to use the deposition at trial, and an objection is made, you should rephrase the question to eliminate the problem.

Third, an objection can be made on the grounds of privilege or harassment. If made on privilege grounds, the witness will probably refuse to answer, since the witness' lawyer will direct the witness not to answer

43. See T. Mauet, Fundamentals of Trial Techniques ch. 5 (2d ed. 1988) on establishing foundations for various types of exhibits.

the question.[44] If on harassment grounds, an objection can be made along with a demand under Rule 30(d) that the deposition be suspended in order to make a motion to limit or terminate the deposition. When objections are made on privilege or harassment grounds, the witness will probably refuse to answer, leaving you, the lawyer taking the deposition, with two options. First, you can terminate the examination and move to compel answers. Second, you can ask other questions not objected to and finish the examination to the extent possible.

Regardless of how you react to the witness' refusal, you must decide whether to seek an order compelling an answer. You can discuss the legal issue with the lawyer making the objection to learn the reason for it, and then either rephrase the question or ask the lawyer to withdraw the objection. If the witness persists in refusing to answer, the information you seek is important, and you wish to force the issue, you must make a clear record. The question, the witness' refusal to answer, and the grounds for the refusal should be clearly spelled out, since the court reporter must provide a transcript of that portion of the deposition that you will attach to your motion to compel discovery.[45]

Example:

Q. Mr. Jones, you were the maintenance man at XYZ Leasing during this time, correct?

A. Yes.

Q. You talked to people about the problem, didn't you?

A. Yes.

Q. That included the company lawyer, Mr. Johnson?

A. Yes.

Q. Tell us what you told Mr. Johnson about the problem.

Jones' lawyer: Objection. Mr. Jones, don't answer that question. That question calls for the disclosure of attorney-client communications, which are privileged.

Q. Mr. Jones, do you refuse to answer the question?

A. Yes.

Q. Your refusal is based on your assertion of the attorney-client privilege?

A. Yes.

In this way you will have made a clear record of the witness' refusal to answer and the reason for it. Ask the court reporter to mark this part of the deposition and transcribe it later so you can attach it to your motion to compel.

Finally, it is an unfortunate fact in litigation that some lawyers misuse objections to coach the deponent into making more desirable responses.

44. See discussion in §6.2.

45. Asking the court reporter to "certify the question," while not necessary to raise the matter in a motion to compel answers, lets the court reporter know that this question should be on a list of questions the witness refused to answer that will be appended to the end of the deposition transcript. This is a common practice in state courts.

Where this repeatedly occurs, you should note your objection to the opposing lawyer and make sure the court reporter records it. If this conduct persists, you may want to terminate the deposition and bring the matter to the court through a motion to compel discovery or for sanctions. If past experience with a particular lawyer suggests this may happen, it may be effective to take a video deposition, because it will graphically capture the lawyer's conduct and sometimes will even act as a deterrent to such conduct. The videotape will show the misconduct more vividly than a written transcript, particularly when the lawyer is improperly harassing the witness.

j. How should I prepare and represent a deponent?

When you receive a notice for deposition of your client, preparing the client for the upcoming deposition may well be the most important single event in the litigation process. The opposing lawyers will use the deposition to determine what your client knows, develop admissions and impeachment, pin your client down to details about what he does or does not know, and generally size up your client as a trial witness. If the deposition goes well, the settlement value of the case will rise as well. Hence, preparation for the deposition is critical.

Shortly before the deposition date, have your client come to your office with enough time allocated to prepare him thoroughly. Scheduling this for the early afternoon, as the last appointment for the day, is a good idea since you will not be rushed by other appointments. On the other hand, some lawyers prefer to schedule such interviews in the morning, when they and the clients are fresh.

First, have the pleadings, discovery, documents, records, reports, photographs, diagrams, and sketches available for the client to review. However, show the client only his statements, not those of others. Showing your client other persons' statements will always create the impression, particularly at trial, that your client has tailored his testimony to be consistent with other witnesses, or has used the other statements to acquire information he himself does not personally have. This may also make such statements disclosable at trial, since under FRE 612 an adverse party may be able to obtain any documents used to refresh the witness' recollection, even if used before trial; the party may be able to use them during the witness' cross-examination and to introduce in evidence relevant portions of the documents. It is usually better to avoid this problem by not showing your client other witnesses' statements. You can always refer to reports and statements of other witnesses and still deal with any inconsistencies.

Second, review what a deposition is, what its purpose is, why it is so critical, and what the procedure will be. Explain to the client that once the deposition begins, you will be relatively inactive, except to make objections to preserve error when necessary, or to instruct him not to answer if critical to do so. Make sure the client knows to dress appropriately for his background. There are commercial videotapes on deposition preparation available, and some are very useful to show what actually goes on during a deposition.

Third, review how your client should answer questions accurately. Impress upon him that even though the atmosphere will probably be informal, he must answer carefully. Standard advice includes the following:

  (i)   Make sure you understand the question. If you don't, say so and ask that the question be rephrased.
 (ii)   If you know the answer, give it. If you don't know, say so. If you know but can't remember just then, say so. If you can only estimate or approximate, say so. However, give positive, assertive answers whenever possible.
(iii)   Don't volunteer information. Answer only what the question specifically calls for. Don't exaggerate or speculate. Give the best short, accurate, truthful answer possible.
 (iv)   Answer questions only with what you personally know, saw, heard, or did, unless the question asks otherwise.
  (v)   Be calm at all times. Avoid arguing with the lawyers or getting upset over the questions. I will be there to protect you from unfair questions and procedures by making objections and instructing you on what to do and say.

Fourth, discuss how objections will be handled. Explain that many objections are made "for the record," and that usually the witness must answer despite the objection, which is made for possible later use at trial. However, be sure the client knows not to answer when an objection is made and you tell the client not to answer. This will be the case if the objection is based on privilege or harassment grounds, where answering the question may waive any error.

Fifth, review with the client what questions the lawyers are likely to ask. This involves creating a short outline as discussed previously. Make sure that the client can accurately respond to those expected questions in a positive, convincing manner whenever possible. Let the client know that other lawyers present may ask additional questions, but that you will probably not ask questions unless necessary to correct a mistake or clarify something ambiguous.

Finally, explain that the client has a right to review the deposition if it is transcribed, noting any corrections and the reasons for them, and to sign it. Explain why that right should not be waived, stressing the importance of correcting any errors in the transcript.

§6.7. *Physical and mental examinations*

In some cases, primarily personal injury cases, the physical and mental condition of a party is a critical fact affecting both liability and damages. Under those circumstances, that party should be examined to evaluate the genuineness of the condition, its extent and causes, and to develop a prognosis. Rule 35 governs this process.

1. Law[46]

Rule 35 applies to physical and mental examinations of a party and of a "person in the custody or under the legal control of a party." The Rule clearly applies to minors and other legally incapacitated persons who are not the actual named parties, but are the real parties in interest.

A court order is required for such examinations, unless the person to be examined voluntarily agrees to the examination, which is permitted under Rule 29 so long as there is a written stipulation. In other situations you must move for a court order and give notice to the person and all parties. For the court to order an examination, the physical or mental condition of a party or related person must be "in controversy," and you must show "good cause" for requesting it.

The good-cause requirement has sometimes caused difficulty. In most cases, however, typically personal injury cases or paternity cases where the physical condition of a party is important, there are few problems and the parties often informally arrange for the necessary examinations. In these types of cases the need for the examinations is apparent from the pleadings. However, issues such as testimonial competency will not be apparent from the pleadings; therefore, the moving party must make a sufficient showing of need in the motion to satisfy the good cause requirement.[47]

The court's order must specify the date, time, place, manner, conditions, and scope of the examination, as well as the person or persons who will perform it. The scope of the examination is determined by the nature of the claims, defenses, and facts and issues in controversy. However, Rule 35 is silent on who should perform the examination. In practice the moving party usually suggests a physician and the court ordinarily approves the selection unless another party, or the person to be examined, has a serious objection. The court has discretion to approve or disapprove, and some districts have local rules that provide for the selection of "impartial experts" from approved lists.[48]

The party moving for the examination must, upon request by the examined party, deliver a detailed written report of the examining physician setting out findings, results of tests, diagnoses, and conclusions, as well as reports of all earlier examinations for the same conditions. The party moving for the examination can then, upon request, get any previous or future reports about the same person for the same condition, un-

46. Wright §88; James & Hazard §5.6; Friedenthal §7.12; Moore's Manual §15.11; Shepard's Manual §§5.195-5.198; Moore's Federal Practice §§35.01-35.07; Wright & Miller §§2231-2239.

47. Moore's Manual §15.11; Shepard's Manual §5.196; Moore's Federal Practice §35.03(5); Wright & Miller §§2232, 2234.

48. Note that FRE 706 also gives the court authority to appoint and compensate experts.

less, where a nonparty is examined, the party shows he cannot obtain the report. This procedure essentially provides for reciprocal discovery when one side requests a report from the examining physician. When the party examined requests a copy of the report of the physician who examined him, this operates as a waiver of the doctor-patient privilege not only as to that physician, but also as to any other physician who has or may later examine him as to the same conditions.

These disclosure requirements and waiver effects apply regardless of whether the examinations are made pursuant to a court order or through agreement of the parties, unless that agreement expressly provides otherwise. In addition, the discovery permitted under Rule 35 does not restrict other permissible discovery. However, Rule 35 is the only rule that can compel discovery where otherwise the doctor-patient privilege would prevent disclosure.

2.   Practice approach

Since the situations in which physical and mental examinations can be compelled are usually obvious, these examinations are frequently arranged informally between the parties. Even where there is an informal agreement, however, it is always a good idea to put it in a letter or, even better, in a stipulation under Rule 29 that is then filed with the court.

Where an arrangement cannot be worked out, you must move for a court order compelling the desired examination. To comply with Rule 35, the motion must (1) ask for the examination of a party or a person in the custody or control of the party, (2) allege a genuine controversy about that person's physical or mental condition, (3) demonstrate good cause for the examination, (4) request the date, time, place, manner, conditions, and scope of the examination, and (5) designate the physician who should conduct it.

Example:

[Caption]

MOTION FOR ORDER COMPELLING PLAINTIFF'S PHYSICAL EXAMINATION

Defendant moves under Rule 35 of the Federal Rules of Civil Procedure for an order compelling plaintiff to submit to a physical examination. In support of her motion defendant states:

1. Plaintiff's physical condition is genuinely in controversy, since plaintiff's complaint on its face alleges that "as a result of this collision, plaintiff has suffered severe and permanent injuries to his back and legs."

2. Since plaintiff alleges that his physical limitations are compensable, there exists good cause for a physical examination to evaluate the

plaintiff's current physical condition, physical limitations, and prognosis.

3. William B. Rudolf, M.D., a board certified orthopedic surgeon, has agreed to examine the plaintiff at his offices at 200 Main Street, Suite 301, Washington, D.C., on August 15, 1985, at 4:00 P.M., or at another time if directed by this court.

WHEREFORE, defendant requests that this court enter an order directing the plaintiff to be examined on the terms set forth above.

_____

Attorney for Defendant

If the court grants the motion, an order must be entered. In federal courts the practice is for the court clerk to prepare orders, which the judge then signs. Where permitted, however, it is always a useful approach to draft an appropriate order in situations where a nonparty, here the physician, is involved because the physician will want a copy of the order before conducting the examination.

Example:

[Caption]

<u>ORDER</u>

This matter being heard on defendant's motion to compel the physical examination of plaintiff, all parties having been given notice, and the court having heard arguments, it is hereby ordered that:

1. Plaintiff John Williams be examined by William B. Rudolf, M.D., at 200 Main Street, Suite 301, Washington, D.C., on August 15, 1985, at 4:00 P.M., unless the plaintiff and Dr. Rudolf mutually agree to an earlier date and time.

2. Plaintiff shall submit to such orthopedic examinations and tests as are necessary to diagnose and evaluate the plaintiff's back and legs, so that Dr. Rudolf may reach opinions and conclusions about the extent of any injuries, their origin, and prognosis.

3. Dr. Rudolf shall prepare a written report detailing his findings, test results, diagnosis and opinions, along with any earlier similar reports on the same conditions, and deliver it to defendant's attorneys on or before September 15, 1985.

Entered:

Dated: _____   _____

United States District Judge

Finally, keep in mind the reciprocal discovery provisions of Rule 35(b)(1). If the examined party requests a copy of the doctor's report, the party moving for the examination has the right to receive from the examined party other reports dealing with the same conditions, regardless of when made; however, you must request those reports. Perhaps the safer approach is to send that party a document entitled "<u>REQUEST FOR MEDICAL REPORTS</u>," show that it is made under the provisions of Rule 35(b)(1), and file the request with the court. If the other party fails to deliver, or later attempts to use such reports, you have made a record of your request and can object to the introduction of those reports at trial because the party did not comply with Rule 35.

§6.8. Requests to admit facts

A request to admit facts and the genuineness of documents is the fifth method of discovery permitted under the federal rules, and is usually the last employed during the litigation process, although it is frequently coupled with interrogatories as a device to get a prompt answer. Its purposes are to sharpen trial issues, streamline trials, and eliminate the need to formally prove controverted facts.

1. Law[49]

Requests to admit facts and the genuineness of documents, governed by Rule 36, apply only to parties. Admissions made in response to the requests are admissions for the purposes of the pending action only and cannot be used for any other purposes. This encourages a party to admit facts without worrying about collateral consequences.

Requests may be served on other parties at any time after service of the summons or complaint on that party or, as to the plaintiff, after commencement of the action. Like other discovery provisions, requests can be employed essentially at any time during the litigation process.

A request can be directed to three categories: the truth of facts, the genuineness of documents, and the "application of law to fact." The general scope of these requests is the same as for discovery in general; they apply to anything that is relevant but not privileged. Each request must be separately stated.

After a request has been served on a party, that party must serve a response within 30 days or the matters requested will be deemed admitted. This automatic provision of Rule 36 makes it a formidable weapon because inertia or inattentiveness can have an automatic, and usually devastating, consequence. Hence, there is one cardinal rule for practice

49. Wright §89; James & Hazard §5.7; Friedenthal §7.10; Moore's Manual §15.12; Shepard's Manual §§5.199-5.215; Moore's Federal Practice §§36.01-36.08; Wright & Miller §§2251-2265.

under this provision: Make sure you respond and serve the response within the 30-day period.

There are four basic responses permitted. First, you can object to a matter in the request, in which case you must state the reasons for the objection. Second, you can admit the matter; if admitted, the matter is deemed conclusively established, unless the court allows withdrawal or amendment in accordance with Rule 16. Third, you can deny the matter. Fourth, you can neither admit nor deny because the matter is genuinely in dispute, or because after reasonable inquiry you do not have sufficient information to determine if the matter is true or not, setting forth the reasons.

How you respond, and whether your response is justified under the circumstances, determines whether Rule 37 sanctions can be imposed. Rule 37(c) usually provides that the expenses — including attorney's fees — incurred in proving a denied matter can be taxed as costs against the losing party. However, if you neither admit nor deny on the basis of there being a genuine issue for trial, or because of genuine insufficient knowledge, Rule 37 sanctions cannot be imposed.[50]

Once a response has been received, you can move the court to review the adequacy of the objections and responses. The Rule requires that a response must specifically deny the matter or set forth in detail why the answering party cannot admit or deny after making a reasonable inquiry. A denial must fairly meet the substance of the requested admission. The better practice is to make a motion to determine the sufficiency of an answer and see if the court will deem the matter admitted. This will avoid surprises at trial. The court can enter an order compelling an answer or amended answer if appropriate, order that the matter be deemed admitted, or continue the motion to the pretrial conference or to another date.

2. Practice approach

Since the scope of Rule 36 is so broad, using and responding to requests to admit are principally tactical concerns that must be part of your overall discovery strategy. Requests for admissions are best seen not as a method for getting additional facts, but as a technique for eliminating the need for formal proof and for determining what facts opposing parties intend to contest at trial.

a. Timing

Rule 36 permits requests to admit at practically any time, so the decision on when to use it is controlled by practical considerations. Frequently, however, the requests are used at the end of the discovery stage. When you have received interrogatory answers and records pursuant to document requests, have deposed the parties and necessary witnesses,

50. See Wright §90; Moore's Manual §15.13; Shepard's Manual §5.229; Moore's Federal Practice §§36.03(7), 36.07; Wright & Miller §§2265, 2288, 2290.

and, where appropriate, have completed physical and mental examinations, discovery is essentially complete. Requests for admissions are most commonly served at this point because the existing discovery will identify what still remains in issue. The requests should focus on the remaining facts still in issue and be served after other discovery has been completed but before the pretrial conference is scheduled or summary judgment motions are made. Requests to admit served at that time will help determine what facts the other side will concede, or contest if the case goes to trial.

Another approach is to serve requests to admit early in the discovery process, sometimes coupled with interrogatories and documents requests, to bring the potential Rule 37 sanctions into play. This forces your opponent to decide what facts and issues she intends to dispute and allows later discovery to become more focused. If a party denies a fact in a request to admit, without a substantial basis for the denial, and that fact is later proved at trial, the party proving the fact can receive as court costs the reasonable expense of proving the denied fact at trial, including attorney's fees. By making requests to admit early, you start the period for which you may be entitled to get Rule 37 costs. Where you think the opposing party will use dilatory tactics or avoid serious settlement discussions on a case that should be settled quickly, making a request to admit early raises the risks for the party using those tactics. This can be quite effective in forcing your opponent to admit facts.

b. What to request

To determine what to request, look first at the elements of your claims. Second, analyze each "fact" you will need to prove to meet your burden of proof at trial on each element. This is what every trial lawyer must do in preparing for trial. Once this is accomplished, you can organize those "facts" into the three categories permitted under Rule 36: (1) genuineness of documents, (2) truth of facts, and (3) application of law to facts. Third, review the pleadings, to see what has been admitted, and your discovery results, to see what facts are conceded. Reviewing the discovery is particularly critical, since a fact, when conceded in interrogatory answers or by a party deposition, is only an admission by a party opponent, which is *not* the same thing as a conclusive admission. The party admitting a fact can still present contrary evidence at trial. To avoid this, focus on matters opposing parties have admitted in previous discovery. Those parties are likely to admit the facts in a request to admit if they have previously admitted them. The advantage is that when a matter is admitted under Rule 36, it is deemed conclusively established for purposes of that pending action, unless the court permits amendment or withdrawal.

c. Drafting the requests

The cardinal rule for the drafting of requests for admissions is to keep it simple. A lengthy, complicated request practically begs to be denied, objected to, or responded to with a lengthy, equivocal response. This will merely generate further motions and probably achieve nothing.

Simplicity requires that a request be short and contain a single statement of fact. Such requests are difficult to quibble with, and they stand the best chance of being admitted outright. They should also comply with admissibility rules such as those concerning relevance and hearsay.

Example (documents):

[Caption]

REQUESTS TO ADMIT FACTS
AND GENUINENESS OF DOCUMENTS

Plaintiff Ralph Johnson requests defendant Marian Smith to make the following admissions, within 30 days after service of this request, for the purposes of this action only:

That each of the following documents is genuine:

1. A contract, attached as Exhibit A, is a true and accurate copy of the contract signed by plaintiff and defendant on August 1, 1984.

Example (facts):

That each of the following facts is true:

1. The signature on the contract, attached as Exhibit A, purporting to be that of the defendant, is in fact that of the defendant.

2. The defendant signed the original of Exhibit A.

3. Defendant signed the original of Exhibit A on August 1, 1984.

Requests to admit can also ask for "opinions of fact" and the "application of law to fact." This is a problematic area since questions of "pure law" cannot be asked. For instance, a request that asks a party to admit negligence or culpability is objectionable. Where the line is between "opinions of fact" and "application of law to fact," as against "pure law" remains unclear.[51] Regardless of where that line is, treading close to it will probably draw objections. Accordingly, it is usually better to be on the safe side and leave the legal disputes for resolution at trial. Common situations where the application of law to fact is raised are issues of title, ownership, agency, and employment.

Example (application of law to fact):

That each of the following statements is true:

1. Defendant was the legal titleholder of a lot commonly known as 3401 Fifth Street, Tucson, Arizona, on August 1, 1984.

---

51. See Wright §89; Moore's Manual §15.12; Moore's Federal Practice §36.04(4); Wright & Miller §§2255, 2256.

2. On August 1, 1984, William Oats was an employee of XYZ Corporation.

3. On August 1, 1984, William Oats was authorized to enter into sales contracts on behalf of XYZ Corporation.

The requests to admit should be signed by the lawyer, served on each party, and filed with the court. Service is made by any permitted method under Rule 5, most commonly by mailing a copy to the lawyers of the other parties. The original requests to admit, with an attached proof of service statement, is then filed with the clerk of the court.

d. Choosing a response

A party on whom requests to admit have been served must respond, usually within 30 days of receiving the requests, or else the matters in the requests will automatically be deemed admitted. There are four basic responses to a request.

First, you can object to the request. As with discovery generally, you can object that the matter requested is irrelevant or privileged. In addition, you can object and seek a protective order if the request is unduly burdensome or harassing.

Second, you can admit the request. When you do so, you conclusively admit the matter for the purpose of the pending action only. Such an admission prevents you from presenting contrary evidence at trial.

Third, you can deny the request. The denial must be based on good faith. If the requesting party later proves the denied matter at trial, under Rule 37 that party may get expenses, including attorney's fees, involved in proving the matter. The response can, of course, admit to some parts of a request and deny others.

Fourth, under certain circumstances you can neither admit nor deny. This is allowed if the answering party has made a "reasonable inquiry" in an effort to acquire necessary information for responding to the request but is still unable to respond. In addition, if the answering party considers the requested matter to be a genuine trial issue, it can either deny or set forth reasons for neither admitting nor denying.

When you have decided what the appropriate response should be, actually drafting the response is very similar to drafting answers to complaints. However, the better format is that used for interrogatory answers, where the answers and interrogatories both appear together.

Example:

[Caption]

RESPONSE TO REQUESTS FOR ADMISSIONS

Defendant Marian Smith responds to plaintiff Ralph Johnson's requests for admissions as follows:

Request No. 1: A contract, attached as Exhibit A, is a true and accurate copy of the contract signed by plaintiff on August 1, 1984.

Answer: Admit.

Request No. 2: Plaintiff performed all his obligations under the contract.

Answer: Deny.

Request No. 3: On August 1, 1984, William Oats was authorized to enter into sales contracts on behalf of XYZ Corporation.

Answer: Objection. Responding to this request would disclose the substance of conversations between William Oats, an attorney, and the XYZ Corporation, which are protected from disclosure by the attorney-client privilege.

Request No. 4: Mary Doyle was the sole titleholder of a lot commonly known as 3401 Fifth Street, Seattle, Washington.

Answer: Defendant can neither admit nor deny this request. Public records neither confirm nor deny, and defendant has no access to any documents that could confirm or deny it.

The response to requests to admit should be signed by the party's lawyer, served on each party, and filed with the court. Service is made by any permitted method under Rule 5, most commonly by mailing a copy to the lawyers for the other parties. The original response, with an attached proof of service statement, is then filed with the clerk of the court.

e. Requestor's responses

When a party has made and served responses to requests for admissions on the requesting party, the requesting party can do two things: move to review the sufficiency of an answer; second, move to review the propriety of an objection. Both of these are directed to the court's discretion. The court can enter any appropriate order, such as deeming a matter admitted, requiring an amended answer, or continuing the issue to the pretrial conference or other time.

§6.9. Discovery motions

Discovery under the federal rules is largely executed without judicial intervention. Except for physical and mental examinations and depositions of experts, discovery can be conducted without prior court approval. Only when there is a dispute over discovery need the courts become involved.

Three points should be remembered. First, many districts have local rules that require the moving party's lawyer to certify what good faith efforts have been made to resolve a dispute before the courts will intervene. While such efforts should be made in any event, those districts with such a rule require that an appropriate certification be signed by the attorney and attached to the motion. Second, discovery abuse has probably been the subject of more controversy and proposals than any other aspect of the litigation process. Courts have responded to the problem by becoming more involved in discovery, particularly by having discovery plan conferences and by dealing more actively with abuses and imposing stiffer sanctions. Third, recent amendments to Rule 26 give courts additional powers to regulate discovery. Rule 26(b)(1) gives courts the power to limit discovery where it is unnecessarily cumulative or duplicative, or is obtainable from other sources with less effort and expense. Rule 26(f) gives courts power to hold discovery conferences and impose a discovery plan. Rule 26(g) parallels the Rule 11 requirements that the lawyer's signature is a certification that he has read the discovery document; has made a reasonable inquiry; and that the document is consistent with the rules and law, is not made for any improper purpose, and is not unreasonably burdensome or expensive. In today's climate, abusing discovery by filing frivolous, needless, or unduly burdensome discovery requests, responses, or motions often results in severe sanctions.

There are two principal types of discovery motions, those for protective orders and those for orders compelling discovery.

1.   Protective orders[52]

Rule 26(c) and, in the case of oral depositions, Rule 30(d) govern protective orders. Whenever an entity or person from whom discovery is sought feels that it is being subjected to annoying, embarrassing, oppressive, unduly burdensome, or unduly expensive discovery demands, the appropriate procedure is to move for a protective order. Both parties and nonparty deponents can seek protective orders.

The motion must usually be brought in the district where the action is pending. However, where a deposition has been terminated so that a protective order can be obtained, the proper jurisdiction under Rule 30(d) is either the district where the action is pending or the district where the deposition is being taken. The latter may well be proper where a nonparty deponent is seeking the protective order, since the deposition is usually taken where the deponent resides or does business.

The moving party must show "good cause." While grounds for protection are obviously numerous, the most common grounds are that the discovery requested is so lengthy and detailed that it is unduly oppressive and expensive; for example, discovery involving lengthy or repetitive in-

52. Wright §83; James & Hazard §5.13; Friedenthal §7.15; Moore's Manual §15.02(1)(d); Shepard's Manual §§5.94-5.105; Moore's Federal Practice §§26.67-26.79; Wright & Miller §§2035-2044.

terrogatories and depositions, and overly detailed documents requests and requests to admit. Another common ground is the serving of notice for depositions on high corporate officers who have no firsthand knowledge of any relevant facts. If the dominant purpose of the discovery is not to develop information reasonably necessary to prepare for trial or settlement, but to spend the opposition into submission, Rule 26(b)(1) is violated and the protective order is appropriate. Other motions frequently seek to limit disclosure, such as restricting persons present at depositions and preventing the disclosure of business secrets to persons outside the litigation.

Keep in mind that many discovery matters come up by motions to compel after a party has objected to discovery requests. Objections are permitted in answers to interrogatories, document requests, and requests to admit. In these circumstances the objection protects the responding party. The requesting party must move for an order compelling discovery, and there is no need for the responding party to move for a protective order.

If a protective order is appropriate, Rule 26(c) provides a variety of remedies that can protect a party or person from embarrassment, oppression, and undue burden or expense. These include barring the requested discovery; regulating the terms, conditions, methods and scope of discovery; limiting persons present at the discovery; requiring the sealing of depositions and documents; and regulating or barring disclosure of trade secrets and confidential information.

The motion for a protective order must be prepared like any other motion, and must include statements of the facts as well as a request for the relief sought.

Example:

[Caption]

MOTION FOR PROTECTIVE ORDER

Plaintiff Willard Johnson requests that this court enter a protective order pursuant to Rule 26(c) against defendant Clark Johnson, and in support of his motion states:

1. On August 8, 1985, defendant took plaintiff's first deposition. This deposition took approximately four hours and generated a transcript of 238 pages. The transcript has been filed with the clerk of this court.

2. On April 15, 1986, defendant again took plaintiff's deposition. This deposition took approximately three hours and generated a transcript of 181 pages. This transcript has also been filed with the clerk of this court.

3. On July 2, 1986, plaintiff was served with another notice of deposition. On that date the undersigned counsel called defendant's counsel and asked why a third deposition was necessary. The only offered

explanation was that counsel "wanted to make sure he'd covered all the bases."

4. This pending action involves a simple intersection collision. The two previous depositions have exhaustively covered what plaintiff knows about the collision, what happened afterwards, his medical treatment, and all claimed damages.

5. The notice for a third deposition, under these circumstances, constitutes an attempt to annoy, oppress, and place undue burdens on the plaintiff, and has no proper purpose. Since plaintiff lives out of state, another deposition will again impose significant financial and time expenses.

WHEREFORE, plaintiff Willard Johnson requests that this court enter a protective order barring defendant Clark Johnson from taking further depositions of the plaintiff or, in the alternative, restricting this deposition to such matters as counsel can demonstrate are relevant and were not inquired into at the previous depositions.

_____

Attorney for Plaintiff

Example:

[Caption]

MOTION FOR PROTECTIVE ORDER

Plaintiff Nancy Jones moves, pursuant to Rule 26(c), for a protective order against defendant XYZ Corporation, and in support of the motion states:

1. The pending case is a product liability case involving a rubber hose manufactured by defendant XYZ.

2. Plaintiff has previously served a motion to produce the rubber hose involved for the purposes of inspection and testing. Defendant's response stated that the rubber hose has already been shipped to ABC Laboratories for testing.

3. There is a substantial danger that any testing by ABC Laboratories will alter or destroy the rubber hose and forever prevent plaintiff from inspecting and testing it.

WHEREFORE, plaintiff requests this court to enter a protective order against defendant as follows:

(a) prevent anything from being done with or to the rubber hose until plaintiff has had a reasonable opportunity to inspect and photograph it;

(b) prevent any tests that would destroy or affect the appearance and integrity of the rubber hose;

(c) if destructive testing is necessary, order that such testing be conducted at a time and place so that plaintiff's experts can be present and participate;

(d) award payment of reasonable expenses, including attorney's fees, to plaintiff incurred as a result of making this motion.

Attorney for Plaintiff

After the motion is prepared and signed, a copy along with a notice of motion must be served on every other party under Rule 5. The original of the motion and notice of motion, with a proof of service, must be filed with the clerk of the court. Keep in mind that many federal judges delegate discovery matters to magistrates, so make sure your notice of motion correctly specifies who will hear the motion.

2. Compelling discovery[53]

Rule 37(a) governs motions for orders compelling discovery. A party seeking to compel discovery must move for an appropriate order in the district where the action is pending, except if the matters relate to a deposition, in which case the motion must be brought in the district where the deposition is being held.

Many local rules require good faith attempts to resolve discovery disputes. When such a rule exists, the attorney for the moving party must attach a certification to the motion showing what steps were taken to resolve the dispute.

A party can move for an order compelling discovery whenever a party fails to answer or gives evasive or incomplete answers to proper discovery. Frequently the issue arises when a party responds by objecting to an interrogatory, request to produce, or request to admit. A motion to compel must then be made to determine whether the objection is proper. The issue also frequently arises when a party fails to answer interrogatories, produce documents after being served with a request to produce, refuses to designate a deponent on behalf of a corporate party, or, in the case of deponents, refuses to appear, be sworn, or answer questions.

Under Rule 37(a)(4), the court has authority to award reasonable expenses, including attorney's fees, to the prevailing party. Therefore, be sure that your motion to compel has merit and stands a good chance of being granted, in whole or in part, before serving it.

The most common motions to compel usually involve either a party's failure to respond to discovery at all, or responding with evasive or incomplete answers that do not fairly meet the substance of the request.

53. Wright §90; James & Hazard §5.13; Friedenthal §7.16; Moore's Manual §15.13; Shepard's Manual §§5.216-5.235; Moore's Federal Practice §37.02; Wright & Miller §§2281-2293.

Example:

[Caption]

MOTION TO COMPEL DISCOVERY

Defendant Alfred Jenkens moves that this court enter an order compelling plaintiff Thomas Smith to answer interrogatories, and in support of his motion states:

1. On June 5, 1986, defendant served his first set of interrogatories on plaintiff.

2. On July 15, 1986, defendant by letter reminded plaintiff's lawyer that answers to interrogatories were overdue and had not yet been received. A copy of this letter is attached as Exhibit A. No response to this letter has been received.

3. Over 100 days have passed since defendant served interrogatories on plaintiff and to date no answers have been received.

WHEREFORE, defendant requests the court to order plaintiff to serve interrogatory answers within five days and award reasonable expenses, including attorney's fees, to defendant incurred as a result of making this motion.

_____

Attorney for Defendant

Where a certification of compliance with a local rule that requires good faith efforts to resolve discovery disputes is required, it should be attached to the motion to compel.

Example:

CERTIFICATE OF COMPLIANCE WITH LOCAL RULE _____

I, Allan Smith, attorney of record for defendant Alfred Jenkens, certify that I have complied with the requirements of Rule _____ by doing the following:

1. On July 15, 1986, I sent a letter to plaintiff's attorney reminding her that her interrogatory answers were overdue. I received no response to this letter.

2. Approximately three times during the past month I have called plaintiff's attorney and left messages requesting the overdue answers.

3. Three days ago I left a message with plaintiff's attorney advising her that I would make a motion to compel unless I received answers

within 48 hours. I received no response of any kind from plaintiff's attorney or her office.

Dated: _____   _____
                            Attorney for Defendant

After the motion is prepared and signed, a copy along with a notice of motion must be served on every other party under Rule 5. The originals of the motion and notice of motion, with a proof of service, must be filed with the clerk of the court. Keep in mind that many judges delegate discovery matters to magistrates, so make sure your notice of motion correctly specifies who will hear the motion.

3. Sanctions for abuse[54]

Rule 37 provides for the enforcement of discovery orders by permitting a wide range of sanctions for discovery abuse. In recent years courts have been much more active in imposing sanctions, a trend that has received support from the Supreme Court.[55]

The basic discovery abuse sanctions are contained in Rule 37(b). However, before any of those sanctions can be imposed, there must be an actual order following a motion that has been made and heard pursuant to Rule 37(a). Once an order has been properly entered and a party or deponent fails to comply with it, the Rule 37(b) sanctions can be imposed. Hence, getting Rule 37(b) sanctions imposed usually requires two motions: moving for an order compelling discovery and, if the order is not complied with, moving for the actual imposition of sanctions.

Rule 37(b) has a hierarchy of sanctions and the level of the sanction should be appropriate to the level of the abuse.[56] The commonly imposed sanctions, which are appropriate for most abuses, include ordering that certain facts be deemed admitted, barring a party from presenting evidence, and striking pleadings or staying proceedings. In addition, the court can hold a party or deponent in contempt. In extreme cases, where bad faith or willfulness exists, the court can dismiss a case or enter a default judgment.[57]

With the sanctions permitted by Rule 37(b), it should be obvious that the court has the power and discretion to impose such sanctions as will be an effective response to discovery abuse. The difficult decisions, however, involve those situations where the discovery abuse was not caused by the

54. Wright §90; James & Hazard §5.14; Friedenthal §7.16; Moore's Manual §15.13; Shepard's Manual §§5.216-5.235; Moore's Federal Practice §§37.03-37.09; Wright & Miller §§2281-2293.

55. Roadway Express, Inc. v. Piper, 447 U.S. 752 (1980); National Hockey League v. Metropolitan Hockey Club, Inc., 427 U.S. 639 (1976); Societe Internationale v. Rogers, 357 U.S. 197 (1958).

56. Societe Internationale v. Rogers, 357 U.S. 197 (1958).

57. National Hockey League v. Metropolitan Hockey Club, Inc., 427 U.S. 639 (1976).

party itself, but by the party's lawyer. Under these circumstances, it may be unjust that a party who may have a meritorious claim should suffer adverse consequences due to abuse by his lawyer. For that reason, Rule 37(b) also allows, as an alternative or additional sanction, the imposition of reasonable expenses, including attorney's fees, against the abusing party or his lawyer, or both, unless there was a substantial justification for the noncompliance. This permits the court to fine the lawyer directly if the lawyer was the principal cause of the failure to comply.

Conversely, a lawyer must protect himself from the possible imposition of sanctions when the client is the reason for a failure to comply with a discovery order. The common problem involves a client who fails to provide documents or information necessary to respond to discovery, or a client who fails repeatedly to submit to a deposition. When this occurs, the lawyer must make it clear to the judge and the other lawyers that his client is the cause of the problem. This can be done orally in conversations with the other lawyers, and perhaps through letters to them explaining what steps you have taken to try to comply with their discovery. If you do this, the other lawyers will probably ask for discovery abuse sanctions only against your client. If the other lawyers ask for sanctions directly against you, you must, both in a written response to the motion and at the hearing on the motion, detail the efforts you personally have made to comply with the discovery.

Rule 37(c) also permits the award of reasonable expenses, including attorney's fees, incurred as a result of proving matters that were denied in a Rule 36 request for admissions, unless there was a good reason for the failure to admit. A party denying a proper Rule 36 request does so at the risk of being responsible for the expenses later incurred to prove it. Reasonable expenses would include the attorney's time and witness expenses, such as travel and housing, that are necessary to prepare and prove the denied fact at trial.

Finally, under Rule 37(d) a party failing to act properly in responding to a discovery request may be subjected to certain sanctions for abuse, including ordering that facts be deemed admitted, barring a party from presenting evidence, striking pleadings and staying proceedings. The difference between Rule 37(d) sanctions and those under Rule 37(b) is that the sanctions under subsection (d) do not require a prior order under Rule 37(a). For this reason, the sanctions permitted do not include contempt, dismissal, and default.

VII
MOTIONS

§7.1.   Introduction

"Motion practice" is a significant part of the litigation process. Motions are used to regulate the routine "housekeeping" matters in litigation, such as the rescheduling of discovery, hearings, and other deadlines. Motions are also used to reach dispositive results, such as motions to dismiss or motions for summary judgment. Every litigated matter will involve motions, so knowing when and how to present appropriate, well-drafted motions is an essential skill for every litigator.

A motion is simply an application to a court for an order. Presenting an effective motion, however, involves both technical requirements, such as format and service rules, and substantive requirements, which control how the body of a motion should be organized and constructed so that the motion will be persuasive to the judge. This chapter discusses both routine housekeeping and dispositive motions. However, pleadings motions, principally governed by Rule 12, are discussed in §5.4; discovery motions, principally governed by Rule 37, are discussed in §6.9.

§7.2.   General requirements for motions

Rules 5 through 11 govern how motions are made. However, local rules must always be checked because they often detail matters such as page size, page limitations, format, organization, supporting memoranda and exhibits, and special service times. While motions may present numerous matters and seek a wide variety of relief, their basic requirements are generally the same.

1. Form

Under Rule 7(b), a motion must meet three basic requirements. It must be in writing, must "state with particularity the grounds therefor," and must state the relief or order requested. Within these broad requirements a great deal of flexibility is allowed, and how a particular motion is structured is controlled primarily by tactical considerations.

The format requirements for motions are identical to those for pleadings. A motion must have a caption showing the name of the court, the names of the parties to the action, and a designation of the motion involved. Where there are multiple parties, the name of the first party on each side, with an "et al." designation, is sufficient.

Every motion must be signed by a lawyer representing the moving party. The motion must show the lawyer's name and address, and will customarily include a telephone number. While some lawyers put the original of all court papers on a blue-backed sheet, Rule 7 does not require it and local rules usually dispense with this formality.

Example:

UNITED STATES DISTRICT COURT
FOR THE DISTRICT OF IOWA

John Smith, 　　　　Plaintiff 　　　v. Johnson Corporation, et al., 　　　　Defendants	No. 85 C 182

MOTION TO RESET HEARING DATE

Plaintiff John Smith moves this Court for an order continuing the hearing on defendant's motion for discovery sanctions, presently set for July 1, 1986, for ten days.

In support of his motion, plaintiff states:

1. . . .
2. . . .
3. . . .

WHEREFORE, plaintiff John Smith requests the Court to enter an order continuing the hearing, presently set for July 1, 1986, to July 11, 1986.

　　　　　　　　　　　Attorney for Plaintiff
　　　　　　　　　　　Address
　　　　　　　　　　　Telephone

In some jurisdictions the practice required by local rule is to state only the motion itself and put all supporting points, authority and agreement on an attached memorandum. Where they exist, these format formalities obviously must be followed.

2. Notice, service, and filing

Rule 6(d) requires that a written motion, any supporting affidavits, and notice of the motion and hearing be served on every party at least five days before the hearing date, unless the federal rules or a court order alters the time requirement.[1] As a practical matter, all documentation that accompanies a motion should be attached to and served with the motion. Service by mail adds three days to the notice requirement.

Example:

[Caption]

NOTICE OF MOTION

To: Alfred Jackson
Attorney for Johnson Corporation
100 Madison St., Suite 1400
Chicago, Illinois 60602

Please take notice that on June 15, 1986, at 9:30 A.M., or as soon as the case will be called, plaintiff will appear before the Hon. Prentice Marshall in Courtroom No. 2303, United States Court House, 219 S. Dearborn St., Chicago, Illinois, and present a motion to reset a hearing date. A copy of the motion, with supporting memorandum and exhibits, is attached to this notice.

_____
Attorney for Plaintiff
Address
Telephone

For the convenience of the court and other parties, it is good practice to give more notice than the minimum required by Rule 6 when possible under the circumstances.[2] It is also good practice to call the other lawyers to select a mutually agreeable hearing date, if possible, before sending

1. For instance, a motion for summary judgment must be served at least ten days before the hearing date. See §7.8.
2. Lawyers sometimes give only the required minimum notice, without prior contact, when the motion involved is routine or when the lawyer on the other side is using delaying tactics or other improper conduct.

out the written notices. This gives the court time to read the motion, avoids disputes over whether notice was adequate, minimizes continuances, and fosters a good working relationship with the other lawyers in the case.

A motion can be served in any of the ways set out in Rule 5(b). The standard methods are to mail the motion and notice of motion to a lawyer for each party or have the motion and notice delivered to them or someone at their offices. Following service, the originals of the notice and motion should be filed with the clerk of the court along with a proof of service. Filing must occur "within a reasonable time" after service, but obviously must be done before the date set for the hearing. The usual procedure is to file the originals immediately after service. Be sure you get a copy of the motion, notice, and proof of service stamped "filed" and dated by the clerk to keep in your files.

Proof of service is merely a certificate, issued by a lawyer or a nonlawyer, that states that service on the other parties has been made in a proper way. The federal rules do not have proof of service rules, but local districts usually do. These should be checked since some rules provide for a certificate from an attorney, while a nonattorney may be required to make a declaration under penalties of perjury or a notarized affidavit of service. The certificate of service is usually attached to the end of the motion.

Example:

CERTIFICATE OF SERVICE

I, James Brown, state that I served the above motion for a continuance by mailing a copy to the attorney for defendant Johnson Corporation at 100 Madison St. on June 7, 1986.

_____

Attorney for Plaintiff

How do you select the day for the hearing on the motion? Check with the clerk of the court to determine on what days the court hears motions, since practices vary widely. Some judges hold daily court calls; others hear motions on only designated days. Find out what your judge's practice is so that the date you select will be one on which the motion can be heard. Finally, check with the clerk the day before the hearing to make sure the case will actually appear on the next day's motion calendar and to find out when you should be in the courtroom. Many judges arrange their court calendars to hear uncontested and routine cases first and contested matters afterwards.

3. Content of the motion

Under Rule 7(b), a motion must be in writing, must "state with particularity the ground therefor," and must state the relief or order requested. Since the Rule permits a great deal of flexibility, the content of a motion is principally governed by tactical considerations: What will be an effective way to present this motion?

The usual procedure is to draft a concise motion summarily setting out the matter and the relief requested, to supplement it with a memorandum of law if appropriate, and to attach any necessary exhibits and supporting documents. In this way a judge can scan the motion quickly, then review the more detailed supporting materials. This format is required by many local rules.

The usual practice must be modified, however, for the relative seriousness and complexity of the motion and for local practice. For example, a motion to reset a hearing date because you will be on trial in another case should be brief. The motion need only point out when the hearing is presently scheduled, state where and when the conflicting trial is scheduled, and how long that case will take to try, and then suggest a new date for the hearing. In this situation the judge will want brevity, and the factual representations by counsel in the motion should be enough.

At the other extreme, a motion for summary judgment usually must be a thorough presentation of both law and facts. You will probably need to make a motion that sets out the background of the case, the relief requested, and incorporates by reference a memorandum that thoroughly discusses the applicable law and existing facts. The memorandum should also contain excerpts from the pleadings and discovery, exhibits such as documents and records, and witness statements in affidavit form. The motion and accompanying materials should be a self-contained package having everything the judge will need to decide the motion.

Learn what your judge's personal preferences on oral argument are and modify your written motion accordingly. Some judges dislike oral argument, and prefer to get everything in writing; others at best skim the written motions, preferring to have oral arguments set out the details. While you must always comply with the Rule 7 requirements and protect your record by having the essential matters in your motion, there is no point in not acceding to your judge's preferences.

In short, drafting a motion requires a flexible approach. The relative complexity of the motion, local custom in presenting motions, and even the preferences of the judge all come into play. Motions that are specifically tailored to these considerations, which do not mechanically follow a set blueprint, have a much better chance of succeeding.[3]

---

3. The motion should be drafted with precision the first time, since no rule expressly allows amendments of motions; Rule 1.5 applies only to pleadings. In practice, however, amendments of motions are sometimes permitted.

4. Responses to motions

Once served with a motion, the respondent has two choices: the respondent can either oppose or not oppose the motion. If the motion is a routine one, a common practice, if you do not oppose the motion, is to notify the opposing lawyer of your position, who will tell the judge at the hearing on the motion that you have no objection to the motion. This will eliminate your having to come to court. However, you should file a statement that says you have no opposition to the motion, since it is good practice to have a written record of your position and this should eliminate the danger that your position is misrepresented.

Example:

[Caption]

STATEMENT OF NONOPPOSITION TO DEFENDANT'S MOTION FOR ADDITIONAL TIME TO ANSWER

Plaintiff John Smith does not intend to oppose defendant's motion for additional time to answer, nor does he intend to appear at the hearing on this motion presently set before the Hon. Prentice Marshall on June 15, 1986, at 9:30 A.M.

_____

Attorney for Plaintiff

Another approach is to agree to a "consent order," in which both parties draft an agreed upon order that disposes of the motion. While this does not guarantee that the judge will sign it, in practice the judge usually will. This approach is common in state courts, but not in federal court.

On the other hand, if you decide to oppose the motion, serve and file your response in advance of the hearing. The response should set out the reasons for your opposition and include case law and other authority you will want the judge to consider.

Example:

[Caption]

DEFENDANT'S OPPOSITION TO PLAINTIFF'S MOTION FOR LEAVE TO FILE A SECOND AMENDED ANSWER

Defendant Wilbur Johnson opposes plaintiff's motion for leave to file a Second Amended Answer, presently set before the Hon. Prentice

Marshall on June 15, 1986, at 9:30 A.M., for the following reasons:

    1. . . .

    2. . . .

    3. . . .

WHEREFORE, defendant Wilbur Johnson requests the Court to enter an order denying plaintiff's motion for leave to file a second amended answer.

_____

Attorney for Defendant

5. Hearing and argument

On the date set for the hearing, check whether an order has already been entered. Many judges will enter orders granting routine and uncontested motions in advance of the hearing day. This is particularly likely where both parties jointly make the motion or the court has been notified in advance that the motion is unopposed. Check with the clerk before the motion calendar starts to determine if the motion has been ruled on. Some courts post a list of motions that have been ruled on outside the courtroom. If yours has already been decided, make sure you get a copy of the order from the court clerk. Most clerks mail copies of the order to the lawyers in the case.

If your motion is still pending, the case eventually will be called by the clerk. The usual practice is for the lawyers to approach the bench when their case is called, state who they are, and which party they represent. If the motion is a routine one, the judge will usually let the lawyers make brief comments, make a decision from the bench, and immediately enter an appropriate order. If a significant motion is involved, the judge will probably permit lengthier arguments and take the case "under advisement," meaning the judge will research and consider the issues further before deciding the motion.

To prepare for oral argument at the hearing, it is critical to learn what your judge's practice is. Some judges disfavor oral argument and dispense with it altogether for routine motions or, for other motions, give the lawyers very little time to argue. Other judges use oral argument principally as an opportunity to ask the lawyers questions about the law or facts. In this situation you obviously must make all your points in the written motion. At the other extreme are judges who at best scan written motions and rely heavily if not exclusively on oral argument in deciding whether to grant a motion. Preparing for oral argument depends a great deal on knowing what the judge wants to hear. If you don't know, ask lawyers familiar with the judge, or watch a motion calendar in that judge's courtroom and see how the judge conducts the hearing.

If the judge's practice is to allow substantial oral argument, you need to decide what will persuade the judge to rule in your favor. Sometimes the weight of prevailing law will be persuasive, at other times the facts. Whatever it is, don't repeat the contents of the motion unless the judge tells you he needs his memory refreshed. Many judges begin the hearing by telling the lawyers that they have read the motion and response, and then ask the lawyers if they have anything to add. Take heed of this request, since usually a motion has an important point that will persuade the judge. It may be the law, facts, basic fairness, or the result of a particular ruling. Basic fairness or the results of a ruling can frequently be argued more persuasively orally.

Regardless of what points you have selected to argue orally, act confident and professional. Address your comments to the judge, not opposing counsel. Above all, don't interrupt or argue with counsel. The judge will usually ask the movant to argue first, and then give the respondent an opportunity to argue. Nothing is as unprofessional and ineffective as two lawyers bickering with each other, yet unfortunately this is an all too common event during motion calls.

As the movant, standard procedure is to approach the lectern positioned before the bench, introduce yourself, state what party you represent, give the other lawyers a chance to identify themselves and their parties, state what your motion is for, and then go immediately to the points you have selected to emphasize. When you are finished, the other lawyers can respond. When they are through, you may, depending on the judge's practice, have a short opportunity to rebut. Always be prepared to answer any questions the judge may ask.

The key to making effective oral arguments is always remembering that the argument must be thought through in advance, coordinated with the written motion, and must supplement the motion by emphasizing the important points that, in your judgment, will present your side in its best light.

6. Order

Regardless of when the motion is decided, the court will enter an order. In federal court, routine motions are usually decided by a "minute order," which is merely a form on which the clerk makes an entry reflecting the ruling. The minute order is then signed by the judge or stamped with his signature, and a copy is mailed to the lawyers. If the motion is important, the judge may prepare a written opinion and order explaining the reasons for the ruling.[4] Make sure that every pending motion is ultimately decided by an order, that the order accurately reflects the court's ruling, and that you obtain a copy of the order.

The court may refer certain motions to a U.S. magistrate, since magistrates are empowered to hear routine civil pretrial matters.[5] In recent years it has become particularly common for magistrates to supervise the discovery process in civil cases. The motion procedure before a magistrate is identical to that before the judge.

4. This practice may differ from state practice, where the prevailing lawyer sometimes prepares a draft order reflecting the court's ruling, which the judge then signs.
5. See Magistrate's Act, 28 U.S.C. §§631 et seq.

§7.3.   *Extensions of time and continuances*

The kinds of motions that can be presented to the court are limited only by the movant's imagination. Practically, however, the routine housekeeping motions invariably deal with time and date modifications. These are the motions for extensions of time, continuances, and new hearing and trial dates.

Rule 6(b) governs extensions of time. If a motion to extend time is made before the expiration of the applicable time period, the court may grant the motion for "good cause." However, if the motion is made after the applicable time period had expired, the court may grant the motion only where the failure to act timely was caused by "excusable neglect."

What constitutes "good cause" or "excusable neglect" is addressed to the court's discretion, and must be evaluated in the context of the pending case. Courts have generally been realistic and accommodating in permitting extensions of time where the applicable period has not yet run. Usually any reason other than one involving bad faith and actual prejudice to an opponent will result in the court's granting a reasonable extension of time.[6]

Excusable neglect, on the other hand, is judged on a substantially higher standard. Courts have usually denied extensions of time where the failure to act within the required time limitations was caused by the lawyer's inadvertence or ignorance of the applicable rule or by a lawyer's busy case load and other work demands.[7] It is usually an extraordinary situation involving good faith, such as the death or serious illness of a lawyer, a delay by a client in forwarding a complaint and summons, or difficulties in substituting proper parties or different lawyers, that must be present before a court will find excusable neglect and permit an extension of time.

Some time periods for post-trial matters usually cannot be enlarged. These include a motion for judgment n.o.v. (Rule 50(b)), motion for new trial after a judgment n.o.v. has been granted (Rule 50(c)(2)), motion to amend findings and judgment (Rules 52(b) and 59(e)), motion for a new trial (Rule 59(b)), motion to set aside a judgment for reasons such as mistake, fraud, or newly discovered evidence (Rule 60(b)), and appeals from magistrates' decisions (Rule 74(a)).

Make the motion and have it decided within the applicable time period. Give the court solid reasons why an extension is necessary, and ask only for such additional time as is reasonably needed. Above all, avoid missing a deadline. Some time periods cannot be enlarged at all; others can only be enlarged after expiration upon a showing of excusable neglect. This is not a situation you want to find yourself in. The best way to avoid having these disasters arise in the first place is by creating, maintaining, and following a reliable docket control system, which will remind you of all significant dates for each case you are handling. These vary

6. See Wright & Miller §1165.
7. See Wright & Miller §1165.

from simple calendars to sophisticated computer systems, but are critical for every litigation lawyer.

Routine motions for extensions of time or continuances should be structured simply. The pertinent information that forms the basis for the motion can ordinarily be put in the body of the motion.

Example:

[Caption]

MOTION FOR ADDITIONAL TIME
TO ANSWER OR RESPOND

Defendant Robert Johnson moves this court for an order granting defendant an additional 10 days to answer or respond to plaintiff's complaint. In support of his motion defendant states:

1. Defendant was served with the summons and complaint on June 1, 1986. Under the rules defendant's answer is due on or before June 21, 1986.

2. Defendant's attorney received the complaint on June 13, 1986.

3. Plaintiff's complaint has five counts and is based on an alleged series of contracts with the defendant.

4. To answer the complaint, defendant's attorney will have to evaluate numerous business records, which the defendant is presently locating, and review them with defendant.

5. Defendant's attorney believes he can prepare and serve an answer or otherwise respond if an additional 10 days to answer or respond is granted.

WHEREFORE, defendant requests that this court enter an order extending defendant's time to answer or respond to July 1, 1986.

_____

Attorney for Defendant

Note that the motion asserts facts in the body of the motion that are based on the lawyer's own knowledge, or on information already contained in the court file. In this situation the facts do not need to be stated in affidavit form. Where the facts that are the basis of the motion are within someone's knowledge other than the attorney, the facts must be in affidavit form and attached to the motion.

§7.4. *Substitution of parties*

During the pendency of an action, occurrences may take place that will require that a named party be replaced by another. Such a substitution of parties can be required when a party dies, becomes incompetent, or loses all legal interest in the action. A public official, named as a party, can die, resign, or be voted out of office. In these situations Rule 25 provides for substitution with a successor party. Unless death abates the action, the court, upon notification and demonstration of the change, will order a substitution. In the case of public officials, the substitution is automatic.

The usual procedure is to make a motion for substitution of parties, state the reason for the substitution in the body of the motion, and attach any necessary documents as exhibits. For example, if a party dies and will be substituted by the administrator of the estate, attach a copy of the death certificate and the probate court order appointing the administrator of the estate.

§7.5. *Temporary restraining orders and preliminary injunctions*

Injunctions are of three types: temporary restraining orders, preliminary injunctions, and permanent injunctions. A permanent injunction is a remedy that can be ordered only after a trial on the merits of the case. Temporary restraining orders and preliminary injunctions, governed by Rule 65, are provisional remedies whose purpose is to maintain the status quo and avoid irreparable injury to the plaintiff until the rights of the parties can be adjudicated. A temporary restraining order can be granted without notice to the other side, and can be granted only until a hearing for a temporary injunction can be held. Its purpose is to avoid an immediate irreparable injury to the petitioning party. A preliminary injunction, by contrast, can be issued only after an adversarial hearing; it maintains the status quo until the case is tried.

Both preliminary injunctions and temporary restraining orders are forms of injunctions. Since an injunction is an equitable remedy, it can only be granted if the legal remedies are inadequate. Accordingly, make sure that the underlying complaint asks for injunctive relief and that such relief would be proper if the complaint's allegations are ultimately proved. While Rule 65 governs temporary restraining orders and preliminary injunctions, local rules often have additional requirements that must be met.

1. Temporary restraining orders[8]

a. Law

A temporary restraining order is governed by Rule 65(b). Its purpose is to maintain the status quo until a hearing upon notice can be held. Since this is an extraordinary procedure, the Rule's requirements must be followed precisely.

---

8. Moore's Manual §10.07(2); Friedenthal §15.4; Shephard's Manual §7.101; Moore's Federal Practice §§65.05-65.08; Wright & Miller §§2951-2953.

First, a "TRO" can be granted without notice to the opposing party, but only if three requirements are met. The motion must be supported by affidavit or a verified complaint alleging specific facts that show that "immediate and irreparable injury, loss or damage will result" unless the order is issued before the opposing side can be heard. In addition, the attorney representing the applicant must file an affidavit stating the "efforts, if any, which have been made to give notice" and the "reasons supporting his claim that notice should not be required." Finally, the applicant for a TRO must post security in an amount the court deems sufficient to cover the costs and damages that may be incurred if the party restrained is found to have been wrongfully restrained. All three of these requirements must be met. Although Rule 65(b) expressly requires only that an applicant for a TRO show an "immediate and irreparable injury," case law generally holds that the applicant must make the same showing, at least on a preliminary basis, as that required for a preliminary injunction.[9] That is, the applicant must show, in addition to an irreparable injury, that there is a likelihood of success on the merits of the case, that the threatened injury to the applicant exceeds any foreseeable injury to the adverse party if the order is granted, and that any order will not be against the public interest. As a practical matter, a court will not enter a TRO unless these considerations, taken as a whole, appear to weigh heavily in the applicant's favor.

Second, if a TRO is granted, the order must specify the injury, why it is irreparable, why it was granted without notice, and describe in reasonable detail the acts that are enjoined. It is limited to the duration set by the court, which cannot exceed 10 days, although it can be extended for another 10 days for good cause.

Third, the court must set a date for a hearing on a preliminary injunction at the earliest possible time whenever a TRO is granted without notice. The party against whom the TRO was issued can, with 2 days notice, move to have the TRO dissolved.

b. Practice approach

Apply for a TRO only under appropriate circumstances. There is a great deal of work involved, and the court cannot properly issue a TRO unless an immediate and irreparable injury will occur without it. Since a TRO is a powerful and extraordinary judicial step, courts are necessarily reluctant to grant it except in the most compelling of circumstances.

Demonstrating an immediate and irreparable injury and an inadequate remedy at law is understandably difficult. Common situations involve threatened damage to unique property and proprietary interests. For example, if someone is about to cut down mature elm trees on another's property, if a magazine is about to release personal photographs of a private person without authorization, or if a former employee is about to sell trade secrets to a business competitor a TRO may be appro-

---

9. Moore's Manual §10.07(2); Shephard's Manual §7.101; Moore's Federal Practice §65.06; Wright & Miller §2951.

priate because in these situations the wronged party cannot be made whole through money damages.

Second, make sure that the court has both subject matter jurisdiction over the claim and personal jurisdiction over the defendant. Lack of subject matter jurisdiction will result in dismissal of the complaint. Lack of personal jurisdiction will make any injunctive relief ordered unenforceable.

Third, moving for a TRO requires that you prepare, file, and ultimately serve several things at nearly the same time. These include:

i. complaint and summons
ii. application for TRO and preliminary injunction
iii. attorney's affidavit of attempted notice
iv. witness affidavits
v. security for costs and damages
vi. court order

i. Complaint and summons

Where a TRO is being sought, the allegations in the complaint will form the factual basis for the motion and must be coordinated with it. The relief requested should include a TRO, preliminary injunction, and permanent injunction. The factual allegations should, like any complaint, show that the pleader is entitled to the relief requested if the allegations are proved. Finally, although not required, the allegations should be verified by the party, since this has the same evidentiary effect as an affidavit. A complaint is verified when it contains a statement that the party has read the complaint, personally knows the facts, and states that the facts are true. Also, the statement must be sworn to before a notary public.

The complaint is usually filed at the same time as the application for the TRO. This means that the summons will not yet have been served. However, since the Rules require that the attorney state how notification on the adverse party has been attempted, you should always try to have service of the complaint and summons expedited, especially since Rule 4 now permits service by private individuals.

The complaint, application, and supporting documents are usually filed with the emergency judge, an assignment that is usually rotated among the active judges. Find out who the present emergency judge is, and notify the judge's clerk of the situation.

ii. Application for TRO and preliminary injunction

The application for a TRO should be combined with a request for a preliminary injunction, since under Rule 65(b) a hearing on a preliminary injunction must be scheduled as soon as possible after a TRO without notice is granted.

The application must allege that an immediate and irreparable injury will occur unless the TRO is granted. Since the application must be supported by facts, it usually refers to the verified complaint and accompanying witness affidavits for factual support. As with motions generally, the application itself is usually drafted briefly and refers to the supporting material for the substance.

Example:

[Caption]

APPLICATION FOR TEMPORARY RESTRAINING ORDER AND PRELIMINARY INJUNCTION

Plaintiff applies, pursuant to Rule 65, for a temporary restraining order and requests that a hearing for a preliminary injunction be set. In support of his application plaintiff states:

1. Plaintiff will suffer an immediate and irreparable injury unless his application for temporary restraining order is granted.

2. In support of his application for a preliminary injunction and a hearing date, plaintiff states:

    (a) defendant will perform the threatened acts, as more fully set out in the complaint, unless enjoined;

    (b) defendant's threatened action, if carried out, will result in irreparable injury to plaintiff;

    (c) a preliminary injunction will not injure or inconvenience the defendant.

3. In support of his application, plaintiff incorporates by reference the allegations of his verified complaint and the facts as set forth in the witness affidavits attached as Exhibits A through C.

4. Plaintiff's attorney's certificate showing her efforts to give notice to the adverse party, and why notice to the defendant should not be required, is attached as Exhibit D.

5. Plaintiff is ready to provide security in such amount as the court determines is necessary to cover the costs and expenses incurred by the defendant in the event the defendant is found to have been erroneously restrained and enjoined.

WHEREFORE, Plaintiff requests that the court enter a temporary restraining order against defendant and set a hearing for a temporary injunction at the earliest practical time.

———————————————
Attorney for Plaintiff

    iii.   Attorney's certificate regarding notice

Rule 65(b) requires that the attorney for the moving party certify in writing "the efforts, if any, which have been made to give the notice and the reasons supporting his claim that notice should not be required." Notice here includes informal as well as formal notice. The court will clearly prefer any notice over none at all, such as a telephone call to the adverse party, his lawyer if known, or an agent. Accordingly, the lawyer's certificate should show all the reasonable steps she took to give some advance notice to the adverse party.

Example:

[Caption]

CERTIFICATE OF ATTORNEY IN SUPPORT OF APPLICATION FOR TEMPORARY RESTRAINING ORDER WITHOUT NOTICE

I, Terry Anton, attorney for plaintiff, make this certificate, in accordance with Rule 65(b), in support of plaintiff's application for a temporary restraining order without notice to the defendant.

1. On June 1, 1986, at approximately 1:00 P.M. I was first informed of defendant's imminent conduct as set forth in the complaint. I immediately began drafting the complaint, this application, and the supporting documents.

2. At the same time I telephoned defendant at his place of business to advise him of this application, but could not personally contact him. I left a message with his answering service, but have received no call from him.

3. I have attempted to locate the defendant's residence and present whereabouts without success.

4. I have no knowledge of any attorney who may presently represent the defendant, and have attempted to learn this without success.

_____

Attorney for Plaintiff

iv.   Witness affidavits

Rule 65 requires that the applicant for a TRO show specific facts, through a verified complaint or witness affidavits, that demonstrate the required "immediate and irreparable injury." Accordingly, you should review the verified complaint and determine what additional facts must be shown, and put them in affidavit form. The affidavit should show who the witness is and demonstrate that the witness has firsthand knowledge of all the facts recited in the affidavit.

Example:

AFFIDAVIT

I, William Jones, having been first duly sworn, state:

1. I am the plaintiff in this action. I live at 123 Maple Lane, Denver, and am the owner of that property.

2. On June 1, 1986, at approximately 8:30 A.M. I saw ...
3. ...
4. ...

_____

Name of Affiant

Signed and sworn to
   before me on June 2, 1986.

_____

Notary Public

My commission expires on _____.

v.   Security for costs

Rule 65(c) requires that a TRO cannot be issued unless the applicant provides adequate security to cover any costs and damages that may be incurred by the adverse party if the TRO is wrongfully issued. Accordingly, thought must be given to the likely security requirement. Ordinarily this means posting a cash bond with the clerk of the court, although the court can set any other security requirement. Since the court will not issue the TRO until the security has been set and met, you should always have the plaintiff prepared to deposit the likely cash bond immediately if the TRO is granted. Check with the clerk's office to determine its requirements for receiving bonds and other security.

vi.   Order and service

It is the usual procedure in federal court for the judge or his clerk to issue orders, either minute or full written orders. However, since with a TRO time is critical, it is useful to prepare a draft order for the judge in advance so that it can be immediately signed if the judge grants the TRO. Rule 65(b) requires that the order specify the date and time issued, define the injury, state why the injury is irreparable, state why the TRO was granted without notice, specify the terms and duration of the order, and set a hearing date for the temporary injunction at the earliest possible time.

Example:

[Caption]

ORDER

This cause being heard on the application of plaintiff for a temporary restraining order and preliminary injunction, the plaintiff appearing ex parte without notice to the defendant, the court having considered the verified complaint, witness affidavits, and the attorney's certificate attached as exhibits to plaintiff's motion,

THE COURT FINDS:

1. Plaintiff's threatened injury as described in the verified complaint is irreparable because. . . .
2. This order is being granted without notice to defendant because. . . .

THE COURT ORDERS:

1. The defendant is hereby restrained from. . . .
2. This order shall remain in effect until June 4, 1986, at 5:00 P.M.
3. A hearing on plaintiff's motion for a preliminary injunction is set for June 4, 1986, at 2:00 P.M. and the defendant is hereby ordered to appear in this courtroom at that time.
4. A copy of this order, along with copies of the complaint, summons, motion, and supporting documentation, shall be served forthwith on the defendant.

SO ORDERED:

_____

Judge

Date: _____

Time: _____

Since the court's order is not enforceable until the defendant receives actual notice of it, you should attempt to notify the defendant by telephone of the court's order and arrange for immediate proper service of the order under Rule 4.

2. Preliminary injunctions[10]

a. Law

Preliminary injunctions are governed by Rule 65(a). The purpose of this Rule is to maintain the status quo until a trial on the merits can be held, and it has several requirements.

10. Moore's Manual §10.07(2); Friedenthal §15.4; Shepard's Manual §7.100; Moore's Federal Practice §65.04; Wright & Miller §§2947-2950.

First, the Rule requires notice to the adverse party. Although it does not specify the necessary time period, it is likely that the usual five-day notice period for motions under Rule 6(d) applies. Also, notice of the motion must include service of the complaint and summons.

Second, the movant must post security in an amount the court deems proper for the payment of costs and damages that may be incurred if the party is found to have been wrongly enjoined.

Third, the movant has the burden of showing, through verified pleadings or testimony and other evidence at the hearing, that: (1) if the injunction is not ordered, the movant will suffer an irreparable injury; (2) the movant will likely succeed on the merits of his claims at trial; (3) the threatened injury to movant exceeds any threatened injury to the adverse party; and (4) a preliminary injunction would not be against the public interest.

Fourth, if the court orders a preliminary injunction, the order must be specific and state in reasonable detail what acts are enjoined.

The court can consolidate the hearing on the motion for a preliminary injunction with a trial on the merits. If consolidation is not ordered, evidence presented at the hearing on the motion for a preliminary injunction need not be repeated at the trial on the merits. Consolidation is frequently ordered where injunctive relief is the principal remedy sought and the evidence at the hearing for the preliminary injunction would be largely the same as at the trial.

An order granting or denying a preliminary injunction and permanent injunction is appealable. An order granting or denying a TRO is not appealable.[11] Since the issuance of injunctive orders is addressed to the court's discretion, the order will be reversed on appeal only if it was erroneous as a matter of law or the order was improvidently granted.

b. Practice approach

A preliminary injunction can come before the court in two ways. First, it can be set by the judge as part of an order granting an application for a TRO. Second, the plaintiff can move for a preliminary injunction.

Regardless of how a motion for a preliminary injunction comes before the court, several considerations must be remembered. First, the adverse party must have notice of the motion, which must be given in accordance with the usual notice requirements. Second, the hearing is an adversary one, with each party entitled to call and cross-examine witnesses. Third, the plaintiff has the burden of proving that an irreparable injury will occur unless the status quo is maintained during the pendency of the action, that there is a likelihood of ultimate success on the merits, that the threatened injury to the plaintiff exceeds any threatened injury to the defendant, and, where appropriate, that the relief requested will not adversely affect the public interest. Fourth, the plaintiff must provide security for costs and damages before a preliminary injunction can be

11. See Wright §102.

issued. Fifth, if a preliminary injunction is granted, it is in effect until a final trial on the merits, although the court can modify or vacate the order if warranted.

The critical point to remember is that the hearing on the preliminary injunction is, as a practical matter, often the determinative proceeding in an injunction case. Proof presented at the hearing need not be duplicated at a later trial. Furthermore, the court can advance the trial on the merits and consolidate the trial with the hearing. Where injunctive relief is the sole or principal remedy sought, the court will often accelerate and consolidate the trial and hearing. The court will frequently order that discovery be expedited. As the plaintiff's lawyer this means you must be prepared to go to trial quickly and present your entire case on short notice.

If you decide to present a motion for a preliminary injunction, it should be drafted both to allege the legal requirements for such relief and to specify precisely what acts are sought to be enjoined.

Example:

[Caption]

MOTION FOR PRELIMINARY INJUNCTION

Plaintiff moves for a preliminary injunction enjoining defendant, his officers, employees, agents and any persons working with him, until a trial on the merits is held and final order is entered in this action. In support of his motion plaintiff states:

1. Defendant will act in the manner alleged in the complaint unless enjoined.

2. Defendant's threatened action if carried out will result in irreparable injury, loss and damage, as more fully alleged in the complaint.

3. The injury to plaintiff, if defendant is not enjoined, will substantially exceed any foreseeable injury to the defendant.

WHEREFORE, plaintiff requests that the court enter a preliminary injunction enjoining defendant from [specify and describe conduct sought to be enjoined].

_____
Attorney for Plaintiff

§7.6. Removal

1. Law

The right of a defendant to remove a case from state to federal court is a statutory right governed by 28 U.S.C. §§1441-1450 and the applicable law is discussed in §3.5 supra.

2. Practice approach

A defendant considering removal must ask several questions before preparing a petition for removal.

a. Should I remove?

Removal is nothing more than a change from a state to a federal forum. Consequently, there is no point in removing unless the defendants will benefit from the change. The potential advantages include a quicker trial date since federal courts frequently have less of a backlog than state courts. Many federal districts, however, make diversity cases the lowest priority on the trial calendar. Another potential advantage is the procedural differences that may exist between the state and federal courts. For example, the pleading possibilities may be greater and the discovery rights broader in federal court. Also, the Federal Rules of Evidence may be more relaxed on admissibility issues than state evidence rules. Removing to federal court is also a way of getting the case away from an unfavorable judge. Also, federal jury panels are usually from a larger geographical pool and may have different characteristics than a state jury panel. Finally, changing to federal court may result in different substantive law being applied in diversity cases. These types of strategic possibilities must be carefully evaluated before proceeding further.

b. Can I get codefendants to remove?

Removal cannot be granted unless all defendants, except nominal or fraudulently joined ones, petition for removal. There is no point in filing a removal petition unless your codefendants agree to join in the petition.

c. Can I remove all claims?

Under §1441(c) a defendant can sometimes have a nonremovable claim removed to federal court if such a claim is related to a removable claim. Such a determination is addressed to the discretion of the court, which can permit removal of all claims or remand the claims not within the court's original jurisdiction. This can be a complicated issue, and the law should always be researched thoroughly. Where fewer than all the claims are removable, however, you must decide whether removing some but not all the claims is strategically advantageous. The advantages are the potential benefits of removal that were discussed previously. The disadvantages concern the time and costs expended by litigating in the two different forums.

d. What are the procedural requirements for removal?

If after considering the relevant issues you decide that removal is the proper course, make sure you follow the procedure set out in 28 U.S.C. §§1446-1450, since case law requires that the procedures be closely followed. There are several basic steps that are requirements of the removal process.

i.   Timing

The petition for removal must, under §1446(b), be filed in the federal district court in the division in which the state action is pending within 30 days after the defendant receives a copy of the plaintiff's initial pleading, or summons if served without the complaint, whichever is shorter. If an amended pleading is the first indication that the case is removable, the defendant must file the petition within 30 days of the receipt of such pleading.

ii.   Petition for removal

Each defendant in the case who has been served must sign and file a verified petition for removal, except nominal or fraudulently named defendants. The petition itself must contain a "short and plain statement of the facts" entitling the defendant to removal. This necessarilly means that the jurisdictional requirements for removal must be alleged in the petition since plaintiff's state court complaint will not usually allege them. This is particularly important where diversity is the basis for removal, in which case the petition must allege the diversity jurisdiction requirements of both complete diversity and the jurisdictional amount. However, regardless of the jurisdictional basis, whether federal question, diversity, or actions against the federal government, it must be alleged accurately and completely since the appropriateness of the removal petition depends principally on this allegation. Where more than one ground for removal exists, each should be alleged.

Example:

[Federal court caption]

Mary Jones,
          Plaintiff-respondent
 	
          v.
 	
John Smith,
          Defendant-petitioner
	No. _____

PETITION FOR REMOVAL

To: The United States District Court for the District of Arizona:

Defendant John Smith requests that the above captioned case be removed from the Superior Court of Pima County, Arizona, to the United States District Court for the District of Arizona, Southern Division. In support of his request defendant states:

1. Plaintiff Mary Jones commenced this action against defendant John Smith in the Superior Court of Pima County under the caption of "Mary Jones, Plaintiff v. John Smith, Defendant," Docket No. 86 C 10478, by serving a copy of the complaint and summons on defendant on June 1, 1986.

2. A copy of the complaint and summons is attached to this petition. No other pleadings or other proceedings have been filed or taken to date.

3. This action is a civil action and is one over which this court has original jurisdiction under 28 U.S.C. §1331 [and/or §1332, etc.] and is an action that can be removed on the petition of defendant to this District Court pursuant to 28 U.S.C. §1441.

4. [If federal question:] This court has original jurisdiction over this action because it appears from plaintiff's complaint that this is a civil action that arises under the _____ Act, _____ U.S.C. §_____, [or Constitution or treaty] because plaintiff claims that. . . .

5. [If diversity:] This court has original jurisdiction over this action because it appears from plaintiff's complaint that this is a civil action, and:

(a) Plaintiff, both when this action was commenced and now, was and is a citizen of the State of California;

(b) Defendant, both when this action was commenced and now, was and is a citizen of the State of Nevada. Defendant was not, when this action was commenced, nor is he now, a citizen of the State of Arizona.

(c) The amount in controversy, exclusive of interest and costs, exceeds $10,000.

6. Defendant has filed a bond with good and sufficient surety, as required by 28 U.S.C. §1446(d), conditioned that he will pay all costs and disbursements incurred if this case is not removable or improperly removed.

WHEREFORE, defendant John Smith requests that this case be removed from the Superior Court of Pima County, Arizona, to the United States District Court for the District of Arizona, Southern Division.

_____
Attorney for Defendant

[Verification]

iii.   Bond

Section 1446(d) requires the defendant to post a bond "with good and sufficient surety" that guarantees the payment of all costs and disbursements in the event removal was improper.

Most clerk's offices have bond forms that can be filled out and filed at the same time the petition and accompanying state court papers are filed. The usual surety is a commercial surety company. These bonds ordinarily use the following language.

Example:

[Caption]

BOND

_____ as principal and _____
_____ as surety, jointly and severally promise to pay plaintiff
_____ such sum, in United States currency, as the United States District Court for the District of Arizona may determine shall be paid to plaintiff to reimburse her for all costs and disbursements in the event the court determines that this case was not removable or was improperly removed. If defendant pays all costs and disbursements, if and as ordered by the court, this obligation will be void; otherwise, this obligation shall remain in effect.

Date: _____   _____
                                                Defendant-principal

                                                _____
                                                Surety

Rule 65.1 requires that each surety submit to the jurisdiction of the court. If the bond goes into effect because the defendant does not pay the costs, the plaintiff on motion can enforce the bond.

iv.   Notice to adverse parties

Section 1446(e) requires that each adverse party be notified promptly of the filing of the removal petition. This is done in the same way that notice is customarily given.

Example:

[Caption]

NOTICE OF FILING REMOVAL PETITION

To: [*attorney for plaintiff*]

Please take notice that on June 10, 1986, defendant John Smith filed a Petition for Removal and Bond in the United States District Court for

the District of Arizona, Southern Division. Copies of the petition and
bond are attached to this notice.

_____

Attorney for Defendant

The original notice should be filed with the clerk of the court after
copies of the notice have been sent to the attorneys of all adverse parties.

v.   File petition in state court

The final step in the removal process is filing a copy of the removal
petition with the clerk of the state court. This act terminates the jurisdiction
of the state court.

vi.   Further proceedings

Once the above steps are completed, removal is complete. There is
no order required to effect removal. The district court retains jurisdiction,
unless and until the case is remanded, and can proceed as with any
other case.

The usual status of affairs after a case has been removed is that the
defendant who has been served has not yet responded to the complaint,
and other defendants have not been served. The served defendant must,
under Rule 81(c), answer or otherwise plead within 20 days of receipt of
the initial pleading or summons, or within five days of filing the removal
petition, whichever is longer. The answer or other response must comply
with the federal pleading rules. If plaintiff has not served all defendants
before the removal petition is filed, service must be made in compliance
with Rule 4. In short, all action taken after removal must be taken under
the federal rules.

§7.7.   _Judgment on the pleadings_[12]

Motions for judgment on the pleadings are governed by Rule 12(c). After
the pleadings are closed, but sufficiently before trial so that trial will not
be delayed, any party can move for judgment on the pleadings. The motion
determines if, based on the allegations in the pleadings, the moving
party is entitled to judgment. For purposes of the motion, the movant's
well-pleaded allegations that have been denied are deemed false, while
the opponent's allegations are deemed true. In short, the pleadings are
viewed in the light most favorable to the opponent. It is only when the
undisputed facts as pleaded show that the movant is entitled to judgment

12. James & Hazard §5.18; Friedenthal §9.1; Shepard's Manual §§4.31-4.34; Moore's
Manual §16.01; Wright & Miller §§1367-1372; Moore's Federal Practice §12.15.

that the motion should be granted.[13] If a party presents matters outside the pleadings and the court decides to receive them, the motion is treated as one for summary judgment.

The motion for judgment on the pleadings is usually made only in cases where "legal" defenses, such as the statute of limitations, are clearly shown to exist. Since under the federal rules answers need not be responded to, allegations in the answer cannot be the basis for judgment on the pleadings.

Example:

[Caption]

MOTION FOR JUDGMENT ON THE PLEADINGS

Defendant Johnson Corporation moves this Court to enter judgment on the pleadings in favor of the defendant. On the undisputed facts in the pleadings, defendant is entitled to judgment, under Rule 12(c), as a matter of law.

In support of its motion defendant states:

1. . . .
2. . . .
3. . . .

WHEREFORE, defendant Johnson Corporation requests the Court to enter judgment on the pleadings in favor of the defendant.

_____

Attorney for Defendant

Rule 15 provides that motions to amend pleadings should be "freely given when justice so requires." Therefore, if it appears likely that a motion for judgment on the pleadings will be granted, the plaintiff should move for leave to amend, if the defect can be cured. Under these circumstances the motion for leave to amend should be attached to the proposed amended pleading. Where the motion is made before substantial discovery has been conducted, it should ordinarily be granted, despite the pendency of a motion for judgment on the pleadings.[14]

The motion for judgment on the pleadings is closely related to the motion to dismiss under Rule 12(b).[15] Of the seven grounds for a Rule 12(b) motion, the most commonly asserted one is Rule 12(b)(6): failure to state a claim upon which relief can be granted. A Rule 12(b)(6) motion should be made after the defendant has received the plaintiff's complaint and before answering. If the motion is granted, the plaintiff will usually

---

13. See Moore's Manual §16.01.
14. See Shepard's Manual §4.33.
15. See §5.4.3.

be given leave to file an amended complaint; usually the plaintiff can cure the defect. The litigation then continues.

By contrast, a motion for judgment on the pleadings is made after the pleadings are closed and it has become evident that there is a legal bar, such as an applicable statute of limitations, that will prevent plaintiff from recovering anything. For this reason, a motion for judgment on the pleadings should not be made unless it is clear from the facts in the pleadings, in light of applicable substantive law, that plaintiff cannot recover on his claim. Such motions are infrequently made.

§7.8. Summary judgment[16]

Summary judgment is governed by Rule 56. It is designed to be an efficient method of deciding a case when there are no genuine disputes over any material facts. A motion for summary judgment can be made on any claim — complaint, counterclaim, cross-claim, or third-party claim — and on a complaint for declaratory judgment. Partial summary judgment can be granted on fewer than all counts, or on one of several issues within a count, such as liability.

1. When made

A complaining party may move for summary judgment on its claim 20 days after the action has been commenced or after an adverse party has moved for summary judgment. A defending party on whom any such claim has been asserted may move for summary judgment at any time. A motion for summary judgment must be served on all other parties at least 10 days before the hearing date.

Since Rule 56(a) allows motions for summary judgment early in the litigation process, when to bring such a motion is principally a matter of litigation strategy. While the Rule permits early motions, as a practical matter they have little chance of success before the pleadings have been closed. The motion is usually made after substantial discovery has been conducted, the important facts become known, and it becomes increasingly apparent that there are no serious disputes over the essential facts.

2. Standards and matters considered

A moving party is entitled to summary judgment only if "there is no genuine issue as to any material fact" and "the moving party is entitled to a judgment as a matter of law." The motion merely asks the court to decide if there are any material facts in issue and whether the substantive law

16. Wright §99; James & Hazard §5.19; Friedenthal §§9.1-9.3; Moore's Manual §§17.01-17.19; Wright & Miller §§2711-2742; Moore's Federal Practice §§56.02-56.04; Shepard's Manual §§4.35-4.42.

entitles the moving party to judgment. It is not the court's function here to determine what facts are true. In deciding if material facts are in dispute, however, the court can consider the pleadings, discovery, and witness affidavits.

What facts are material is determined by the claim involved and the allegations in the pleadings. The court will review the movant's motion and supporting matters and determine if any material facts remain disputed. The court will resolve any doubts against the moving party. Keep in mind, however, that the formal pleadings are not controlling. If the pleadings show a dispute, but the discovery and affidavits show that no dispute over any material fact exists, the motion should be granted.

If the motion fails to demonstrate that summary judgment should be granted, the opponent theoretically need do nothing. As a matter of practice, of course, the opposing party always responds to the motion with a memorandum and, if possible, affidavits showing why the motion should not be granted. However, if the motion with accompanying materials shows that the motion should be granted, the opponent ordinarily must, if able to, present a response and opposing affidavit to show that disputes over material issues still remain.[17] If the court then finds that disputed issues remain, the motion will be denied.

3. Hearing, order, and appealability

At the hearing on the motion for summary judgment the judge will usually allow oral argument, and then ordinarily will take the case under advisement and enter a written order at a later time. The order will set out whether the motion is granted or, if partial summary judgment is requested, on what issues the motion is granted or denied. It will also set out the findings and reasoning that are the basis of the order.

Appealability of the order depends on whether the order disposes of all or only part of the case. When an order granting the motion disposes of the entire case, the order is final and appealable.[18] Where the order grants only partial summary judgment, either for some but not all parties or for some but not all claims, the order may be appealable, depending on whether the court makes it an appealable one under Rule 54(b). That Rule permits the judge to make the order appealable "only upon an express determination that there is no just reason for delay" and the judgment is expressly entered.

When the motion is denied, the usual reason is that material facts are still in dispute. An order denying summary judgment on that basis is not final and cannot be appealed.[19]

17. See Celetex Corp. v. Catratt, 106 S. Ct. 2548 (1986), where the Court rejected the notion that the moving party must always support the motion with affidvits showing the absence of a genuine dispute over a material fact. Where a party has the burden of proof on an essential element and fails to make a sufficient showing to establish that element after an adequate time for discovery, there is no genuine dispute over a material fact and the other party may be entitled to summary judgment without a further factual showing.
18. See Moore's Manual §17.19(1).
19. See Moore's Manual §17.19(2).

4. Practice approach

A motion for summary judgment is most frequently successful in simple cases where the "facts" cannot be disputed, such as actions on contracts and notes where the signatures are conceded to be either genuine or fraudulent. The motion is unlikely to be granted in cases where a mental state or a witness' credibility is critical.

Motions for partial summary judgment should also be considered in more complex cases, where at least one count, or one issue in a count, can possibly be disposed of. This may at least streamline the case and make the remaining counts or issues easier to try. For example, parties in personal injury cases frequently move for summary judgment on the issue of liability, so that the trial will focus only on the amount of damages.

If you decide to make a motion for summary judgment, keep several points in mind. First, serve and file the motion well in advance. While the Rule permits service to be made only 10 days before the hearing, or 13 days before if service is by mail, the court will need more time to evaluate a serious motion. In addition, since the opposing party has a right to respond, setting a hearing date well in advance will allow the other party to prepare and present a response. This approach will minimize continuances.

Second, present the motion well before trial. While Rule 56 sets no limits on how close to a trial date a summary judgment motion can be presented, as a practical matter a late motion will be viewed with suspicion. The usual time to present the motion is when discovery has been completed, but before a trial date has been set, since at this stage you should have all the essential information on which the motion will be based.

Third, prepare the motion in an organized, progressive way. The better practice is to have the motion itself simply state on what issues summary judgment is being sought. A supporting memorandum should then detail the material facts involved in those issues and refer to the pleadings, discovery, and affidavits to demonstrate that there is no genuine issue over those facts. Finally, an exhibits section should contain those documents and witness affidavits that are referred to in the memorandum.

Example:

[Caption]

MOTION FOR SUMMARY JUDGMENT

Plaintiff Albert Smith moves, pursuant to Rule 56, for an order entering summary judgment in plaintiff's favor on:

1. Count I of the complaint for the relief requested;
2. Count II on the issue of liability only;

on the ground that there is no genuine issue as to any material fact in
Count I, and no genuine issue as to any material fact regarding the issue
of liability in Count II, and that plaintiff is entitled to summary judgment
to the extent requested as a matter of law.

In support of his motion, attached are the following:

1. memorandum of law and fact
2. excerpts from the pleadings
3. excerpts from the interrogatories and answers
4. excerpts from depositions
5. excerpts from requests to admit and responses
6. three witness affidavits, marked Exhibits A, B and C.

WHEREFORE, plaintiff Albert Smith requests the Court to enter an
order for summary judgment in favor of plaintiff on Count I, and on
Count II on the issue of liability.

_____
Attorney for Plaintiff

Witness affidavits must be carefully prepared for the motion, and
particular care must be taken that they conform to the requirements set
out in Rule 56(c). Affidavits are sworn statements by witnesses, and their
contents should be drafted so that the facts asserted would be admissible
at trial. Accordingly, the witness must be shown to be competent and to
have firsthand knowledge of the facts. The facts asserted must comply
with all other evidence rules. The testimony of each witness is usually set
out in statement form, although in some situations a question and answer
format may be appropriate. The statement is then sworn to before a notary public showing that the witness has personal knowledge of the facts
and that they are true. The notary's attestation and seal should be on the
affidavit.

Example:

AFFIDAVIT IN SUPPORT
OF MOTION FOR SUMMARY JUDGMENT

I, Gloria Patterson, having first been sworn, state under oath:

1. I am a resident of Tucson, Arizona, and have resided there for
eight years.

2. Since January 1, 1980, I have been the President of Cross-Country Transportation, an Arizona corporation having its principal place
of business in Tucson, Arizona. As President of Cross-Country, I have
overall responsibility for its operation, including entering in and approving contracts on behalf of Cross-Country.

3. On June 1, 1986, at approximately 10:00 A.M., I was at the office of Smith Corporation at 100 Main Street, Tucson, Arizona, for a meeting with John Smith, president of Smith Corporation, the defendant in this case. Also present was Adam York, the plaintiff in this case.

4. At that meeting, I saw John Smith sign his name to a contract, a copy of which is attached to this affidavit as Exhibit A. The signature at the bottom page 5 of Exhibit A as that of John Smith, the defendant.

5. I have seen John Smith sign his name to various documents about 25 times over the past five years. Based on this previous experience, I recognize the signature on page 5 of Exhibit A as that of John Smith, the defendant.

Gloria Patterson

State of Arizona | SS.
County of Pima |

Signed and sworn to before me on _____.

Notary Public

My commission expires on _____.

5. Opponent's responses

What should the opponent of a motion for summary judgment do? Rule 56(e) expressly states that an opposing party cannot rely on denials in the pleadings to resist the motion. Of course, if the motion on its face fails to show that the movant is entitled to relief, the adverse party theoretically need not do anything. As a practical matter, however, the adverse party should present an opposing memorandum with supporting affidavits to demonstrate that issues of material fact remain. The supporting affidavits will usually present testimony that contradicts the movant's affidavits on some material facts, thus creating an issue of witness credibility. Credibility issues that exist concerning material facts can only be decided by a trial, so the motion should be denied. If the movant's witness affidavits contain information that the witness would not be able to testify to because of evidentiary objections or because the affidavit is improperly sworn to or notarized, these defects should be raised in the opposing memorandum.

§7.9. *Dismissals and defaults*[20]

Dismissals are governed by Rule 41. There are two types of dismissals, voluntary and involuntary. While the Rule speaks only of plaintiffs, it is clear that the Rule applies to any claimant and therefore to any claim, counterclaim, cross-claim, or third-party claim. It permits dismissals of fewer than all claims against fewer than all parties.[21]

1. Voluntary dismissals

There are two ways to obtain a voluntary dismissal. First, if an answer or summary judgment motion has not yet been filed, a plaintiff can simply file a notice of dismissal with the clerk of the court. No court order is required. The rationale is that this Rule permits a plaintiff to withdraw a lawsuit that is ill-considered or prematurely brought without incurring penalties.

Example:

[Caption]

NOTICE OF DISMISSAL

Please take notice that on June 15, 1986, plaintiff Wilbur Jackson filed this Notice of Dismissal to dismiss plaintiff's complaint without prejudice, pursuant to Rule 41, with the clerk of the Court.

_____

Attorney for Plaintiff

Second, if all parties who have appeared in the action agree on a dismissal, the plaintiff need only file with the clerk of the court a stipulation of dismissal signed by all parties. Again, no court order is required. This is the usual method for terminating a lawsuit following a settlement.

---

20. Wright §97; James & Hazard §12.14; Friedenthal §§9.4-9.5; Shepard's Manual §§7.5, 7.63; Moore's Manual §§19.01-19.11; Wright & Miller §§2362-2376; Moore's Federal Practice §§41.02-41.07.

21. Rule 15, governing amendments of pleadings, and Rule 21, governing joinder, overlap Rule 41 and should always be checked. See Moore's Manual §19.04.1.

Example:

[Caption]

STIPULATION OF DISMISSAL

The parties, plaintiff Wilbur Jackson and defendant Frank Johnson, agreed on June 15, 1986, to dismiss the above-captioned action, without prejudice, and for each party to bear its costs of suit.

_____

Attorney for Plaintiff

_____

Attorney for Defendant

In all other circumstances, plaintiff may obtain a voluntary dismissal only by court order. The court has power to impose terms and conditions that are appropriate under the circumstances, which may include the payment of costs, expenses, and attorney's fees to the defendant. Under ordinary circumstances the motion should be granted, unless the defendant can show that some actual legal prejudice would result from a second lawsuit.

As a tactical matter, plaintiff should simply file and serve a motion for a voluntary dismissal of the action, stating reasons for granting the relief. If the court will only grant the motion upon terms that seem unduly harsh or expensive, plaintiff should consider withdrawing the motion and continuing with the action.

Regardless of whether the voluntary dismissal was obtained through a notice of dismissal or court order, the dismissal is without prejudice unless otherwise stated. The claim can then be refiled later. However, under Rule 41(d), if a plaintiff later files the same claim against the same defendant, the court can order the plaintiff to pay the costs of the previously dismissed action to the defendant, and can order a stay of the new action until plaintiff complies with the order for payment of costs.

Where the dismissal is made by notice of dismissal, the first one is without prejudice. However, to avoid abuse of this Rule by repeated filings and dismissals of actions, Rule 41(a)(1) has a "two dismissal rule." A notice of dismissal is with prejudice and constitutes an adjudication on the merits if the second dismissal is based on the same claim previously dismissed in any federal or state court.

The court ordinarily will not look into the plaintiff's motivation in seeking a voluntary dismissal. The only issues are whether a dismissal would create a legal prejudice to the defendant and what terms the order should include so that defendant's costs and expenses will be reasonably reimbursed. For instance, a plaintiff may dismiss an action that has been removed to federal court even if the only purpose of the dismissal is to defeat the removal and resulting federal jurisdiction, since a defendant has no absolute right to have a case tried in federal court.[22]

Under Rule 41(a)(2), a voluntary dismissal of a claim will not be allowed if a counterclaim has been pleaded before the plaintiff has served a motion for voluntary dismissal, if the counterclaim has no independent jurisdictional basis, or if the defendant objects to the dismissal. The reasoning behind this Rule is that the plaintiff, having previously decided to sue, cannot now use a voluntary dismissal to avoid the counterclaim. Where the defendant's counterclaim does have an independent basis for federal jurisdiction, the plaintiff may dismiss his complaint.

2.   Involuntary dismissals

Involuntary dismissal provides a method for terminating a claim where the plaintiff or other claimant has been guilty of misconduct. While the Rule mentions only a defendant's motion to dismiss, it is clear that the court on its own motion may dismiss.[23] There are several grounds for an involuntary dismissal.

First, a plaintiff's failure to prosecute a claim can result in dismissal. This depends on the nature of the case, but includes a plaintiff's lack of diligence in litigating, such as failing to respond to motions or to appear at hearings, and other repeated dilatory behavior. Involuntary dismissal is a drastic remedy and will normally not be imposed unless other remedies are inadequate. The difficult cases often involve situations where the plaintiff's inaction is a result of his attorney's misconduct, but the plaintiff may have a valid claim. In these situations the court will usually do something short of involuntary dismissal.

Second, the court can involuntarily dismiss where the plaintiff fails to comply with rules of procedure or with court orders. Keep in mind that most failures to comply involve discovery. The Supreme Court has held that only Rule 37 controls sanctions for discovery abuse.[24] Hence, Rule 41 will govern only situations involving failures other than in discovery.

Third, an involuntary dismissal may be entered at trial where the evidence presented by the plaintiff fails to demonstrate that the plaintiff is entitled to any relief. This is permissible only during a bench trial after plaintiff has rested his case in chief. This motion performs the same function as a motion for a directed verdict in a jury trial. However, since the judge during a bench trial is also the trier of fact, the judge may evaluate the facts that the plaintiff has presented; while in a motion for a directed verdict under Rule 50, the judge must consider the evidence in the light most favorable to the plaintiff.

An involuntary dismissal is with prejudice unless otherwise ordered. Hence, it is a final and appealable order.

22. See Moore's Manual §19.05.
23. See Moore's Manual §19.08.
24. See Societe Internationale v. Rogers, 357 U.S. 197 (1958).

3. Defaults

Closely related to dismissals are defaults, governed by Rule 55. This Rule allows any claimant to obtain a default judgment against a party that fails to plead or take any steps to defend against the pending action. The usual situation involves a defaulting defendant.

Defaults are allowed only when the claim seeks affirmative relief. If the claim is for a specific sum, or a sum that can be computed to a specific amount, a default judgment can be entered by the clerk of the court, provided the defendant is not an infant or incompetent. The plaintiff must present an affidavit to the clerk of the court setting out the facts showing default and the sum due. The affidavit should be in the same form as any notarized witness affidavit.[25]

In all other cases the claimant must make a motion for default at least three days before the hearing. If the defaulting party has appeared in the case, you must serve a notice of motion on that party at least three days before the hearing. Even if the defaulting party has never appeared in the case, it is a good practice to serve a notice of motion anyway. At the hearing the court will determine if the allegations of the claim are true and, if plaintiff is entitled to judgment, what the proper amount of damages is.

Example:

[Caption]

MOTION FOR DEFAULT

Plaintiff Joan Franklin moves for an order finding defendant Thomas Johnson in default, finding that the defendant owes plaintiff the sum of $24,246.80 plus costs, and for judgment against defendant in that amount. In support of her motion plaintiff states:

1. On March 1, 1985, defendant Thomas Johnson was personally served with the summons and the complaint, as shown by the affidavit of service on the summons.

2. Defendant has failed to answer the complaint, has failed to make an appearance, or in any way respond or defend, although over 90 days have passed since service upon him.

3. Defendant has not responded to three letters sent to him by plaintiff's attorneys. Copies of these letters are attached as Exhibits A, B, and C.

4. Plaintiff is prepared to testify to her reasonable damages, which total $24,246.80.

WHEREFORE, plaintiff requests that the court find defendant Thomas Johnson in default, hold a hearing to determine the exact

25. See §7.9.3.

amount due plaintiff, and enter judgment for plaintiff and against defendant in that amount.

_____

Attorney for Plaintiff

Defaults are most commonly obtained in simple cases where a defendant who has been properly served fails to respond in any way to the lawsuit, and enough time has passed so that it becomes obvious the defendant does not intend to defend against the claim.

If the sum due is clear, such as in a contract action for past due rent or in an action for an unpaid bill for purchased merchandise, an affidavit to the clerk of the court is appropriate. In many cases, however, the full damages can only be determined at a hearing, requiring that a motion for default judgment be made.

At the hearing on the motion, commonly called a "prove up," you should be prepared to show that service on the defaulting party was proper, that the allegations of the complaint are true, and what the proper damages are. While judges vary on the formality of the prove-up hearing, you should have all your documentation available and any witnesses on hand that may be necessary to prove your case. For example, in an action on a contract, you should be able to prove proper service with the proof of service in the court file. If necessary, have the person who served the complaint and summons testify. You can prove the existence and execution of the contract by calling a witness who was present at its execution. Another witness along with exhibits can prove performance by the plaintiff, typically payment of the contract price. Other witnesses and records can show nonperformance by the defendant and the extent of the plaintiff's damages. Although the court may not require them, or permit witnesses to summarize what they know in a narrative fashion, it is always safer to have all your witnesses available and prepared to testify as if the proceeding were a trial.

A defaulting party can only have the default judgment set aside if any of the reasons under Rule 60(b), principally excusable neglect, are shown. For that reason, you should take certain steps to minimize the chances that a default will be vacated. First, serve the defendant by the most direct of the permitted service methods. Second, wait an appropriate period of time, at least 60 to 90 days, before seeking a default. Third, during this time you should send the defendant periodic letters asking for a response and spelling out the consequences of a default. Finally, send the defendant a notice of motion for the default motion, even though this is required only if the defendant has previously appeared in the case. Taking these steps now will support the motion itself and will make it less likely that the defaulted defendant will succeed in having the default judgment set aside later. The defendant will usually try to vacate the judgment only when you take steps to execute the judgment against the defendant's property, such as garnishing a savings account, and the matter suddenly becomes "serious."

Moving for a default judgment as soon as permitted under the Rules usually has the effect of stimulating action by the defendant. If you think the defendant really wants to defend, but is just dragging his feet, making a quick motion for default is frequently an effective technique for getting the lawsuit going.

§7.10. Consolidation and separate trials[26]

Under Rule 42 the court may consolidate separate cases for trial, or have parts of a single case tried separately.

1. Consolidations

Consolidation is governed by Rule 42(a) and has several elements. First, actions can be consolidated only when all actions are "pending before the court." This means that the cases have all been filed and are presently pending in the same district court. Second, the actions must have "common questions of law or fact." Typical are personal injury actions by several plaintiffs arising out of a single accident. Third, the court may decide to consolidate only certain issues for hearing or trial, such as the liability issues. This is a discretionary matter for the court and is usually decided after discovery has been completed and the cases are scheduled on the trial calendar.

2. Separate trials

Under Rule 42(b), the court may also order separate trials. This is permitted where separation will create convenience, avoid prejudice, or permit a case to be tried more efficiently and economically. The court has broad authority to separate claims, counterclaims, cross-claims, and third-party claims and to separate issues in any claims, or to separate parties. The typical situation involves unrelated permissive counterclaims or third-party claims where it makes sense to try unrelated claims later or spin off third-party actions to keep the trials simpler. This decision is also usually made only when discovery is complete and the case is on the trial calendar. Frequently a decision to sever is made at the pretrial conference.

While the court has authority to separate issues, a problem often arises because the Rule expressly reserves a party's rights to a jury trial. The case law is still unclear as to when a court may order separate trials

26. Wright §97; Friedenthal §6.2; Shepard's Manual §§7.3-7.4; Moore's Manual §20.01; Wright & Miller §§2382-2390; Moore's Federal Practice §§42.02-42.03.

of issues before different juries.[27] Separate trials on liability and damages issues before the same jury cause no problems, but there is some dispute over different juries deciding the separate issues.[28]

27. See Wright §97.
28. See Wright & Miller §2390.

VIII

PRETRIAL CONFERENCES AND SETTLEMENTS

§8.1. Introduction

More than 90 percent of civil cases filed in court settle before trial. The
law prefers settlement and has created several methods to accomplish it.
Judges prefer settlement, and the trend has been toward greater judicial
involvement, principally by using pretrial conferences to get the adversaries together to discuss settlement possibilities. Finally, most clients ultimately prefer settlement over the increased expenses and uncertainties of
a trial. Small wonder, then, that lawyers settle most cases before trial.

This chapter discusses both pretrial conferences and settlement because the two are closely related in most cases. Judges are increasingly
using pretrial conferences to force settlement discussions as a case nears
trial. Although lawyers can and do discuss settlement at other times, once
a case has been filed in court the most common point at which settlement
is discussed is after discovery has been completed but before trial preparations have begun. Since this is when pretrial conferences are commonly
scheduled, it makes sense to discuss both pretrial conferences and settlements as interrelated parts of the litigation process.

§8.2. Pretrial conferences[1]

1. Procedure

Pretrial conferences are governed by Rule 16, which gives the trial court
broad authority to hold pretrial conferences on a wide spectrum of matters and to enter comprehensive pretrial orders. Rule 16 is not manda-
tory, however, and trial judges vary widely in how they use the Rule.
Many districts and individual judges have also adopted local rules and
instructions further regulating pretrial conferences. Hence, in preparing
for a pretrial conference, you must comply not only with Rule 16, but

1. Wright §91; James & Hazard §§5.16-5.17; Friedenthal §§8.1-8.3; Moore's Manual
§§18.01-18.09; Shepard's Manual §§6.1-6.18; Moore's Federal Practice §§16.07-16.22;
Wright & Miller §§1521-1530.

also with applicable local rules, and be aware of your judge's special instructions on, and attitude toward, pretrial conferences.

Rule 16(a) permits holding pretrial conferences for two basic purposes. First, a judge can order a pretrial conference to set cut-off dates for motions and discovery. This is usually done early in the litigation process. Second, a pretrial conference held after motions and discovery are completed can force the parties to sit down with the judge and discuss settlement possibilities, force the parties to narrow the issues that will actually be tried, and streamline the presentation of evidence by obtaining stipulations, evidentiary rulings, and limitations on witnesses. The usual time contemplated by Rule 16(d) for the latter conference is a few weeks before trial. By this time pleadings will be closed, discovery completed and most motions will have been ruled on.

The conference must be attended by each party's counsel, who should have authority to settle and to make stipulations and admissions. If settlement will be discussed, the clients should either be present at the conference or be available by telephone.

Judges vary widely in how they conduct pretrial conferences. Some will merely have an informal meeting in chambers, without the court reporter, to discuss the general nature of the lawsuit and explore the possibilities for settlement. At the other end of the spectrum are judges who will hold a formal conference, sometimes in open court, and conduct a formal, detailed review of the pretrial memorandum, make all possible rulings, and detail them in an extensive pretrial order. Some judges actively encourage settlements, others do not. Also, some judges are flexible and let the lawyers participate in deciding what type of conference would be most productive in a particular case. Learn how your judge conducts pretrial conferences and prepare accordingly. If you do not know your judge's practice, ask around. The judge's law clerk is usually a good place to start.

2. Pretrial memorandum

Once you have determined your judge's expectations for the pretrial conference, you should prepare the pretrial memorandum. How detailed to make the memorandum depends on the particular judge's procedures; some require only a short, general memorandum, a few require none at all, while others expect a detailed review of the case. The trend is toward requiring a detailed pretrial memorandum that is prepared jointly by the parties. Keep in mind that many jurisdictions have local rules concerning the contents of the memorandum. Many judges also issue instructions that specify how the memorandum must be prepared. The following subjects are ordinarily included in a pretrial memorandum and discussed at the conference.

a. Simplifying issues

A principal purpose of the pretrial conference is to reduce issues to those that will actually be tried. Pleadings often assert many possible claims and defenses against every possible party. At the pretrial conference, then, the judge will usually require each party to state the claims and defenses that will actually be presented at trial as well as those that will be waived. At this time the judge may also permit amendments to the pleadings so that the pleadings accurately reflect the disputed trial issues.

Keep in mind that where multiple claims are involved, the judge has authority under Rule 42(b) to order separate trials when it will promote the orderly and efficient presentation of evidence. In addition, as a trial strategy matter it is often preferable to pursue only the strongest claim without presenting alternative theories of recovery, particularly if they are factually or logically inconsistent.

b. Agreed and contested facts

To avoid unnecessary formal proof and to focus on disputed facts, the judge will usually require that each party state what facts it agrees to and what facts it contests. Where facts are agreed upon, they may be introduced at trial through stipulations. While a judge has no authority to force the parties to stipulate to facts, as a practical matter it is often in everyone's best interests to do so. Keep in mind that if you do not admit a fact, your opponent can then serve a request for admissions. If you do not admit it in your response to the request and your opponent later proves that fact at trial, the court under Rule 37(c) may award costs and attorney's fees expended to prove it.

c. Witness lists

The judge will usually require a list of lay and expert witnesses, along with addresses, that will be called for each party's case in chief. Judges also frequently require a summary of each witness's expected testimony and the qualifications of each side's experts. This requirement does not usually extend to impeachment or rebuttal witnesses. Each party may be asked to state whether it intends to object to any witness' testimony; also, the judge may eliminate cumulative or repetitive witnesses.

d. Exhibit lists

Parties will usually be required to prepare lists of all exhibits they will introduce in evidence at trial. Opposing parties may be required to state whether they object to any of the exhibits and, if so, provide the legal basis for the objection. This requirement essentially operates as a motion in limine on objections to evidence. If there is no objection to an exhibit, the judge will usually treat the exhibit as admitted in evidence. Where objections exist, the judge may be able to rule on them before trial. Keep in mind, however, that some objections, such as foundation objections, cannot be ruled on in advance of trial. However, the judge is at least alerted to the objections that will be heard at trial and thus will be able to decide them more efficiently.

e. Damages proof

In certain types of cases the judge may direct that evidence on damages issues be presented separately. Other parties will be required to state whether they object to the evidence or the amounts asserted. Certain special damages, such as lost wages and medical bills, are often not contested and can be admitted at trial through stipulations.

f. Instructions

The judge usually requires that each party submit proposed jury instructions and state whether it intends to object to the opponent's instructions, and, if so, provide the basis for each objection. While the judge often cannot decide whether to give an instruction before evidence has been presented at trial, the judge can usually rule on the wording of proposed instructions. Since this can be a time consuming task, reviewing the instructions at a pretrial conference can often avoid substantial delay at trial. If the case is one in which special interrogatories or verdict forms will be submitted to the jury, the same procedure can be followed.

g. Voir dire questions

The most common practice in federal court today is for the judge to ask the voir dire questions during jury selection. Where this is the practice, the lawyers are asked to submit proposed voir dire questions to the judge, who then decides whether to ask the questions during the jury selection process. Frequently judges will direct the parties to list their proposed voir dire questions in the pretrial memorandum.

h. Trial briefs

Most judges today expect the parties to submit a trial brief discussing the applicable substantive law and likely evidentiary issues. The trial brief alerts the judge and parties to anticipated procedural and evidentiary issues, reviews applicable law, and permits the judge to schedule hearings and make rulings on motions in limine. The advantage to both sides should be apparent, since each side has an interest in presenting its case in chief in a smooth, uninterrupted way. Jurors are annoyed by constant side bar conferences and recesses. Trial briefs, coupled with pretrial motions and motions in limine, will minimize trial interruptions and benefit everyone.

A simple joint pretrial memorandum is usually drafted by the lawyers for each of the parties, with each party contributing those portions that reflect its own witnesses, exhibits, and objections to the other side's evidence. This has the obvious benefit of putting all the necessary information in one document.

Example:

[Caption]

JOINT PRETRIAL MEMORANDUM

Counsel for plaintiff Frances Johnson and defendants Robert Jones and Lisa Roberts submit the following Joint Pretrial Memorandum:

I

Uncontested Facts

The accident occurred on June 1, 1986, at approximately 2:00 P.M. Plaintiff Frances Johnson was a passenger in a 1981 Honda Accord owned and driven by defendant Robert Jones. Jones was driving north on Kolb Road intending to turn left (west) on 22d Street. As he was executing this turn, the defendant Lisa Roberts, who was driving her 1983 Buick Skylark south bound on Kolb Road, struck Jones' vehicle. The intersection is controlled by a traffic light. Both defendant Roberts and defendant Jones claim to have had a green light favoring their direction of travel. At the time of the accident, the plaintiff Johnson was employed as a bank teller by the First National Bank.

II

Contested Issues of Fact and Law

1. Which of the defendants, if either, were negligent?
2. Were both defendants negligent?
3. If the plaintiff was injured as a result of the negligence of one or both defendants, what amount of money is she entitled to recover for her damages?

III

Exhibits

A. *Plaintiff Johnson's Exhibits:*   *Objections to Admissibility, if any:*

1. Medical expenses totaling $848.26 as evidenced by vouchers in support of each expenditure contained in a blue brochure with a cover

sheet listing the medical expenses.

2. The Police Department official report of the accident.   Objected to by defendant Jones.

3. St. Mary's Hospital emergency room records of the plaintiff.

4. Photographs of the plaintiff showing her shoulder deficit.

5. X rays taken of the plaintiff.

6. Photographs and diagrams of the intersection involved.

B.   *Defendant Jones' Exhibits:*   *Objections to Admissibility, if any:*

1. Plaintiff's hospital and medical records.

2. X rays.

3. Plaintiff's employment records.

4. Bills concerning property damage.

5. Time sequence of signal lights.

6. Photographs of the vehicles.

7. The police report as far as it is admissible.

C.   *Defendant Roberts' Exhibits:*   *Objections to Admissibility, if any:*

1. Police report of accident.

2. Photographs of vehicles involved.   Objected to by plaintiff and by defendant Jones, for the reasons stated in the attached Memorandum of Law

3. Plaintiff's medical records.

IV

Witnesses

A. *Plaintiff Johnson's Witnesses:*

1. Plaintiff.

2.   Richard Martin, M.D.
3.   Ernest Jackson, M.D.
4.   Philip Wigmore, a bystander.
5.   Bernie Sullivan, plaintiff's supervisor at First National Bank.
6.   Investigating police officer Frank Johnson.
7.   Defendants.

B.   *Defendant Jones' Witnesses:*

1.   The parties to this action.
2.   Investigating police officer Frank Johnson.

C.   *Defendant Roberts' Witnesses:*

1.   The parties to this action.
2.   Doctors who have seen or treated plaintiff.
3.   Richard Hollister, a bystander.
4.   Officer Horn, Police Department.
5.   Glenda Sylvester, accident reconstruction expert.

V

Jury Instructions

Plaintiff and defendants' proposed jury instructions are attached.

1. Plaintiff Johnson objects to Jones' instructions numbers 4, 7, and 9, and objects to Roberts' instruction number 6 for the reasons stated in the attached Memorandum of Law.

2. Both defendants object to plaintiff Johnson's instructions numbers 6, 7, 8, and 13 for the reasons stated in the attached Memorandum of Law.

RESPECTFULLY SUBMITTED this 1st day of June, 1988.

By _____
Attorney for Plaintiff Johnson

By _____
Attorney for Defendant Jones

By _____
Attorney for Defendant
Roberts

3. Pretrial order

Rule 16(e) requires that the judge enter an order reciting the actions taken at the pretrial conference. The Rule is silent on who prepares the order and practices vary widely. Some judges prepare the order, either by stating the results of the conference in open court so the court reporter will record it, or by preparing a written pretrial order. Other judges have the parties draft an agreed order, which the judge then reviews and signs.

The content of the pretrial order is critical, since the order controls the trial. If the pretrial order incorrectly recites the disputed issues, witnesses, exhibits, or other matters, it must be promptly corrected. The best time to do this, when possible, is while the order is in draft form and not yet signed by the judge. Once entered, the order can be modified "only to prevent manifest injustice."

A simple pretrial order, based on the joint pretrial memorandum, might look like the following.

Example:

[Caption]

FINAL PRETRIAL ORDER

The following are the results of pretrial proceedings in this cause held pursuant to Rule 16 and IT IS ORDERED:

I

This is an action for damages arising out of a collision involving vehicles driven by defendant Jones and defendant Roberts, which ocurred on June 1, 1986, at the intersection of Kolb Road and 22d Street.

II

Jurisdiction is based on diversity of citizenship under 18 U.S.C. §1332. Plaintiff is a citizen of California, defendant Jones is a citizen of Arizona, and defendant Roberts is a citizen of Nevada.

III

The following facts are admitted by the parties and require no proof:

1. The collision occurred on June 1, 1986, at the intersection of Kolb Road and 22d Street.

2. Defendant Jones was the owner and operator of a 1981 Honda Accord that was involved in the collision.

3. Defendant Roberts was the owner and operator of a 1983 Buick Skylark that was involved in the collision.

4. Plaintiff Johnson was a passenger in defendant Jones' vehicle at the time of the collision.

IV

The following facts, though not admitted, will not be contested at trial by evidence to the contrary:

1. Plaintiff was absent from work from June 1, 1986, through June 14, 1986.

2. Plaintiff was admitted to St. Mary's Hospital Emergency Room on June 1, 1986, and was discharged from the hospital on June 3, 1986.

3. Plaintiff's hospital bill was $492.83.

4. Plaintiff's doctor bills to date total $978.21.

V

The following are the issues of fact to be tried and determined upon trial:

Issue: Whether the defendants used due care in operating their vehicles?

Plaintiff contends that both defendants were speeding, not driving safely, and were not keeping a proper lookout.

Defendant Jones contends that he was driving within the speed limit and operating his vehicle safely.

Defendant Roberts contends that she was driving within the speed limit and operating her vehicle safely, and that defendant Jones failed to yield the right of way.

VI

The following are the issues of law to be tried and determined upon trial:

Issue: Whether the defendants, or either one of them, were negligent?

Plaintiff contends that both defendants were negligent and that their negligence jointly and directly caused plaintiff's injuries.

Defendant Jones contends that he was not negligent, and that his conduct caused no injuries to plaintiff.

Defendant Roberts contends that she was not negligent, that she did not violate any statutes, and that her conduct caused no injuries to plaintiff.

VII

a. The following exhibits are admissible in evidence in this case and may be marked in evidence by the Clerk:
(1) Plaintiff's exhibits: (see attached List number 1)
(2) Defendants' exhibits: (see attached Lists numbers 2 and 3)
b. As to the following exhibits, the party against whom the same will be offered objects to their admission upon the grounds stated:
(1) Plaintiff's exhibits: (see attached List number 4)
(2) Defendants' exhibits (see attached Lists numbers 5 and 6)

VIII

The following witnesses will be called by the parties upon trial:
(a) On behalf of plaintiff: (see attached List number 7)
(b) On behalf of defendants: (see attached lists numbers 8 and 9)

IX

A jury trial has been requested, and was timely requested. It is anticipated that the case will require three trial days.

APPROVED AS TO FORM:

_____
Attorney for Plaintiff Johnson

_____
Attorney for Defendant Jones

_____
Attorney for Defendant
Roberts

The foregoing constitutes the Final Pretrial Order in the above case. All prior pleadings in the case are superseded by this Order, which shall not be amended except by consent of the parties and by order of this court.

_____
United States District Judge

Dated: _____

The pretrial order bars parties from raising any claims or defenses not permitted by the order, and restricts the witnesses, exhibits, objections, and any other matters to those contained in the order. While Rule 16(e) permits modification to prevent manifest injustice, the granting of such a motion is discretionary with the judge, and counsel must ordinarily present a persuasive reason for amending the order.

Since pretrial orders are not usually final orders, they cannot be appealed under 28 U.S.C. §1291 until the case is disposed of by a final judgment.[2] However, an appeal following a final judgment can raise errors in the pretrial order.

§8.3.   Settlements[3]

Settling a case involves three basic steps: determining the case's settlement value, selling your assessment to the opposing side, and having the client agree. While a case can be settled at any time, settlement possibilities are almost always explored when a case nears the pretrial conference stage and a trial is just around the corner. Discovery will be complete at this point, and there is sufficient information to accurately assess the case.[4]

For this reason, you should take stock of your case again when the final pretrial conference is first scheduled. Preparing the pretrial memorandum necessarily will involve reviewing the pleadings, discovery, contested issues, witnesses, exhibits, and potential factual and legal problems. Since the pretrial conference will ordinarily explore settlement possibilities, you might as well review the case for its settlement potential in a systematic way.

1.   Case evaluation[5]

You need to evaluate the case in a clear, progressive way so that you reach an accurate and realistic assessment of its strengths and weaknesses. The sequence to use for your case evaluation should include the following, which parallel the way you have used a litigation chart to structure your litigation plan.[6]

a.   List elements of proof

Look at the elements instructions for liability, special damages, general damages, and defenses for every claim you intend to pursue at trial.

2. Under a few special circumstances an interlocutory appeal may be permitted. See 28 U.S.C. §1292; Moore's Manual §18.08.
3. See G. R. Williams, Legal Negotiations and Settlement ch. 5, pp. 90-109 (1983); J. Jeans, Handbook on Trial Advocacy ch. 18, pp. 425-465 (1975).
4. Obviously, settlement should be explored earlier as well, for instance just before or just after filing suit, or after the plaintiff's deposition has been taken, when the costs both in terms of time delay and litigation expenses can be held down.
5. See J. Jeans, Handbook on Trial Advocacy ch. 17, pp. 395-424 (1975).
6. See §2.2.

The elements instructions will itemize exactly what facts must be proved. This, of course, should already be on your litigation chart.

b. List sources of proof

List all lay and expert witnesses, with a summary of their testimony; all exhibits; and any other anticipated proof, such as stipulations and judicial notice. Include only evidence that you reasonably believe will be admissible at trial.

c. Relate proof to elements

Now list the various witnesses and exhibits with the specific facts that must be proved for each claim and defense. Do this for your opponent's proof as well. This approach will organize the evidence and show what evidence there is to prove and refute for each element of the claims and defenses.

d. Review credibility of the proof

Once you have organized the evidence and related it to the elements of the claims and defenses, you must take the critical step of realistically assessing whether it will be considered credible to a jury. How persuasive will the witnesses be? How probative are the exhibits?

Assessing credibility of proof is largely a function of trial experience, but there are other ways to get a "feel" for your case. Do the witnesses have good personal, family, and employment backgrounds that will make them believable to a jury? Do they tell stories that make sense? Are their stories consistent with our common experience in life? Are the witnesses consistent with each other? A good practice for any lawyer, regardless of experience, is to try out your case, giving an objective summary of your side's proof as well as the other side's proof. This can be done before experienced trial lawyers, colleagues, friends, and spouses. Their reactions to the case and assessment of the case's strengths and weaknesses will usually be good indicators of how the proof will be viewed by a real jury.

e. Evaluate your case's jury appeal

Cases, of course, are not presented in a perfect, dispassionate world. A major consideration is whether your case, or your opponent's, has jury appeal. This must be assessed whenever any party has made a jury demand. Granted, "jury appeal" is an elusive concept, but it is extremely important to consider both before filing a demand for a jury trial with your initial pleading and before reviewing the case for settlement purposes. The basic components of jury appeal are the claims, the parties, and the lawyers.

The claims have much to do with whether a jury will be sympathetic to, or offended by, the conduct of either side. For the most part, juries are sympathetic to the unassuming individual who has been victimized. For example, a simple negligence case involving property damage or a routine contract action usually has little jury appeal. A negligence case against a drunk driver, however, or a contract action by a home owner against a home builder charging faulty construction will have substantial appeal.

Jury appeal is influenced by who the parties are. Similar cases can have widely varying verdicts, depending on the appeal of the parties. A plaintiff who is physically attractive, speaks well, and has a middle-class background will have considerable appeal. A trial involving a wealthy defendant, or a corporate or government defendant, will usually generate substantially higher verdicts for the plaintiff.[7]

Finally, the particular trial lawyer will obviously have some impact. Experienced trial lawyers with a proven record for obtaining good verdicts in similar types of cases can be expected to get better verdicts than other lawyers. Accordingly, you should always investigate your opponent's actual jury trial experience and reputation as a trial lawyer, and add this information to the overall analysis.

f. Review jury verdict reporters

Some jurisdictions, usually those with large metropolitan populations, have jury verdict reporter services that periodically report the facts of cases tried and the verdicts obtained.[8] By researching these services, not only for your jurisdiction but similar ones, you can at least learn the range of verdicts realistically attainable in similar cases. Keep in mind, however, that verdicts can vary widely depending on the jurisdiction, judge, lawyers, and facts — factors not readily apparent in the reports.

g. Review the trial expenses

Trials are expensive, both emotionally and financially. The client must realize the emotional toll a trial can take, and must be aware of the significant demands a trial will make on his time, demands that must take priority over all other obligations. Give the client a projection of how much of his time you will need in order to prepare and try the case, and what he will be doing during those hours. Where a client is unwilling to make the necessary commitment, or is unprepared to handle the emotional stresses and uncertainties of a trial, settlement is the obvious course.

The client should also be aware of the trial expenses involved, because they can be substantial. This is a good time to review your litigation budget with your client.[9] If you are being compensated on an hourly ba-

7. There are numerous psychological studies that have identified factors that affect witness credibility. See, e.g., Applying Social Psychological Research to Witness Credibility Law, in 2 Applied Social Psychology Annual (1980).

8. Frequently used national services are the ATLA Law Reporter and Jury Verdict Reports, which report the monetary range of successful plaintiff's verdicts.

9. See §2.2.5.

sis, you should give the client a current estimate of the trial preparation and trial time involved. Experienced trial lawyers usually need at least one day of preparation for each day of trial, and often more. With hourly rates frequently exceeding $100 per hour, a five day trial, requiring five preparation days, can easily cost a client $10,000 in lawyer fees alone. Where a statute permits awarding attorney's fees to the winning party, this will significantly increase the costs to the losing side.

Witness fees, particularly for experts who expect to be compensated for their time and expenses, and travel and housing expenses, can be substantial since medical and other technical experts usually command an hourly rate comparable to that of lawyers. For example, doctors usually insist on being compensated at the same hourly rate they would receive in their practice; taking a doctor away from his practice for even half a day can cost several hundred dollars. Flying an expert in to testify at trial will obviously be substantially more expensive. Finally, court costs and other expenses cannot be overlooked, since they can add up during a protracted jury trial. Court costs, including the initial filing fees and the daily juror fees, can become substantial in any lengthy trial.

h. Consider preparing a settlement brochure

In recent years it has become fashionable among plaintiff's personal injury lawyers to prepare so-called settlement brochures in major cases. These brochures essentially set out the background of the plaintiff and family along with the evidence showing liability and damages. The fact summaries are usually supplemented by photographs and documents such as employment records, hospital and other medical records, bills, and medical and economic expert reports detailing the extent of injuries, the degree of permanent physical losses, and the plaintiff's economic future. Some lawyers believe that developing such a brochure is the most effective way of presenting the plaintiff's case before trial and obtaining a favorable settlement, since it can graphically show the nature and extent of the injuries, summarize the quality of the plaintiff's case, and demonstrate the jury appeal of a plaintiff.

i. Determine the settlement value

Your case evaluation is not complete, of course, until you have reached a dollar amount, or range, that represents a realistic settlement figure that you can recommend your client accept. This means that you must translate the case evaluation into a final dollar amount. Of course, there are many factors other than a monetary analysis that may affect the way a case is settled. These include the amount and coverage of the defendant's insurance, whether any of plaintiff's damages have been paid by other sources, the defendant's ability to pay a judgment if little or no insurance coverage is available, each party's ability to bear the costs of litigation, the willingness of the parties to go to trial, the effect of litigation on the parties' business and personal interests, and whether publicity surrounds the litigation. While these can significantly affect the settlement of any case, most cases are settled principally on an evaluation in monetary terms, and there are several steps in this process.[10]

First, you need to establish the dollar amount of a likely verdict if the plaintiff were to prove both liability and damages. In some cases, such as contract actions, it may be possible to reach a specific figure. In others, such as personal injury actions, it is probably better to use a dollar range for a likely verdict. Make the same determination for any counterclaims.

Second, you need to determine the probability that the plaintiff will succeed on the question of liability; this probability is expressed as a percentage. For example, if you conclude that the plaintiff is as likely to prevail on liability as lose on it, the likelihood of success is 50 percent. This means that the "value" of the case for settlement purposes is 50 percent of the probable verdict. Make the same kind of analysis for any counterclaims. For example, if a personal injury case is being tried under comparative negligence, you need to determine the likelihood of the jury concluding that the defendant was also negligent, express it as a percentage, and reduce the value of the case by that amount.

Third, analyze the additional costs the client will incur if the case goes to trial. These costs will include lawyer fees and other trial expenses, such as the cost of having experts testify. Of course, if you are being paid on a contingency or flat fee basis, there will be no additional legal fees. When you are being paid on an hourly basis, however, you will need to estimate the hours required to finish preparing and to try the case and then multiply that number by your hourly rate. Those additional legal fees and trial expenses reduce the value of the case if it goes to trial and should be discounted for settlement evaluation purposes.

Fourth, you need to take into account the time value of money. Money received now is worth more than the same amount of money received one year from now. As the plaintiff in the case, you will need to discount the "value" of the case to reflect the benefit of receiving an amount of money now rather than after a trial. The discount, expressed as a percentage, depends on how much sooner the plaintiff will get the money and the increased value of getting it now. For instance, if the plaintiff would get a certain amount of money after a verdict but the case will not be tried for a year, and the investment yield on a prudent investment is currently 7 percent, that amount of money received next year is worth about 7 percent less than if received now. Plaintiff needs to discount the value of the case by these time value considerations; a defendant would add the same amount, since deferring payment of a judgment is a benefit.[11]

Fifth, see if the defendant's insurance coverage, or other ability to pay, will create a practical limit on what the plaintiff can realistically hope to recover. Where insurance coverage is low and the defendant has no substantial assets that could help satisfy a judgment, the policy limit may

10. During the past few years, litigation support firms have developed computer models that attempt to quantify the various parts of a case analysis for reaching a settlement value. While this may be cost effective only in large cases, it indicates a general recognition that settlement values must be analyzed systematically.

11. This assumes that there is no prejudgment interest applicable.

be the only amount the plaintiff can ever recover. In this situation the defense may simply "tender the policy" to settle the case against that defendant.

Example:

You represent the plaintiff in a personal injury case on a contingency basis. The applicable state's law uses comparative negligence. Your settlement value analysis should go along the following lines:

(1) Assuming liability, you assess the probable verdict range at $20,000 to $30,000.

(2) You assess the likelihood of proving liability at 80 percent. However, you conclude that the jury will find the plaintiff 33 percent responsible for his injuries.

(3) Since you are representing the plaintiff on a contingency basis, a trial will not create additional legal costs. However, you estimate that the plaintiff will have to pay $2,000 for trial expenses, principally expert fees and costs.

(4) You estimate the case will not be tried for 18 months; the current rate of return for safe investments is 6 percent.

The value of the case computes as follows:

(1) Median "value" of the case is $25,000 (the midpoint of your verdict range).

(2) Your 80 percent recovery chances reduce the value to $20,000; the comparative negligence likelihood of 33 percent reduces the value to approximately $13,000.

(3) Your estimated trial expenses of $2,000 reduce the value of the case to $11,000.

(4) Finally, the 18 months to trial and investment rate of 6 percent per year reduces the value to about $10,000.

These figures show a current settlement value of approximately $10,000 to the plaintiff. In other words, plaintiff should consider accepting any settlement that exceeds $10,000. Since discovery has already revealed that the defendant has an applicable insurance policy with $25,000 coverage, collecting the judgment should not be a concern.

The defendant, of course, should be making the same type of analysis. Because the defendant will usually be paying legal fees on an hourly basis and can expect to pay several thousand dollars in lawyer's fees if the case goes to trial, her settlement value will frequently be higher than the plaintiff's. When the plaintiff and the defendant have analyzed the likely jury verdict in a similar fashion, a dollar range is usually created that makes settlement attractive to both sides. Settlement is then likely to be reached on a figure that is higher than the plaintiff's settlement value but lower than the defendant's. For example, if plaintiff has valued the case at $10,000 and the defendant has valued it at $13,000, any settlement figure between these two extremes would be beneficial to both parties.

2.   Negotiating a settlement

The dynamics of negotiation, in the litigation arena as well as in other fields, has received increasing attention in recent years. This has occurred, in part, because litigation and trial costs have made settlement more desirable, but also because there is a growing awareness that learning negotiating methods can improve a lawyer's ability. The literature on negotiation methods for lawyers is rapidly expanding, and a number of books are particularly useful for litigators.[12] Although this text obviously cannot summarize this literature, some generalizations about negotiations may still be useful.

First, trying a case inherently involves risks, since neither party can ever predict with absolute certainty what a jury will decide in a given case. Settlements are simply the way in which lawyers eliminate the risks in the litigation process.

Second, since risks are at the core of the process, you need to do whatever you can to minimize them. This requires that you adequately prepare the case for trial, since the more you know about the case, the fewer the uncertainties and unknown factors, and hence the less risk. It also requires that you realistically evaluate the case for settlement purposes.

Third, the more relative uncertainty there is in your opponent's mind, the more flexible and compromising he is likely to be. Factors that increase uncertainty in your opponent's mind are your own thorough preparation of the case and willingness and ability to go to trial if necessary, and your client's willingness and preparedness for trial. In communications with your opponent, you need to stress the strong points of your case, probe for the weak spots in your opponent's case, and see if you can glean your opponent's true attitude about the case. Much of this can be accomplished through your contacts during the discovery and motions stages.

Fourth, negotiation styles are as varied as lawyers are numerous. They range from the "take it or leave it" approach to an approach that involves making an initial high demand or low offer that will be followed by protracted negotiations. Nevertheless, there are two basic approaches that are commonly followed.[13] The first approach is competitive: the lawyer makes an initial high demand, keeps the pressure on the opponent, and makes as few concessions as possible. The atmosphere is entirely adversarial, and the projected attitude is one of strength. This approach, perhaps the traditional way in which settlement negotiations were conducted, has benefits, principally that any settlement reached will probably be a good one for the client of the more competitive lawyer. Its drawback

---

12. G. Bellow & B. Moulton, The Lawyering Process: Negotiation (1981); H. T. Edwards & J. J. White, Problems, Readings and Materials on the Lawyer as a Negotiator (1977); R. Fisher & W. Ury, Getting to Yes (1983); X. M. Frascogna & H. L. Hetherington, Negotiation Strategy for Lawyers (1984); R. S. Haydock, Negotiation Practice (1984); K. F. Hegland, Trial and Practice Skills in a Nutshell (1978); G. R. Williams, Legal Negotiation and Settlement (1983).

13. See G. R. Williams, Legal Negotiation and Settlement (1983).

is that probably a lower percentage of cases settle under this approach. A possible conclusion to draw is that this approach is effective where you have a strong case and don't need to compromise.

The other approach is more cooperative: the lawyer makes a more realistic initial demand, emphasizes the parties' shared interests, and shows a willingness to make concessions. The atmosphere is conciliatory. The benefit to this approach is that probably more cases get settled. On the negative side, the settlement may not be as good for your client, since the other side may try to take advantage of your attitude. Accordingly, this approach may be effective where both parties are equally strong.

The cooperative approach is becoming more accepted, probably because it seems to improve the possibilities of reaching an eventual agreement. While it has several characteristics,[14] the key to the cooperative approach is to avoid taking rigid "positions." Instead, the lawyers who are negotiating focus on the mutual interests of their clients, avoid personalizing the conflicts, and expand the possible solutions before objectively culling through the solutions to settle on a resolution of the problem. This approach, by avoiding personalities and rigid posturing, becomes a joint effort to reach solutions. Where the parties have a complex set of interests, this approach may be useful.

Regardless of which negotiating approach you use in a particular case, the question of which side should first raise the possibility of settlement must be considered. Many lawyers avoid raising it first, on the theory that it suggests weaknesses in the case. Where you have obviously prepared your case thoroughly, however, and show a capacity and willingness to try the case if necessary, no such implication should arise.

Which side should make the initial offer? Frequently both sides are reluctant to state the first dollar figure, on the theory that since the initial figure will be the starting point for later compromises it is better to get the other side committed first. The result is often unrealistically high or low initial offers, which the other side can easily reject. The more effective approach usually is to make a realistic initial offer because this will put pressure on the opponent. The last thing the opponent wants is to get a serious offer, reject it, and end up with a less favorable result following a trial. A realistic offer puts pressure on the opponent to evaluate it seriously.

Finally, remember that the possibilities for settlement frequently track litigation stages. The opposing clients are often unwilling to compromise when litigation begins, the stage when emotions are high. As time passes, however, emotions subside and the costs of litigation become realities to the clients. Still, the lawyers are often unwilling to discuss settlement until discovery is complete, a point when the ability to evaluate the case is greater. Consequently, the pretrial conference stage is where most serious settlement negotiations occur. The clients are increasingly willing to settle, the lawyers are able to assess the case, and substantial cost savings can still occur if a trial is avoided. Finally, if the plaintiff's latest demand is reasonably close to the defendant's last offer, the judge

14. See R. Fisher & W. Ury, Getting to Yes (1983).

can enter the picture and help the parties reach an agreement. For that reason, negotiation is more accurately seen as an ongoing process that can, and does, come into play throughout the preparation for litigation.

3. Client authorization

Before you begin negotiations on behalf of a client, you must have authority to settle. The law in almost all jurisdictions is that an agreement to represent a client does not confer authority to settle. Therefore, the client must expressly authorize his lawyer to settle.[15] A client cannot give a valid consent unless he is fully informed concerning the terms of the proposed settlement, understands the terms and the reasons for them, and expressly consents to them. The best way to accomplish this is to schedule a meeting with the client to discuss the upcoming settlement possibilities; candidly give the client your present assessment of his case, explaining what you believe a reasonable settlement would be and why. If the client agrees to settle the case on those terms, you should still obtain his written authorization for that settlement. This is best done by sending a letter that recites the terms of the settlement proposal to the client. He should sign and return a copy of the letter acknowledging and approving its terms. When time is short, authorization by phone will suffice, but this should be followed up with a letter reciting the details of the authorization, as in the example below.

Example:

Dear Mr. Johnson:

As we discussed yesterday, the defendant's lawyer in your case asked us to consider the possibility of settling your case without a trial. I am writing to make sure you understand what is involved in a settlement and to obtain your permission to reach a settlement with the defendant.

Trials involve risks, and it is impossible to predict with certainty how your case will look to a jury and what verdict the jury will return. Nevertheless, based on the present state of your case, it is my judgment that if a jury were to find the defendant liable, it would return a verdict in the $30,000 to $40,000 range. However, I feel that there is perhaps an even likelihood that a jury would find no liability at all. In addition, we must consider that the expenses of going to trial will be in the $2,000 range, which primarily involves the costs of having the medical experts testify. Finally, keep in mind that my fee for representing you in your case is one-third of any recovery.

The "value" of your case for settlement purposes, then, is approximately as follows: a potential verdict of $30,000 to $40,000, discounted by 50 percent to reflect the possibility the jury will find that no liability exists, and reduced by the $2,000 trial expenses. This comes to a total in

15. 30 A.L.R.2d 944.

the $13,000 to $18,000 range. Of course, by settling the case, you will avoid having to pay the trial expenses.

Based on these considerations, I recommend that you settle your case for not less than the sum of $15,000, which, after deducting my fee, would result in your actually recovering $10,000. Each side will pay its own court costs, which for us have been approximately $150 to this date. Yesterday you told me to go ahead and try to settle your case for not less than $15,000. Of course, I will negotiate with the defendant's lawyer and try to get a higher settlement.

If you still authorize me to settle your case for not less than $15,000, please sign the copy of this letter in the space provided and return it to me as soon as possible. I will keep you fully informed of the settlement negotiations as they progress.

Sincerely,

_____

John Lawyer

Authorized:

_____

William Johnson

Date: _____

When representing a defendant where insurance coverage is involved, remember that your client is the party, not the insurance company. While insurance contracts customarily permit the insurer to select defense counsel and control the conduct of the defense, case law has increasingly upheld the client's right to authorize any settlement.[16] In short, you must represent the best interests of the insured, and the insurer usually cannot settle a case against the insured's wishes. If this occurs, the client can usually have the settlement set aside, since under these circumstances it is not binding.[17]

4. Settlement contracts

Since settlements are simply agreements between parties, general contract law principles apply. Good practice generally requires that the agreement be in writing and signed by each party, and some local rules require it.

16. See §8.3.4(g) on insurer good faith requirements.
17. This conflict between a client and the client's insurer is a complex area of law and must be researched thoroughly. See, e.g., R. E. Keeton, Basic Text on Insurance Law ch.7 (1971).

Settlements are generally made using either a release, a covenant not to sue, or a loan receipt. The agreement is then presented to the court, and the case is dismissed with prejudice. It is extremely important to understand the legal differences between the various settlement methods. The choice of method is influenced by the types of legal claims and the number of parties involved, whether the settlement is intended to be complete or partial, the type of court action or approval that may be necessary, and the applicable law of contribution. You must know the law of the jurisdiction that governs the settlement contract because statutes and case law concerning releases, covenants not to sue, and loan receipts vary among the jurisdictions. Also, the drafting of the agreement is important, since you need to ensure that it is treated under the applicable law in the way you want it treated, and that it has the effect you intend. This is particularly important in cases with joint tortfeasors, where issues of contribution among the tortfeasors may arise.

a. Releases, covenants not to sue, and loan receipts

A basic common law release operates as a discharge of all claims against the parties to the release as well as against any persons against whom the same claims are or could have been asserted. In short, a release is a complete discharge, or satisfaction, of an action. For this reason a release is used only when there is a settlement of the entire lawsuit involving every claim and every party.

A covenant not to sue does not discharge any parties. It is simply a contract between two or more parties in which the plaintiff agrees not to sue or to pursue an existing claim against one or more defendants. For this reason a covenant not to sue is used when there is a partial settlement not involving every party.

The need for covenants not to sue has an historic basis. Since under common law a release was a discharge of all joint tortfeasors, a plaintiff could not use a release when he wished to settle a tort claim with fewer than all defendants. The covenant not to sue solved this problem. Today the effect of the common law release rule has been eliminated in those jurisdictions that have adopted the Uniform Contribution Among Joint Tortfeasors Act.[18] However, the laws of the states are not uniform, and the relevant laws must be understood to determine the effect on contribution whenever the settlement involves a tort claim having multiple joint tortfeasors. A simple covenant not to sue does not prevent a nonsettling defendant from later bringing a contribution claim against the settling defendant after a final judgment, unless a statute (like the Uniform Contribution Among Joint Tortfeasors Act) in the applicable jurisdiction prevents this result. Therefore, it is critical that you know how your jurisdiction deals with the question of contribution.

In recent years the loan receipt, sometimes called a "Mary Carter agreement,"[19] has been used to generate some contribution among joint

---

18. W. L. Prosser & P. Keeton, The Law of Torts §§49-50 (5th ed. 1984).
19. Booth v. Mary Carter Paint Co., 202 So. 2d 8 (Fla. App. 1967). See also Vermont Union School Dist. No. 21 v. Cummings Const. Co., 143 Vt. 416, 469 A.2d 742 (1983); City of Tucson v. Gallagher, 108 Ariz. 140, 493 P.2d 1197 (1972).

tortfeasors. Under this settlement approach, one defendant agrees to "loan" a certain amount to the plaintiff. The plaintiff in turn agrees to dismiss the case as to that defendant only, pursue the case against the other defendants, and repay the loan to the settling defendant from any recovery against the remaining defendants. Through the loan receipt approach a defendant can settle for a given amount, which might be recouped after trial. Plaintiff for her part gets an early partial recovery and a cooperative defendant. The legality of this basic settlement technique has been upheld in most jurisdictions over public policy objections, but courts have also generally required that the existence and terms of a loan receipt be disclosed to the remaining defendants and have allowed it to be used to show the bias and interest of a witness who testifies at trial if the witness is associated with the settled defendant.[20]

Any number of variations of the basic loan receipt formula are possible. In some situations the loaning defendant is not dismissed as a defendant but is kept as a nominal party who "agrees" to defend the suit. Sometimes the loaning defendant is dismissed with prejudice, sometimes without. The choices are numerous and are affected by the extent to which the details of such arrangements are admissible at trial, and whether the jurisdiction's law of contribution among joint tortfeasors is affected by any particular agreement's structure. The jurisdictions vary widely on the validity and enforceability of the numerous variations of Mary Carter agreements. It should be apparent that you should never enter into a loan receipt agreement unless you are familiar with the particular jurisdiction's applicable law.

b. Drafting the agreement

Regardless of which type of settlement is used, care obviously must be taken in drafting the agreement to ensure that it is specifically tailored to the case involved. First, the agreement should clearly state whether it is a release, covenant not to sue, or loan receipt, and state what matters it does and does not resolve. Second, the agreement should describe the events involved in the case, since the discharge will only be for those events. Third, the agreement should recite the claims of liability and damages and the defendant's denial of them, since it is the compromise of these disputed claims that constitutes the mutual consideration in the agreement. Fourth, the agreement should specify how the pending court case is to be terminated. Fifth, the agreement can contain a choice of law clause and specify the details of any contribution in a covenant not to sue, if appropriate and permitted under the applicable jurisdiction's law.

The following are simple examples of a release, covenant not to sue, and loan receipt. They should be modified to fit the facts of any particular situation and the particular law of the applicable jurisdiction.

---

20. See Reese v. Chicago, Burlington & Quincy R.R. Co., 5 Ill. App. 3d 450, 283 N.E.2d 517 (1972) aff'd, 55 Ill. 2d 356, 303 N.E.2d 382 (1973).

Example:

RELEASE

In consideration of the sum of \$ _____ , which Plaintiff acknowledges receiving, Plaintiff _____ agrees to release Defendants _____ and _____ _____ and their heirs, survivors, agents, and personal representatives from all claims, suits, or actions in any form or on any basis, because of anything that was done or not done at any time, on account of the following:

All claims for personal injuries, property damage, physical disabilities, medical expenses, lost income, loss of consortium, and all other claims that have been or could be brought, including all claims now known or which in the future might be known, which arise out of an occurrence on or about _____*(date)*_____ , at _____ _____*(location)*_____ , when Plaintiff claims to have sustained injuries as a result of a collision between an automobile driven by Plaintiff and automobiles driven by the Defendants.

As a result of this collision, Plaintiff has brought suit against the Defendants for damages. The Defendants have denied both liability and the claimed extent of damages. This release is a compromise settlement between Plaintiff _____ and the Defendant _____ _____ and Defendant _____ _____ .

This agreement is a release and shall operate as a total discharge of any claims Plaintiff has or may have arising out of the above occurrence against these Defendants and any other persons.

Plaintiff _____ and Defendant _____ _____ and Defendant _____ also expressly agree to terminate any actions that have been filed, particularly a claim by this Plaintiff against these Defendants currently filed as civil action no. _____ in the United States District Court for the District of _____ , in _____ . Plaintiff and these Defendants agree to execute a Stipulation of Dismissal, with prejudice, and file it with the Clerk of the above Court, thereby terminating that action in its entirety, within seven days of the execution of this agreement.

Date: _____   _____
                                 Plaintiff

                                 _____
                                 Defendant

                                 _____
                                 Defendant

Example:

COVENANT NOT TO SUE

In consideration of the sum of $_____ , which Plaintiff acknowledges receiving, Plaintiff _____ agrees not to institute, pursue, or continue any claim, suit, or action in any form or on any basis, because of anything that was done or not done at any time, against Defendant _____ and his heirs, survivors, agents, or personal representatives on account of the following:

Any claims against Defendant _____ for personal injuries, property damage, physical disabilities, medical expenses, lost income, loss of consortium, and any other claims that have been or could be brought, including all claims now known or which in the future might become known, which arise out of an occurrence on or about _____*(date)*_____ , at _____*(location)*_____ , when Plaintiff claims to have sustained injuries as a result of a collision between an automobile driven by Plaintiff and an automobile driven by Defendant.

As a result of this collision, Plaintiff has brought suit against Defendant for damages. Defendant has denied both liability and the claimed extent of damages. This covenant not to sue is a compromise settlement between Plaintiff _____ and Defendant _____ _____ .

This agreement is a covenant not to sue, and not a release or an accord and satisfaction. Nothing in this agreement shall operate as a discharge against any other persons, and Plaintiff _____ _____ expressly reserves the right to pursue any claims against any other persons other than Defendant _____ and his heirs, survivors, agents, and personal representatives.

Plaintiff _____ and Defendant _____ _____ also expressly agree to terminate any actions between them, particularly a claim by Plaintiff against this Defendant currently filed as civil action no. _____ in the United States District Court for the District of _____ , in _____ _____ . Plaintiff and Defendant agree to execute a Stipulation of Dismissal, with prejudice, and file it with the Clerk of the above Court, to terminate that action against this Defendant only, within seven days of the execution of this agreement.

Date: _____   _____

                                  Plaintiff

                                  _____

                                  Defendant

Example:

LOAN AGREEMENT

Plaintiff _____ and Defendant _____ _____ enter into the following agreement:

Plaintiff _____ has filed suit against Defendant _____ and other Defendants. This suit, civil action no. _____ , is pending in the United States District Court for the District of _____ in _____ _____ . Defendant _____ and the other Defendants have denied the claims.

Plaintiff's pending suit is based on a collision that occurred on or about _____*(date)*_____ at _____*(location)*_____ in which Plaintiff claims to have suffered injuries as a result of a collision between an automobile in which Plaintiff was a passenger and other automobiles. Defendant _____ was the driver of the automobile in which Plaintiff was a passenger. Defendant _____ _____ has denied liability for Plaintiff's claimed injuries.

Plaintiff wishes to dispose of her claim against Defendant _____ _____ and continue her claims against the other Defendants in the pending suit. Defendant _____ wishes to dispose of Plaintiff's claim against him. Plaintiff _____ _____ and Defendant _____ agree to the following:

Plaintiff _____ agrees to dismiss the complaint only against Defendant _____ in the above action, with prejudice, and continue her action against the remaining defendants until her action is terminated by settlement or judgment.

Defendant _____ agrees to loan Plaintiff the sum of $_____ . This loan is without interest. Plaintiff promises to repay the loan from any judgment or settlement Plaintiff actually receives and collects from any of the remaining Defendants in the above action. Plaintiff will be obligated to repay the loan only to the extent of any recovery actually collected from any of the remaining Defendants, and in any event Plaintiff shall have no obligation to pay Defendant _____ any sum exceeding $____*(loan amount)*____ .

Date: _____   _____
                                                                   Plaintiff

_____
Defendant

When drafting a settlement contract, you must research the law of the applicable jurisdiction to determine the validity and effect of these settlement devices,[21] and you must keep the following basic concepts clear. First, a common law release terminates all of plaintiff's claims against all existing and potential defendants, not just the settling defendant. As a plaintiff, never agree to a release unless you intend to terminate all present and future litigation. Second, a covenant not to sue, first created to avoid the effect of the common law release rule, technically keeps the claims alive against the settling defendant since the plaintiff only agrees not to enforce the claims against that defendant. As a result, a settling defendant is still exposed to contribution claims by the other defendants who are still in the lawsuit. As a defendant, never agree to a covenant not to sue unless you have adequate protection against later contribution claims, either by statute or by the settlement agreement. Third, remember that contribution among joint tortfeasors is not the same thing as indemnification. Contribution does not affect valid indemnification claims against any parties. Fourth, many states by statute protect a settling joint tortfeasor defendant by providing that any judgment against the nonsettling defendants be reduced by the amount the settling defendant paid the plaintiff, and by discharging the settling defendant from any later contribution claims by nonsettling defendants and other joint tortfeasors (the Uniform Contribution Among Joint Tortfeasors Act so provides). However, not all states have such statutes, so the settling defendant must know the applicable jurisdiction's law to assess his exposure to later contribution claims. Fifth, the settlement agreement can usually specify what jurisdiction's law will apply to the agreement. Such a choice of law clause can then apply more favorable law to the contribution issues. Sixth, jurisdictions vary in how they define a defendant's pro rata share of any judgment against joint tortfeasors. If the jurisdiction does not protect a settling defendant from contribution claims, the defendant should make sure that the settlement agreement adopts the applicable jurisdiction's definition of a pro rata share and insist that the defendant get a "credit" for either the amount paid to the plaintiff to settle or a pro rata share of any ultimate judgment plaintiff gets, whichever is greater. Finally, if the lawsuit involves both contract and tort claims, make sure you know how much of the settlement amount will be allocated to each type of claim. This is important, because contribution exists only in tort, not contract. Shifting the allocation of the settlement amount between the contract and tort claims will affect the amount of contribution the nonsettling defendants may be entitled to later.

It should be apparent that the drafting of a settlement can be complex, particularly in situations involving multiple joint tortfeasors. In general, every plaintiff wants a guaranteed dollar amount from the settling defendant, wants to keep claims alive against the nonsettling defendants, and wants no relief from contribution for the settling defendant. Every

---

21. For an excellent discussion of this area along with illustrations of potential problems, see Dewey, Traps in Multitortfeasor Settlements, 13 Litigation (No. 1, Summer 1987).

settling defendant, by contrast, wants to get out of the case with a guaranteed dollar amount to cap his exposure, and wants adequate protection from later contribution claims, if a statute does not already provide it. A careful lawyer must know the legal effect of these settlement devices, the contribution law that applies to the tort claims, and must prepare a carefully drafted instrument that fits the particulars of the case so that the final agreement achieves what the lawyer needs in order to adequately protect his client.

c. Structured settlements

In recent years so-called structured settlements have become common, particularly in the personal injury area when plaintiffs have been seriously and permanently injured. A structured settlement is simply a settlement under which the plaintiff receives periodic payments rather than one lump sum. The benefit to the plaintiff is that she is assured of support over a period of years. Defendant's insurance companies are also benefited, since paying a settlement over a number of years reduces the true cost of the settlement. Socially, structured settlements help ensure that the plaintiff will not become indigent and depend on the state for support. Under §104(a)(2) of the Internal Revenue Code, periodic payments receive the same tax treatment as lump sum payments.[22]

The most frequently used approach in structured settlements is to provide for an initial lump sum and a series of periodic payments. The lump sum is large enough to cover the plaintiff's attorney's fee, other legal expenses, and the plaintiff's unpaid bills. The periodic payments cover either a fixed period of years or the lifetime of the plaintiff; the periods are either annual or a shorter time. If the payments may extend over a number of years, they may be tied to the inflation rate by providing for increases based on the Consumer Price Index or other measure of inflation rates. The defendant's insurer usually funds the periodic payments by purchasing an annuity from an established life insurance company that will automatically make the payments required under the agreement.

d. Terminating the suit

After a settlement agreement has been reached, the lawsuit must be terminated. The standard method is to file a stipulation to dismiss with the clerk of the court. Under Rule 41 a court order is no longer necessary.

Make sure the stipulation to dismiss is with prejudice as to the settling defendant, since this bars the plaintiff from refiling the claim later. If the settlement is only partial, as is the case with a covenant not to sue or a loan receipt, the stipulation must clearly show which party is being

22. This change came about through the Periodic Payment Settlement Act of 1982, Pub. L. No. 97-473, effective as of Jan. 14, 1983 (amending §104(a)(2)). In general, §104 excludes from gross income damages for personal injuries, whether paid as lump sums or periodic payments.

dismissed and which parties remain in the case. The stipulation is signed by the lawyers for the parties who have agreed to settle.

Example:

[Caption]

STIPULATION OF DISMISSAL

Plaintiff _____ , Defendant _____ _____ , and Defendant _____ agree to dismiss this action with prejudice, and each party will bear its costs.

Date: _____   _____
                                          Attorney for Plaintiff

                                          _____
                                          Attorney for Defendant

                                          _____
                                          Attorney for Defendant

Example:

[Caption]

STIPULATION OF DISMISSAL

Plaintiff _____ and Defendant _____ _____ agree to dismiss this action with prejudice as to Defendant _____ only, and the action shall continue as to the remaining Defendants.

Date: _____   _____
                                          Attorney for Plaintiff

                                          _____
                                          Attorney for Defendant

In certain types of cases court approval is needed for any settlement. Settlements in class actions must have court approval under Rule 23(e). Also, settlements involving decedents' estates or incapacitated parties such as minors and incompetents usually require court approval. In these situations the action will be brought in the name of the representative party, such as a guardian, guardian ad litem, conservator, administrator, or executor. Local statutes and rules must always be checked to ensure compliance with technical requirements. The usual procedure is to present a petition to the court having jurisdiction over the party, usually a probate or family court, and to serve notice to all parties and other interested persons. A hearing is then conducted on the proposed settlement and, if approved, an appropriate court order authorizing the settlement will be entered.

e.   Offers of judgment

Rule 68 provides that a party defending a claim can serve an offer of judgment upon the opposing party more than 10 days before the trial. The purpose of Rule 68 is to encourage settlements where reasonable offers to settle have been made. If the offer is refused and a judgment following trial is the same or less favorable to the plaintiff than the pretrial offer of judgment, the plaintiff becomes responsible for the defendant's "costs" incurred from the time of the offer.

In the past few years Rule 68 has become a prominent weapon in the settlement stage of the litigation process and has generated substantial case law. Rule 68 applies whenever a final judgment is in a plaintiff's favor but is less favorable than the offer to settle made by a defendant.[23] The defendant's offer to settle must be reasonably certain in amount and must be unconditional, but there is no requirement that the settlement and cost amounts be itemized.[24]

The principal difficulty in applying Rule 68 has concerned the meaning of the term "costs." It is clear that costs include clerk and marshall fees, witness fees, and court reporter fees,[25] but less so concerning attorney's fees. In Marek v. Chesney,[26] the Supreme Court held that "costs" refers to all costs that can be awarded under applicable substantive law. In that case, a 42 U.S.C. §1983 civil rights action, §1988 allowed attorney's fees to the prevailing party. However, the plaintiff's judgment was not as favorable as the defendant's pretrial offer of judgment. Therefore, plaintiff could not recover as part of costs any attorney's fees incurred from the date of the defendant's offer. Since this included the attorney's fees for the entire trial, plaintiff could not collect attorney's fees amounting to over $100,000.

Case law to date has generally rejected a similar argument, in attorney's fees cases, that the plaintiff who gets a judgment less favorable than a previous offer should also be required to pay defendant's post-offer attorney's fees.[27]

23. Delta Air Lines v. August, 450 U.S. 346 (1981).
24. Marek v. Chesney, 473 U.S. 1 (1985).
25. See 28 U.S.C. §§1920 et seq.
26. 473 U.S. 1 (1985).
27. Crossman v. Marcoccio, 806 F.2d 329 (1st Cir. 1986).

The present usefulness of Rule 68 to defendants depends largely on whether "costs" include attorney's fees. Where they include only court costs and the like, these are likely to be sufficiently small in most cases that they will not exert much pressure on a plaintiff to settle. Where costs include attorney's fees because a statute expressly so provides, Rule 68 affords substantial leverage against a plaintiff since, if the later judgment is less favorable than defendant's offer of settlement, the plaintiff will forgo recovering attorney's fees from the date of the offer. As Marek v. Chesney illustrates, this can be a substantial amount. Because of this disparity between cases where costs include attorney's fees and those that do not, various proposals to amend Rule 68 have been raised. Most call for Rule 68 costs to include attorney's fees in all cases, but no such proposal has been adopted to date.

If a defendant wishes to make an offer of judgment to the plaintiff, this must be done more than 10 days before trial begins. Make sure the offer is actually delivered to the plaintiff's attorney within the permissible time.

Defendants usually make settlement offers under Rule 68 when settlement negotiations have broken down and a trial is to begin soon. However, the offer can be made at any time, and you should consider making it earlier if you can realistically assess the case's value, particularly where attorney's fees are included as costs. The offer can be made in a letter, sent by registered mail or hand delivered, or in a formal offer with an attached copy of service.

Example:

[Caption]

OFFER OF JUDGMENT

To: ___*(attorney for plaintiff)*___

Defendant Johnson Corporation, pursuant to Rule 68, offers to allow judgment to be entered against it, in favor of plaintiff Frank Jones, in the amount of fourteen thousand ($14,000) dollars, and costs of suit incurred to the date of this offer.

This offer is made under Rule 68 of the Federal Rules of Civil Procedure and Rule 408 of the Federal Rules of Evidence, is made as a settlement offer, and is not to be taken as an admission of, or any indication of, liability on the part of this defendant.

Date: _____   _____
                                          Attorney for Defendant
                                          Johnson Corporation

If the plaintiff elects to accept the offer of judgment, he simply sends a notice to the defendant that he accepts the offer. Judgment can then be entered on the accepted offer.

f.   Evidence rules

Under Rule 408 of the Federal Rules of Evidence, compromises and offers of compromise are not admissible to prove liability or damages. Rule 408 is broadly drafted to bar settlement discussions from being introduced at trial on those issues. The Rule, however, does not prevent admission of such evidence for other purposes, principally to expose bias and interest of a testifying witness. The law is clear that a party that has settled and later becomes a witness at the trial of the same case can be cross-examined on the existence and content of the settlement. The same Rule has generally been applied to Mary Carter agreements, since they usually show bias and interest.[28]

g.   Insurer good faith requirements

In civil litigation a defendant will often have some insurance coverage. The insurance contract normally has language under which the insurer reserves the right to manage the defense and negotiate a settlement. However, courts have usually imposed a duty on the insurer to deal fairly and in good faith to protect the interests of the insured. This duty comes about because the interests of the insurer sometimes conflict with those of the insured. The insured naturally wants the company to stand behind her and defend vigorously or, if a settlement is reached, to settle within the policy limits. The insurer also has an interest in defending vigorously, but in a settlement situation only has a financial interest in settling the case under the policy limit. Hence, the insurer and insured's interests come most sharply in conflict where there is a risk of exposure over the policy limits since, once the policy limit is reached, only the insured has additional exposure. Because of this conflict, courts have imposed a good faith obligation on the insurer to manage the case fairly and to adequately protect the insured's interests. In other words, the insurer has a fiduciary duty and must conduct the defense in the best interests of the insured as though there were no policy limits.[29]

Any settlement offer from the plaintiff should be communicated to the insured's lawyer, since the insured is the actual party. Case law is not uniform on whether failure to notify the party of a settlement offer is a breach of good faith, but some courts have so held.[30] It is obviously a good practice to notify your client of every settlement offer, regardless of how unrealistic it is. Where a duty to defend in good faith has been

---

28. Johnson v. Moberg, 334 N.W.2d 411 (Minn. 1983); Hegarty v. Campbell Soup Co., 214 Neb. 716, 335 N.W.2d 758 (1983).
29. See G. R. Williams, Legal Negotiation and Settlement ch. 5, pp. 105-106 (1983).
30. See G. J. Couch, Couch on Insurance (2d ed. 1982).

breached, the insurer is generally liable for the entire judgment, regardless of policy limits.[31]

For the defense counsel the message from case law should be clear. The defense counsel's client is the insured, and counsel's professional and ethical obligation is to serve the best interests of the client. That counsel was selected, and will have fees paid, by the insurance company does not alter the professional obligations. Where settlement negotiations are in progress, both the insured and insurer must be kept informed of its progress. Whenever possible, the insured and insurer should both agree in writing to any settlement. Since the lawyer serves the client, not the insurer, the lawyer must accept a reasonable settlement, even when it involves the policy limits, if it is in the best interests of the client. Where exposure above the policy limits is involved and you, as lawyer, cannot get both the insured and the insurer to agree to a settlement, you must always research the status of the law in your jurisdiction to determine what the rights, duties, and liabilities of the insured and the insurer are in such circumstances.

h. Enforcing settlements[32]

Although uncommon, a party may sometimes breach a settlement. Since a settlement agreement is a contract, the settlement can always be enforced in a separate contract action, but this is not the preferred method. Under Rule 60(b), the wronged party can move to enforce the judgment. The motion must be made in the same court, preferably before the same judge to whom the case had been assigned. You may need to have the case restored to the court's active calendar before you make the motion. At the hearing on the motion, be prepared to prove up the breach of the settlement agreement.

---

31. See 49 A.L.R.2d 711.
32. Wright & Miller §§2860 et seq.

APPENDIX

LITIGATION FILE: *JONES v. SMITH*

This appendix is part of the litigation file in *Jones v. Smith*, an automobile collision case. It illustrates each basic step in the pleadings, discovery, motions, and settlement stages of the litigation process.

FACTS

John Jones, a 23-year-old delivery truck driver, was involved in a collision with Susan Smith. The collision occurred on September 2, 1986, at the intersection of 40th Street and Thomas Road in Phoenix, Arizona. Jones injured his stomach, neck, back, a shoulder, and an ankle and was out of work for a month. His car was also damaged.

Jones brings suit in federal court in Phoenix, Arizona. He claims that Smith negligently ran a red light at the intersection and crashed into his car (he was not operating a delivery truck at the time). Jones is a citizen of Arizona; Smith is a citizen of Nevada. The lawsuit was filed on January 1, 1987.

UNITED STATES DISTRICT COURT
FOR THE DISTRICT OF ARIZONA

The "Caption" includes the Court, the parties, and the case number.

John Jones,
      Plaintiff,

v.

Susan Smith,
      Defendant

NO. _____

Civil Action

**JURY TRIAL
DEMANDED**

The jury demand is usually put in the caption as well as at the end of the complaint.

COMPLAINT

Plaintiff John Jones complains of defendant Susan Smith as follows:

1. Jurisdiction in this case is based on diversity of citizenship and the amount in controversy. Plaintiff is a citizen of the State of Arizona. Defendant is a citizen of the State of Nevada. The amount in controversy exceeds, exclusive of interest and costs, the sum of ten thousand ($10,000) dollars.

This is the standard jurisdictional allegation in diversity cases. It should be the first paragraph of the complaint.

2. On September 2, 1986, at approximately 2:00 P.M., plaintiff John Jones ("Jones") was driving a vehicle northbound on 40th Street toward the intersection of 40th Street and Thomas Road in Phoenix, Arizona. Defendant Susan Smith ("Smith") was driving a vehicle eastbound on Thomas Road toward the same intersection.

The factual allegations should be clear and simple. This makes it more likely that they will be either admitted or denied outright, making the pleadings easier to understand.

3. Smith failed to stop for a red light at the intersection of 40th Street and Thomas Road, and negligently drove her vehicle into Jones' vehicle.

4. As a direct and proximate result of Smith's negligence, Jones injured his stomach, neck, back, a shoulder, an ankle, and other bodily parts, received other physical injuries, suffered physical and mental pain and suffering, incurred medical expenses, lost income, and will incur further medical expenses and lost income in the future.

The negligence and causation claims are kept single. This is adequate under "notice pleading" requirements.

The injury allegations are usually spelled out in some detail.

WHEREFORE, plaintiff John Jones demands judgment against defendant Susan Smith for the sum of $100,000, with interest and costs.

Many complaints simply ask for "a sum in excess of $10,000," the jurisdictional limit.

Dated: January 1, 1987

Anne Johnson

Anne Johnson
Attorney for Plaintiff
100 Congress Street
Phoenix, AZ 85001
882-1000

PLAINTIFF DEMANDS TRIAL BY JURY

This avoids requesting unrealistic damages. The danger of exaggerated damages is that, unless amended, the pleadings can be read to the jury at trial, making the plaintiff look greedy.

Most jurisdictions also require submitting a jury demand form and paying a jury demand fee to preserve the right to a jury trial.

UNITED STATES DISTRICT COURT FOR THE DISTRICT OF ARIZONA

John Jones,
       Plaintiff

    v.   NO. _____

Susan Smith,
       Defendant

SUMMONS

TO THE ABOVE-NAMED DEFENDANT:
Susan Smith
200 Palmer Way
Las Vegas, Nevada

You are hereby summoned and required to serve upon Anne Johnson, plaintiff's attorney, whose address is 100 Congress Street, Phoenix, AZ, 85001, an answer to the complaint which is herewith served upon you, within 20 days after service of this summons upon you, exclusive of the day of service.

If you fail to do so, judgment by default will be taken against you for the relief demanded in the complaint.

_____
Clerk of the Court

[Seal of U.S. District Court]

Dated: January 1, 1987

A good practice is to give the person who serves the complaint and summons any additional information about the defendant that may help make an effective service.

In this case service must be made under the Arizona long-arm statute. Make sure that the service complies with the statute, since this is required by Rule 4(e).

The person making the service must prepare an Affidavit of Service showing how service on the defendant was actually made.

The Affidavit of Service form is frequently attached to the summons form.

UNITED STATES DISTRICT COURT
FOR THE DISTRICT OF ARIZONA

John Jones,
   Plaintiff,

    v.   No. 87 C 1000

Susan Smith,
   Defendant

ANSWER

Defendant Susan Smith answers the complaint as follows:

 1. Admit
 2. Admit
 3. Deny
 4. Defendant denies plaintiff was injured as a result of any negligence by the defendant, and is without knowlege or information sufficient to form a belief as to the truth of all other allegations in Par. 4, and therefore denies them.

Simple responses are more likely to be made since the complaint's allegations are correspondingly simple.

First Defense

Plaintiff's claimed injuries and damages were caused by plaintiff's own negligence, which was the sole proximate cause of any injuries and damages plaintiff may have received.

WHEREFORE, defendant requests that plaintiff receive nothing, and that judgment be entered for the defendant, including costs of this action.

Each defense should be set out separately.

Dated: <u>January 15, 1987</u>

<u>William Sharp</u>
William Sharp
Attorney for Defendant
100 Broadway
Phoenix, AZ 85001
881-1000

AFFIDAVIT OF SERVICE

I, Helen Thompson, having been first duly sworn, state that I served a copy of defendant's Answer on plaintiff by personally delivering it to Anne Johnson, attorney for plaintiff, at 100 Congress Street, Phoenix, Arizona, on January 15, 1987.

Helen Thompson
_____
Helen Thompson

Signed and sworn to before me on January 15, 1987

Ned Fark
_____
Notary Public

My commission expires on December 31, 1987

[Seal]

After the complaint has been served, every other court paper must be served on every other party in accordance with Rule 5. The usual service is personal delivery or mailing to the party's attorney of record.

An affidavit or certification of service should always be attached to every court paper showing how proper service was made.

All court papers must be filed with the court either before service or within a reasonable time after service.

In practice, court papers are usually filed with the court clerk the same day service is made.

UNITED STATES DISTRICT COURT FOR THE DISTRICT OF ARIZONA

John Jones,
          Plaintiff

          v.   NO. 87 C 1000

Susan Smith,
          Defendant

DEFENDANT'S INTERROGATORIES TO PLAINTIFF

Pursuant to Rule 33 of the Federal Rules of Civil Procedure, defendant Smith requests that plaintiff Jones answer the following interrogatories under oath, and serve them on the defendant within 30 days:

1. Describe the personal injuries you received as a result of the occurrence described in the complaint (hereafter "this occurrence").

2. State the full names and present addresses of any physicians, osteopaths, chiropractors, and other medical personnel who treated you as a result of this occurrence, each such person's areas of specialty, the dates of each examination, consultation or appointment, the amount of each such person's bill, and whether each bill has been paid.

3. Were you confined to a hospital or clinic as a result of this occurrence? If so, state the name and address of each such hospital or clinic, the dates of your confinement at each facility, the amount of each such facility's bills, and whether each bill has been paid.

4. Have you incurred other medical expenses, other than these requested in Interrogatory Nos. 2 and 3, as a result of this occurrence? If so, state each expense incurred, the nature of each expense, when the expense was incurred, to whom it was incurred, and whether each expense has been paid.

5. Have you incurred any expenses as a result of this occurrence other than medical

Interrogatories will usually be the first discovery device the parties serve on each other.

In this example, the defendant served interrogatories on plaintiff two weeks after answering the complaint. (Many defendants serve interrogatories with the answer.)

Note how each interrogatory deals with a separate, defined category and asks for all relevant data for the category. This will usually generate more complete answers. It also gives the answering party the opportunity of answering the interrogatory by producing the relevant records that contain the answers.

expenses? If so, state the nature of each expense, the date incurred, the amount of each expense, the reason for incurring each expense, and whether each expense has been paid.

6. Were you unable to work as a result of this occurrence? If so, state the dates during which you were unable to work, each employer during these dates, the type of work you were unable to do, and the amount of lost wages or income from each employer.

7. Have you recovered from the claimed injuries that resulted from this occurrence? If not, state the claimed injuries from which you have not recovered and any present disability.

The plaintiff's current condition and medical history are important areas that should be explored thoroughly. This can then be verified during the plaintiff's deposition.

8. During the 10 years preceding September 2, 1986, have you suffered any other personal injuries? If so, state when, where, and how you were injured and the name and address of each medical facility where, and physicians by whom, you were treated for these injuries.

9. During the 10 years preceding September 2, 1986, have you been hospitalized, treated, examined, or tested at any hospital, clinic, physician's office, or other medical facility for any conditions other than those requested in Interrogatory No. 8? If so, state the name and address of each such medical facility and physician and the dates of such services and the medical conditions involved.

10. State the full name and address of each person who witnessed, or claims to have witnessed, the collision between the vehicles involved in this occurrence.

Occurrence witnesses are obviously important in this kind of case. It's a good practice to break them up by category in appropriate cases.

11. State the full name and address of each person who has any knowledge of the facts of the collision other than those persons already identified in Interrogatory No. 10.

12. Describe your vehicle involved in this occurrence, any damages to your vehicle as a result of this occurrence, the name and address of any firm repairing your vehicle, the amount billed for repairs, when such repairs took place, and whether the repair bills have been paid. If your vehicle has not been repaired, state where it is presently located and its condition.

13. Identify, by date, description, and source any medical records and any other records or documents of any kind in your or your attorney's possession or control that relate in any way to this occurrence and the injuries and damages you claim resulted from this occurrence.

Medical records are obviously critical in this kind of case. The descriptions you get will be used to send production requests to the plaintiff and subpoenas to third-party sources.

This interrogatory tracks the language of Rule 33.

14. For each expert expected to testify at trial, state:

(a) the expert's full name, address, and professional qualifications;

(b) the subject matter on which the expert is expected to testify;

(c) the substance of the facts and opinions to which the expert is expected to testify; and

(d) a summary of the grounds of each opinion.

Dated: February 1, 1987

A proof of service must be attached.

William Sharp

William Sharp
Attorney for Defendant
100 Broadway
Phoenix, AZ 85001
881-1000

UNITED STATES DISTRICT COURT
FOR THE DISTRICT OF ARIZONA

John Jones,
     Plaintiff

    v.   NO. 87 C 1000

Susan Smith,
     Defendant

PLAINTIFF'S ANSWERS TO INTERROGATORIES

Plaintiff John Jones answers Defendant's interrogatories as follows:

Interrogatory No. 1: Describe the personal injuries you received as a result of the occurrence described in the complaint (hereafter "this occurrence").

Answer: Cervical, dorsal and lumbar sprain and strain; cerebral concussion; multiple contraction headaches and concussion headaches; left hemiparesis with ataxia; ankle sprain; numbness; multiple contusions and abrasions.

Interrogatory No. 2: State in full the names and present addresses of any physicians, osteopaths, chiropractors, nurses, or other medical personnel who treated you as a result of this occurrence, each such person's areas of specialty, the dates of each examination, consultation, or appointment, the amount of each such person's bill, and whether each bill has been paid.

Answer:
Doctors Hospital
1947 East Thomas Road
Phoenix, Arizona 85016

Leo L. Lang, M.D.
333 East Campbell Avenue
Phoenix, Arizona 85016

Frank Hoffman, M.D.
222 West Thomas
Suite 100
Phoenix, Arizona 85013

The usual way of answering interrogatories is to set out the questions and the answers, making it easy to correlate the two.

J. Franks, D.C.
55 North 27th Avenue
Phoenix, Arizona 85007

(Answer may be supplemented as discovery and investigation continues.)

Interrogatory No. 3: Were you confined to a hospital or clinic as a result of this occurrence? If so, state the name and address of the hospital or clinic, the dates of your confinement at each facililty, the amount of each facility's bills, and whether each bill has been paid.

Answer: No; treated, but not confined, at Doctors Hospital.

Interrogatory No. 4: Have you incurred other medical expenses, other than those requested in Interrogatory Nos. 2 and 3, as a result of this occurrence? If so, state each expense incurred, the nature of each expense, when the expense was incurred, to whom it was incurred, and whether each expense has been paid.

Answer:

Doctors Hospital	$257.18
Leo Lang, M.D.	39.70
Frank Hoffman, M.D.	140.00
J. Franks, D.C.	697.80
Walgreen Pharmacy	23.13

Those bills have been paid.

(Answer may be supplemented as discovery and investigation continues.)

Interrogatory No. 5: Have you incurred any expenses as a result of this occurrence, other than medical expenses? If so, state the nature of each expense, the date incurred, the amount of each expense, the reason for incurring each expense, and whether each expense has been paid.

Answer:

Broken wristwatch	$75.00
College tuition and books	
(tuition $110/books $52)	162.00

Here the plaintiff has prepared partial answers, and acknowledges that further information will generate supplemental answers later. However, these partial answers were prepared within the 30-day requirement of Rule 33.

Wristwatch repair bill has been paid.

Interrogatory No. 6: Were you unable to work as a result of this occurrence? If so, state the dates during which you were unable to work, each employer during these dates, the type of work you were unable to do, and the amount of lost wages or income from each employer.

Answer: Yes. September 2, 1986 to October 1, 1986. Devo Wholesale Florist. Delivery truck driver. $700 — one month's salary.

This is a typical interrogatory answer. It provides all the facts requested, does so efficiently, and does not volunteer anything not asked for.

Interrogatory No. 7: Have you recovered from the claimed injuries that resulted from this occurrence? If not, state the claimed injuries from which you have not recovered and any present disability.

Answer: Plaintiff still experiences headaches, neck pain, and lower back pain.

Interrogatory No. 8: During the 10 years preceding September 2, 1986, have you suffered any other personal injuries? If so, state when, where, and how you were injured, and the name and address of each medical facility where, and physicians by whom, you were treated for these injuries.

Answer: No.

Interrogatory No. 9: During the 10 years preceding September 2, 1986, have you been hospitalized, treated, examined, or tested at any hospital, clinic, physician's office or other medical facility for any conditions other than those requested in Interrogatory No. 8? If so, state the name and address of each such medical facility and physician, the dates of such services, and the medical conditions involved.

Answer: No.

Interrogatory No. 10: State the full name and address of each person who witnessed, or claims to have witnessed, the collision between the vehicles involved in this occurrence.

Answer:

John Jones, plaintiff

Susan Smith, defendant
Carol Brown, 42 E. Cambridge, Phoenix, AZ
Mary Porter, 42 E. Cambridge, Phoenix, AZ
Officer Steven Pitcher, Phoenix Police Department

(Answer may be supplemented as discovery and investigation continues.)

Interrogatory No. 11: State the full name and address of each person who has any knowledge of the facts of the collision, other than persons already identified in Interrogatory No. 10.

Answer: See persons listed in answer to Interrogatory No. 4; John Jones, Sr., and Mary Jones, plaintiff's parents; James Devo, plaintiff's employer.

(Answer may be supplemented as discovery and investigation continues.)

Interrogatory No. 12: Describe your vehicle that was involved in this occurrence, any damage to your vehicle as a result of this occurrence, the name and address of any firm repairing your vehicle, the amount billed for repairs, when such repairs took place, and whether the repair bills have been paid. If your vehicle has not been repaired, state where it is presently located and its condition.

Answer: 1984 Toyota Corolla four-door sedan. Extensive damage to left and front side of car. Jack's Auto Repair, 2000 E. Valley Road, Phoenix. $1,213. Repairs completed about September 30, 1986. Repair bill has been paid.

Interrogatory No. 13: Identify, by date, description, and source any medical records, and any other records or documents of any kind in your or your attorney's possession or control, that relate in any way to this occurrence and injuries and damages you claim resulted from this occurrence.

Answer:

Employment records of Devo Wholesale Florist
Doctors Hospital records
Dr. Lang's office records

Witness lists must frequently be supplemented over time, since the ongoing investigation will often uncover additional witnesses.

This is another typical answer. It provides the facts called for, yet does not volunteer anything.

Dr. Hoffman's office records
Dr. Franks' office records
Medical bills
X rays taken by the above health care pro-
 viders
Phoenix Police Department Accident Report
Photographs of the scene of the accident

(Answer may be supplemented as discovery
and investigation proceeds.)

Interrogatory No. 14: For each expert expected to testify at trial, state:

- (a) the expert's full name, address, and
   professional qualifications;
- (b) the subject matter on which the expert is expected to testify;
- (c) the substance of the facts and opinions to which the expert is expected
   to testify; and
- (d) a summary of the grounds of each
   opinion.

Answer:

Frank Hoffman, M.D.,
222 W. Thomas
Suite 100
Phoenix, AZ 85013

J. Franks, D.C.
55 North 27th Avenue
Phoenix, AZ 85007

Leo L. Lang, M.D.
333 East Campbell Avenue
Phoenix, AZ 85016

(Answers may be supplemented as discovery
and investigation continues.)

Dated: February 25, 1987

John Jones

John Jones, Plaintiff

The initial answer to this standard inter-rogatory is frequently "None known at pre-sent — investigation continues," on the ba-sis that the answering party has not yet de-cided whom its testify-ing experts will be.

Here the treating phy-sicians will obviously be witnesses at trial, so their names are dis-closed, with supple-mental answers to follow.

State of Arizona
County of Maricopa | SS.

I, John Jones, being first duly sworn, state that:
I am the plaintiff in this case. I have made the foregoing Answers to Interrogatories and know the answers to be true to the best of my knowledge, information and belief.

Interrogatory answers must be signed under oath by the party making them.

_____
John Jones, Plaintiff

Subscribed and sworn to before me this 25th day of February 1987, by John Jones, Plaintiff.

_____
Mary Ryan, Notary Public

My commission expires on
    December 31, 1987

[Seal]

Like any court papers, the answers must be served on every party. A proof of service, showing how service was made, must be attached to the answer.

UNITED STATES DISTRICT COURT
FOR THE DISTRICT OF ARIZONA

John Jones,
          Plaintiff

          v.   NO. 87 C 1000

Susan Smith,
          Defendant

REQUEST FOR PRODUCTION
OF DOCUMENTS

Pursuant to Rule 34 of the Federal Rules of Civil Procedure, defendant requests that plaintiff produce within 30 days, in the law offices of William Sharp, 100 Broadway, Phoenix, AZ 85001, the following documents for inspection and copying:

1. All medical reports, records, charts, X-ray reports, and all other records regarding any medical examinations and treatment received by plaintiff for the injuries claimed in the complaint.

2. All United States Income Tax returns filed by plaintiff for the years 1982, 1983, 1984, 1985, and 1986.

3. All exhibits plaintiff will offer at the trial of this case.

Dated: February 1, 1987

William Sharp
William Sharp
Attorney for Defendant
100 Broadway
Phoenix, AZ 85001
881-1000

Note that this documents request was served at the same time as were the interrogatories.

Documents requests usually depend on interrogatory answers to identify the relevant documents. Here, however, what the defendant wants is both simple and obvious, so the defendant decides to serve the requests with interrogatories.

These kinds of records should already be in the plaintiff's possession.

A proof of service must be attached.

UNITED STATES DISTRICT COURT
FOR THE DISTRICT OF ARIZONA

John Jones,
      Plaintiff

    v.   NO. 87 C 1000

Susan Smith,
      Defendant

PLAINTIFF'S RESPONSE TO REQUEST FOR PRODUCTION OF DOCUMENTS

Plaintiff responds to defendant's Requests for Production of Documents as follows:

1. Plaintiff will produce copies of all reports in plaintiff's possession regarding medical examinations and treatment of plaintiff for his injuries. These copies will be delivered to defendant's attorney on or before March 1, 1987.

2. Plaintiff herewith produces his U.S. Income Tax Returns for the years 1982 through 1986.

3. Plaintiff to the extent known at present will produce copies of all exhibits he will offer at the trial of this case. These copies will be delivered to defendant's attorney on or before March 1, 1987.

Dated: February 25, 1987

Anne Johnson

Anne Johnson
Attorney for Plaintiff
100 Congress
Phoenix, AZ 85001
882-1000

A response to a production request should be filed so there is a court record that shows how and when the request was complied with. If photocopying will be expensive, the requesting party will usually have to pay for the photocopying charges.

Since plaintiff may have additional trial exhibits, the notation "investigation continues" may be appropriate. A supplemental response may then need to be filed as plaintiff decides on additional exhibits.

A proof of service must be attached.

UNITED STATES DISTRICT COURT
FOR THE DISTRICT OF ARIZONA

John Jones,
       Plaintiff

    v.   NO. 87 C 1000

Susan Smith,
       Defendant

SUBPOENA DUCES TECUM

TO: James Devo, President
      Devo Wholesale Florist
      3731 40th Street
      Phoenix, AZ 85010

    YOU ARE HEREBY COMMANDED to appear and give testimony under oath at the law office of William Sharp, 100 Broadway, Phoenix, AZ 85001 on March 15, 1987 at 1:30 P.M. You are also commanded to bring the following:

    All records relating to the employment of John Jones at Devo Wholesale Florist, from the first day of employment through the present date, including but not limited to records showing wages received, hours worked, and the condition of John Jones' health.

Dated: <u>March 1, 1987</u>

[Seal]

John Clark
_____
Clerk of the Court

A deposition subpoena that also requires the party to bring specified records is the only discovery method that can be used to obtain records from non-party witnesses.

Make sure that you serve a Notice of Deposition on every other party, because other parties always have a right to attend any deposition and question the deponent.

UNITED STATES DISTRICT COURT
FOR THE DISTRICT OF ARIZONA

John Jones,
            Plaintiff

        v.   NO. 87 C 1000

Susan Smith,
            Defendant

NOTICE OF DEPOSITION

TO: PLAINTIFF JOHN JONES

Please take notice that the undersigned will take the deposition of John Jones, Plaintiff, on March 15, 1987, at 2:00 P.M. at 100 Broadway, Phoenix, AZ 85001. You are hereby notified that the plaintiff is to appear at that time and place and submit to a deposition under oath.

Dated: March 1, 1986

William Sharp

William Sharp
Attorney for Defendant
100 Broadway
Phoenix, AZ 85001
881-1000

Two weeks notice is appropriate in this type of case.

A subpoena is not necessary since the deponent is a party.

A proof of service must be attached.

UNITED STATES DISTRICT COURT FOR THE DISTRICT OF ARIZONA

John Jones,
      Plaintiff

      v.   NO. 87 C 1000

Susan Smith,
      Defendant

DEPOSITION OF JOHN JONES

DEPOSITION OF John Jones, taken at 2:13 P.M. on March 15, 1987, at the law offices of William Sharp, at 100 Broadway, Phoenix, AZ 85001, before Nancy Post, a Notary Public in Maricopa County, Arizona.

Appearance for the plaintiff:

Anne Johnson
100 Congress St.
Phoenix, AZ 85001

Appearance for the defendant:

William Sharp
100 Broadway
Phoenix, AZ 85001

JOHN JONES

Called as a witness, having been first duly sworn, was examined and testified as follows:

EXAMINATION BY MR. SHARP:

Q. This is the deposition of the plaintiff, John Jones, being taken in the case of John Jones v. Susan Smith, Case No. 87 C 1000 in the United States District Court for the District of Arizona. It is being held at the law office of William Sharp, 100 Broadway, Phoenix, Arizona 85001. Today's date is March 15, 1987. Present in addition to Mr. Jones are myself, William Sharp, attorney for defendant Smith, Anne Johnson, attorney for plaintiff Jones,

This is a standard introductory statement.

and Nancy Post, a certified court reporter and notary public. Mr. Jones,
you were just sworn to tell the truth
by the court reporter, correct?

A. That's right.

Q. It's important that you understand the
questions and give accurate answers.
If there's anything you don't understand, or anything you don't know or
aren't sure of, you let us know, all
right?

A. Yes.

Q. Please tell us your full name.

A. John J. Jones.

Q. How old are you?

A. I'm 23.

Q. Are you married or single?

A. Single.

Q. Where do you live?

A. 1020 North 50th Street, Phoenix, Arizona.

Q. How far did you go in school?

A. I graduated from high school — Central High, 1982.

Q. What did you do after high school?

A. I joined the army.

Q. Tell us about your army experience.

A. After basic training, I was sent to an
infantry division, and did most of my
three years in Germany. I was a cor-
poral when I received my honorable
discharge. That was in August 1985.

Q. What did you do after that?

A. I came back to Phoenix, moved into
my parents' house, and started working for Devo Wholesale Florist.

Q. Where is that located?

A. It's at 3731 40th Street, Phoenix.

Q. What kind of work do you do there?

A. I started as a sales clerk, then I
became a driver on one of their
trucks.

Q. What do you do as a driver?

A. I deliver flowers from the store to cus-
tomers in the Phoenix area.

Q. What were your hours in August and
September 1986?

A. It varied, but it was usually 6:00 A.M.
to 2:00 P.M.

a. Personal back-
ground.

Note the form of the
questions and the tone
of the examination.
The principal pur-
poses of this deposi-
tion are to acquire
information and assess
the plaintiff as a trial
witness. Accordingly,
the questions are usu-
ally open-ended,
designed to elicit in-
formation and have
the plaintiff do the
talking. The questions
are asked in a pleas-
ant friendly way.

b. Work experience.

Q. Were those your hours the day of the accident?

A. Yes.

Q. Other than your job for Devo Florist, did you have any other jobs or activities in September 1986?

A. I didn't have any other job. I was a part-time student at Glendale Community College.

Q. Mr. Jones, were you ever involved in an automobile accident before September 2, 1986?

A. No.

Q. Did you ever receive personal injuries of any kind before September 2, 1986?

A. No.

Q. During the past 10 years, other than for this accident, did you ever see a physician for any reason?

A. Well, our family doctor is Dr. Hoffman. I would see him from time to time for check ups, shots, and things like that. But I never had any serious injury or illness that I went to Dr. Hoffman for.

Q. Mr. Jones, tell me each injury you feel you've received as a result of the accident on September 2.

A. Okay. I hurt the left side of my neck, my lower back, my left ankle, my left shoulder, and my stomach.

Q. Let's start out with the left side of your neck. What injuries did you receive there?

A. I think I whipped my head to the side when the car crashed into me and I strained my neck. I had these shooting pains in my neck whenever I tried to move it.

Q. How long did that pain continue?

A. Well it was pretty severe for about a week, and then it started getting better. I still get pains there from time to time.

Q. Tell me about the injuries to your lower back.

c. Accident and health history must be explored, since preexisting injuries would affect the damages picture.

d. Each claimed injury should be explored in detail.

The "tell me" form of questions are used to get the witness to disclose everything.

If the plaintiff at trial tries to claim additional injuries, he can hardly say he didn't mention all his injuries during the deposition because the lawyer didn't give him a chance to do so. Since pain and suffering will probably be the largest single element of damages, these questions are important to "pin down" the witness and prevent later exaggeration at trial.

A. Well, that was sort of the same thing. I must have wrenched my back from the force of the collision. Just like my neck, it was stiff and hurt for a while. After about a week it started getting better, and today I only get the pain from time to time, especially toward the end of the work day.

Q. Tell me about your left ankle.

A. I sprained my ankle during the accident. That was probably the worst injury. I had to stay off my feet for about two weeks, and I really couldn't start walking on it for three or four weeks. That's the injury that kept me out of work for a month.

Q. When did your ankle start getting better?

A. About a month after this happened it was well enough so I could start working, although I was still limping for quite a while. It probably took about four months before the ankle healed up completely.

Q. Tell me about the injury to your left shoulder.

A. I got some cuts and scratches and bruises on my left shoulder when I crashed into the dashboard of the car. That hurt for maybe two weeks, and then went away.

Q. Finally, tell me about the injuries to your stomach.

A. I guess I injured my stomach when I smashed against the steering wheel. It was just painful inside of my stomach. That went away after a few days.

Q. Other than these injuries to your neck, lower back, ankle, shoulder, and stomach, did you receive any other injuries?

The "any other injuries" question is always useful. Again, it prevents later exaggeration.

A. Oh yeah. I received a concussion on the left side of my head. That's what the doctor told me.

Q. Mr. Jones, let's talk about the medical treatment you received for these injuries following the accident. First, how did you get to Doctors Hospital?

e. Medical treatment.

Note how this deposition is organized chronologically (with

A. An ambulance came to the intersection and they put me on a stretcher and drove me to the hospital.

Q. What happened when you arrived at Doctors Hospital?

A. The ambulance attendants took me into the emergency room, and some nurses checked me over, took my pulse and blood pressure, and stuff like that. After a while one of their doctors examined me. I think his name was Dr. Lang. I told Dr. Lang where I hurt and about the accident.

Q. What kind of treatment did you receive at the hospital?

A. Well, they examined me, x-rayed, cleaned-up some of the cuts on my shoulder and chest, and put my ankle in a cast. It wasn't one of those big plaster casts, it was a cast that went around the back of my ankle and foot and was surrounded with an elastic bandage. I must have been there a couple of hours, and by that time my parents had come to the hospital, and they took me home.

Q. Did you receive any medication prescription?

A. The doctor gave a prescription for Tylenol with codeine, which my mother picked up at the drug store. The doctor told me to follow instructions on the bottle and take the medication if I needed it for the pain.

Q. Mr. Jones, tell us about the month you spent before you went back to work.

A. Well, the first week I pretty much spent in bed. Sometimes I got up and lay on the couch and watched TV. At that time everything was aching, my neck hurt, my head hurt, my stomach hurt, my ankle was swollen up. I spent all my time with my foot up to keep the swelling down, and I was taking the medicine to keep the pain down.

Q. How long was it before you were able to move around the house?

A. I'd say the first week or 10 days I pretty much spent on my back. After that period of time the pain in my

the exception of the accident itself). This is usually the best way to organize the questions, unless you have a specific reason for doing it another way.

f. Recovery period.

head, shoulder and stomach started going away, and the swelling in my ankle was starting to go down. I got a pair of crutches and started moving around the house a little bit. I couldn't stay on my feet very long before the foot would swell up if I stood up for any length of time.

Q. At the end of September, 1986, what was your physical condition like?

A. The scratches and bruises had gone away. The pains in my neck, shoulder, stomach and leg, and back, had started to get better. The only places that really kept on hurting was my lower back and my ankle.

Q. Tell me about those.

A. Well my back would have these stabbing pains from time to time. It felt real stiff. My ankle was stiff. My ankle was still swollen, and I couldn't walk on it yet. Dr. Hoffman, my family doctor, had removed the cast about three weeks after the accident and I could start walking without crutches, but I was still limping and the ankle would get sore if I walked on it for any length of time.

Q. When did you see Dr. Hoffman?

A. My mom took me to Dr. Hoffman about three weeks after the accident. He checked me out, removed the soft cast from my ankle, and told me it was okay to start walking around without the crutches if I could stand it.

Q. When did you stop using the crutches?

A. I stopped using them when I went back to work at the beginning of October.

Q. What did you see Dr. Franks, the chiropractor, for?

A. Well, my mom thought that going to a chiropractor might help my back and ankle. My back still hurt, and my ankle was still sore. She thought that it might be a good idea to get some physical therapy to see if that might help. That's why I went to Dr. Franks.

Since the defendant's purpose is to minimize the extent and length of the pain, these questions are important. Again, they prevent later exaggeration.

The history of the plaintiff's treatments is, of course, available from the medical records, which the defendant will have before the deposition. Nonetheless, these questions test the witness' recall and propensity to exaggerate.

Q. How many times did you see Dr. Franks?

A. I went to him for the first time around October 1st. I went to see him maybe twice a week for the next couple of months.

Q. What kind of treatment did Dr. Franks perform?

A. He would give me physical therapy. That involved bending my back, stretching it, applying heat treatments, things like that. The same thing was true for the ankle.

Q. Did it help?

A. Yes. About two months later, maybe by Christmas, most of the stiffness and pain had gone away.

Q. From December 1986 to the present day, describe your physical condition.

A. It's better. I still have pain from time to time in my back and ankle.

Q. When do you get the pain there?

A. Well, it depends on how much or how hard I work. The more I work the more likely I am to get those pains.

Q. How often do you get those pains?

A. It's maybe once a week for an hour or two, usually at the end of the work day.

Q. When was the last time you took Tylenol with codeine?

A. I took that stuff for maybe six weeks.

Q. Did you ever take any painkillers other than Tylenol with codeine?

A. I sometimes take aspirin when I get these pains.

Q. Other than what you've told me about, do you have any other injuries or problems that you feel were caused by this accident?

A. No, you pretty much covered it.

Q. Mr. Jones, let's talk about some of the bills involved here. First the medical bills. Your interrogatory answers show that the bills from Doctors Hospital, Dr. Lang, Dr. Hoffman, and Dr. Franks have all been paid. Who paid those bills?

A. I'm not sure. I know they were paid

These questions effectively limit the damages.

g. Expenses and lost income.

by my health insurance. I think my mother paid the Walgreen pharmacy bill.

Q. Who paid for the wristwatch repair?

A. My mom paid that. I'm supposed to pay her back.

Q. You claim college tuition and books expenses in the amount of $162. Tell us about that.

A. Well, I was a part-time student at Glendale Community College. I had already paid the tuition and bought the books for the two courses I was taking. When I got injured, I couldn't take the courses I signed up for.

Q. How much income did you lose as a result of this accident?

A. I get paid $700 a month salary from Devo Florists. I went back to work October 1, 1986. The way I figure it, I lost one month's salary, or $700.

Q. The $700 is your gross income, isn't it?

A. Yes.

Q. What's your take-home pay?

A. We get paid on the first and fifteenth of the month. My take-home for half a month is about $270.

Q. Mr. Jones, let's talk about how this accident happened. Describe the vehicle you were driving.

A. It's a 1984 Toyota Corolla four-door. I bought it when I got out of the service. It was in really good shape, because I took good care of it.

Q. Is the title to that car in your name?

A. Yes.

Q. The accident happened around 2:00 P.M.?

A. Yes.

Q. At the time of the accident, where were you coming from?

A. I was coming from work at the flower shop.

Q. Where is that flower shop located?

A. On 40th Street and Thomas Road.

Q. 40th Street is the north-south street, correct?

While the fact that most of the bills have been paid by insurance is not admissible at trial, it will have some effect on the settlement picture.

n. The accident.

Note that here the questioner has saved the accident as the last topic. Some lawyers save the most important part of a deposition for the end, on the theory that the lawyer then has a better "feel" for the witness and the witness' guard will be down by that time.

These scene description questions are useful to see how effectively the plaintiff can describe the scene, and are good questions to see how effective a trial witness he will make.

A. Yes.

Q. Where is the flower shop in relation to the intersection?

A. It's not right at the corner. It's on 40th Street maybe 300 feet south of Thomas.

Q. Which side of 40th Street is the flower shop on?

A. It's on the east side.

Q. Tell me how you went from the flower shop north on 40th Street.

A. My car was parked in the lot next to the flower shop. When I got out of work, I pulled out of the lot and started going north on 40th Street.

Q. Describe what 40th Street looks like.

A. It's a pretty wide street. It has three lanes of traffic in each direction. In addition, it has left-turn lanes at the major intersections.

Q. There are traffic lights at the corner of 40th Street and Thomas, right?

A. Yes.

Q. Where are they located?

A. I think there's one at each corner and on the median strips.

Q. How many lights face the northbound traffic on 40th Street?

A. Probably around three.

Q. When you pulled onto 40th Street, which lane did you pull into?

A. I got into the inside lane, right next to the median strip.

Q. Mr. Jones, when was the first time you looked at the traffic lights at the corner of 40th Street and Thomas?

A. When I first pulled onto 40th Street and got in the inside lane.

Q. How far were you from the intersection at that time?

A. I guess around 100 feet.

Q. How fast were you going at that time?

A. Maybe 20 or 25 miles per hour.

Q. What was the color of the traffic lights at that point?

A. Green.

Q. What happened as you went northbound on 40th Street?

A. Well, it all happened really quickly. As

This is a useful answer since he was only about three seconds from the intersection before he looked at the lights.

I went north, the light turned yellow just before I got into the intersection. I was going through the intersection on the yellow light when suddenly I got smashed by another car from the driver's side.

Q. How long had the light been yellow at the time the other car collided with you?

A. It couldn't have been more than two or three seconds.

Q. How fast were you going when you were hit?

A. Maybe 25 or 30 miles per hour.

Q. Did you ever see the car that hit you before the impact?

A. Not really. I first saw it just before it was about to smash into me. It couldn't have been more than 10 or 15 feet from me. Before I could even put on my brakes, the car hit me.

Q. Tell us what happened from the moment the two cars hit?

A. Well, I remember putting on my brakes, I kind of skidded in the intersection, and the other car seemed to be stuck against the side of my car. I can remember getting bounced around inside the car and smashing my head and chest against the inside of the car and the steering wheel.

Q. Were you wearing a seat belt at that time?

A. No.

Q. Did your car have seat belts?

A. Yes.

Q. What happened when your car came to a stop?

A. I was pretty much numb. I can remember people coming up to me when I was in the car telling me not to move. I wasn't going to move anyway. I just hurt all over. I don't know how long it was, but after a while an ambulance came and they got me out of the car and put me on a stretcher.

Q. Mr. Jones, just before the impact, describe exactly what you were doing.

This answer is also useful since it suggests that the plaintiff was not paying much attention as he entered the intersection.

Note how the questions become more specific. The questioner's purpose now is to "pin down" the witness to specific facts.

This is important, since in some jurisdictions this fact is admissible to show plaintiff's own negligence or failure to prevent damages.

A. Well, I remember starting into the intersection. Since the light was yellow, I remember looking to the right to make sure that there weren't any cars taking a turn that might get in my way. I just looked to my right and then looked back up the road, then I saw the other car coming from my left just before it crashed into me.

Q. Did you ever put on your brakes before the impact?

A. No, I don't think so, there wasn't time to react.

Q. Mr. Jones, is there anything you remember about how this accident happened that you haven't told me about this afternoon?

A. No, nothing that comes to mind. I think I've pretty much told you everything.

Q. That's all the questions I have at this time. Do you have any questions, Ms. Johnson?

Ms. Johnson: No.

Mr. Sharp: Will you waive signature?

Ms. Johnson: No, we'd like to see the transcript.

(The deposition was concluded at 3:06 P.M.)

_____
John Jones

Some lawyers always ask this kind of question, since it's potential impeachment if the plaintiff "remembers" more at trial.

The party deponent should not waive signature, since he should review the transcript for accuracy.

Note that the plaintiff's lawyer asked no questions. This is the usual practice, unless the party gave incorrect or confusing answers that need to be corrected or clarified.

Note also that the plaintiff's lawyer made no objections during the deposition. The questions were proper so objections were unnecessary. The lawyer did not make objections for the purpose of coaching the plaintiff on desired responses, ethically questionable conduct some lawyers unfortunately engage in.

State of Arizona
County of Maricopa | SS.

The foregoing deposition was taken before me, Nancy Post, a Notary Public in the County of Maricopa, State of Arizona. The witness was duly sworn by me to testify to the truth. The questions asked of the witness and the answers given by the witness were taken down by me in shorthand and reduced to typewriting under my direction. The deposition was submitted to the witness and read and signed. The foregoing pages are a true and accurate transcript of the entire proceedings taken during this deposition.

The court reporter must arrange a meeting with the deponent so he can review the transcript, note any claimed inaccuracies, and sign the transcript. Any claimed inaccuracies are usually put on a separate sheet and attached to the transcript.

Dated: April 1, 1987

Nancy Post
—————————————
Notary Public

My commission expires on
   December 31, 1987.

UNITED STATES DISTRICT COURT
FOR THE DISTRICT OF ARIZONA

John Jones,
      Plaintiff

     v.   NO. 87 C 1000

Susan Smith,
      Defendant

NOTICE OF MOTION

TO: Anne Johnson
       Attorney at Law
       100 Congress Street
       Phoenix, AZ 85001

PLEASE TAKE NOTICE that on June 10, 1987, at 9:00 A.M., or as soon as counsel can be heard, defendant in the above-captioned matter will present the attached Motion to Compel Discovery before the Hon. Joan Howe, Courtroom No. 4, United States Court House, Phoenix, Arizona.

Even with service by mail, this is adequate notice. As a professional courtesy, however, it's a good idea to call the opposing lawyer and let him know you're serving the motion.

Dated: June 1, 1987

William Sharp
_____
William Sharp
Attorney for Defendant
100 Broadway
Phoenix, AZ 85001
881-1000

UNITED STATES DISTRICT COURT
FOR THE DISTRICT OF ARIZONA

John Jones,
          Plaintiff
 	
          v.
 	
Susan Smith,
          Defendant
	NO. 87 C 1000

MOTION TO COMPEL DISCOVERY

Defendant moves for an order compelling plaintiff to answer in the full interrogatories previously served on plaintiff, pursuant to Rule 37 of the Federal Rules of Civil Procedure. In support of her motion defendant states:

   1. Defendant served interrogatories on plaintiff on February 1, 1987.

   2. Plaintiff partially answered these interrogatories on February 25, 1987. Many of the answers are incomplete and do not provide the facts called for.

   3. Plaintiff's answers to Interrogatory Nos. 2, 4, 10, 11, 13, and 14 stated that "answers may be supplemented as discovery and investigation continues."

   4. To date plaintiff has neither supplemented his interrogatory answers nor advised defendant that no additional answers will be forthcoming, although defendant has requested, by telephone and letter, that plaintiff submit supplemental answers.

          WHEREFORE, defendant requests the court to order plaintiff to serve supplemental interrogatory answers within 10 days and award reasonable expenses, including attorney's fees, incurred by defendant as a result of this motion.

Since over three months has passed since plaintiff served incomplete answers to interrogatories, this motion should be brought.

In many jurisdictions local rules require that a motion must be supplemented by a memorandum of points and authorities. In other jurisdictions this is done only for complicated or contested motions, such as for summary judgment. You should always show what efforts you have made to get compliance before filing the motion.

Keep in mind that many jurisdictions require a lawyer to certify compliance with local rules that require that the parties first try to resolve discovery disputes informally.

Dated: June 1, 1987

William Sharp

William Sharp
Attorney for Defendant
100 Broadway
Phoenix, AZ 85001
881-1000

Note that Rule 37 allows the court to award the reasonable costs incurred in being forced to bring this motion. This includes attorney's fees. Asking for perhaps $150 here would be reasonable.

AFFIDAVIT OF SERVICE

I, Helen Thompson, having been first duly sworn, state that I have served a copy of the attached Notice of Motion and Motion to Compel Discovery on plaintiff's attorney by mail at 100 Congress Street, Phoenix, Arizona 85001, on June 1, 1987.

Helen Thompson

Helen Thompson

Signed and sworn to before me on June 1, 1987.

Ned Lark

Notary Public

My Commission expires on December 31, 1987.

[Seal]

UNITED STATES DISTRICT COURT
FOR THE DISTRICT OF ARIZONA

John Jones,
     Plaintiff

    v.   NO. 87 C 1000

Susan Smith,
     Defendant

REQUESTS FOR ADMISSION OF FACTS AND GENUINENESS OF DOCUMENTS

Plaintiff requests defendant, pursuant to Rule 36 of the Federal Rules of Civil Procedure, to admit within 30 days the following facts and genuineness of documents:

1. Defendant was the owner of a 1984 Buick Skylark sedan on September 2, 1986.

2. Defendant was driving the 1984 Buick Skylark sedan when the collision occurred on September 2, 1986.

3. Defendant was a driver licensed by the State of Nevada at the time of the collision.

4. Each of the following documents, attached as exhibits to this request, is authentic:

Exhibit No.	*Description*
1.	Phoenix Police Dept. accident report.
2.	Title and registration documents from the Nevada Dept. of Transportation showing defendant to be the owner of a 1984 Buick Skylark sedan.
3.	Driver's license issued to defendant by the Nevada Dept. of Transportation.

Dated: June 1, 1987

Anne Johnson

Anne Johnson
Attorney for Plaintiff
100 Congress Street
Phoenix, AZ 85001
882-1000

If this case will go to trial, the plaintiff will need to establish basic facts. These requests cover facts that the defendant will probably not contest, and that will streamline the plaintiff's case during trial.

A proof of service must be attached.

UNITED STATES DISTRICT COURT
FOR THE DISTRICT OF ARIZONA

John Jones,
         Plaintiff

         v.   NO. 87 C 1000

Susan Smith,
         Defendant

DEFENDANT'S ANSWER TO PLAINTIFF'S REQUESTS FOR ADMISSION OF FACTS AND GENUINENESS OF DOCUMENTS

Defendant answers plaintiff's Requests for Admission of Facts and Genuineness of Documents as follows:

Request No. 1: Defendant was the owner of a 1984 Buick Skylark sedan on September 2, 1986.

Answer: Admits.

Request No. 2: Defendant was driving the 1984 Buick Skylark sedan when the collision occurred on September 2, 1986.

Answer: Admits.

Request No. 3: Defendant was a driver licensed by the State of Nevada at the time of the collision.

Answer: Admits.

Request No. 4: Each of the following documents, attached as exhibits to this request, is authentic:

Exhibit No.	Description
1.	Phoenix Police Dept. accident report.
2.	Title and registration documents from the Nevada Dept. of Transportation showing defendant to be the owner of a 1984 Buick Skylark sedan.

Like interrogatories, the usual practice in answering is to set out both the request and the answer. This avoids confusion.

3.   Driver's license issued to defen-
        dant by the Nevada Dept. of
        Transportation.

<u>Answer:</u> Admits

Dated: <u>June 20, 1987</u>

William Sharp

William Sharp
Attorney for Defendant
100 Broadway
Phoenix, AZ 85001   A proof of service
881-1000   must be attached.

UNITED STATES DISTRICT COURT
FOR THE DISTRICT OF ARIZONA

John Jones,
         Plaintiff

         v.   NO. 87 C 1000

Susan Smith,
         Defendant

OFFER OF JUDGMENT

Pursuant to Rule 68 of the Federal Rules of Civil Procedure, defendant offers to allow judgment to be taken against her in the amount of SEVEN THOUSAND FIVE HUNDRED and 00/100 DOLLARS ($7,500.00), and costs of suit incurred to the date of this offer.

This offer is being made under Rule 68 of the Federal Rules of Evidence and Rule 408 of the Federal Rules of Evidence.

By this time defendant has sufficient facts to assess the case's settlement value. The offer of judgment will put additional pressure on the plaintiff to consider a realistic settlement.

Dated: August 1, 1987

William Sharp

William Sharp
Attorney for Defendant
100 Broadway
Phoenix, AZ 85001
881-1000

A proof of service must be attached.

UNITED STATES DISTRICT COURT FOR THE DISTRICT OF ARIZONA

John Jones,
      Plaintiff

v.   NO. 87 C 1000

Susan Smith,
      Defendant

MOTION FOR ORDER TO COMPEL PLAINTIFF'S PHYSICAL EXAMINATION

Defendant moves under Rule 35 of the Federal Rules of Civil Procedure for an order compelling plaintiff to submit to a physical examination. In support of her motion defendant states:

1. Plaintiff's physical condition is genuinely in controversy since the complaint alleges a variety of physical injuries.

2. Plaintiff during his deposition stated that he still suffers from the consequences of the accident that is the basis for his complaint. These include periodic pain in his back and ankle.

3. There exists good cause, in light of the above, for a physical examination of the plaintiff to evaluate the plaintiff's current physical condition and prognosis.

4. Rudolf B. Anton, M.D., a board certified neurologist, has agreed to examine and evaluate the plaintiff at his medical office located at 4401 N. Scottsdale Road, Scottsdale, Arizona, on September 15, 1987, at 5:00 P.M., or at another time, as directed by this court.

WHEREFORE, defendant requests that the court enter an order directing the plaintiff to be examined on the terms set forth above.

Dated: September 1, 1987

William Sharp

William Sharp
Attorney for Defendant
100 Broadway
Phoenix, AZ 85001
881-1000

Since plaintiff has not accepted the offer of judgment, defendant must continue her trial preparations. Getting a current evaluation of the plaintiff's medical condition and prognosis from a physician who has not previously seen the plaintiff is vital.

Keep in mind that many jurisdictions require a lawyer to certify that he has complied with local rules that require that the parties first try to resolve discovery disputes informally.

A proof of service must be attached.

UNITED STATES DISTRICT COURT
FOR THE DISTRICT OF ARIZONA

John Jones,
   Plaintiff

   v.   NO. 87 C 1000

Susan Smith,
   Defendant

JOINT PRETRIAL MEMORANDUM

Pursuant to Local Rule, plaintiff and defendant submit the following joint pretrial memorandum:

Judges frequently have instructions on what the memorandum should contain and how it should be organized.

I

Uncontested Facts

Plaintiff Jones and defendant Smith were involved in a vehicle collision on September 2, 1986. The collision occurred at the intersection of 40th Street and Thomas Road in Phoenix, Arizona, at approximately 2:00 P.M. At the time of the collision Jones was driving his car, a 1984 Toyota Corolla four-door sedan, northbound on 40th Street; Smith was driving her car, a 1984 Buick Skylark sedan, eastbound on Thomas Road. The intersection is controlled by traffic lights.

On September 2, 1986, Jones was employed as a delivery driver by Devo Wholesale Florist and was being paid gross wages of $700 per month.

These facts have all been admitted in the pleadings or during discovery.

II

Contested Issues of Fact and Law

1. Did Smith run a red light?
2. Did Jones run a red light?
3. Was Smith negligent?
4. Was Jones negligent?

III

Exhibits

A. *Plaintiff Jones' Ex-*   *Objections, if any*
   hibits
   1. Doctors Hospi-
      tal records
   2. Dr. Lang's of-
      fice records
   3. Dr. Hoffman's
      office records
   4. Dr. Franks' of-
      fice records
   5. All bills for
      above
   6. X rays taken by
      above
   7. Devo Wholesale
      Florist employ-
      ment records
   8. Phoenix Police   Objection, for   If any evidence is ob-
      Dept. reports   reasons stated   jected to, the judge
                          in attached   may rule on the objec-
                          memorandum.   tions, if possible to do
                                                so, during the pretrial
                                                conference.

   9. Accident scene   If objections are
      photographs   made, the objecting
   10. Jack's Auto Re-   party should state the
       pair records   basis for the objection,
       and bill   with supporting cita-
   11. Watch repair   tions.
       bill
   12. Glendale Com-
       munity College
       bills
   13. Walgreen phar-
       macy bill
   14. Accident scene
       diagrams

B. *Defendant Smith's Ex-*   *Objections, if any*
   hibits
   1. Plaintiff's hos-
      pital and medi-
      cal records

    2. Rudolf Anton,
       M.D., medical
       records
    3. Accident scene
       photographs
    4. Accident scene
       diagrams
    5. Phoenix Police
       Dept. reports
       to extent ad-
       missible

IV

Witnesses

A. *Plaintiff Jones' Witnesses*
    1. Plaintiff
    2. Carol Brown, 42 E. Cambridge, Phoenix
    3. Mary Porter, 42 E. Cambridge, Phoenix
    4. Dr. Lang
    5. Dr. Hoffman
    6. Dr. Franks
    7. James Devo, Devo Wholesale Florist
    8. John Jones, Sr., and Mary Jones, plaintiff's parents
    9. Officer Steven Pitcher, Phoenix Police Dept.
   10. Defendant
   11. Personnel from Jack's Auto Repair, to qualify exhibits
   12. Personnel from above hospitals and physicians, to qualify exhibits

B. *Defendant Smith's witnesses:*
    1. All of plaintiff's witnesses
    2. Dr. Rudolf Anton

V

Jury Instructions

Plaintiff's and defendant's proposed jury instructions are attached.

1. Plaintiff objects to defendant instruction Nos. 6, 7, and 9, for the reasons stated in plaintiff's attached memorandum.

2. Defendant objects to plaintiff instruction nos. 2, 3, 4, and 6, for the reasons stated in defendant's attached memorandum.

RESPECTFULLY SUBMITTED,

Date: November 1, 1987

Anne Johnson

Anne Johnson
Attorney for Plaintiff

William Sharp

William Sharp
Attorney for Defendant

Pretrial memoranda frequently also contain a memorandum of law from each party that discusses any legal issues that the judge will need to resolve before or during trial.

The judge's final pretrial order will usually track the language and organization of the memorandum and contain all rulings on admissibility issues that were made at the conference.

RELEASE

In consideration of the sum of twelve thousand dollars ($12,000), which plaintiff acknowledges receiving, Plaintiff John Jones agrees to release Defendant Susan Smith and her heirs, survivors, agents, and personal representatives from all claims, suits, or actions in any form or on any basis, because of anything that was done or not done at any time, on account of the following:

All claims for personal injuries, property damage, physical disabilities, medical expenses, lost income, loss of consortium, and all other claims that have been or could be brought, including all claims now known or that in the future might be known, which arise out of an occurrence on or about September 2, 1986, at 40th Street and Thomas Road, in Phoenix, Arizona, when plaintiff claims to have sustained injuries as a result of a collision between an automobile driven by plaintiff and an automobile driven by defendant.

A release would be the standard way of settling this case, since it is a complete settlement by all the parties.

The parties would usually execute a separate settlement agreement detailing the terms of the settlement.

As a result of this collision plaintiff has brought suit against defendant for damages. Defendant has denied both liability and the claimed extent of damages. This release is a compromise settlement between Plaintiff John Jones and Defendant Susan Smith.

This agreement is a release and shall operate as a total discharge of any claims plaintiff has or may have, arising out the above occurrence, against this defendant and any other persons.

Plaintiff John Jones and Defendant Susan Smith also agree to terminate any actions that have been filed, particularly a claim by this plaintiff against this defendant currently filed as civil action No. 87 C 1000 in the United States District Court for the District of Arizona, in Phoenix, Arizona. Plaintiff and defendant agree to execute a Stipulation of Dismissal, with prejudice, and file it with the Clerk of the above Court, thereby terminating that action in its entirety, within five days of the execution of this agreement.

Date: <u>December 1, 1987</u>

_____
John Jones, Plaintiff

The parties, not their lawyers, must sign the release.

_____
Susan Smith, Defendant

UNITED STATES DISTRICT COURT
FOR THE DISTRICT OF ARIZONA

John Jones,
         Plaintiff

         v.   No. 87 C 1000

Susan Smith,
         Defendant

STIPULATION OF DISMISSAL

Plaintiff John Jones and Defendant Susan Smith agree to dismiss this action with prejudice, and each party will bear its costs.

The stipulation of dismissal terminates the lawsuit. No court order is necessary.

Dated: December 2, 1987

Anne Johnson
_____
Anne Johnson
Attorney for Plaintiff

William Sharp
_____
William Sharp
Attorney for Defendant

INDEX

353

FUNDAMENTALS
OF PRETRIAL TECHNIQUES